How to Grade for Learning

Fourth Edition

To my wife, Marilyn, and my children, Jeremy and Bronwyn, who have provided me with the ongoing support and encouragement that made it possible for me to write this book four times.

To Elliot Hugh and Vivian Ruth O'Connor, born July 10, 2007, and Emmeline Florence Mason, born December 31, 2016, with the hope that they are experiencing or will truly experience assessment for learning and receive "good" grades.

To the thousands of teachers and administrators who I've had the pleasure of working with over the last twenty years, especially those in the school districts where I had the opportunity to work on an ongoing basis.

To David Chojnacki (the recently retired brilliant executive director), Bridget Doogan and Gail Seay, who have a superb professional development vision for NESA (the Near East Council of International Schools) and who have kindly included me in the wonderful learning experiences at NESA conferences and institutes.

To the Standards-Based Learning and Grading Facebook group and the #sblchat, #caflnchat, and #colchat Twitter chats that have dramatically opened communication on grading and reporting issues and that have provided me with many new understandings and professional friends.

To Damian Cooper and Lorna Earl, my longtime friends and professional colleagues, for their devotion to assessment for learning and for including me in the development and launching of the Canadian Assessment for Learning Network.

How to Grade for Learning

Linking Grades to Standards

Fourth Edition

Ken O'Connor

Forewords by Garnet Hillman and Rick Stiggins

CORWIN
A SAGE Publishing Company

FOR INFORMATION:

Corwin
A SAGE Company
2455 Teller Road
Thousand Oaks, California 91320
(800) 233-9936
www.corwin.com

SAGE Publications Ltd.
1 Oliver's Yard
55 City Road
London EC1Y 1SP
United Kingdom

SAGE Publications India Pvt. Ltd.
B 1/I 1 Mohan Cooperative Industrial Area
Mathura Road, New Delhi 110 044
India

SAGE Publications Asia-Pacific Pte. Ltd.
3 Church Street
#10-04 Samsung Hub
Singapore 049483

Program Director: Jessica Allan
Associate Editor: Lucas Schleicher
Editorial Assistants: Katie Crilley and
                        Mia Rodriguez
Production Editor: Melanie Birdsall
Copy Editor: Jared Leighton
Typesetter: Hurix Systems Pvt. Ltd.
Proofreader: Theresa Kay
Indexer: Marilyn Augst
Cover Designer: Janet Kiesel
Marketing Manager: Nicole Franks

Printed in the United States of America

Library of Congress Cataloging-in-Publication Data

Names: O'Connor, Ken, author.
Title: How to grade for learning: linking grades to standards / Ken O'Connor; forewords by Garnet Hillman and Rick Stiggins.

Description: Fourth Edition. | Thousand Oaks, California: Corwin, A SAGE Company, [2018] | Includes bibliographical references and index.

Identifiers: LCCN 2017030479 | ISBN 9781506334158 (Paperback : acid-free paper)

Subjects: LCSH: Grading and marking (Students) | Education—Standards.

Classification: LCC LB3060.37 .O27 2018 | DDC 371.27/2—dc23 LC record available at https://lccn.loc.gov/2017030479

This book is printed on acid-free paper.

17 18 19 20 21 10 9 8 7 6 5 4 3 2 1

Contents

Foreword by Garnet Hillman

Ken O'Connor has touched the lives of countless educators and students through his work as a teacher, administrator, consultant, and author. His charge to improve grading practices in order to support student learning has consistently pushed the thinking of teachers and administrators to challenge the status quo of grading. To shed light on the fact that grading can move beyond a process of mathematical algorithms, *How to Grade for Learning* shows how grades can clearly reflect and communicate academic achievement while recognizing the importance of a separate means for reporting behaviors and habits. Ken highlights the value of including students in the process of grading to maximize their impact and effectiveness. Student involvement creates an environment where students are inspired to demonstrate their learning. While the book is centered on grading, it is essential to remember that grading is not a simple end-of-term mathematical process. It is an ongoing, thoughtful, and reflective practice guided by professional judgment. This book provides guidance for teacher reflection and thought and fodder for conversations that grapple with the sometimes tenuous issues of grading, followed by guidelines for practical implementation.

This fourth edition of *How to Grade for Learning* includes many powerful stories and examples from current practitioners that give a pulse to the reality of grading reform. There are more than forty contributions from a wide variety of professionals in the educational community. Providing so many different voices makes this robust edition a vital contribution to the literature in this field. The diverse contributions provided come from a variety of grade levels and content areas and hail from around the globe. *How to Grade for Learning* is not an idea that only works in particular situations or only on paper. *How to Grade for Learning* affords a worldwide audience practical guidelines and strategies to bring grading practices into a realm of meaning, accuracy, and relevance.

While there are many publications that address why it is essential for grades to reflect learning, Ken O'Connor goes one step further by adding practical advice and specific examples of how to put those strategies into effective classroom practice. I have often encountered educators who are enthusiastic about changing grading practices but have no idea where to get started. They can easily internalize and concur with the guidelines proposed in the book but struggle to discern how to implement the practice. For example, the third guideline speaks to basing grades on individual achievement without the interference of effort, participation, attitude, and other behaviors. As educators, who doesn't want a student's grade to be based on his or her individual achievement? However, when putting this practice into play, it becomes clear that this is easier said than done. Questions abound, such as, If effort is not part of the grade, what will we do with it? If students are working in groups, how can I grade them, and are the grades truly accurate? The questions that undoubtedly arise are answered in the pages that follow each guideline. They are answered not only in theory but also in practice, which is vital to a successful change in grading.

Ken O'Connor's work has played a critical role in my own career in education. As a beginning teacher, I had no training or coursework in the areas of assessment and grading. I never considered that there could be more than one way to grade students, nor had I thought about the impact that grading has on students. I was under the common impression that everything (I mean everything) in the classroom must have a grade associated with it—that everything was *worth* something and inclusion in the grade was how to show what was valued. Thankfully, after a few years, I was able to reflect on this topic and search for a new way to grade. I found Ken's writings, among others, and, in turn, began my own journey to reform grading for the benefit of my students and their learning. I realized early on that I was looking at the purpose of grading with good intentions but bad results. By including everything, my grades were not clearly communicating anything. Over time, my grades transitioned to represent students' academic achievement with a separate communication about behaviors. I found that grading was not a way to show importance or value; value in learning comes from relevance, engagement, and personal impact. After a few years of implementation at the classroom level, I was able to take my learning and practices to a new district and support the transition on a larger scale.

Teachers and administrators at all levels will benefit from this new edition of *How to Grade for Learning*. The ideas presented can easily be taken and suited to fit varied classrooms, schools, and districts. This is not a compilation of examples that must be taken verbatim in order to be successful. Rather, the ideas inspire change and are ready to adapt to diverse settings. It is only when we take an idea and make it our own that we are set up for success. This book opens the path forward. How we choose to take that path, with whom, and by which means—those decisions are up to us.

—**Garnet Hillman**
Instructional Coach, Deerfield Public Schools District 109
Assessment Associate, Solution Tree
Crest Hill, IL

Foreword by Rick Stiggins

Early in our daughter Krissy's third-grade school year, she arrived home after school with a paper in her hand and a tear in her eye. She was carrying a "story" she had written. Her assignment was to write about something or someone that she cared about. She gave it to her mom and me with obvious trepidation.

As we read, we found the touching tale of the kitten named Kelly who came to be a part of our family briefly and then had to go home to the farm because of allergies and because she was just too aggressive. Krissy had wanted a kitten so badly and was so sad about losing her special new friend. The story clearly reflected the work of an emergent writer. As unsophisticated as it was, it captured the emotions of the event. It was quite touching. Krissy's six or seven sentences filled about two-thirds of the sheet of paper. In the space below the story, at the bottom of the sheet, there appeared a very big, very red F. So naturally, my wife and I asked why Krissy had been assigned a failing grade.

Her reply triggered some very strong emotions within both of us. Krissy said sadly, "The teacher told us that we were to fill the page, and I didn't do that. And so she said I didn't follow directions, and I failed. I don't think I'll ever be a good writer anyway . . ." As our disappointed little writer walked off, my wife and I could only shake our heads in wonder and fury.

We both know and understand that all classroom teachers face immense classroom assessment, record-keeping, and communication challenges. We empathized. First, they must establish rigorous but realistic achievement expectations for each student. Then, they must provide opportunities for students to learn to meet those expectations. Next, they must transform those achievement targets into high-quality assessments to determine the level of student success. Finally, teachers must transform assessment results into accurate information for those who need access to it and communicate that information in a complete, timely, and understandable form to those users.

Each of these steps can be carried out using either sound or unsound practices. If teachers use sound practices, students can prosper. If they use unsound practices, students suffer the consequences. In other words, if achievement expectations are inappropriate (e.g., too high or too low) for a student, the learning environment will be counterproductive. If assessments are of poor quality, inaccurate information and poor instructional decisions will follow. When communication procedures fail, students will have great difficulty succeeding academically.

Krissy's teacher made it partway through this gauntlet of challenges. She wanted her students to write well—an important achievement target. She obviously provided her students with opportunities to write because Krissy had written her story. The assessment could have been of high quality because she relied on a direct performance assessment of writing proficiency. But from here on, the teaching, assessment, and communication processes clearly broke down.

In this book, Ken O'Connor gives voice to many of the things that went wrong in this case. Although he centers on the process of communicating about student achievement through the use of report card grades, Ken puts the grading process into a larger context. He gives attention to each of the other keys to success. He argues convincingly for an open and honest educational system—a system in which there are no surprises and no excuses. He advocates the careful articulation of appropriate achievement expectations and the unconditional sharing of those targets with students and their families. He demands rigorous achievement standards and accurate ongoing classroom assessments of student success. Finally, Ken spells out concrete procedures for transforming assessment results into grades that communicate in a timely and understandable way.

The practical guidelines offered in this book help teachers design and conduct grading practices that help students feel in control of their own academic success. These guidelines can keep students from feeling that sense of hopelessness that Krissy felt. Every teacher's goal must be to implement grading practices that lead students to feel that they can succeed if they try.

—Rick Stiggins
Founder, Assessment Training Institute
Portland, OR

Preface

In May 1992, I had the good fortune to attend a train-the-trainer workshop given by Rick Stiggins in Toronto, Canada. This sparked in me a general interest in classroom assessment, but the aspect of the workshop that really "turned me on" was the part on grading. Since then, I have read everything that I could find about grading. I also watched the passage of my own children through the school system, and I'm now watching the passage of my grandchildren. Each of these influences convinced me that what is needed is a practical set of grading guidelines that support learning and that teachers can apply at the classroom level—that is, in their gradebooks and computer grading programs.

I began to think seriously about guidelines for grading when I became one of three authors of *Assess for Success* for the Ontario Secondary School Teachers' Federation (Midwood, O'Connor, & Simpson, 1993). What really motivated me to develop the guidelines was a journal article that I read in April 1994, which I thought was both wrong and internally inconsistent. I wrote to the editor making these criticisms, and she wrote back suggesting I write an article. At first, I ignored this suggestion, but several months later, she sent me the author's response to my criticism and again suggested that I write an article. Twice challenged, I had to respond, so I spent most of my 1994 Christmas vacation writing an article, which appeared in the May 1995 edition of the *NASSP* (National Association of Secondary Schools Principals) *Bulletin*.

I then created staff development workshops based on the article, and the positive response to my presentations made me want to try to reach a wider audience by turning my article and workshops into a book on grading. This I did with the first edition, which I completed in September 1998. Three years later, it was time to update and revise the book, especially to reflect the increasing move to learning goals, or a standards-based approach to teaching and learning. This resulted in the second edition that was published in June 2002. Further developments over the next six years led to the revised and updated third edition, which was published in 2009. Now, eight years later, there has been an explosion of activity and ideas about grading, so it is time for a fourth edition that I hope will be a worthwhile addition to the literature on effective grading practices.

WHAT'S THE PURPOSE OF THIS BOOK?

Much of what teachers do is because that is the way it was done to them; this is no longer good enough. It is my hope that this book will lead teachers to examine critically their grading practices. Some of the ideas in this book challenge long-held beliefs and practices and create considerable cognitive dissonance.

Over twenty years ago, Glickman (as cited in Bailey & McTighe, 1996) said, "There are profound questions about current educational practices that need to debated" (p. 119). There have been many significant advances since then, but this is still true in 2017. The quotations on the first page of the introduction in this book demonstrate clearly that grades and grading need to be debated. Even though there are many books and journal articles on the topic, grading is an aspect of education that practitioners have traditionally discussed very little. I believe it is *the most important ignored topic in education*, and to illustrate this, I suggest you look at the programs for major educational conferences, and you will find that out of hundreds of sessions, there may be three or four on grading. Also, one major barometer of educational issues is SmartBrief, published daily, Monday to Friday, by ASCD. Every day, there are brief summaries of articles about education issues from journals and newspapers with links to the articles. From January 1 to April 30, 2017, there were almost eight hundred linked articles and approximately 160 links to ASCD programs and publications, and only *three* mentioned grades. It appears that teachers have considered grading to be a private activity, thus "guarding [their] practices with the same passion with which one might guard an unedited diary" (Kain, 1996, p. 569). Fortunately, with the help of social media, this has changed considerably over the last few years, and I now see a much greater willingness on the part of teachers to reflect on their grading practices and to discuss them openly with their colleagues on Facebook groups like Standards Based Learning and Grading and Twitter chats like #sblchat and #colchat.

This book examines the many issues around grading and provides a set of practical guidelines that teachers can use to arrive at grades for their students. Teachers from kindergarten to college can use the ideas in this book to examine and perhaps change their own grading practices and, even more importantly, to focus their discussion of this complex, confusing, and difficult issue with colleagues.

HOW IS THIS BOOK ORGANIZED?

An introduction sets the big picture for this book and gives readers an opportunity to identify and examine grading practices and the issues that arise from these practices. These practical grading issues lead to the need for guidelines, and subsequent chapters provide eight guidelines. These are practical guidelines, not just broad general principles. They are important to consider as a set, but each also needs to be considered individually. Chapters 1 through 8 do this, with each of these chapters addressing three questions: What is the purpose of the guideline? What are the key elements of the guideline? What is the bottom line? In all chapters except Chapter 7, there are contributions from educators who lead, teach about, or practice standards-based grading.

At the end of each of these guideline chapters, a reflection activity, What's My Thinking Now?, asks readers to think about the guideline and its importance and meaning to them. An example of one person's reflections on that particular guideline concludes the chapters on guidelines.

Chapter 9 examines a number of additional grading issues, including grade point average calculation, the use of computer grading programs, how to grade exceptional students, and legal concerns. Chapter 10 examines the broader aspects of communicating student achievement, considering topics such as expanded-format reporting, informal communications, and student-involved conferencing. Chapter 11 provides a variety of approaches to implementing the change to more effective grading practices. Conclusions and recommended actions are provided in Chapter 12. In the appendices, there are a powerful testimonial about a teacher's journey to assessment for learning and on to standards-based grading, expanded guidelines for grading in standards-based systems, a proposed grading policy based on the guidelines, an example of a district grading policy, a letter to parents about student-led conferencing, a glossary, and other additional information for the reader. Also included are extensive references and a section of additional resources.

CHANGES IN THE FOURTH EDITION

One of the objectives I started with in writing this edition was to shorten the book, but this hasn't happened because in the "world" of grading, a lot has changed over the last eight years, and a lot more people have had a lot to say about grading, especially online. I have tried to capture those changes in this edition. Standards-based grading and reporting have become very common in elementary schools across North America (and beyond) and have become reasonably common in middle schools; they are starting to make inroads into high schools, especially in the New England states that have mandated proficiency-based graduation requirements and in a few other states, notably Iowa and Oregon. Many teachers are trying hard to implement standards-based grading at the high school level, but I am frequently disappointed by the lack of willpower of administrators at school and district levels to push for changes that they acknowledge are needed; at the first sign of resistance by teachers or parents, too many administrators give up on their principles, "fold up the tent," and say, "Not now, maybe later." This illustrates that a great need persists to focus on the "why" issues, but there is also increasing need to focus on "how."

Throughout the book, there are numerous quotes to introduce or support a viewpoint that I discuss. I have attempted to update these quotes to be from sources in the last five years, but if I couldn't find one that is equal or better than the existing quotes, then the "old" quote stays.

In this edition, the biggest changes are as follows:

1. The inclusion of forty-eight "Educator Contributions" from educators from the United States, Canada, and a number of international schools. The contributors include nationally and internationally known authors and consultants, among them Carol Commodore, Damian Cooper, Myron Dueck, Lorna Earl, Tom Hierck, Lee Ann Jung, Douglas Reeves, and Rick Wormeli.

2. The content of the previous Chapter 9 has been incorporated into Chapter 6, with the previous Chapter 10 becoming Chapter 9 and the previous Chapter 11 becoming Chapter 10.

3. A completely new Chapter 11 on implementing changes in grading and reporting has been added.

4. About one hundred new references

Other changes are the rewriting of some of the scenarios that introduce each guideline and significant rewriting of the What's My Thinking Now? sections that complete the discussion of each guideline.

The main chapter by chapter changes are as follows:

Introduction

- An almost entirely new set of quotes on page 1

- New sections on motivation, mindset, fairness, and professional judgment

- A reduction in the number of case studies from ten to seven, with some rewritten

- Three new pieces providing student voice on grading

- Two educator contributions

Chapter 1

- A detailed examination of the Next Generation Science Standards leading to the determination of gradebook and reporting categories for a science

- A gradebook based on the Grade 5 Common Core math standards

- The addition of the "Big Ideas" approach to identifying grading and reporting standards

- Five educator contributions

Chapter 2

- Significantly rewritten with a new organizing structure

- An expanded section on the contentious issue of the specificity of performance standards for classroom assessment and grading

- A new section contrasting achievement, growth, and progress

- Three educator contributions

Chapter 3

- A rewritten section on academic dishonesty, with a new example

- More information about support periods in the timetable

- Three educator contributions

Chapter 4

- A focus on formative assessment as a process, not as events

- An expanded section on homework

- Four educator contributions

Chapter 5

- Expanded sections on reassessment and yearlong grading periods

- Four educator contributions

Chapter 6

- Inclusion of content from previous Chapter 9

- New sections on using logic rules and student involvement in the determination of grades

- Student questions about determining grades

- Six educator contributions

Chapter 7

- Some rewriting and new graphics

Chapter 8

- Reorganized into two parts, one focusing on student understanding of assessment and grading and one on student involvement in assessment and grading

- Seven educator contributions

Chapter 9

- Previously Chapter 10

- Seven issues but only four are the same; new sections on competency-based education/grading, college grading and admissions, and athletic eligibility

- One educator contribution

Chapter 10

- Previously Chapter 11

- Two new report card examples

- Five educator contributions

Chapter 11

- New chapter

- Eight educator contributions

Chapter 12

- Significantly rewritten, with two interesting new high school transcripts

- One educator contribution

This edition also incorporates many other small changes, including minor edits, to improve readability.

HOW CAN THIS BOOK BE USED?

The most important way to use this book is with an open mind; regardless of how many or few years of experience teachers have, they can use this book to critically examine their own practices. Throughout the book, readers will find reflection opportunities, which, it is hoped, they will use to engage themselves more thoroughly with the text. Consider creating a journal to record your thoughts in response to the questions posed in these reflection activities.

Engaging with the text can be done individually, but it is more beneficial if done in groups (e.g., the whole staff in a small school, learning teams, department or division groups). This is particularly important for the detailed analysis of each guideline at the end of Chapters 1 through 8. Remember, when changing practices, start small; adapt, do not adopt; and work together. When you have finished the book, you are encouraged to use the rubric in Appendix H to evaluate your own grading practices. For this book to be of real value, teachers must use it to examine critically and discuss the sometimes taboo subject of grading. It is hoped that this exploration will lead teachers to use grading practices presented in the eight guidelines. To further encourage your interest, here are my top-twelve readings, which I think will be particularly helpful to you (see References and Additional Resources for more resources):

Top-Twelve Readings

Boaler, J. (2016). *Mathematical mindsets: Unleashing students' potential through creative math, inspiring messages, and innovative teaching.* San Francisco, CA: Jossey-Bass.

Cameron, C., & Gregory, K. (2014). *Rethinking letter grades: A five-step approach for aligning letter grades to learning standards* (2nd ed.). Winnipeg, MB, Canada: Portage and Main Press.

Chappuis, J., Stiggins, R., Chappuis, S., & Arter, J. (2012). *Classroom assessment for student learning: Doing it right—doing it well* (2nd ed.). Boston, MA: Pearson.

Chappuis, S., Commodore, C., & Stiggins, R. (2017). *Balanced assessment systems: Leadership, quality, and the role of classroom assessment.* Thousand Oaks, CA: Corwin.

Cooper, D. (2011). *Redefining fair: How to plan, assess, and grade for excellence in mixed-ability classrooms.* Bloomington, IN: Solution Tree.

Dueck, M. (2014). *Grading smarter, not harder: Assessment strategies that motivate kids and help them learn.* Alexander, VA: ASCD.

Guskey, T. R. (2013). The case against percentage grades. *Educational Leadership, 71*(1), 68–72.

Guskey, T. R. (2015). *On your mark: Challenging the conventions of grading and reporting.* Bloomington, IN: Solution Tree.

Kagan, S. (1995). Group grades miss the mark. *Educational Leadership, 52*(8), 68–71.

Reeves, D. (2016). *Elements of grading: A guide to effective practice* (2nd ed.). Bloomington, IN: Solution Tree.

Schimmer, T. (2016). *Grading from the inside out.* Bloomington, IN: Solution Tree.

Wormeli, R. (2006). *Fair isn't always equal: Assessing and grading in the differentiated classroom.* Portland, ME/Westerville, OH: Stenhouse/NMSA.

Acknowledgments

First, I must thank the fifty-two educators who were willing to share their experience and expertise and put the time and effort into producing the excellent educator contributions for the book. Almost all of the contributions that were submitted are included, although some couldn't be used because they were duplicated by other contributions or for space reasons. This book is immensely better than it would have been without their contributions, and I'm very grateful to all of them.

During the past twenty-seven years, I have been on a journey—a journey of learning about assessment, grading, and reporting. This journey has been assisted by many people; it was initiated and supported over the years by Lorna Earl, formerly the research director of the Scarborough Board of Education; it was jump-started by attending train-the-trainer workshops given by Rick Stiggins, who has continued to nurture my journey by his interest in and encouragement for my work; and it was moved forward by attending workshops given by Kay Burke and Jay McTighe and by the opportunity to learn from professional friendships with Kay and Jay, as well as with Judy Arter, Kathy Busick, Jan Chappuis, Steve Chappuis, Nancy McMunn, and Patricia Schenck.

I also benefited greatly from my ongoing collaboration with Damian Cooper, then with the Halton Board of Education, and Dale Midwood, of the then Frontenac County Board of Education. I also gratefully acknowledge the Ontario Secondary School Teachers' Federation, which gave me my first assessment "immersion" opportunity when I was chosen to be one of the authors of *Assess for Success*.

There are many people whose work I admire and have learned from over the years, and I thank them for their contributions—Robert Lynn Canady, Art Costa, Myron Dueck, Rick DuFour, Robin Fogarty, Forest Gathercoal, Tom Guskey, Karen Harvey, Garnet Hillman, Lee Ann Jung, Garth Larson, Becca Lindahl, Marvin Marshall, Ken Mattingly, Sherri Nelson, Jim Popham, Douglas Reeves, Spence Rogers, Tom Schimmer, Carol Ann Tomlinson, Matt Townsley, Grant Wiggins, Dylan Wiliam, and Rick Wormeli.

Although I gratefully acknowledge the contributions of all people mentioned, the responsibility for the views expressed in this book is mine and mine alone. The clarity of these views, however, is only partly due to my writing; I must acknowledge the huge contribution of my editors, Dara Lee Howard, Anne Kaske, Kathy Siebel, Paula Fleming, and Jared Leighton. It has been a delight to work with them and to see what professional editors can do to improve the original manuscript. I would also like to acknowledge Sue Schumer and Jean Ward, the acquisitions editors who made this book possible, Hudson Perigo at Corwin, who pushed me for the third edition, and to Jessica Allan, Dan Alpert, Jacob Bruno, and Nicole Franks, Katie Crilley, Melanie Birdsall, and Lucas Schleicher at Corwin, who have provided encouragement and valuable assistance as this fourth edition has developed.

About the Author

Ken O'Connor is an independent classroom assessment consultant with a special interest in grading and reporting. An internationally recognized speaker who has presented in forty-seven states in the United States, nine provinces and one territory in Canada, and twenty-four other countries, he has also consulted for schools, districts, and state and provincial departments of education. He had twenty-three years of classroom experience, from Grade 7 to Grade 12, and ten years of experience as a curriculum coordinator for a large school district. Ken was born in Melbourne, Australia, but has lived most of his life in the east end of Toronto, Canada.

Introduction

"Developing meaningful, reasonable, and equitable grading policies and practices will continue to challenge educators at all levels." —Guskey (2015, p. 81)

"If I were asked to enumerate ten educational stupidities, the giving of grades would be at the top of the list." —DeZouche (1945, p. 339)

"It is far better to prevent failure than endure it." —Nagel (2015, p. 128)

"Grading on standards for achievement means a shift from thinking that grades are what students earn to thinking that grades show what students learn." —Brookhart (2011, p. 13)

"Reassessment is both the most important and most misunderstood practice of grading reform." —Schimmer (2016, p. 64)

"Students will be more inclined to seek help in a supportive, mastery-oriented environment that values failure and struggle as part of the learning process." —Stuart Karabenick in McKibben (2016, p. 4)

"We're not interested in getting into a spitting contest about whether or not homework should be given at all." —Sackstein and Hamilton (2016, p. 171)

"We know the practices that work; implementation is the key." —Depka (2015, p. 109)

"The ultimate goal of formative assessment . . . is that both the teacher and the student know what actions to take to keep learning on a successful track." —J. Chappuis (2015, p. 10)

"Teacher quality is the single most important variable in an education system." —Wiliam (2011, p. 22)

"In a perfect world, standards-based grades would be the norm and letter grades and percentages would be a thing of the past." —Vatterott (2015, p. 71)

"Fail early, fail often, but always fail forward. Turn your mistakes into stepping-stones for success." —Maxwell (2000, p. 203)

Traditional grading, grades as adults mostly knew them, is grading based on assessment methods and giving or taking away points for almost everything students did and then calculating the mean for those points should—and to a considerable extent is—fading away. I would have no difficulty if there were no grades, but we don't live in a perfect world, so I believe that for the foreseeable future, we will continue to have grades, especially in almost all high schools and colleges. That being the case, we have to make them better, and better for me means making grades accurate, consistent, meaningful, and supportive of learning.

WHAT GRADING TERMINOLOGY IS NEEDED?

As the quotes about grading show, grading raises many concerns. One communication concern is grading terminology. The term *grading* carries different meanings for different people while other words, such as *marking* and *scoring*, may sometimes mean grading, too. As McTighe and Ferrara (1995) state, "Terms [are] frequently used interchangeably, although they should have distinct meanings" (p. 11). Discussion of any issue or principle must proceed from a clear understanding of the meaning of the terms being used. In support of this goal, a glossary is provided in Appendix I. At this point, readers need a shared understanding of three critical terms: *grades* (or grading), *marks* (or marking), and *scores* (or scoring). These terms are often used almost interchangeably, although *grading* is used more frequently in the United States and *marking* more commonly in Canada.

The main problem is that these terms, especially *grades* and *grading*, are often used with two meanings. For careful analysis, it is critical to have a clear meaning for each term. In this book, *grade(s)/grading*, *mark(s)/marking*, and *score(s)/scoring* are used as follows:

> **Grade(s) or grading**—The number or letter reported at the end of a period of time as a summary statement of student performance

> **Mark(s) or marking and score(s) or scoring**—The number, letter, or words placed on any single student assessment (test, performance task, etc.)

I make this distinction because there are two very different processes involved; when a teacher evaluates an individual piece of student assessment evidence and gives it a mark or level score, that is very different from what happens at the end of the grading period when the marks or level scores are summarized as a grade. As the processes are so different, I believe we communicate more clearly when we use separate terms with specific meaning.

Airasian (1994) uses *grading* to mean "making a judgment about the quality of a pupil's performance, whether it is performance on a single assessment or performance across many assessments" (p. 281). In most writings, the context makes clear which of these two meanings is intended. However, this is not always the case, and when the meaning is not clear, confusion and lack of clarity in analysis and discussion requires that the two activities be distinguished by using separate terms.

Anderson and Wendel (1988) define *marks* and *grades* oppositely to the definitions used here. They agree, though, that defining terms is essential so that "everyone operates under the same assumptions and knows exactly what meanings underlie those assumptions" (pp. 36–37).

An example of the confusion that can arise is provided by a group of teachers who believe that feedback, not marks, should be given on all assessments, regardless of purpose. They have labeled their cause—and Facebook group—Teachers Throwing Out Grades, but they really mean teachers throwing out marks/scores because almost all of them have to ultimately come up with grades for their students.

An entertaining definition is provided by Paul Dressel (as cited in Kohn, 1993b):

> A grade can be regarded only as an inadequate report of an inaccurate judgment by a biased and variable judge of the extent to which a student has attained an undefined level of mastery of an unknown proportion of an indefinite amount of material. (p. 201)

WHAT IS THE CONTEXT OF GRADING?

> The mission of schools most [of] today's adults grew up in was to begin the process of sorting students into various segments of our social and economic system. Assessment's role in those days was to provide evidence upon which to rank those who remained in school at the end of high school based on academic achievement (as represented by grades, GPA's and class rank). However we have come to realize that many students who drop out or finish low in the rank order fail to develop the academic and lifelong learning skills needed to succeed in an ever-evolving world of work. And so schools were required to become accountable to leave no child behind; schools and all students were expected to meet high standards, reduce dropout rates and make all students ready for college or workplace training (and to compete in the global economy). (Chappuis, Stiggins, & Commodore, 2017, p. 3)

This quote from Chappuis, Stiggins, and Commodore eloquently summarizes the shift that has taken place in our economic and social systems and in the role of schools since the 1960s, and so, a different understanding is needed about the schooling that is required. It is no longer sufficient to have a successful few; we must have as our objective that all students are successful self-directed *learners*. A different understanding is also needed about the role of assessment. "Instead of just providing evidence for grading and ranking students, assessments must go beyond tests and tools to include processes and strategies that encourage and support greater student achievement" (Chappuis et al., 2017, p. 3). This change has led to the understanding that it is essential to make clear distinctions between assessment *for* learning and assessment *of* learning and that schools and districts must ensure a balance between both purposes in the assessments used in classrooms. This distinction has been taken a step further by Lorna Earl and Steven Katz (2006) in the document they wrote for the Manitoba Ministry of Education, Citizenship and Youth titled *Rethinking Classroom Assessment*, where they make distinctions between assessment for, of, and as learning. In this view of the purposes of assessment, assessment *for* learning has been split into two:

1. Assessment *for* learning—Basically done by others who provide students with descriptive feedback to move their learning forward

2. Assessment *as* learning—Basically done by the students themselves through reflection, self-assessment, and goal setting

The result of this is that it is essential that each teacher is assessment literate; she or he must be able to collect accurate information about student achievement and must be able to use the results effectively to support learning and to communicate appropriately about student performance (doing it right, using it well) (see Figure 7.1, Keys to Quality Assessment).

The context of grading early in the twenty-first century has also been influenced by the widespread development of the use of standards and new and/or increased understanding about how learning takes place and factors that impact learning, such as motivation, growth mindset, multiple intelligence and learning styles, relationships and beliefs about fairness, and the role of professional judgment.

1. Standards

The 1990s saw a huge change in how curriculum is determined. By the end of that decade, forty-nine of fifty American states, most educational jurisdictions in Canada, and many jurisdictions in other parts of the world had developed mandatory standards for curriculum content. Subsequently, the National Governors Association Center for Best Practices (NGA Center) and the Council of Chief State School Officers (CCSSO) coordinated the development of the Common Core Standards that were voluntarily adopted by most states. "A recent analysis found that of the 46 states that adopted the standards, eight states have officially repealed or withdrawn, 21 states have finalized revisions—many of them minor— or have revision processes underway, and 17 states have not yet made any changes" (Strauss, 2017). Voluntary national standards in the United States have also been developed for science, fine arts, physical education and health, the social sciences, and technology. (For details, see Education World, 2017.) These standards have a variety of titles, including *standards, expectations, outcomes, learning results,* or *learning goals* (all used virtually interchangeably in this book). They describe, with varying degrees of clarity and specificity, what students are expected to know and be able to do at different stages in K–12 schooling. The distinguishing characteristic of these statements, as compared with previous organizers for curriculum content, is that the focus is on outputs—what students will know and do— rather than on inputs—the opportunities that will be provided to students and/or what teachers are expected to do. Generally speaking as shown in Figure 0.1, standards consist of *content standards* at various grade levels—the what—and *performance standards*— descriptions of how good is good enough. These two types of standards should form the basis of both classroom-level and large-scale assessment.

There is widespread agreement that standards provide a number of benefits:

- Clear focus on what students should know and be able to do

- Common direction for all schools in an educational jurisdiction

FIGURE 0.1 Assessment, Evaluation, and Reporting Connections Chart

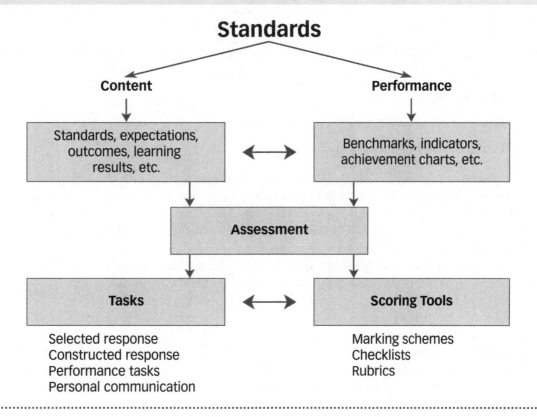

- Greater equity in learning goals for all students

- Consistent basis for communication about student achievement to and among stakeholders

- Explicit and external basis for judging the success of teaching and learning

There isn't universal support for standards, as some educators believe that they lead to standardization that takes spontaneity and creativity out of the learning process. I believe, however, that the standards determine the *what*, but teachers still have great freedom in determining the *hows*. It is appropriate to have some limits on teachers' individual freedom in curricular decision-making so that students have genuine opportunities to learn what needs to be learned, not just what the teacher likes to teach.

Improvements have been made in standards since they were first released, when they were often long lists that could not have been covered in K–12, let alone K–16. Considerable efforts have been made by those developing the standards to identify the essential learning for each subject, often by grade level or grade band, and to provide frameworks for the development of curriculum, instruction, and assessment.

To be effective, standards-based reform requires an approach to lesson and unit design that replaces teachers' absolute individual freedom and the tyranny of the textbook with a "design-down" or backwards design approach. This involves the following sequence:

1. Selection of the standard(s) as a base for planning

2. Identification of how and how well students will be expected to demonstrate their knowledge and skills

3. Instructional planning that is focused on "how to get them there"—that is, the instructional strategies, topics, theme, and resources that will be used to illuminate the standards

The logic of "design down" suggests a planning sequence for curriculum. This sequence has three stages:

1. Identify desired results.

2. Determine acceptable evidence of achievement.

3. Plan learning experiences and instruction.

It is important to remember that "[achievement] standards can be raised only by changes that are put into effect by teachers and students in classrooms" (Black & Wiliam, 1998, p. 148). The move to standards-based systems holds promise, if teachers are assisted appropriately in aligning curriculum instruction, assessment, grading, and reporting. If this alignment occurs, teachers will truly be able to "work smarter, not harder." It will also be easier for teachers to separate their dual classroom roles of coach/advocate and judge because of the clear focus on publicly articulated learning goals known to all. In this context, it should also be easier for students to see assessment as something that is done *with* them (to improve their learning) rather than something that is done *to* them (to find out what they don't know). For maximum benefit to be obtained, the purpose for grades and reporting must clearly be the communication of achievement of the standards. "If grading and reporting do not relate grades back to standards, they are giving a mixed message. Our grading practices must reflect and illuminate those standards" (Busick, 2000, p. 73).

Standards-Based Mindset

Busick was advocating for what has come to be known as standards-based grading and reporting, but what has become clear since she wrote in 2000 is that in order to effectively move to standards-based grading and reporting, educators must have a "standards-based mindset." This concept has been most clearly articulated by Tom Schimmer (2016) who says, "We need a completely new paradigm to replace the traditional view of grades as a commodity or reward. The new grading paradigm shifts grades from something the teacher randomly doles out to a reflection of learning that a student earns" (p. 3). Schimmer says we need this paradigm shift because (like me) he has seen many schools develop new report cards based on standards and then seen implementation struggle. "Without first establishing a standards-based mindset, many teachers still (find) themselves entrenched within traditional grading thought processes" (p. 4).

For Schimmer, the standards-based mindset has "three components that, when put together, reshape the grading paradigm." They are

1. Give students full credit for what they know.

2. Redefine accountability.

3. Repurpose the role of homework.

Each element and the interconnections between them can be seen in Figure 0.2.

Schimmer examines each of these three elements in detail in Chapters 5 through 7 (pp. 59–105). (They are also closely related to the guidelines presented in this book. Giving students full credit for what they know requires Guideline 5 specifically but also 1, 2, 6, 7, and 8);

redefining accountability is related to Guideline 3, and repurposing the role of homework is dealt with by Guideline 4.)

FIGURE 0.2 The Standards-Based Mindset

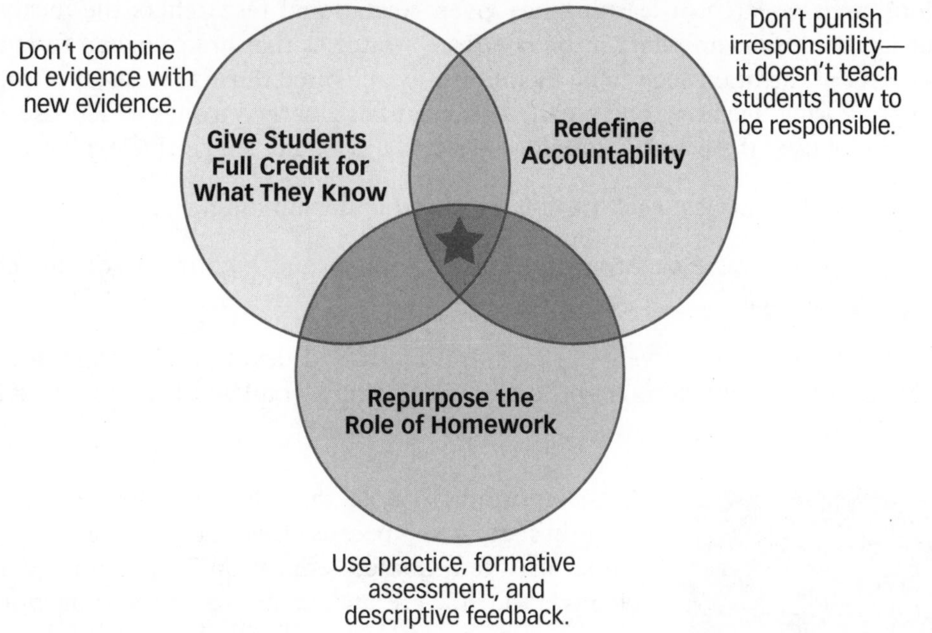

Don't combine
old evidence with
new evidence.

**Give Students
Full Credit for
What They Know**

**Redefine
Accountability**

Don't punish
irresponsibility—
it doesn't teach
students how to
be responsible.

**Repurpose the
Role of Homework**

Use practice, formative
assessment, and
descriptive feedback.

SOURCE: Schimmer (2016).

2. Constructivist Theories of Learning

Another important understanding has been the widespread acceptance of constructivist theories of learning. Constructivism recognizes that learning is a process in which the learner builds personal meaning by adding new understanding to old on the basis of each new experience. We have come to understand that learning is different for every student, in that it occurs in different ways and at a different pace. Individuals experience meaningful learning when they have the opportunity to process information and relate it to their own experiences. This has significant implications for how the teaching/learning process takes place in schools.

Each of these approaches requires more complex assessment than traditional approaches, which emphasize simple scoring of answers or behaviors as right or wrong. More varied approaches to assessment imply that teachers will not always have neat numbers that can be "crunched" and converted into grades. Grading, therefore, also becomes a more complex activity. Teachers need to consider carefully how they will incorporate data from a broader array of assessments into the determination of their students' grades. Guidelines presented in this book help teachers do this because they are designed to support varied approaches to learning and assessment and to encourage student success, however it is demonstrated.

3. Brain-Based Research

The constructivist view of learning has been supported and expanded by what is often called *brain-based research*. This research has demonstrated that the way the brain works is much more complex than theories of learning previously acknowledged. Brain research shows that the ability to learn is significantly influenced by coping with emotions and the environment, by being taught the skills of thinking, and by the encouragement of metacognition—that is, thinking about thinking.

Some of the best ideas about the brain and learning come from the work of Judy Willis (2007), who is both a neurologist and a teacher. She states,

> Brain-based research in learning has given educational researchers the means to translate neuroimaging data into classroom strategies that are designed to stimulate parts of the brain seen to be metabolically activated during stages of information processing, memory, and recall. And what has emerged from the neuroscience of learning over the past two decades is a body of highly suggestive evidence that
>
> • successful strategies teach for meaning and understanding, . . .
>
> • learning-conducive classrooms are low in threat and high in reasonable challenge, and that
>
> • students who are actively engaged and motivated devote more brain activity (as measured by metabolic processes) to learning. [bulleted list format added] (p. 698)

> "Two rules of thumb come from the field of brain research and enrichment. One is to eliminate threat, and the other is to enrich like crazy."
>
> —Jensen (1998, p. 2)

It is important to note that she says the evidence is only "highly suggestive" because there are reservations about the value of "brain-based education." Wiliam (2011) says claims about it "are at best premature and at worst disingenuous, many 'neuromyths' still abound" (p. 31).

To the extent that neuroscience evidence is applicable, it suggests that teachers need to be very flexible in their approach to assessment and grading. If teachers are more flexible, then a greater variety of information will be available to incorporate into their summary judgments. The guidelines in this book are designed to provide teachers with an approach to grading that allows for more than mere number crunching.

4. Multiple Intelligences and Learning Styles

When I wrote the third edition of this book, multiple intelligences and learning styles were "hot," and lots of professional development was taking place to get teachers to understand and apply them in the classroom. In the intervening nine years, enthusiasm has cooled, but the basic idea of recognizing individual differences in students and how they learn remains as an influence on decisions about instruction and assessment.

Gardner (1983) suggested that rather than one fixed entity of intelligence, there are at least eight intelligences:

- **Verbal/linguistic**—Words, listening, speaking, dialogues, poems
- **Visual/spatial**—Images, drawings, doodles, puzzles, visualization
- **Logical/mathematical**—Reasoning, facts, sequencing, judging, ranking
- **Musical/rhythmic**—Melody, beat, rap, pacing, blues, classical, jingles
- **Bodily/kinesthetic**—Activity, try, do, perform, touch, feel, participate

- **Interpersonal**—Interact, communicate, charisma, socialize, empathize

- **Intrapersonal**—Self, solitude, create, brood, write, dream, set goals

- **Naturalist**—Nature, observe, classify, hike, climb, trees, ecosystem

Learning styles are related to these intelligences but are normally limited to three or four preferences, such as visual, auditory, or kinesthetic. According to Goodwin and Hein (2017), "More than 70 different learning-styles frameworks exist . . . [but all of] these frameworks seem to capture more or less the same concepts, but with competing terminology" (p. 80).

Without getting too involved in the details, the idea that the focus should be on "how one is smart," not just on "how smart" is powerful, and should be on helping teachers help children learn by building on their strengths.

Each of these areas of understanding—constructivism, brain-based research, and multiple intelligences and learning styles—has contributed to the realization that, in the past, educators have held a very narrow view of learning and knowledge and that this view now needs to be broadened dramatically. Teachers, for example, have focused most commonly on only two intelligences, verbal/linguistic and logical/mathematical, to the exclusion of the other six; students whose strengths are in the other intelligences have frequently not done well in school.

5. Motivation

The classroom traditionally has been a haven for extrinsic motivation, starting with stickers and gold stars in kindergarten through Grade 3 for sitting quietly on the mat to money and product rewards from parents and grandparents for grades deemed worthy in upper elementary through Grade 12. Also, in some communities, stores give ice cream or donuts or pizza for "good" grades. Alfie Kohn has railed against these practices for decades starting most notably with his book *Punished by Rewards* (1993). More recently, in an article titled "A Case Against Grades" (Kohn, 2011), he identifies the negative impact of using grades as motivators, as "grades tend to diminish students in whatever they're learning," "grades create a preference for the easiest possible task" (p. 29), and "grades tend to reduce the quality of students' thinking" (p. 30).

Carrots and Sticks: The Seven Deadly Flaws

1. They can extinguish intrinsic motivation.

2. They can diminish performance.

3. They can crush creativity.

4. They can crowd out good behavior.

5. They can encourage cheating, shortcuts, and unethical behavior.

6. They can become addictive.

7. They can foster short-term thinking (Pink, 2009, p. 59).

My go-to source for help on understanding motivation has become Daniel Pink's (2009) superb book *Drive: The Surprising Truth About What Motivates Us*. He identifies three types of motivation. Motivation 1.0 is the things we do to survive. Motivation 2.0 is motivation based on punishments and rewards (i.e., extrinsic motivation). He calls punishments and rewards "if-then" motivators, as in, "*If* you do this, *then* you get that" (Pink, 2014, p. 12). He says they are "pretty effective for simple, short-term algorithmic tasks," but they "are far less effective for more complex, creative tasks" (Pink, 2014, p. 12). Motivation 3.0 is motivation based on "the drive to do something because it is interesting, challenging and absorbing" (p. 46) (i.e., intrinsic motivation). Pink identifies being extrinsically motivated as *Type X behavior* and being intrinsically motivated as *Type I behavior*. He notes that "for Type X's the main motivator is external rewards; any deeper satisfaction is welcome, but secondary. For Type I's the main motivator is freedom, challenge, and purpose of the undertaking itself; any other gains are welcome, but mainly as a bonus" (p. 78).

In a section of the book aimed at parents and educators, Pink makes some strong statements that may create discomfort for some teachers and parents.

> All kids start out as curious, self-directed Type I's. But many of them end up as disengaged, compliant Type X's. (p. 174)

> We need to break Motivation 2.0's grip on education and parenting. (p. 174)

> There is a mismatch between what science knows and what schools (and parents) do. (p. 174)

> We're bribing students into compliance instead of challenging them into engagement. (p. 174)

These are strong indictments of traditional teaching and parenting based on punishments and rewards, and he says, "If we want to equip young people for the new world of work—and, more important, if we want them to lead satisfying lives" (p. 174), we have to raise Type I students.

Fortunately, his review of modern psychological research allows him to tell us what the keys to intrinsic motivation are, and he makes suggestions for how to put those keys into teaching and parenting practices (pp. 175–184).

The keys to intrinsic motivation and developing Type I behavior are *autonomy*, *mastery*, and *purpose*. Autonomy means choice (at least some of the time) in what we do, when we do it, how we do it, and whom we do it with. Mastery means "the desire to get better and better at something that matters" (p. 111). Purpose means that we have to be clear about the value and goal(s) of what we are doing. In summing up how these three keys work, Pink states, "The science shows that the secret to high performance isn't our biological drive or our reward-and-punishment drive, but our third drive—our deep seated desire

> to direct our own lives,

> to extend and expand our capabilities, and

> to live a life of purpose. (p. 145)

The implications for teachers who want to support learning are that

1. some of the time, students must be given choice in what they do and how they do it and how they show what they know, understand, and can do;

2. students must know what getting better looks like and where they are on a learning continuum; and

3. the purpose for each learning and assessment activity must be clear to students.

Number 1 suggests that there is an important role for project-based learning (Cooper & Murphy, 2016) and the assessments that give students choices about how to show their learning.

Number 2 means that both the what and how well of learning goals must be clear and that the self-assessment capabilities of students must be developed from an early age.

Number 3 requires that teachers spend time on "hooking" students into learning and help them in developing their learning goals.

I believe that far too many teachers, especially at the high school level, and many parents still believe that punishment and rewards are effective. Most have not been exposed to the modern psychological research synthesized by Pink, and so, schools/districts need to use professional development to inform teachers and various means of communication to inform parents about the type of motivation that is most effective.

6. Mindset—Fixed or Growth

As hot as multiple intelligences and learning styles were in the 1990s, the hot idea of this decade has been "mindset," which comes from the work of Carol Dweck, a professor of psychology at Stanford University. Her book *Mindset: The New Psychology of Success* was published in 2008. Her work is "part of a tradition in psychology that shows the powers of people's beliefs" (p. ix). Dweck says that

> for twenty years, my research has shown that *the view you adopt for yourself* profoundly affects the way you lead your life. . . . Believing that your qualities are carved in stone—the *fixed mindset*—creates an urgency to prove yourself over and over. If you only have a certain amount of intelligence, a certain personality, and a certain moral character—well then you'd better have a healthy dose of them. (p. 6)

She says that as a child, she was focused on being smart, but she had a fixed mindset that "was really stamped in by Mrs. Wilson, (her) sixth-grade teacher" (p. 6), who seated the class around the room in IQ order and doled the important tasks to the highest IQ students. The other mindset sees "the hand you're dealt is just the starting point for development. This *growth mindset* is based on the belief that your basic qualities are things you can cultivate with your efforts" (p. 7).

Writing seven years later, Dweck (2015) says,

> We found that students' mindsets—how they perceive their abilities—played a key role in their achievement and motivation, and we found that if we changed students' mindsets, we could boost their achievement. . . . when students learned from a structured program that they could "grow their brains" and increase their intellectual abilities, they did better. Finally, we found that having children focus on the process that leads to learning (like hard work or trying new strategies) could foster a growth mindset and its benefits. (p. 1)

Many educators have applied the mindset principles with great success, but there have been pitfalls and misunderstandings, so Dweck shares some things she has learned. First, she says that "a growth mindset isn't just about effort" (p. 1). It also requires the use of new strategies and a willingness to seek the help of others, so it isn't appropriate to praise effort when they don't learn. "When they're stuck teachers can appreciate their work so far but add, "Let's talk about what you have tried and what you can try next" (p. 2). Second, "teachers who understand the growth mindset do everything in their power to unlock that learning"

(p. 2) and don't just blame the student's fixed mindset. Third, she has found teachers—and parents—who say they support a growth mindset but who see "children's mistakes as though they are problematic or harmful, rather than helpful," which leads "their children [to] develop more of a fixed mindset about their intelligence" (p. 2). Fourth is "let's legitimize the fixed mindset" because "we're all a mixture of fixed and growth mindsets" (p. 2), and "if we want to move closer to a growth mindset . . . we need to stay in touch with our fixed mindset thoughts and deeds" (p. 3).

There are important applications of mindset that relate to grading. Traditional grading, with everything counting from day one regardless of purpose, leads toward a fixed mindset while the grading guidelines in this book, especially not including formative assessment in grades and emphasizing more recent evidence, are aligned with growth mindset.

What is important is that teachers try to use the learning process to minimize fixed mindsets and maximize growth mindsets. When I reflect on this I think I did a much better job as a coach than as a teacher because with my teams, I focused on improvement individually and collectively by my players, not on winning, although, of course, when we got better, we won more. In the classroom, I was focused on my students getting better, but my basic approach of teach, test, and calculate grades acted against a growth mindset for many students.

A very interesting article describes how growth mindset can be used in what the authors identify as the *learning zone* and in the *performance zone* in sports (Frith & Briceno, 2017). The learning zone is "where an athlete (or student) must focus on a level of competence beyond that already mastered, which means there will be a higher level of challenge and more feedback and analysis than during the game (summative assessment). . . . Of course, after the game, feedback and analysis of the performance are very valuable, which again is the Learning Zone" (p. 2). The performance zone is obviously the game, but "players and coaches (students and teachers) are often stuck in the Performance Zone—focused on what they know and minimizing mistakes—even during practice, when they need to be in the Learning Zone" (p. 2). The authors provide an interesting graphic (see Figure 0.3) that shows how a growth mindset should be operationalized in both the learning and performance zones, and I think this is a fascinating practical application of mindset that has equal applicability in the classroom.

A very practical application of growth mindset in an area where it is desperately needed is the work of Jo Boaler in the teaching of mathematics. Students often have the belief drilled into them by parents, teachers, and peers that they are "just not good at math," and this generally prevents students from being successful. In her groundbreaking book *Mathematical Mindsets*, Boaler (2016) says,

> My work on mindset and math over recent years has helped me develop deep appreciation of the need to teach students about *mindset* inside mathematics, rather than in general. Students have such strong and often negative ideas about math that they can develop a growth mindset about everything else in their life but still believe that you can achieve highly in math or you can't. To change these damaging beliefs, students need to develop mathematical mindsets, and this book will teach you ways to encourage them. (p. ix)

Boaler writes about the power of mistakes and struggle, the importance of thinking conceptually, the necessity of rich mathematical tasks, eliminating or at least changing the nature of homework, replacing scores with descriptive feedback, developing student self-awareness and responsibility through reflection and self- and peer assessment, and valuing depth over speed. All of these are closely aligned with the guidelines that this book is about.

FIGURE 0.3 Growth Mindset in the Learning and Performance Zones

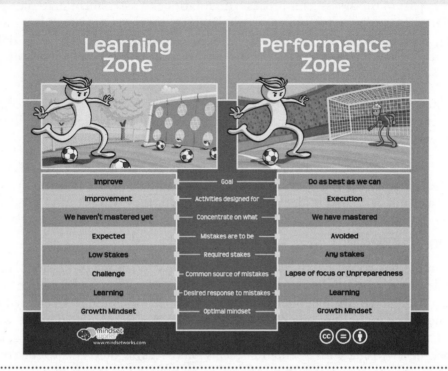

SOURCE: This graphic is available at https://www.zazzle.ca/learning_zone_vs_performance_zone_poster-228426858198203621. Accessed on April 26, 2017.

Other interesting ideas about what contributes to whether children succeed or not can be found in Paul Tough's interesting book *How Children Succeed* (2012).

Jo Boaler's Advice on Grading

1. Always allow students to resubmit any work or test for a higher grade.

2. Share grades with school administrators but not with students.

3. Use multidimensional grading.

4. Do not use a 100-point scale.

5. Do not include early assignments from math class in the end-of-class grade.

6. Do not include homework, if given, as any part of grading. (Boaler, 2016, pp. 167–168)

---

7. Fairness

Teachers have often justified their assessment and grading practices by saying that they are designed to be fair, but when you examine their practices, you find that by fair, they mean uniform. When people are different—and our students certainly are different—treating them uniformly is actually unfair because people who are different should be treated according to their needs. Fairness is not uniformity; it is *equity of opportunity*, and it means doing whatever we can to help each student to be successful.

The best short statement I've seen that captures fairness in assessment as equity of opportunity is this from the Ministry of Education in the province of Manitoba. It stated,

All students are given an *equal opportunity* to demonstrate what they know and can do as part of the assessment process. Adaptations to assessment materials and procedures are available for students including *but not restricted to* students with learning disabilities, to allow them to demonstrate their knowledge and skills, provided that the adaptations do not jeopardize the integrity or content of the assessment. [My italics for emphasis]

The first sentence emphasizes equal opportunity. The second sentence acknowledges individual differences and stresses that accommodations should be available for all students, not just students who have been identified as having learning disabilities.

Teachers tend to think parents see fairness as uniformity and continue to use it that way so as to not upset parents, but I'm convinced that parents actually see it as equity of opportunity because as soon as a need is identified for their child, they want it for their child.

8. Professional Judgment

When I was in the classroom, I abdicated my responsibility to use my professional judgment when I was determining grades for a number of years to a calculator and then to a computer grading program that did nothing but calculate the mean for the numbers I entered into the program. There was more than one occasion when I knew the calculated grade was inaccurate and made no sense, but when I was challenged, I justified it by saying the calculator/computer was never wrong with calculations. This was actually anathema to the concept of being a professional because one of the hallmarks of a profession is that you use your craft knowledge, and if challenged, you defend it without being defensive. (Think about the reaction of the first doctor if you say that you are going to get a second opinion.)

This statement from Damian Cooper captures the essence of professional judgment:

I define professional judgment as

"decisions made by educators,

in light of experience,

and with reference to

shared public standards and

established policies and guidelines." (Cooper, 2011, p. 13)

Each piece of this description is essential, which is why I put each on a separate line. It is important to recognize that professional judgment doesn't give teachers permission to do whatever they want because the decisions they make are constrained by shared public standards and established policies and guidelines. It does mean, however, that when the right to use professional judgment is acknowledged, for example, in the determination of grades, teachers are being recognized as the professionals we are and not just as bookkeepers.

Fortunately, the role of professional judgment is being recognized by policy makers and is increasingly being written into principles and policy documents. For example, the policy document for schools in Ontario, appropriately titled "Growing Success," states that "teachers' professional judgements are at the heart of effective assessment, evaluation and reporting of student achievement" (p. 8).

Damian Cooper expands on his definition of professional judgment in the following educator contribution.

Educator Contribution

Damian Cooper
President, Plan, Teach, Assess Consulting
Mississauga, Ontario

Professional Judgment

When I began teaching in the late '70s, we spoke only about evaluation and grading. The word *assessment* was only used in the context of special education (i.e., conducting an assessment of a child with special needs). My view of evaluation, learned in teachers' college and from the more experienced teachers around me, was that it was a mathematical process. I did not question the practice of applying the same percentage scale to measure the quality of argumentative discourse as contained in a twenty-page term paper and a history examination containing one hundred multiple-choice questions. Heaven knows how I determined that one paper would receive a grade of 78 percent while another received 80 percent! Back then, my colleagues and I certainly didn't develop a rubric for the essay before assigning the task. Neither did we ever engage in moderated marking in order to monitor and increase the reliability of our evaluations. But of course, we were not actually evaluating the merits of each paper, per se. Instead, we were ranking the papers, one against another, having begun by reading the two papers that we expect to define the extremes of the range of performance on the essay-writing task. And since the purpose of the evaluation task, back then, was to rank-order a set of papers, having one hundred points at one's disposal was most helpful! It followed that this paper is just slightly better than the one I just marked—a 79 percent, as opposed to an 80 percent.

My goodness, we've come a long way! It is now common practice for teachers to develop a rubric that communicates to students the performance standards for a given task before they begin to work on it. But with the use of tools that identify the *qualitative* features of a product or performance—as opposed to *quantifiable* features—the potential for measurement error increases. When an assessor observes a product or performance and judges its quality relative to the criteria and associated descriptors on a rubric, the potential for measurement error is greater than is the case when an assessor simply counts the number of items correct on a multiple-choice test—hence, the need for processes such as moderated marking and the use of anchors and exemplars to improve the reliability of rubric-based assessment.

When a group of teachers collaborate in the assessment of student products or performances, they discuss differing interpretations of the performance standards represented by the rubric and anchors in light of the samples of work in front of them. "Outlying" interpretations are "moderated" by more commonly held views. As teachers engage in this process over time, they are able to design more valid assessment tasks, they are able to create rubrics that increasingly reflect the essential criteria of those tasks, and they gain a clearer understanding of the myriad ways students respond to the demands of those tasks. Simply put, the quality of their professional judgments improves with experience. This is why I define *professional judgment* as "decisions made by educators, in light of their

(Continued)

experience, and with reference to shared public standards and established policies and guidelines."

In my work, I frequently encounter teachers who are uncomfortable with the notion of professional judgment. Not mincing words, I point out that teacher certification is a professional qualification. With this certification come numerous responsibilities and expectations, including the responsibility for assessing the progress and achievement of student learning. And despite attempts to render assessment as an exact science, it remains what Ruth Sutton (1991) described as "a human process, conducted by and with human beings, and subject inevitably to the frailties of human judgement. . . . It is, after all, an exercise in human communication."

As adults, we rely almost daily on the professional judgments of doctors, engineers, mechanics . . . As professionals in their given fields, we trust that they have the necessary knowledge and skills to look at our unique needs and recommend a course of action. Heeding Ruth Sutton's wise counsel, we must accept the fact that assessment of student learning is not a matter of precise numerical measurement. Assessment requires thoughtful, reflective observation of individual students, while referencing collaboratively developed performance standards. And just as we may ask for a second medical opinion concerning our personal health, students and parents are completely within their rights to ask for a second opinion regarding a mark or grade.

9. World Economy

The world economy changed dramatically in the 1990s, and the pace of the change has continued into this new century. Globalization has given unprecedented freedom based on comparative advantage to the flow of capital and jobs between countries. For the developed world, the manufacturing sector has declined, and the service, or tertiary, sector, which requires higher levels of skill and knowledge, has enjoyed a huge increase. Thus, far fewer jobs are available for those who do not complete high school.

The sorting function of schools—creating categories of those who leave early and find low-skill jobs, those who complete high school, and those who go on to postsecondary education—does not have the value that it did in the past. What schools now have most commonly is the orientation and expectation that students will succeed. Educators consider themselves to be in "the success business," ensuring that students have real opportunity available to them and that the economy has sufficient skilled and knowledgeable people to continue to function efficiently and effectively. This means that, at least at the school and classroom levels, we have to operate a criterion-referenced system in which the standards are absolute, and all can succeed (or fail), *not* a norm-referenced system where standards are relative. The result of a norm-referenced system is a dependable rank order in which a somewhat fixed percentage of students are successful, and some students fail regardless of their actual level of performance. Everyone, especially parents, must be helped to understand that in a standards-based, criterion-referenced system, we compare each student's performance to the standard, not to other students or groups of students, and that there is no place for the normal, or bell, curve in twenty-first-century schools.

HOW DO THESE CONCEPTS AFFECT CLASSROOM ASSESSMENT?

Global economic changes, together with the development of standards and our new understandings about learning, are leading to significant changes in the ways children are taught and the ways in which they are assessed. There has been a move to authentic learning—learning that is relevant to students and to the real world—and to authentic assessment—assessment that provides students with opportunities to demonstrate what they know, can do, and are like. These approaches have moved classroom assessment away from emphasis on paper-and-pencil methods (especially an almost exclusive reliance on multiple-choice questions) toward the use of a broader array of assessment methods, with an emphasis on performance assessment.

Reflecting on . . . Assessment Methods

Use the checklist shown in Figure 0.4 to identify the assessment methods you use in your classroom.

FIGURE 0.4 Assessment/Evaluation Checklist

Types of Student Assessment

Personal Communication
- ❏ Instructional questions
- ❏ Conferences
- ❏ Questionnaires
- ❏ Response journals
- ❏ Learning logs
- ❏ Oral tests/exams

Performance Assessment (using rubrics, checklists, rating scales, and anecdotal records)
- ❏ *Written Assignments*
  - ❏ Story
  - ❏ Play
  - ❏ Poem
  - ❏ Paragraph(s)
  - ❏ Essay
  - ❏ Research paper
- ❏ *Demonstrations* (live or taped)
  - ❏ Role-play
  - ❏ Debate
  - ❏ Reading
  - ❏ Recital
  - ❏ Retelling
  - ❏ Cooperative group work

- ❏ *Presentations* (live or taped)
  - ❏ Oral
  - ❏ Dance
  - ❏ Visual (photos or video)
- ❏ *Seminars*
- ❏ *Projects*
- ❏ *Portfolios*

Paper-and-Pencil Tests/Quizzes
- ❏ True/false
- ❏ Matching items
- ❏ Completion items
- ❏ Short answer
- ❏ Visual representation
- ❏ Multiple choice
- ❏ Essay style

SOURCE: Adapted from Burke, Fogarty, and Belgrad (2001).

All of these changes and their impact on schools lead to the conclusion that "the primary . . . purpose of classroom assessment [must now be] to inform learning, not to sort and select or justify a grade" (McTighe & Ferrara, 1995, p. 11).

The focus of traditional grading practices is to sort, select, and justify. Traditional grading practices emphasize the use of scores from assessments that are easy to quantify, such as selected-response items, especially multiple-choice questions. This approach was consistent with the competitive mentality prevalent in schools and society. However, as McTighe and Ferrara suggest, this approach is not compatible with the role grading could play, given what is now understood about the nature of learning and the type(s) of assessment that encourages and supports real learning. It is, therefore, necessary to move away from traditional grading and, as much as possible, use grading in the service of learning. This book provides many suggestions about ways in which grading can be used to inform learning.

WHY GRADE?

Reflecting on . . . Grading Purposes

Reflect on why educators grade students and their achievement. List as many purposes as you can. When you have finished your list, number each purpose in your order of priority (1 for highest priority).

Purpose

Through such reflection and discussion with colleagues, you will almost certainly recognize that clarity about purpose is critical to everything we do. Purpose is like a compass—it provides direction. If there is ever any doubt about what we should do, if we are thinking logically, we focus on our agreed-upon purpose, and what we should do usually becomes clear. Your reflection and discussion will lead you to find that there are many purposes for grading. To understand this fully, it is helpful to consider classifications from two sources. According to Gronlund and Linn (1990) in their classic text *Measurement and Evaluation in Teaching*, there are four general uses for grading:

1. Instructional uses—To clarify learning goals, indicate students' strengths and weaknesses, inform about students' personal-social development, and contribute to student motivation

2. Communicative uses—To inform parents/guardians about the learning program of the school and how well their children are achieving the intended learning goals

3. Administrative uses—To include "determining promotion and graduation, awarding honors, determining athletic eligibility, and reporting to other schools and prospective employers" (Gronlund & Linn, 1990, p. 429)

4. Guidance uses—To help students make their educational and vocational plans realistically

A second source, Guskey (1996), summarizes the purposes of grading as follows:

- *Communicate* the achievement status of students to parents and others.

- *Provide information* that students can use for self-evaluation.

- *Select, identify, or group* students for certain educational paths or programs.

- *Provide incentives* to learn.

- *Evaluate* the effectiveness of instructional programs. (p. 17)

Both of these classifications were developed relative to the broader, double meaning of grading. However, when the narrower, single meaning of grading employed in this book is used, all of the purposes still apply, although some uses apply more to marks than to grades—for example, self-assessment. Also note that the use of grades, especially traditional grades, for accountability purposes is of limited value.

It is clear from these two classifications that grades have served many different purposes. Therein lies the basic problem with grades—to serve so many purposes, one letter or number symbol must carry many types of information (achievement, effort, behavior, etc.) in the grade. Putting together such a variety of information makes it very difficult to clearly understand what grades mean. To achieve this clarity, a definitive prioritization of the purpose of grades, such as "the primary purpose for grading . . . should be to communicate with students and parents about their achievement of learning goals" (Brookhart, 2004, p. 5) is needed.

> Communication is also the purpose that best fits with what grades are—symbols that summarize achievement over a period of time.

The premise on which this book is based is that communicating student achievement is the primary purpose of grades. If clear communication about student achievement does not occur, then none of the other purposes of grades can be effectively carried out. Communication is also the purpose that best fits with what grades are—symbols that summarize achievement over a period of time. Communication is most effective when it is clear and concise; grades are certainly concise, and they can be clear communication vehicles if there is shared understanding of how they are determined and, thus, what they mean. Instructional and guidance uses not only need to be based on grades with clear meaning but also are best served by much more information than symbols provide. The administrative uses of grades are really a form of communication and are best served when communication is clear. The other purposes of grades are also best served when communication is the focus. Clarity about student achievement enables all the participants in the educational endeavor to do what is needed to support learning and encourage success.

Acknowledging that the primary purpose of grades is communication helps to point teachers in some very clear directions concerning the ingredients of grades and the use of grades at different levels within the school system. It is essential that there be a shared understanding, at least at the school level but preferably at the district level, about this primary purpose. It is critical, therefore, that teachers have opportunities for professional dialogue about purpose so this shared understanding can be developed. Emphasizing communication about achievement means that clarity is also needed about what achievement is (see Chapter 3). This emphasis is reflected in the analysis of grading and the grading guidelines presented in this book.

WHAT ARE THE UNDERLYING PERSPECTIVES ON GRADING?

The following sections explore seven perspectives, which were developed from a variety of assessment specialists, over the last twenty-three years. They provide both a clear indication of the philosophy that underlies the approach to grading advocated in this book and a vehicle for addressing some of the myths about grades and criticisms of grading.

Without reading any further, what is *your* reaction to the seven perspectives listed at the top of the next page? With what perspectives do you agree? Disagree? Which ones are you not sure about? Keep a record of your initial reaction as you read the rest of this section.

Reflecting on . . . the Seven Perspectives

1. Grading is not essential.

2. Grading is complicated.

3. Grading is subjective—and no apologies are needed.

4. Grading is inescapable.

5. Grading has a limited but expanding research base on how to grade.

6. Grading has an emerging consensus about best practice.

7. Grading that is faulty damages students—and teachers.

Perspective One: Grading Is Not Essential

Although many teachers appear from their actions to believe otherwise, "teachers do not need grades or reporting forms to teach well, and students can and do learn well without them" (Guskey, 1996, p. 16). Proof of this can be found in cocurricular activities, such as teams and clubs, and in interest courses, such as noncredit night school classes. In each of these situations, excellent teaching and superb learning take place—without grades. The problem in the school system is that as soon as grades are introduced, teachers, parents, and students emphasize grades rather than learning. As noted before, the issue of motivation and learning is of vital importance in this analysis of grading. It is therefore important to acknowledge the following:

- Teachers need to learn more about motivation so that they can use knowledge, rather than perception, to guide their practices.

- Students—and parents—have been taught to overvalue grades. Although it will not be easy, if teachers assess and grade better, both may learn to value grades more appropriately.

- Good grades may motivate, but poor grades have no motivational value. In fact, the only grades that motivate are those that are higher than a student expects or usually receives.

- Educators must recognize that learners are doing the learning and are responsible for their learning. It is then clear that the learner must have intrinsic interest and understand the worth of what is being learned, not by the carrot-and-stick approach that emphasizes gold stars and A's. Students' responsibility for their own learning can be achieved most effectively by consciously involving students in the assessment process. Students should be involved in designing or selecting assessment strategies, developing criteria, keeping records of their achievement, and communicating about their learning. (More information about student involvement is provided in Chapter 8.)

Perspective Two: Grading Is Complicated

Much grading is done in a mechanistic way, using formulas and/or computer grading software to produce the final grade merely as the result of arithmetic calculations. Teachers and students, therefore, come to believe that grading is simple; in fact, it is extremely complicated. Grades are shorthand; they are symbols that represent student performance. To arrive at grades, hundreds of decisions must be made along the way; the final grade could be very different if any of those choices is made differently. In particular, the decisions that are made about how the numbers are "crunched," or manipulated, are critical. This issue is addressed in Chapter 6, with suggestions about how to manipulate numbers in ways that support student learning better than traditional grading practices.

> "The question is not whether it is subjective, but whether the scoring system is defensible and credible."
>
> —Wiggins (2000)

Perspective Three: Grading Is Subjective—and No Apologies Are Needed

Rather than looking at the volume and complexity of the decisions about calculations, this perspective focuses on decisions about what is included in grades and the why of calculations. Because grades are usually the result of at least some numerical calculation, teachers often claim that grades are objective measures of student performance.

Grades are as much a matter of values as they are of science; all along the assessment trail, the teacher has made value judgments about what type of assessment to use, what to include in each assessment, how the assessment is scored, the actual scoring of the assessment, and why the scores are to be combined in a particular way to arrive at a final grade. Most of these value judgments are professional ones; these are the professional decisions that teachers are trained (and paid) to make. I wish I had a dollar for every time I've heard a teacher say they are striving to be objective or imply that objective is good, and subjective is bad. We have to stop using "subjective" pejoratively and "objective" as positive and praiseworthy. It must be acknowledged that grades are subjective, not objective, judgments. The issue isn't whether grades are subjective or objective; the issue should be whether our judgments are defensible and credible, and we have to be able to demonstrate that they are.

It should also be acknowledged that although most teachers' decisions are based on professional judgment, some are based on emotion. Teaching is and, it is hoped, always will be an interpersonal activity. How we feel about the individuals and the groups being assessed sometimes affects our judgment. Again, the point here is not that this is wrong but that all involved need to acknowledge that giving and receiving grades has a significant emotional component. The subjective and emotional aspects of grades have implications for how grading is done; grading will contribute to more effective learning when this perspective is acknowledged rather than denied.

Perspective Four: Grading Is Inescapable

Willis (1993) lists the following criticisms of grades:

- Grades are symbols, but what they represent is unclear.

- Grades sort students rather than help them to succeed.

- Grades give little information about student strengths and weaknesses.

- Grades are arbitrary and subjective.

- Grades undermine new teaching practices.

- Grades demoralize students who learn more slowly.

These criticisms all had validity when they were written and are still true today. Many educators believe that grades should be abolished. Although this might be desirable, especially for younger students, and although there are elementary schools, middle schools, high schools, and colleges that are gradeless to varying extents, it simply is not going to happen in the foreseeable future in most educational jurisdictions. In fact, there have been schools or school systems that have tried to remove grades from report cards that have been faced with community reaction so strongly negative that educators have been forced to return to traditional grades.

Wiggins (1996) states,

> Trying to get rid of familiar letter grades . . . gets the matter backwards while leading to needless political battles. . . . Parents have reasons to be suspicious of educators who want to tinker with a 120-year-old system they think they understand—even if we know traditional grades are often of questionable worth. (p. 142)

> "Grading practices are inherently subjective—a fact that constitutes not a denunciation of education but a truth that needs to be told."
>
> —Farr (2000, p. 14)

Getting it backwards means that it is probably counterproductive to focus on trying to eliminate grades; it is more productive to make grades better. Wiggins goes on to say that "what critics of grading must understand [is] that the symbol is not the problem; the lack of stable and clear points of reference in using symbols is the problem" (p. 142). These concerns are addressed in Chapters 1 and 2.

Wiggins (1996) makes another basic point: "Grades or numbers, like all symbols, offer efficient ways of summarizing" (p. 142). Although traditional grades may be of questionable worth, they have a long history. It is not worth fighting against this history; rather, it is worth fighting to make grades meaningful and more supportive of learning. That is what this book is about. What is needed are "thoughtfully designed grading and reporting systems that emphasize the formative and communicative aspects of grades [that] can maintain students' focus on important learning goals" (Guskey & Bailey, 2001, p. 20). Furthermore, "the harmful effects of grades can be eliminated by changes in grading systems that provide more chances for success, more guidance, feedback, re-instruction, and encouragement" (Haladyna, 1999, p. 12).

Perspective Five: Grading Has a Limited but Expanding Research Base on How to Grade

Sue Brookhart and seven colleagues, including Tom Guskey, published an article in late 2016 titled "A Century of Grading Research: Meaning and Value in the Most Common Educational Measure" (Brookhart et al., 2016). The study

> synthesizes findings from five types of grading studies: (a) early studies of the reliability of grades on student work, (b) quantitative studies of the composition of K–12 report card grades and related educational outcomes, (c) survey and interview studies of teachers' perceptions of grades and grading practices, (d) studies of standards-based grading (SBG) and the relationship between students' report card grades and large-scale accountability assessments, and (e) grading in higher education. (p. 1)

They say that "the purpose of this review is to provide a more comprehensive and complete answer to the research question 'What do grades mean?'" (Brookhart et al., 2016), and they conclude that most teachers' grades do not yield a pure achievement measure, but rather a multidimensional measure dependent on both what the students learn and how they behave in the classroom. This conclusion, however, does not excuse low quality grading practices or suggest there is no room for improvement. One hundred years of grading research have generally confirmed large variation among teachers in the validity and reliability of grades, both in the meaning of grades and the accuracy of reporting. (p. 30)

What can be seen from the five types of grading studies and the conclusion is that there is a lot of research about what teachers do but not very much about why and not much that provides direction toward more effective grading practices. Examining the resources in the References and Additional Resources at the back of this book shows that many books, journal articles, and reports have been written on grading, but most of them, including this book, are summaries of previous work and/or the opinion(s) of the author(s) on how grading should be done. Logical and well explained as the books, articles, and reports are, they should be given considerable weight, but they don't have the authority or weight provided by research, especially at a time when one of the mantras we hear constantly is that teachers should use *research-based practices*. Sadly, teachers freely ignore the advice of researchers, even those they acknowledge as experts. Stiggins, Frisbie, and Griswold (1989) identified nineteen grading practices that measurement experts agreed were desirable. When they examined the actual practices of a group of teachers, they found that teachers ignored the expert advice for eleven of these grading practices. Stiggins et al. suggest three reasons for this situation: (1) recommendations may be opinion or philosophical position rather than established fact, (2) recommendations may be unrealistic in terms of actual classroom practice, and (3) recommendations may be outside the knowledge or expertise base of teachers.

Perspective Six: Grading Has an Emerging Consensus About Best Practice

The limited research base and the fact that most methods of grading have advantages and disadvantages means that there is no absolutely right way to grade. The private nature of grading and the dramatic inconsistency in approaches within departments in high schools and colleges and between classrooms in elementary schools means that educators have major problems to address.

This is especially so where grades are *high stakes*—that is, when grades serve as more than communication with students and parents. Thus, when grades are the prime or major component of the decision-making process (e.g., for college admission), there needs to be greater consistency, at least within a school and, preferably, across a school district. Despite the limited research base, "our knowledge base on grading is quite extensive and offers us clear guidelines for better practice" (Guskey & Bailey, 2001, p. 145). There are, therefore, principles that can be agreed on that could lead to consistency across many—or even all—educational jurisdictions. These principles have been articulated as guidelines or directions for more effective grading practices by authors such as J. Chappuis et al. (2012), S. Chappuis et al. (2017), Brookhart (2011), Cooper (2007), Dueck (2014), Guskey and Bailey (2001), Guskey (2015), Reeves (2016a, 2016b), Schimmer (2016), Tomlinson and McTighe (2006), Vatterott (2015), and Wormeli (2006). Although there are some differences among the directions recommended by these authors, a consensus about best practices, previously lacking, has become evident since the year 2000 and increasingly since 2010. It is important to note that these are recommendations mostly by classroom assessment specialists, not just educational measurement experts.

Both the consensus noted previously and the fact that we know what to do is reflected in this book, the basic purpose of which is to provide principled and practical guidelines that all teachers can follow.

Perspective Seven: Grading That Is Faulty Damages Students and Teachers

The following student contribution illustrates some of the problems with traditional grading practices.

Allie
Age 15, High School Freshman

(*Allie is a struggling student who has received interventions her entire life. However, she desires to be successful and sees grades as the affirmation of if she's smart or as she says, "not so much."*)

I have a test tomorrow, and it's 11 p.m. I can't remember what I was supposed to learn in class, so I'll take my test, and I'll fail. I'm stupid. The majority of students can relate to this story. The alternate might be—it's the week before the test, and I begin to study. I relearn everything in a week, and I take my test and maybe even get 100 percent. After the quiz is done, I will never use that knowledge again. I have space in my brain for the information for the time being, and then once I have tested on it, I need to make more room for the other information that I'll be tested on. This is what my teachers call "learning."

As a high school student, I strive to get good grades and be the best. However, I am getting weighed down by the label I'm waiting to tell me if I'm smart or not. A means I'm smart; C means not so much. If I get an F, I might as well just give up. The stress is overwhelming. I have so many other commitments that I cannot meet that I just do what I have to do to get the best possible grade, and I don't care if I'm actually learning it for life; I just need to learn it for the test. Right? Teachers often dedicate the day before a test to model the idea of cramming and holding information for the next twenty-four hours, just so I can get the grade. Just because I am tested on a subject or unit doesn't mean I know the information. It means I can memorize something for a short amount of time.

While my parents crave and value my education, all I care is what my score is. The information doesn't matter to me, but the gradebook does. If I score perfectly, it means I memorized and practiced in advance. It doesn't mean I know all of the information and can use it in everyday tasks.

While I wish I could value the knowledge, instead of the grades, I know that it just isn't going to happen. There is not enough time or enough lesson plans for me to actually learn everything. If I could change something about grades, it would be for us to be tested on what we actually know, rather than what we memorized.

Overemphasis on grades and faulty assessment and grading practices have detrimental effects on student achievement, motivation, and self-concept, as can be seen in this vignette. Faulty grading also damages the interpersonal relationship on which good teaching and effective learning depend. This problem occurs at least partly because of teachers' dual roles as coach and judge. Unfortunately, these roles frequently conflict, and as a result, teacher–student relationships are damaged. Many of the problems illustrated by Allie's story would at least be alleviated and possibly even eliminated if grading practices that support learning and student success are used.

These perspectives on grading contrast with traditional perspectives on grading. Traditional grading is normally seen as being essential for learning ("If I don't give them grades, they won't do the work") and as straightforward and scientific ("The formula says . . .; the calculator shows . . ."). If one followed the first three perspectives to their logical conclusion, a strong case could be made against grading; but the fourth perspective means that, as it is virtually impossible to do away with grades, it is necessary to find ways to make grades more accurate, more consistent, more meaningful, and more supportive of learning. Teachers must not see grades as weapons of control but rather use grading as an exercise in professional judgment to enhance learning. If teachers acknowledge the seven perspectives in their dealings with parents, students, and other teachers, grades can become a positive rather than a punitive aspect of educational practice.

Reflecting on . . . the Perspectives

- Now that you have read about each of the perspectives, what do you think?

- With which perspectives do you now agree? Disagree?

- Which perspectives in the list are you now not sure about?

- How has your thinking changed from when you first read the list?

STANDARDS-BASED GRADING

When I submitted the first edition of this book in 1998, the title I suggested was *Good Grades*. Fortunately, a very clever editor at Skylight Publishing suggested the current title, with the emphasis on learning and standards. This was when the standards "movement" was relatively new and only beginning to gain widespread acceptance, so the idea of linking grades to standards instead of assessment methods was seen as foolish by some and radical by others. Fast forward almost twenty years, and that idea has widespread—but not universal—acceptance. The result is that this book is about what has come to be known as *standards-based grading*. Some prefer to call it *standards-referenced grading*, and others have begun to call it *evidence-based grading*, at least partly because of the backlash against the Common Core standards in the United States.

Standards-based grading and the guidelines described in this book are based on the premise identified earlier that "the primary purpose for grading . . . should be to communicate with students and parents about their achievement of learning goals" (Brookhart, 2004, p. 5); I cannot stress the importance of this purpose enough. It is essential that schools and districts be clear about the purpose of grades and that the procedures that teachers are required to follow are aligned to this purpose—and their mission and vision.

The useful graphic in Figure 0.5 provides a comparison and contrast between standards-based grading and traditional grading. It was developed by Connie Hamilton, who is a curriculum director in western Michigan. I think she is being overly generous to traditional grading in making the links to traditional grading from the middle column. They may be there for some who do traditional grading, but they certainly weren't part of my practice when I was a traditional grader in the classroom from 1967 to 1990.

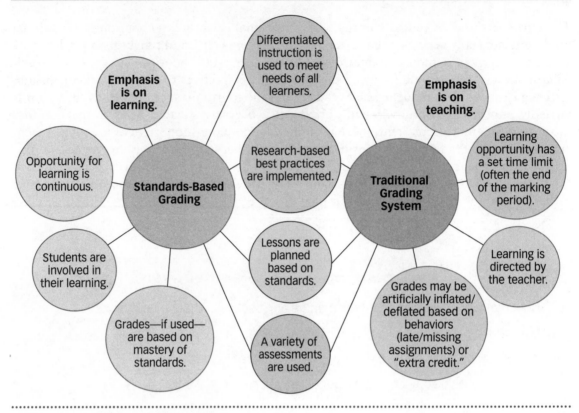

SOURCE: Connie Hamilton, @conniehamilton.

I believe that standards-based grading (SBG) is grading that accurately portrays student proficiency/mastery. In SBG grades are based on

- standards, not assessment methods, and

- levels of proficiency, not points, and they are

- not contaminated by nonachievement factors.

I also believe that there are a number of reasons why standards-based grading should be adopted universally for K–16 education, unless, of course, a school decides to not have grades at all. Those reasons are as follows:

1. **Mandate**—All school/districts now have standards/learning goals that are the base for curriculum, instruction, and assessment, so to maximize the impact of those standards, grading and reporting must be based on those standards.

2. **Support of learning**—School should be about learning, not just the accumulation of points, and learning is the focus when students know the learning goals and are striving for proficiency.

3. **Improved communication**—Standards-based grading and reporting provides a profile of students' strengths and weaknesses on standards that is much better information than a single subject grade.

4. **Consistency/fairness**—Because both the content and performance standards (the what and the how well) are clear, teachers have a base for shared practices that leads to greater consistency and acknowledges individual differences in achieving the learning goals.

5. **Teachers as professionals**—SBG "honors teachers as professionals. Grading is no longer a mechanical, numerical exercise. Rather it becomes an exercise in professional judgment" (O'Connor, 2017, p. 28).

6. **Traditional grading is broken**—Traditional grades usually include a variety of non-achievement factors and are calculated on points for virtually everything students do, regardless of when or why, often to two decimal points. This makes school a competition that is focused on points, not learning.

(Very detailed information about SBG, with some great graphics developed by leaders from the Champlain Valley Union School District in Vermont, can be found at http://cvulearns .weebly.com.)

If you have any doubt about that traditional grading is broken and/or that standards-based grading is essential, consider these student voices: first, the opinions about standards-based grading from Katie Budrow's sixth-grade students at Caruso Middle School in the northern suburbs of Chicago and then the brilliant poem about percentages and traditional grading by Alexa McDonald-Chiazzese, a twelve-year-old seventh-grade student at Strayer Middle School in Quakertown, Pennsylvania.

Educator Contribution

Katie Budrow
Sixth-Grade Science Teacher, Caruso Middle School
Deerfield, Illinois

Student Voices on Standards-Based Grading

"This class is frustrating. It's all about the learning. I can't hide anything. In other classes, I can find loopholes. I can't in here."

"I like that we get to go at our own pace and get to choose what our project is about. If we need help, Mrs. Budrow won't just tell us the answer but will direct us toward the right resource, so we know what to do."

"I think I'm learning way more than I should be for this project. I'm looking at equilibrium and tension."

"The best peer review I got was when my friend said that I didn't meet the second standard and then told me what I could do to get there."

"I like how in this room you get to go at your own pace. Also, when you meet with Mrs. Budrow, and you aren't ready yet, you can keep revising if you need to."

"I like standards-based grading because if I want to improve, I know exactly which part of the activity or project I need to work on."

"This class is very difficult because you can't find loopholes in the system. This is the only class that I feel grasps the concept of standards-based grading. When you do project-based learning, it is hard to find loopholes."

"This is a very self-directed classroom. We do all of our projects independently, but we can still get advice from our peers. They have great brains, just like us. We do several projects

(Continued)

(*Continued*)

a year, and Mrs. Budrow gives us resource documents and help along the way. Although we do all of our projects independently, toward the end of the project, we get peer reviews and get advice on our projects."

"With standards based, people don't have to worry about grades. It is easier to see what you have to improve on."

"I like the way Mrs. Budrow teaches because she grades us on what we learn. We don't just focus on the test and forget everything after that. She doesn't give us tests. We do projects, and she gives us real-world situations."

"We focus on the learning, not the grades."

Poem by Alexa McDonald-Chiazzese

100%
Your standards are high
Three-digit numbers are all you will accept
I got one and now that is the only thing you take

90%
It's not the "best" I can do
And you are disappointed in me
Because I didn't put in 110%
Of my mind, my body, my soul
Into this project

80%
Am I even trying anymore
It feels like you don't care at this point
Even though I spent hours and hours pouring myself into this
Blood, sweat, and tears
There might even be a sample
On the last assignment

70%
Why isn't it higher?
Do I even care about my report card?
This is what I have come to
After days of studying for the big assessment
It's too close to a D
I've disappointed myself

60%
You've convinced me that I'm so bad at this
That it shows in my grades now
I'm trying, I promise
But trying hard enough
I am not
To you, of course

50%
I got an F.
Everyone else did wonderfully
But this was too hard for me
Are you ashamed in me?
I'm sorry

40%
30%
20%
10%
0%
I've given up

You've drained the life out of me
Isn't this what you wanted?
I've found something I'm good at.
Failing.

SOURCE: With thanks to Shawn Storm, a teacher at Alexa's school for posting this on Twitter and for obtaining Alexa and her mother's permission for me to include it in the book.

GRADING "GYM"

This section actively engages readers in analyzing grading practices. Readers examine their own beliefs about grading and their own grading practices. Case studies then provide opportunities to analyze grading practices and identify grading issues: the what, how, and why of grading. Readers might keep a list of the issues that they identify to compare with a list provided in Figure 0.15. Having identified grading issues, one looks for solutions. One solution is practical guidelines that teachers use in their classrooms and in their grade books. A set of eight such guidelines is introduced in this section and examined in detail in Chapters 1 through 8.

How Do You Grade?

"[Grading] practices are not the result of careful thought or sound evidence. . . . Rather, they are used because teachers experienced these practices as students and, having little training or experience with other options, continue their use" (Guskey, 1996, p. 20). This statement may be unfair to some teachers, but it is certainly true for many teachers.

Reflecting on . . . Your Grading Practices

- What are the principles on which your grading practices are based?

- What are your actual grading practices? Do you just crunch numbers?

- What were or are the main influences on your grading principles and practices?

- How do your grading principles and practices compare with those of other teachers in your school?

The best ways to evaluate grading practices (and the principles behind them) are to analyze why we grade, the values on which our grading practices are based, and the sets of marks and/or grades and to identify the issues that arise from such analyses. Following are seven case studies that give us the opportunity to analyze grading practices and discover grading issues.

Case Study 1 begins with reading a short piece written by a high school junior in Michigan. He is obviously a veteran of the grading "wars" and has some very interesting things to say.

Luke
Age 17, High School Junior

(Luke is a classic case of a bright student whose grades don't reflect his capability. After years of educators labeling him with a letter, he has become cynical about grades and school yet still manages to own his learning outside the classroom.)

Grades only matter to teachers—not kids. I used to think grades were what told kids if they were smart or—let's just say "not smart." All through elementary and middle school, I watched as my friends would get anxious about getting their tests back to see how smart they were. I didn't even have to see one of the first six letters of the alphabet followed sometimes by a plus or minus to know what was there. Perceived smart kids with anything below a B quickly stuffed their papers in their backpacks or covered up the score with another sheet of paper. If they received their traditional A or A–, they proudly displayed it for all to see. They would ask questions about problems they got wrong but only if there were just a couple. Any students with many incorrect answers were not interested in figuring out why. It's almost a relief. Something like, "Whew, that's over. Maybe I'll do better next time."

I've always had the opinion that school shouldn't be about grades, but people think I'm crazy and brush it off as just a kid who doesn't get A's and B's and wishes he did. This hunch was recently affirmed during the fall term of my junior year in high school. I was carrying a heavy schedule, and geometry was the class I was having the most difficulty in—and that is probably a bit understated. When my mom and I attended parent–teacher conferences on October 22, the end of the trimester was still over a month away. I knew what I was going to hear; I've heard it for years. "Luke needs to try harder. He's a bright kid; he just needs to study more." But this time, the advice was much different. The teacher told us that my grade was so far behind that it was nearly impossible for me to pass the class. He said I'd have to get 100 percent on every assignment—including the final and that was not likely. He suggested I bring work from another class to geometry to help boost my grades in other classes to help my GPA because failing with a 59 percent was no different than failing with a 29 percent. An F is an F. I was thrilled that the weight of geometry was lifted from me. However, the fury rolled in as I started to rationalize what this professional educator, dedicated to student learning, was actually communicating to me: *It's not even worth trying to learn because the grade is what really matters.*

I'd like to give you a happy ending, telling you I took on the challenge and passed the class despite the lack of faith my teacher showed in me. Truth is I'm currently taking geometry online without a teacher and am on track to get a B . . . whatever that means.

Reflecting on . . . Case Study 1

- What is your reaction to Luke's ideas and the other student viewpoint and the student poem you read?

- What issues does it raise for you in relation to your school/district grading policies?

Case Study 2: Interim Report Card Grade, Grade 11 Science, 1995

Case Study 2 considers the impact of a zero mark on a grade and the possible impact on a student of grade reporting very early in a course/year.

The marks in Figure 0.6 were given to a student in a Grade 11 science class on an interim report card (after four weeks of seventy-six-minute classes) in a school with a semester block schedule.

FIGURE 0.6 Scores for a Student in a Grade 11 Science Class, 1995

TASK	MARK/TOTAL POSSIBLE	PERCENTAGE
Tests (50%)		
Symbols	16/20	80
Matter	0/68 (absent)	0
Reactions	35/50	70
Daily Work (25%)		
Assignment	10/10	100
Homework	9/10	90
Homework	9/10	90
Atom Quiz	9/10	90
Moles Quiz	5/8	62.5
Homework	9/10	90
Lab Work (25%)		
MP/BP	18/20	90
Superation	20/24	83.3
Reactions	7/10	70
Periodicity Check	10/10	100

This case study dramatically illustrates the effect of assigning a zero for a missed test. The student has six marks of 90 percent or higher, two marks in the 80s, and no mark lower than 62.5 percent, but the interim grade was lower than all except the lowest mark! A grade like this could have a devastating effect on students, causing them to give up. This student is achieving well, but the grade suggests otherwise—because of a missed test.

Reflecting on . . . Case Study 2

- What grade would you give the student? Why?

- The actual grade the student received was 68.2 percent. What is your reaction to this grade? Was this grade a fair reflection of the student's overall achievement?

- If the zero were not included, the grade would be 81.6 percent. Would this be a fairer reflection of the student's overall achievement?

- What grading issues arise from this case study?

- How this report would look like in a standards-based gradebook is illustrated in Figure 1.4 (page 55)—which is more accurate and more useful? Why?

Case Study 3: Chris Brown's Science Class

Case Study 3 considers the marks and grades of a teacher using a very traditional approach to grading. The student marks have been arranged so that, for most students, there are some obvious problems with their performance and/or the way it is graded.

The marks and grades in Figure 0.7 are for Chris Brown's science class in Ontario. If you are not a science teacher, put the appropriate items for your subject in place of the lab reports, care of equipment, and so forth. Note carefully the information that is shown: the gradebook extract regarding the miscellaneous items, the way absence is dealt with, and the grading scale.

Enter to the right of the chart the letter grade each student would get using the grading scale in use in your district/school.

In this Ontario class, there is one A, one B, four Cs, and a D—but did they go to the right students? Marg got a D, but on her achievement alone, she probably deserved an A. Lorna got an A but had only a 60 percent average on tests and exams. Is she a weak student who is a teacher's pet—one who receives good marks on the things she can get help on—or is she a very capable student who suffers from severe test anxiety? Kay and Peter have the same grade, but Kay is getting high 80s at the end, whereas Peter is receiving failing marks—is this fair? These are just some of the considerations that arise from an analysis of this case study.

Reflecting on . . . Case Study 3

- Do the grades awarded fairly reflect the results from which they were derived for each student?

- If you answered yes . . . For which students? Why?

- If you answered no . . . For which students? Why?

- What grading issues arise from this case study?

Case Study 4: All or Some

Another aspect of number crunching is presented in this case study.

Imagine you are going to go skydiving. Presumably, you want a parachute that has a very good chance of opening properly. The skydiving company has provided you with the assessment scores of three students who attended a recent parachute-packing course. These three are the only people they employ to pack parachutes, so you have to take a parachute packed by one of them—unless you want to jump without a parachute! Please note the competency/mastery level for each assessment, as shown in Figure 0.8, and carefully consider which student you want to pack your parachute.

FIGURE 0.7 Scores in Chris Brown's Science Class

NAME	LAB REPORTS										TOTAL	TESTS/EXAMS			TOTAL	MISCELLANEOUS*					TOTAL	FINAL TOTAL	FINAL GRADE %	FINAL GRADE LETTER	YOUR DISTRICT
OUT OF	10	10	10	10	10	10	10	10	10	10	100	50	50	100	200	20	20	20	20	20	100	400	%	LETTER	
Robin	6	6	6	5	6	6	7	6	6	6	60	33	39	81	153	15	15	12	0	10	52	265	66	C	
Kay	2	3	5	5	6	6	7	8	9	10	61	11	29	86	126	15	13	18	10	10	66	253	63	C	
Marg	10	A	10	10	10	10	A	A	10	A	60	50	A	100	150	0	0	0	0	15	15	225	56	D	
Dennis	9	8	9	9	10	8	9	9	9	9	89	24	24	49	97	20	17	17	20	20	94	280	70	B	
Peter	10	10	9	9	8	7	6	5	7	8	79	45	36	32	113	20	15	10	5	10	60	252	63	C	
Lorna	10	10	10	10	10	10	10	10	10	10	100	32	29	59	120	20	20	20	20	20	100	320	80	A	
John	8	8	8	7	9	9	8	10	9	8	84	32	30	57	119	20	8	7	0	5	40	243	61	C	

SOURCE: Adapted from Todd Rogers, University of Alberta. Used with permission.

A = Absent = 0 (for Lab Reports and Tests/Exams)

*Miscellaneous: 1—Attendance; 2—Care of Equipment; 3—Attitude/Participation; 4—Notebook; 5—Reading Reports (4 × 5 marks)

Letter Grade Legend (in Ontario): A = 80%–100%; B = 70%–79%; C = 60%–69%; D = 50%–59%; F = 0%–49%

FIGURE 0.8 Parachute-Packing Test Scores

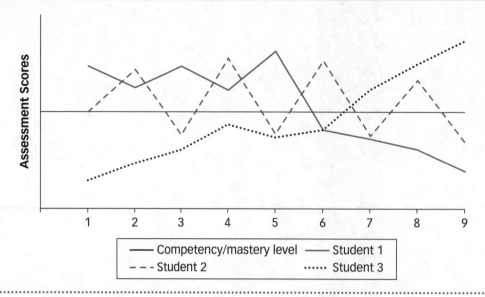

SOURCE: Originally developed by Michael Burger. Adapted from Davies (2000).

Reflecting on . . . Case Study 4

- Which student will you choose to pack your parachute? Why?

- If these were scores in a typical teacher's gradebook, which students would pass? Which students would fail?

- Is there any discrepancy between your answers to the above two questions? If so, why does this discrepancy occur?

Case Study 5: Grading Scales

What does A mean? What does F mean? For more than fifty years, as a student and as a teacher in Australia and in Canada, I have known that an A has been any grade more than 80 percent, and an F has been less than 50 percent. Anything different is very hard for me to comprehend. The familiar becomes the norm—but is it right? Case Study 5 demonstrates that letter grades, honors, and pass/fail mean very different things in different educational jurisdictions.

Figure 0.9 shows grading scales used in North America at five different places. You may use the last row to enter the grading scale used in your district/school.

An A can mean anything from 80 to 95 percent, and a failing grade can be anywhere between 49 and 74 percent. What do these variations mean? For example, is a 49 percent in Ontario the same as 74 percent in the district identified by Canady and Hotchkiss (1989) as having the highest grade equivalents? There is no way of knowing this without comparing marked student work from both jurisdictions, but the wide variation makes one wonder about the meaning of grades.

Reflecting on . . . Case Study 5

- What is your reaction to the wide variation in grading scales?

- What grading issues arise from this case study?

FIGURE 0.9 Grading Scales

SYMBOL CONVERSION					
SOURCE	A	B	C	D	F
Ontario	80–100%	70–79%	60–69%	50–59%	<50%
British Columbia	96–100%	85–92%	50–72%**	—	<50%
Cobb County, GA	90–100%	80–89%	74–79%	70–73%	<70%
South Carolina until 2016–2017	93–100%	85–92%	77–84%	70–76%	<70%
R. L. Canady*	95–100%	88–94%	81–87%	75–80%	<75%
Your School/District					

SOURCE: Canady & Hotchkiss (1989).

* Canady & Hotchkiss (1989).

** British Columbia—C+ = 64–72%, C = 60–63% and C– = 50–59%. Also 20–49% = I = In Progress.

Case Study 6: Grading Practices That Inhibit Learning (Old, but Still Worth Consideration!)

Canady and Hotchkiss (1989) identify twelve grading practices that inhibit learning (see Figure 0.10). Although the article was written almost twenty years ago, many of these are quite common practices that some—maybe even most—teachers would consider acceptable and normal. The fact that Canady and Hotchkiss labeled them as practices that inhibit learning requires teachers to analyze carefully their own grading practices.

The grading practices in numbers 2, 3, 4, 6, and 9 in Figure 0.10 were all part of my practices when I was a classroom teacher. Most teachers will probably admit that they use at least one-third of the practices listed at least some of the time. The grading guidelines presented in this book, when fully implemented, eliminate most of these learning-inhibiting practices.

FIGURE 0.10 Grading Practices That Inhibit Learning

1.	Inconsistent grading scales	The same performance results in different grades, in different schools or classes.
2.	Worshipping averages	All of the math to calculate an average is used, even when "the average" is not consistent with what the teacher knows about the student's learning.
3.	Using zeros indiscriminately	Giving zeros for incomplete work has a devastating effect on averages, and often zeros are not even related to learning or achievement but to nonacademic factors like behavior, respect, punctuality, etc.
4.	Following the pattern of assign, test, grade, and teach	Students are often told to read material and prepare for a test. The real discussion and teaching then takes place—after the test. It is far more logical to teach before testing, but we continue, to an alarming extent, to follow the pattern of assign, test, grade, and teach.
5.	Failing to match testing to teaching	Too many teachers rely on trick questions, new formats, and unfamiliar material. If students are expected to perform skills and produce information for a grade, these should be part of the instruction.
6.	Ambushing students	Pop quizzes are more likely to teach students how to cheat on a test than to result in learning. Such tests are often control vehicles designed to get even, not to aid understanding.

(Continued)

FIGURE 0.10 (Continued)

7.	**Suggesting that success is unlikely**	Students are not likely to strive for targets that they already know are unattainable to them.
8.	**Practicing "gotcha" teaching**	A nearly foolproof way to inhibit student learning is to keep the outcomes and expectations of their classes secret. Tests become ways of finding out how well students have read their teacher's mind.
9.	**Grading first efforts**	Learning is not a "one-shot" deal. When the products of learning are complex and sophisticated, students need a lot of teaching, practice, and feedback before the product is evaluated.
10.	**Penalizing students for taking risks**	Taking risks is not often rewarded in school. Students need encouragement and support, not low marks, while they try new or more demanding work.
11.	**Failing to recognize measurement error**	Very often grades are reported as objective statistics without attention to weighting factors or the reliability of the scores. In most cases, a composite score may be only a rough estimate of student learning, and sometimes, it can be very inaccurate.
12.	**Establishing inconsistent grading criteria**	Criteria for grading in schools and classes often change from day to day, grading period to grading period, and class to class. This lack of consensus makes it difficult for students to understand the rules.

SOURCE: Canady & Hotchkiss (1989).

Reflecting on . . . Case Study 6

- Which practices in Figure 0.10 are ones you never used, used in the past, or still use?

- What grading issues arise from this case study?

Case Study 7: Standards-Based Grading—What Grade Would Emmeline Get?

In standards-based systems, instead of grading each subject by points and percentages based on assessments, as illustrated in Case Study 3, teachers collect evidence for each standard or cluster of learning goals. In the example in Figure 0.11, the strands from a fairly common language arts curriculum have been used. Emmeline's scores on ten assessments in the first grading period have been recorded by strand using a scale where 4 means "excels," 3 means "competent," 2 means "partially competent," and 1 means "well below competency."

Summarizing Emmeline's first-quarter achievement with such an array of data and such variability in the scores is obviously difficult. If her grade(s) were determined by calculating averages, her overall average would be 2.3, while the strand averages are reading, 1.8; writing, 2.4; listening, speaking, and viewing, 4.0; language, 2.4; and literature, 1.0. If we

FIGURE 0.11 Emmeline's First-Quarter Assessment Scores in Language Arts

ASSESSMENTS	1	2	3	4	5	6	7	8	9	10	GRADE
Reading	1		2	2			2			2	2
Writing		1		2		3		3		3	3
Listening, Speaking, and Viewing					4				4		4
Language		1	2			3		3		3	3
Literature							1				

did this but reported by letter grades, we would need a scale to convert the numbers to letters, so a decision would have to be made about what would be an appropriate scale.

An alternative to the numerical, mechanical approach would be to look for the most consistent level of achievement while taking particular notice of more recent achievement. If this approach were used, her overall grade would probably be 3 while the strand grades would be 2 for reading; 3 for writing; 4 for listening, speaking, and viewing; 3 for language; and not enough information for literature. Hopefully, these grades would be left as numbers with a clear explanation of what each number meant, but as with the averaging example before, if reporting by letter grades were required, a conversion chart or logic rule would be needed.

Reflecting on . . . Case Study 7

- What grade should Emmeline get for reading; writing; listening, speaking, and viewing; language; and literature?

- Should Emmeline get an overall grade for language arts or just grades for each strand or standard?

- If Emmeline gets an overall grade for language arts, what should it be?

GRADING ISSUES

The case studies have identified the issues listed below:

- Basis for grades: Standards (learning goals) or assessment methods?

- Performance standards: What is good? How good is good enough?

- Ingredients: Achievement, ability, effort, attitude, behavior?

- Sources of information: Methods, purposes?

- What evidence: All or more recent evidence?

- Number crunching: Calculation method?

- Assessment quality and record-keeping

- Student understanding and involvement

Although this list is general, I believe it includes all of the major grading issues. (An expanded version of this list, with the specific concerns that arise out of each issue, can be found in Figure 0.15.)

Reflecting on . . . Grading Issues

- How does the list of grading issues discussed here compare with your list?
- Which issues that you identified are included?
- Which issues that you identified are not included?

Basis for Grades

Traditionally, grades have been based on assessment methods, but in standards-based systems, this is not the appropriate link. For grades to reflect standards directly and not just by chance, grades must be based directly on the standards. If there are a limited number of standards (no more than ten, preferably less), grades can be based on the standards themselves. In most standards documents, however, there are so many standards that they need to be organized in some way to provide a manageable amount of information. Another important consideration is that the basis for grades is usually also used as the base for reporting—traditionally a single grade for each subject. Basing grades on standards also gives us the most appropriate base for reporting in standards-based systems—a grade for each standard or learning goal.

Performance Standards

For grades to have any real meaning, they must be based on clear performance standards. This requires some point of reference or comparison: norm, criterion, or self-referenced. Traditionally, grades have been norm referenced; that is, they were based on comparing the individual with a group. This frequently involved the use of the bell curve or some modification of the curve.

With the introduction of national, state/provincial, and school standards, grades should be based on these standards and be criterion referenced. Even where there are no published standards, teachers use a criterion-referenced approach when they provide their students with rubrics—scoring scales that clearly indicate the criteria for quality work. Classroom teachers determine most criterion-referenced standards, however, so variability from teacher to teacher is still a major issue. The concerns arising from this problem are discussed in Chapter 2.

Self-referencing, which compares students with their own previous performance, can also provide valuable information.

Ingredients

Teachers have included and mixed many ingredients to arrive at grades. Student characteristics often used in the mix are achievement, ability, effort, attitude, behavior, participation, and attendance. These ingredients are included because grades serve so many purposes. The result is that grades frequently become almost meaningless for their main purpose: communication. This is clearly illustrated in Rick's Mysterious Falling Grade, the case that begins Chapter 3.

To provide effective communication, grades must be clearly understood by the message senders (teachers and schools) and by the message receivers (students, parents, college admissions officers, employers, etc.). "To develop this shared understanding, there must be a consistent and limited basis for what is included in grades; instead of including everything, we must limit the variables or valued attributes that are included in grades" (O'Connor, 1995, p. 94).

Frisbie and Waltman (1992) identified a large set of evaluation variables, which include everything (or almost everything) students do in the classroom and the school. This large set of evaluation variables is reduced to a smaller subset of grading/reporting variables. The size of this subset depends on the type of reporting to parents done by each school district. Care should be taken to ensure that the most highly valued variables are included.

Guskey (1994) provides another approach to identifying the ingredients in grades. He identifies progress criteria (for improvement scoring or learning gain); process criteria (for work habits, attendance, participation, effort, and so forth); and product criteria (for final exams, overall assessments, or other culminating demonstrations of learning).

Frisbie and Waltman's (1992) and Guskey's (1994) concepts are combined in Figure 0.12. Figure 0.12 shows that in Frisbie and Waltman's terms, Guskey's process and progress criteria are the reporting variables, and the product criteria are the grading variables. This combination identifies variables that are separated for grading and reporting purposes. The interaction shown in Figure 0.12, however, is rather simplistic, as some process variables may be assessed over time as part of stated learning goals and, therefore, legitimately may be considered as grading variables. Figure 0.13 on the next page illustrates this more complex and more realistic identification of grading and reporting variables. By definition, in standards-based systems, the content standards now define achievement and should be the only grading variables.

FIGURE 0.12 Reporting and Grading Variables

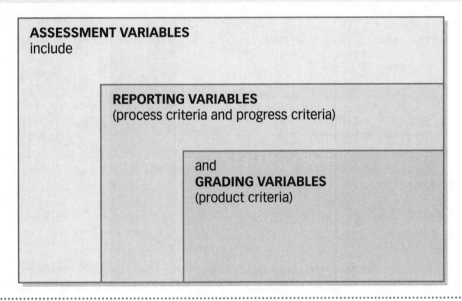

SOURCE: Adapted from O'Connor (1995). Reproduced with permission.

Sources of Information

Teachers have many possible sources of information about student achievement. Teachers use a wide variety of assessment methods, but not all sources of information need be included in grades. They decide which sources of information to include based on the reliability and validity of the data and the purpose of the assessment. Teachers make these decisions consciously and carefully.

What Evidence—All or Some?

Teachers tend to include everything that they score in student grades. The issue to consider is whether all of these data are necessary or appropriate. The amount of data needed is only that which enables confidence that any further information will confirm the previous judgment. Focus should be on the most consistent level of performance, especially toward the end of any learning (grading) period because this is the information that tells whether the learning goals have been met.

FIGURE 0.13 Sum Total of Everything Students Do in School/Classroom

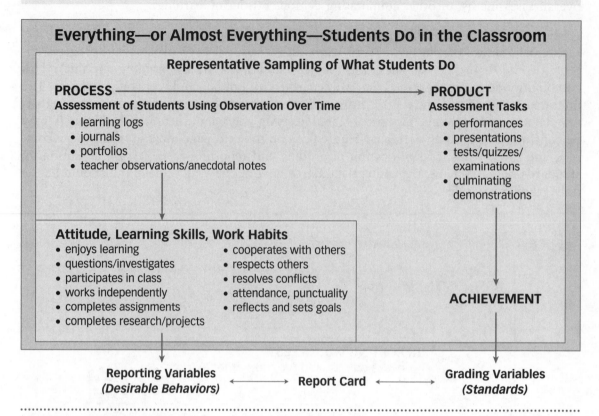

Everything—or Almost Everything—Students Do in the Classroom

Representative Sampling of What Students Do

PROCESS ⟶ **PRODUCT**

Assessment of Students Using Observation Over Time

- learning logs
- journals
- portfolios
- teacher observations/anecdotal notes

PRODUCT

Assessment Tasks

- performances
- presentations
- tests/quizzes/ examinations
- culminating demonstrations

Attitude, Learning Skills, Work Habits

- enjoys learning
- questions/investigates
- participates in class
- works independently
- completes assignments
- completes research/projects

- cooperates with others
- respects others
- resolves conflicts
- attendance, punctuality
- reflects and sets goals

ACHIEVEMENT

Reporting Variables (Desirable Behaviors) ⟷ **Report Card** ⟷ **Grading Variables (Standards)**

SOURCE: Adapted with permission from the work of Ken O'Connor and Damian Cooper, President, Plan, Teach, Assess Consulting, Mississauga, Ontario.

Number Crunching

The case studies demonstrate that numbers can be "crunched" in a variety of ways. They also demonstrate that, depending on the distribution of student scores and the method chosen, students can receive very different grades from the same set of scores. Thus, the methods chosen and the extent to which grading is seen just as a number-crunching activity are very important considerations in the determination of grades.

Assessment Quality and Record-Keeping

Because there are many ingredients in grades, even if only achievement information is used, teachers must ensure that the evidence comes from assessments that meet standards of quality. If, for example, assessment is not matched appropriately to teaching, student achievement will be measured incorrectly, and the evidence used to determine grades will be inaccurate.

Record-keeping is also important. The complexity of learning goals requires that teachers base grades on complete and accurately tabulated records—on paper, on a computer, or both. It is not justifiable for data that go into a grade to come off the top of a teacher's head at the end of the grading period.

Student Understanding and Involvement

Frequently, students do not understand how the grades they receive are determined. This occurs because either the grading procedures are not discussed with them or the procedures are too complicated to be understood. The issue is how teachers may best ensure that students understand their grades. If grades are to serve learning, students must understand and be involved in the whole assessment process.

GUIDELINES FOR GRADING

Grading issues can be addressed in a variety of ways. To avoid the misuse and misinterpretation of grades, a set of grading guidelines that address the practical concerns of teachers is needed. Traditional grading practices need to change so that grading aligns with standards and supports current assessment and evaluation philosophy and practices.

The grading guidelines in Figure 0.14 were developed with these principles in mind. Some of them require radical changes in teacher practices, especially at the high school and college levels, and in school and district policies. The guidelines are organized in approximate order relative to the implementation of standards because once Guideline 1 is implemented, Guidelines 2 through 6 become logical extensions. The order also relates to where most change from traditional grading practices is needed—relatively few teachers using traditional approaches to grading use Guidelines 1 through 6, whereas many (maybe most) teachers already follow Guidelines 7 and 8 to some extent. Each guideline stands on its own, but they interconnect significantly and, together, make a coherent group.

FIGURE 0.14 Guidelines for Grading in Standards-Based Systems

To Support Learning
To Encourage Student Success

1. Relate grading procedures to learning goals (i.e., standards).

2. Use clearly described criterion-referenced performance standards.

3. Limit the valued attributes included in grades to individual achievement.

4. Sample student performance—do not include all scores in grades.

5. Grade in pencil—keep records so they can be updated easily.

6. Determine, don't just calculate, grades.

7. Use quality assessment(s) and properly recorded evidence of achievement.

8. Discuss and involve students in assessment, including grading, throughout the teaching/learning process.

A more detailed version of these guidelines can be found in Appendix B: Guidelines for Grading in Standards-Based Systems.

This set of grading guidelines has been modified considerably from those proposed by Gronlund and Linn (1990), but it is important to acknowledge that their list was the starting point. The guidelines are intended to provide practical guidance to teachers as they decide how to grade students' achievement—and they can actually be used by teachers in their gradebooks or in setting up their computer grading programs. Guidelines also should have school and/or district policy status so that students and parents can understand the grading practices used in their classrooms and so that they can expect grading practices to be consistent among all teachers in each school. Currently, especially in high schools and colleges, teachers are "all over the book"; these guidelines should at least get teachers in the same chapter and, eventually, on the same page!

The specific relationships between the grading issues identified and the guidelines are shown in Figure 0.15. Each issue relates primarily to one guideline. Some of the specific concerns that arise out of each issue also are listed.

FIGURE 0.15 Relationships Between Grading Guidelines and Issues/Concerns

GUIDELINE	ISSUE(S)	CONCERN(S)/QUESTIONS
1	*Basis for grades* Assessment methods or learning goals	Which groupings—standards, strands? How many?
2	*Performance standards* Norm or criterion referenced	How good is good enough? How specific—levels or percentages? General or for each target? To curve or not to curve (bell, that is)?
3	*Ingredients* Achievement, behavior(s)	Learning skills/work habits/effort—where? How? Penalties and bonuses for late assignments/extra credit/academic dishonesty/attendance? Group grades/marks?
4	*Sources of information* Formative, summative methods	How much data? Which data is used in grades—tests? Quizzes? Homework? Variety?—paper and pencil, performance assessment, personal communication
5	*Changing grades*	Recent or all information? Second- or multiple-opportunity assessment?
6	*Number crunching* Mean, median, mode	Calculate or determine? How many points on the scale? Role of professional judgment? Effect of zeros/missed work?
7	*Quality* Record-keeping	Clear targets, clear purpose, sound design Management/tracking system(s)
8	*Student understanding/ involvement*	Clear criteria How much student involvement?

In Chapters 1 through 8, each guideline is examined individually in detail.

Reflecting on . . . the Guidelines

- What is *your* initial reaction to each of the guidelines for grading in Figure 0.14? Why?

- Think in terms of Kagan's PMI strategy—what is *positive*, what is negative (*minus*), and what is *interesting* and needs further thought and/or discussion? List your reflections for later reference.

An excellent visual showing the components involved in "Assessing Student Learning in the Classroom" has been produced by the Alberta Assessment Consortium, and it is included here in Figure 0.16 with my guideline numbers added as another way of showing the relationships between the guidelines and the connections with assessing student learning.

FIGURE 0.16 AAC Key Visual: Assessing Student Learning in the Classroom

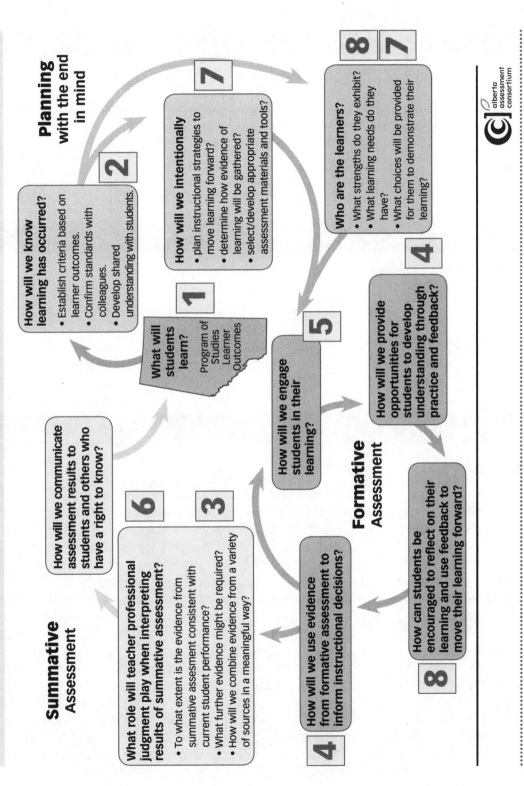

SOURCE: Copyright © 2017 by Alberta Assessment Consortium.

CHAPTER 1

Basing Grades on Standards

A student's grade should reflect what he/she actually knows and can demonstrate on . . . assessment tied to specific learning standards.

—Tarte (2015)

Guideline 1

Relate grading procedures to learning goals.

a. Use learning goals (standards or some clustering of standards [e.g., domains, strands]) as basis for grade determination and grade reporting.

b. Use assessment methods as the subset, *not* the set.

THE CASE OF . . .

Donald's Meaningless English Grade

In Grade 9, all students are required to take a course in English. Donald was not a good reader, and he avoided writing as much as he could. During the course, the students were supposed to read several books, and they also studied a Shakespeare play. He skimmed through the books and the play, but he relied on the CliffsNotes versions (Coles Notes in Canada!), and he regularly copied his homework from his very conscientious and capable friends. School procedures established a highly structured assessment schedule, which provided four days of written exams at the middle and at the end of each semester. School policy also required that a single subject grade be reported for each subject and that exams counted for 50 percent of the final grade. The English teacher taught 120 students each day and only had three days to complete the marking of the exams and determine the grades for the course, so most of the exam was selected response and short answer questions, with only one extended written response. The selected response and short answer questions were easy for Donald because he had a good memory, and he was a good test taker, but he did poorly on the extended written response because his understanding of the books and play was minimal, and his writing was of poor quality. He received thirty out of fifty on each exam, which was added to his homework and quiz scores (all multiple choice) resulting in a grade of B for the course. He didn't deserve that grade, as he hadn't met the reading and writing standards of the course.

WHAT'S THE PURPOSE OF THE GUIDELINE?

This guideline requires that grading procedures be aligned with stated learning goals. This alignment is direct, and ideally, a grade is determined and reported for each learning goal with no overall grade. As is illustrated in the case study, Donald should have received low grades for reading and writing, but because the assessments mostly tested memory and test-taking skills, he received well above a passing grade; determining his achievement based on the assessment methods resulted in a meaningless grade. This is not new, as Tombari and Borich wrote in 1999 that

> the principal limitation of any grading system that requires the teacher to assign one number or letter to represent . . . learning is that one symbol can convey *only* one meaning. One symbol *cannot* do justice to the different degrees of learning a student acquires across all learning outcomes. [emphasis added] (p. 213)

However, in many schools, especially high schools, for the foreseeable future, teachers will be required to determine single-subject grades. Where this is the case, the contribution of each learning goal to the final grade needs to be clear and direct. For example, if the primary learning goal in a course is practical demonstration of skills, then the final grade in that course should be based mostly on direct observation of those skills and evaluation of the products that result from those skills. Unfortunately, for me, this was the case for some teachers a long time ago. In the mid-1950s, I failed Grade 7 woodwork because no self-respecting bird would have wanted to live in the bird boxes that I built. If I could have written about how to build a bird box, I would have passed, but even way back then, in a skill-based course, my grade was determined by my lack of skill in the primary learning goal of the course.

> This guideline requires that grading procedures be aligned with stated learning goals. This alignment is direct, and ideally, a grade is determined and reported for each learning goal with *no* overall grade.

Teachers' record keeping, therefore, must be based on learning goals, not assessment methods.

WHAT ARE THE KEY ELEMENTS OF THE GUIDELINE?

Most schools and school districts and all states and provinces have had clearly stated learning goals for many years. Forty-six states and the District of Columbia signed on to use the Common Core standards, although some have withdrawn, and some states have made minimal changes to the Common Core and labeled them as state standards. Different words are used to name these goals. In most places, *standards* is still the label of choice, but in many places, other words, such as *learning results* or *expectations* or *outcomes*, are used. It does not matter much which word is used; the concept is that at either the local or state level, specific learning goals have been established, often on a grade-by-grade basis. In this book, I use *learning goals* and *standards* interchangeably; however, when other sources are quoted, the alternative terms will be retained.

Learning Goals/Standards

Grades should be effective communication vehicles, and the methods used to determine them need to provide optimum opportunities for student success and to encourage learning. For this to happen, the meaning of grades must be clear, which requires that, in addition to all of the issues dealt with in the other guidelines, grades must be directly related to the learning goals for each grading period in each classroom. Teachers must understand clearly what learning results are expected and then base their assessment and grading plans on these learning goals. Students must also understand clearly what the learning goals are so that they know what they are expected to know, understand, and be able to do.

The learning goals base identifies specific areas of strength and weakness in student learning in place of how they are performing on different assessment tools. It is much more valuable for students to recognize strength or weakness in, for example, reading comprehension or persuasive writing than to identify that they are good at tests but not good at performance assessments.

Planning the Base for Grading (and Reporting)

Lots of details about this process follow, but for those of you who prefer a short version with some direction about where to find more detail, here is a contribution from Carol Commodore:

Educator Contribution

Carol Commodore, EdD
Leadership, Learning and Assessment, LLC
Oconomowoc, Wisconsin

Focus on Standards

If we are going to communicate grades to students, parents, and others, then we need to be clear about the standards being measured. The grades communicate the achievement of the essential standards at the time of grading. The essential standards reflect the heart of the discipline and drive what is taught, learned, assessed, recorded, and communicated to others about the achievement of a student. We design our lessons and our assessments to measure these standards and underpinning learning targets. We record and grade the students' achievement by these standards or targets. A report card communicates a concise list of these essential standards and does not list a tome of standards or learning targets.

To ensure that essential standards are the central focus across the system, school districts need to have determined the essential standards for each of the disciplines and subjects being taught. For assistance in doing so, refer to S. Chappuis, Commodore, and Stiggins (2017, pp. 36–46).

Now for the details.

Off Target: Methods of Assessment

Before discussing an appropriate basis for determining grades, let's briefly discuss what not to use. Simply put, do not base a grading plan on methods of assessment, as illustrated in Figure 1.1.

With this type of plan, it is extremely difficult to identify each learning goal appropriately because the primary focus is on the methods of assessment. Each learning goal may be assessed in a number of ways; for example, there may be questions on tests/exams, written assignments, and demonstrations for each goal. However, to align assessment with the desired emphasis on each goal over several methods of assessment is extremely difficult.

FIGURE 1.1 Traditional Grading Plan

EVALUATION CATEGORY	EXPECTED RANGE
1. **Quizzes/tests/exams**	20–30%
2. **Written assignments** creative or explanatory paragraphs, essays, notes, organizers, writing folios, portfolios	15–25%
3. **Oral presentations or demonstrations** brief or more formal presentations or demonstrations, role-playing, debates, skits, etc.	15–25%
4. **Projects/assignments** research tasks, hands-on projects, video- or audiotaped productions, analysis of issues, etc.	10–20%
5. **Cooperative group learning** evaluation of the process and skills learned as an individual and as a group member	5–15%
6. **Independent learning** individual organizational skills, contributions to class activities and discussions, homework, and notebooks	5–15%
	70–130%

NOTE: Aspects of this plan conflict with other grading guidelines in addition to Guideline 1.

On Target: Learning Goals

A much better approach is to use the learning goals as the basis for grades. In this approach, some aspect of the organizational structure of the learning goals is the basis for grades for the year or for each grading period. This can be determined by teachers working collaboratively; for example, all of the Grade 3 teachers in a school or district or all of the Grade 9 science teachers meet to discuss what is the most appropriate basis for grades. This discussion may be the best professional dialogue teachers engage in because they have to be very clear about what goals are important at what point in the school year, and they have to be prepared to support their own views while respecting the opinions of others. Another important benefit of this approach is that much greater consistency across a school or district will occur than with traditional, largely private approaches to grading.

> Grades must be directly related to the learning goals for each grading period.

This discussion should take place within the parameters established by the district or by the school on a number of issues—what and how many learning goals, the level of specificity of the learning goals, grade-level specific or grade band learning goals, parent- or student-friendly language or official language, and whether there are subject grades or just grades for learning goals. When organizing and reporting by standards, teachers need to communicate this clearly to parents, and you can see an example in Ken Mattingly's contribution on the next page.

What and How Many Learning Goals

Almost all the time when learning goals have been developed at the state or provincial level, there are too many, so they have to be reduced in number and prioritized so that they are manageable and so that the more important standards receive appropriate emphasis. This has been done by some states and school districts through the identification of "power standards" or "essential standards" or "priority standards"—the most important standards from the original, overly long lists.

Educator Contribution

Ken Mattingly
Science Teacher, Rockcastle County Middle School, Mt. Vernon, Kentucky

Letter to Parents: 2016–2017 Science Grading Process

Dear Parents,

During this school year, Mr. Mattingly will be using a grading process that is designed to give students more direct feedback about specific learning objectives. Students will know the areas that they have performed well in and areas that need improvement. The following will outline how this grading system operates and what students can expect.

For each unit, students will receive a list of learning targets that are written in student-friendly language. These targets specify what students need to know, be able to do with what they know, and demonstrate. Lessons will focus on these learning targets, and students will know the learning target that the activity/lesson addresses. Students will be assessed throughout the unit to see how they are doing on their targets. This information will provide feedback to the teacher and student on the progress being made and where to go next.

This grading process allows students to have ownership of their grades. They have the opportunity to know what they need to improve on and how to improve it. Students also discover that it's never too late to learn.

Thanks,
Ken Mattingly

An example of how these learning goals were determined and communicated is provided in the following educator contribution from Laurie Ransom, the director of learning at the International School Yangon (Myanmar).

Educator Contribution

Laurie Ransom
Director of Teaching and Learning
The International School Yangon

Basing Grades on Standards

When the International School Yangon moved to standards-based assessment, grading, and reporting, we first prioritized our standards and indicators to identify the content and skills that should receive greater depth and emphasis and which would be assessed summatively. These would become the standards that would be guaranteed to be taught and assessed at ISY, no matter the teacher. Knowing what is essential has assisted teachers in focusing instruction, assessment, and grading. To help guide the process of prioritizing standards, teams considered the following when determining what was most essential in a set of grade-level standards: the importance for a student's enduring understanding of content, skills, and processes; the importance of the standard/indicator as a prerequisite to the next level of learning; the results of school-wide and grade-level student assessment data; and the standards/indicators that most support our Expected Schoolwide Learner Results—global mindedness, communication, critical thinking and creativity, and lifelong learning. After grade-level and horizontal teams identified essential standards, teams met in vertical grade clusters to help locate gaps and redundancies among the identified essential content, skills, and processes.

Once teams were satisfied with their prioritization of standards and indicators, they documented each course's essential standards in Atlas, our curriculum mapping software. The first "unit" of each course's unit calendar contains only the identified essential standards. This way, all teachers of a given course know what has been deemed essential. At the end of every school year, teams review their essential standards and revise them as needed for the following year.

In order to communicate our prioritized, essential standards to parents, students, and other stakeholders, such as prospective families, we created grade-level curriculum guides that provide readers with a summary of grade-level curriculum that includes an overview and explanation of a standards-based curriculum, course descriptions, and the essential standards for each course of a grade level. We also defined, in this publication, essential standards and pointed readers in the direction of our school's website to view standards in their entirety. During our back-to-school night program at the beginning of the school year, all families receive a curriculum guide for their children's given grade levels. Our curriculum guides are also posted on our website under each school division's page.

S. Chappuis et al. (2017, p. 37) suggest the following characteristics as being necessary for priority standards:

Clear—clearly stated and understandable by teachers and students within the district as well as by the members of the community the district serves

Aligned—where relevant, aligned with state standards for accountability purposes

Essential—reflect what is truly important to learn; what is at the heart of the discipline, what will have leverage in mastering the next level of learning; what will prepare the students not only to do well today but also well into the future

Realistic—the time, the conditions, and the materials are available for students to reach the targets

Measurable—what students have to know or do is measurable and can be assessed accurately

They give this example developed by a group of world language teachers.

"At the end of 12th grade, students will be able to do the following:

• Interpret the spoken words of the target language;

• Communicate orally and fluently with others in the target language;

- Read for comprehension in the target language and for a variety of purposes;

- Write clearly and effectively (in the target language) for different purposes and audiences;

- Compare and contrast the cultures of the target language with their own culture." (S. Chappuis et al., 2017, p. 37)

Guskey and Bailey (2001, p. 38) make a useful distinction between what they call "Curriculum Standards" and "Reporting Standards" in this way:

CURRICULUM STANDARDS	REPORTING STANDARDS
Designed for planning instruction and assessments	Designed for reporting on student learning
Many in number (10–50 per subject)	Relatively few in number (usually 4–6 per subject)
Highly specific	Broad and more general
Complicated and detailed	Clear and understandable
Expressed in complex, educator language	Expressed in parent-friendly language

The reporting standards are what S. Chappuis et al. (2017, p. 37) and others label as "priority standards," and the curriculum standards are often labeled by others as "learning targets."

Guskey and Bailey recommend four to six standards per subject for grading and reporting purposes, and while this is good advice, I would suggest that a minimum of three and a maximum of about ten grading and reporting standards are acceptable. I provided a detailed illustration of this using the Common Core Grade Mathematics standards in *The School Leader's Guide to Grading* (O'Connor, 2013, pp. 38–41). Here, I will use the Next Generation Science Standards to illustrate how standards may be chosen and how a learning goals–based gradebook would look different from the 1995 science gradebook in Figure 0.6 on page 31.

The National Science Education Framework

There are three main components in the framework:

1. Scientific and engineering practices

2. Crosscutting concepts, and

3. Core ideas in four disciplinary areas as follows:

1. Scientific and Engineering Practices

1. Asking questions (for science) and defining problems (for engineering)

2. Developing and using models

3. Planning and carrying out investigations

4. Analyzing and interpreting data

5. Using mathematics and computational thinking

6. Constructing explanations (for science) and designing solutions (for engineering)

7. Engaging in argument from evidence

8. Obtaining, evaluating, and communicating information

2. Crosscutting Concepts

1. Patterns

2. Cause and effect: Mechanism and explanation

3. Scale, proportion, and quantity

4. Systems and system models

5. Energy and matter: Flows, cycles, and conservation

6. Structure and function

7. Stability and change

3. Disciplinary Core Ideas

Physical Sciences

PS1: Matter and its interactions

PS2: Motion and stability: Forces and interactions

PS3: Energy

PS4: Waves and their applications in technologies for information transfer

Life Sciences

LS1: From molecules to organisms: Structures and processes

LS2: Ecosystems: Interactions, energy, and dynamics

LS3: Heredity: Inheritance and variation of traits

LS4: Biological evolution: Unity and diversity

Earth and Space Sciences

ESS1: Earth's place in the universe

ESS2: Earth's systems

ESS3: Earth and human activity

Engineering, Technology, and Applications of Science

ETS1: Engineering design

ETS2: Links among engineering, technology, science, and society (3) (National Research Council, 2012, p. 3)

This means for a physical sciences course, there are nineteen categories—eight scientific and engineering practices, seven crosscutting concepts, and four disciplinary core ideas (DCIs), but the DCIs include thirteen "component ideas," as follows:

Core Idea PS1: Matter and Its Interactions

PS1.A: Structure and Properties of Matter

PS1.B: Chemical Reactions

PS1.C: Nuclear Processes

Core Idea PS2: Motion and Stability: Forces and Interactions

PS2.A: Forces and Motion

PS2.B: Types of Interactions

PS2.C: Stability and Instability in Physical Systems

Core Idea PS3: Energy

PS3.A: Definitions of Energy

PS3.B: Conservation of Energy and Energy Transfer

PS3.C: Relationship Between Energy and Forces

PS3.D: Energy in Chemical Processes and Everyday Life

Core Idea PS4: Waves and Their Applications in Technologies for Information Transfer

PS4.A: Wave Properties

PS4.B: Electromagnetic Radiation

PS4.C: Information Technologies and Instrumentation (105)

The framework states that the

> vision is that students will acquire knowledge and skill in science and engineering through a carefully designed sequence of learning experiences. Each stage in the sequence will develop students' understanding of particular scientific and engineering practices, crosscutting concepts, and disciplinary core ideas while also deepening their insights into the ways in which people from all backgrounds engage in scientific and engineering work to satisfy their curiosity, seek explanations about the world, and improve the built world.
>
> *A major question confronting each curriculum developer will be which of the practices and crosscutting concepts to feature in lessons or units around a particular disciplinary core idea so that, across the curriculum, they all receive sufficient attention.* [my emphasis]
>
> Every science unit or engineering design project must have as one of its goals the development of student understanding of at least one disciplinary core idea. In addition, explicit reference to each crosscutting concept will recur frequently and in varied contexts across disciplines and grades. These concepts need to become part of the language of science that students use when framing questions or developing ways to observe, describe, and explain the world.

Similarly, the science and engineering practices delineated in this framework should become familiar as well to students through increasingly sophisticated experiences with them across grades K–8. Although not every such practice will occur in every context, the curriculum should provide repeated opportunities across various contexts for students to develop their facility with these practices and use them as a support for developing deep understanding of the concepts in question and of the nature of science and of engineering. This will require substantial redesign of current and future curricula. (p. 247)

This means that all of these ideas need to be taken into account when deciding which standards will be the focus of each course or grade level and when planning curriculum and instruction.

Based on the National Science Framework, twenty-six states and their broad-based teams worked together with a forty-member writing team and partners throughout the country to operationalize the vision described above by developing the NGSS. This was done by crafting *performance expectations* (see Figure 1.2) that state "what students should be able to do in order to demonstrate that they have met the standard, thus providing . . . clear and specific targets for curriculum, instruction, and assessment" (NGSS Lead States, 2013, *How to Read the Next Generation Science Standards*, p. 1). The NGSS emphasize that the NGSS are standards, not curriculum, with this statement:

The NGSS are standards, or goals, that reflect what a student should know and be able to do—they do not dictate the manner or methods by which the standards are taught. The performance expectations are written in a way that expresses the concept and skills to be performed but still leaves curricular and instructional decisions to states, districts, school and teachers. The performance expectations do not dictate curriculum; rather, they are coherently developed to allow flexibility in the instruction of the standards. While the NGSS have a fuller architecture than traditional standards—at the request of states so they do not need to begin implementation by "unpacking" the standards—the NGSS do not dictate nor limit curriculum and instructional choices. (NGSS Lead States, 2013, *Executive Summary*, p. 2)

However, to help those curriculum instructional choices, the NGSS provides suggested course maps (NGSS Lead States, 2013, *Appendix K*, pp. 8–12).

Now I will use the Next Generation Science Standards to illustrate how standards may be chosen and how a learning goals–based gradebook would look different from the 1995 science gradebook in Figure 0.6 on page 31.

In the 1995 gradebook (Figure 0.6), science content is identified as Symbols, Matter, Reactions, Atom Quiz, Moles Quiz, MB/BP, Superation, and Periodicity Check. This was handed to me about five weeks into my son's first semester as a high school junior in a parent–teacher conference with his science teacher. At his high school, parent–teacher conferences were limited to *seven* minutes; in this conference about five-and-a-half minutes was spent talking about the subject grade. This was not a productive discussion, and in the end, we agreed to disagree about the accuracy and meaning of his science grade. We then spent a minute and a half talking about what the details showed about my son's strengths and weaknesses in the class; this was a more productive discussion, as we identified that his daily work was very good (except for one little quiz), that his labs were strong, and his variable test performance pointed to a need for better preparation (and attendance) at tests.

FIGURE 1.2 NGSS Performance Expectations

PHYSICAL SCIENCE	LIFE SCIENCE	EARTH AND SPACE SCIENCE
PS1 Matter and Its Interactions	*LS1 From Molecules to Organisms: Structures and Processes*	*ESS1 Earth's Place in the Universe*
PS1A Structure and Properties of Matter	LS1A Structure and Function	ESS1A The Universe and Its Stars
PS1B Chemical Reactions	LS1B Growth and Development of Organisms	ESS1B Earth and the Solar System
PS1C Nuclear Processes	LS1C Organization for Matter and Energy Flow in Organisms	ESS1C The History of Planet Earth
PS2 Motion and Stability: Forces and Interactions	LS1D Information Processing	*ESS2 Earth's Systems*
PS2A Forces and Motion	*LS2 Ecosystems: Interactions, Energy, and Dynamics*	ESS2A Earth Materials and Systems
PS2B Types of Interactions	LS2A Interdependent Relationships in Ecosystems	ESS2B Plate Tectonics and Large-Scale System Interactions
PS2C Stability and Instability in Physical Systems	LS2B Cycles of Matter and Energy Transfer in Ecosystems	ESS2C The Roles of Water in Earth's Surface Processes
PS3 Energy	LS2C Ecosystem Dynamics, Functioning, and Resilience	ESS2D Weather and Climate
PS3A Definitions of Energy	LS2D Social Interactions and Group Behavior	ESS2E Biogeology
PS3B Conservation of Energy and Energy Transfer		
PS3C Relationship Between Energy and Forces	*LS3 Heredity: Inheritance and Variation of Traits*	*ESS3 Earth and Human Activity*
PS3D Energy and Chemical Processes in Everyday Life	LS3A Inheritance of Traits	ESS3A Natural Resources
	LS3B Variation of Traits	ESS3B Natural Hazards
PS4 Waves and Their Applications in Technologies for Information Transfer	*LS4 Biological Evolution: Unity and Diversity*	ESS3C Human Impacts on Earth Systems
PS4A Wave Properties	LS4A Evidence of Common Ancestry	ESS3D Global Climate Change
PS4B Electromagnetic Radiation	LS4B Natural Selection	
PS4C Information Technologies and Instrumentation	LS4C Adaptation	
	LS4D Biodiversity and Humans	

SOURCE: Adapted from https://www.nextgenscience.org/sites/default/files/NGSS%20Combined%20Topics%2011.8.13.pdf

Figure 1.3 shows twelve performance expectations suggested by Ken Mattingly for a high school chemistry course. This is slightly more than the maximum number that I suggest, but if five or six are addressed in each quarter with some overlap, or seven or eight in each half of a semester, again with some overlap, this organization is manageable. Using these performance expectations, the 1995 gradebook would look like Figure 1.4 as a standards-based gradebook in 2017.

FIGURE 1.3 Chemistry Course Performance Expectations

HS-PS1-1; HS-PS1-2; HS-PS1-3; HS-PS1-4; HS-PS1-5; HS-PS1-6; HS-PS1-7; HS-LS1-5; HS-LS1-6; HS-LS1-7; HS-LS2-5; and HS-ETS1-4

SOURCE: As suggested by Ken Mattingly, science teacher, Rockcastle (KY) County Schools.

NOTE: See Appendix E for a list of the details of these performance expectations.

FIGURE 1.4 Science Standards-Based Gradebook 2017

Student: _____

| Standards | Achievement Evidence | | | | | | | Summary |
| | Assessments | | | | | | Strengths, Areas for Improvement/ Observations | |
	9/15 Test	9/22 Lab	9/30 Lab	10/02 Test	10/8 Lab	10/12 Test		
Structure and Properties of Matter (HS-PS1-2)		1	2		2	2 (14/20)		2
Explaining Reaction Rates (HS-PS1-5)		M		M	1			I
Properties and Periodicity (HS-PS1-1)	3 (8/10)				1			NA
Chemical Systems and Equilibrium (HS-PS1-6)		1	4 (20/24)			4 (19/20)		4
Mole Calculations (HS-PS1-7)		1	2	M	4	4 (20/20)		4
Scientific inquiry (HS-PS1-3)	4 (8/10)	2	3	M	4	4 (5/5)		4
Comments:							**Overall Grade: I**	

M = Missing; IE = Insufficient Evidence; NA = Not Assessed; I = Incomplete

N.B., This gradebook is based as accurately as possible on the gradebook in Figure 0.6.

NOTE: Ken Mattingly, science teacher at Rockcastle County (KY) Middle School provided advice to the author on the Next Generation Science Standards and classification for this gradebook.

If I were handed this gradebook, I would have a much richer picture of my son's learning in science. I would know that

1. he was excelling in three standards (Chemical Systems and Equilibrium, Mole Calculations, and Scientific Inquiry), although he had difficulty with two of them at the beginning and was a little inconsistent in the third;

2. he was approaching proficiency in Structure and Properties of Matter;

3. his understanding of Properties and Periodicity was inconsistent, but the teacher had not provided enough summative assessment opportunities to make a summary judgment (NA);

4. his understanding of Explaining Reaction Rates was limited, and again, the teacher could not make a summary judgment because he had missed two summative assessments, so he had provided insufficient evidence (I); and

5. if a subject grade were required, his current grade would be an I for incomplete because he had provided insufficient evidence for one standard.[1] (More about this follows in this chapter and in Chapter 6.)

Clearly this gradebook provides much richer information about my son's science achievement because it is organized by learning goals rather than assessment methods and activities.

This is how teachers should be grading and reporting from kindergarten to Grade 12 (and beyond!). It is being done very commonly by elementary schools in North America and in international schools and is reflected in report cards such the ones in Figures 10.2 (Elementary) and 10.5 (High School). To complete such a report card effectively, ideally, each teacher would need to use a gradebook page like this for each student, with horizontal rows for each of the standards included on the report card (see Figures 1.4 and 1.5). Unfortunately, most teachers have too many students and/or too many subjects to teach to manage tracking of every standard for every student in this way, so they must find alternatives. One alternative is to use spreadsheets, but most often, it means using computer grading programs. Until recently, this was a challenge, as the programs were not friendly to a standards-based approach. But now, the gradebooks in student information systems, like PowerSchool,[2] and stand-alone programs, like JumpRope and FreshGrade, can be used as fully standards-based gradebooks. (There is more about computer gradebooks in Chapter 9.)

One subject in which this approach has often been seen to be difficult is physical education. Melograno (2007) provides helpful direction when he suggests that teachers of this subject should grade and report student achievement based on the standards developed by the U.S. National Association for Sport and Physical Education as follows:

- Competency in Motor Skills and Movement Patterns;

- Understanding of Movement Concepts, Principles, Strategies, and Tactics;

- Regular Participation in Physical Activity;

- Health-Enhancing Level of Physical Fitness;

- Responsible Personal and Social Behavior; and

- Values Physical Activity.

---

[1] This example was originally used in a blog that I wrote for PowerSchool titled "Why Standards-Based Grading? For Parents and Educators."

[2] In order to be ethical and to acknowledge a potential conflict of interest, I must inform readers that I have consulted with PowerSchool for a number of years.

As another example, Figure 1.5 shows the domains for Grade 5 mathematics and a gradebook that a teacher could use to record the achievement evidence for each domain. Each component of every assessment had to link to one of the five domains. A grade can then be determined for each domain, and if required, an overall grade could be determined for mathematics. (There is more about determining subject grades in Chapter 6.)

FIGURE 1.5 Standards-Based Gradebook for Grade 5 Math

Student: _____

| Standards | Achievement Evidence | | | | | | | Summary |
| | Assessments | | | | | | Strengths, Areas for Improvement/ Observations | |
	10/1 Test	10/15 PA	11/7 PA	11/18 PA	12/8 PA	12/17 Test		
Operations and Algebraic Thinking (3)	3 (17/10)	3		3	3	3 (17/20)		3
Number and Operations in Base Ten (7)					1			NA
Number and Operations— Fractions (7)	3 (15/10)		4	2	2	2 (15/20)		2
Measurement and Data (5)	4 (19/20)	4	4	1		4 (19/20)		4
Geometry (4)		1	2	3	4	4 (20/20)		4
Comments:								

It is almost self-evident that standards-based grading also requires standards-based assessment; if tests are used, each test must be on a single learning goal, or the test must be organized by learning goals (or concepts or skills). For example, the Advanced Algebra second-semester final exam developed by Megan Moran had the structure and directions you see on the next page.

Megan Moran
Math Teacher, Schaumberg High School, Illinois

A Standards-Based Algebra Exam Outline

Advanced Algebra Second-Semester Final Exam

The following are the primary standards of second semester. You will need to complete all of the following and show your understanding of these concepts.

I will mark each problem as correct, minor error, or additional evidence needed. When I return the final exam, you will be able to either make corrections or attempt another problem (depending on how I marked it) to demonstrate your understanding.

Unit 7: Graph and Identify Key Characteristics of Rational Functions

three questions

Unit 7: Write and Model Rational Functions

two questions

Unit 8: Determine the Solution Set of Polynomial Equations and Inequalities

three questions

Unit 8: Graph and Identify the Key Characteristics of Polynomial Functions

two questions

Unit 9: Determine the Solution Set of Radical and nth Root Equations

three questions, one with a two-part question

Unit 10: Graph and Identify the Key Characteristics of Logarithmic and Exponential Functions

two questions

Unit 10: Determine the Solution Set of Exponential and Logarithmic Equations

six questions

Unit 11: Determine the Solution Set of the System of Equations or Inequalities

five questions

It is important to emphasize that in this example, no overall score for the test was recorded or reported. The traditional practice of only recording an overall score provides very little information of value and should be discontinued. On a test with questions like this scored with points, a number of students might get twenty out of twenty-six questions correct, with each having a very different pattern of performance on the eight concepts. The valuable information is the profile—the details of the achievement on each concept/learning goal—not an overall score.

Other Ways of Organizing Learning Goals/Standards

There is not one way to organize the standards for grading and reporting, so I'll provide several alternatives.

One different approach can be found in Ontario, Canada. For all elementary and secondary subjects, achievement charts have been developed that provide the performance standards. Each chart has descriptors of four levels of achievement for each of four categories of knowledge and skill—Knowledge and Understanding, Inquiry and Thinking, Communication, and Application (often referred to as KICA). These categories are now consistent across all subjects in Grades 1 to 8 and all of the disciplines included in the secondary curriculum. This approach was developed to

- provide a common framework that encompasses all curriculum expectations for all grades and all subjects/disciplines;

- guide the development of assessment tasks and tools (including rubrics);

- help teachers to plan instruction for learning;

- assist teachers in providing meaningful feedback to students;

- provide a variety of aspects (e.g., use of thinking skills, ability to apply knowledge) on which to assess and evaluate student learning. (Ontario Ministry of Education, 2004, p. 2)

Expectations (as learning goals are called in Ontario) have to be classified into the most appropriate category, and then a gradebook like Figure 1.6 can be used with these categories. The International School of Brussels (ISB) uses a similar approach, as the categories it uses are Knowledge, Skills and Understanding, Conceptual Learning, Language for Learning, and Learning Relationships.

Another possible organizing structure is to use the four categories of learning targets identified by the Assessment Training Institute, namely Knowledge, Reasoning, Skills, and Products. These could be placed in Figure 1.6 instead of the Ontario categories (J. Chappuis, Stiggins, S. Chappuis, & Arter, 2012; Dueck, 2014, pp. 72–78).

The main benefit of the Ontario and the International School of Brussels approaches is that using the same categories for every subject reveals patterns of performance across subjects for students, so it is easier to identify areas of strength and areas that need improvement. Teachers in schools that use this approach report that it is helpful to be able to identify that across the curriculum, e.g., Marilyn is strong in communication but struggles with application.

The "Big Idea" approach, advocated by Caren Cameron and Kathleen Gregory, is also worthy of consideration (Cameron & Gregory, 2014, pp. 21–23). They "start with the question 'What are the five big ideas that you expect your students to learn in . . . ?' (choose one subject area) and invite individuals to respond in their own words from their experiences" (Cameron & Gregory, 2014, p. 21). They do this because they have "learned that going directly to curriculum documents at this point can make us give up before we get started; it is easy to get bogged down by the sheer numbers of learning standards and/or by the specialized and complex language used in curriculum documents" (Cameron & Gregory, 2014, p. 21). They recommend referring to curriculum documents only after the Big Ideas for one subject have been identified. The question to ask then is, "What Big Ideas on our list do we need to add to or change?" (Cameron & Gregory, 2014, p. 23). This process should result in three to five Big Ideas because they have "learned that fewer than three Big Ideas is too general, and having more than five is overwhelming" (Cameron & Gregory, 2014, p. 23).

FIGURE 1.6 Summary of Evidence for Ontario Secondary Subjects or Courses

Student: _____

Achievement Evidence												
Assessments **Knowledge/ Skill Categories**												Summary
Knowledge/ Understanding												
Thinking/Inquiry												
Communication												
Application												
Comments												
									Most consistent level of achievement with consideration for more recent			

The last step in the process is deciding on the words and phrases that make the Big Idea clear for all; for this they insist that each Big Idea be stated as "a short phrase that begins with a verb, such as read or understand" (Cameron & Gregory, 2014, p. 23).

Two examples of their Big Ideas can be seen in Figure 1.7.

FIGURE 1.7 Big Ideas

LANGUAGE ARTS (GRADE 7)	SOCIAL STUDIES: CANADA (GRADES 4–6)
1. Read a wide variety of text using reading and thinking strategies to increase understanding.	1. Understand/explain how (and where) people lived in Canada in the past.
2. Respond to a text as a way to increase understanding, enjoyment, and appreciation of language, literature, and story.	2. Connect the past to the present by explaining what happened in the past influences what we have in Canada today.
3. Communicate in written, visual, and digital media forms for different purposes and audiences.	3. Retell stories from Canada's past to bring to life the vivid/vital aspects of our history.
4. Use oral language to communicate ideas/information for different purposes and audiences.	4. Manage information and ideas.
	5. Communicate ideas, information, beliefs, and perspectives.

These are some of the numerous alternatives for determining how to organize the collection and reporting of evidence of student achievement. It has a great amount of complexity, as we have to try to balance the amount of information with workload for teachers and possible information overload for parents. It is very much related to what and how many learning goals are in the chosen standards, but ultimately, choosing the organizational structure for grading and reporting has to be determined by what is manageable for teachers and understandable and useful for parents and students.

It is important to note, however, that for planning and delivery of instruction and learning activities, the standards have to be deconstructed into learning targets that are the focus of units and lessons. Many authors, such as S. Chappuis et al. (2017), Dueck (2014), Vagle (2015), Westerberg (2016), and White (2017), have addressed this issue and provided valuable advice and examples of how this should be done.

Grade-Level-Specific or Grade Band Learning Goals

This really depends on the structure of the standards chosen for use; some standards documents have at least slightly different standards for each grade while others provide standards for a grade band, say Grade 1 to 3. If it is possible, I believe standards for grade bands is the best approach because it increases the likelihood that teachers and students—and especially parents—will develop a deeper understanding of and appreciation for the standards.

Parent- and Student-Friendly Language or Official Language

This one is easy—we should always translate the official standards language into parent- and student-friendly language whenever that can be done without becoming wordy or complicated. One of the best ways to do this is with the standards written as age-appropriate "I can" statements for students.

Subject Grades or Just Grades for Learning Goals

This one is not easy because of our traditional approach to grading where there is a single grade for each subject, and often, that is all there has been on report cards, especially for high schools. When we have grades for standards, adding a subject grade not only doesn't add to the communication, it also detracts from the value of the communication for three reasons. First, when there is a subject grade as well as standards grades, students and parents—and grandparents—inevitably focus on the subject grade that does no more than give a highly generalized view of the student's achievement rather than the more valuable information provided by the standards grades. Second, if a student's achievement on the standards is consistent at any level, the subject grade is redundant. Third, if a student's achievement on the standards is inconsistent, it is difficult to determine an accurate, meaningful subject grade. The net result is that determining subject grades is work for teachers that has little value, so I believe that there absolutely should be no subject grades until Grade 9—and ideally not until Grade 11. Two years of data are sufficient for the external purposes for which grades are used at the end of high school. I realize that we will probably continue to have subject grades for all four years in most high schools and in many middle schools, so we have to have ways to determine subject grades from standards grades. That issue will be addressed in Chapter 6.

If overall grades are required, another aspect of this approach that teachers need to consider is whether each strand or category is of equal significance or whether some strands or categories are more important for the whole year or for any particular grading period. It is best to start from the position that each standard or category is of equal significance and later make appropriate adjustments if it is obvious from the emphasis in the curriculum or in the way the subject is taught that one or more strands or categories are of greater significance than others. An example of this uneven distribution is the recommendation from the provincial association for physical and health education (PHE) teachers in Ontario that the application category be assigned a weight of 60–65 percent for Grades 9 and 10 PHE.

Learning Goals and Passing Grades

A final issue that needs to be considered in connection with this guideline is whether students should receive credit for a course if they have not demonstrated mastery of the critical learning goals. In the example in Figure 1.4, there are six science standards. Although unlikely, it would be possible for a student to obtain very low scores on two strands while obtaining sufficiently high scores on the other strands to obtain a passing overall grade. Teachers and schools need to decide if this is acceptable. If they really believe all or some strands are critical, then students should not be able to obtain credit unless they have achieved a reasonable level of competence—ideally proficiency—on each of those standards. This is certainly the approach taken with pilots (and plumbers): a student pilot has to be competent in takeoffs, flying the plane in the air, landings, and navigation before receiving certification. It is not acceptable that the pilot be excellent in three of these and less than competent in the fourth, but this is the performance we reward in high schools all the time with traditional grading.

If teachers use this approach, it obviously complicates the grading process, but it supports the concept that grading is an exercise in professional judgment, not just a mechanical, numerical exercise.

It also illustrates the interconnectedness of the grading guidelines because Guidelines 4 and 5 (see Chapters 4 and 5) become absolutely critical. Formative assessment has to be used to provide information to students and to teachers about progress (Guideline 4), and students need to have growth acknowledged appropriately and have varied opportunities to demonstrate competence (Guideline 5). In the educator contribution that follows, Megan Moran describes the requirement that a student must reach proficiency or excel on all of the standards categorized as "primary" to receive credit for the course.

Educator Contribution

Megan Moran
Math Teacher, Schaumberg High School, Illinois

Prioritizing Standards for Determining Proficiency

In my transition to teach, grade, and report with standards, the aspect that has undergone the most continuous change has been the writing and organization of the standards themselves. When I began, I wrote three to five standards per unit for my Algebra 2 course, totalling close to sixty standards for a single year. It was difficult for me to track and too overwhelming for students to tackle when they wanted to show improved understanding on a reassessment. Most students resorted to calling standards by a number (Unit 3 Standard 2) rather than by the name, such as "Graphing Linear Functions." Purpose and communication was lost with having too many standards.

Another issue was converting these approximately thirty standards per semester into a single letter grade that is still required at my school. Coming from twelve years of my own schooling, combined with ten years teaching in a traditional grading system, my instinct was to draw on those experiences when setting the expectation of a student exiting my course. I chose to avoid using an average of the four-point rubric scores from the thirty standards and instead set the expectation that students must reach a proficiency score of three or excel with a score of four and will earn a grade based on the percentage of standards at that score. For example, to pass the course with a D, a student must reach or excel beyond proficiency on 60 percent of the standards. To earn a C, B, or A, students must meet the expectation on 70 percent, 80 percent, and 90 percent of standards respectively.

I soon learned that this was a flawed plan. Paired with the number of standards I had, the predicament was that students got to choose which 60 percent of the standards they would learn and choose to reassess only enough to meet the low bar I set. In addition, these clean percentage cut offs didn't work smoothly in a context of twenty-eight or thirty-one standards. While I was trying to eliminate the "game of school" by implementing standards-based learning, the students adapted and learned to play a "new game of school"—the one I created.

To address the number of standards, I started by listing the standards I taught and the skills that supported each of them. I realized many of my previous sixty standards were actually skills. This step was crucial to reducing the quantity of standards I was teaching and assessing while still acknowledging that I teach much more. Next, I organized the now only thirty standards into three overarching ideas: Solution Sets, Modeling, and Properties. My final step in organization was to rate the priority of the standard. I labeled each standard as primary or secondary. Primary standards are essential for success in upcoming units and the subsequent course, and secondary standards are supportive to the others yet not as crucial.

The most important change came about organically from the primary and secondary standard organization. I set the expectation that to pass the course, a student must reach proficiency or excel on all primary standards, and the other traditional grades—C, B, or A—would be determined by the number of secondary standards a student met proficiency or excelled on. Interestingly, I found that I naturally deemed about 60 percent of

(Continued)

(*Continued*)

the standards as primary. So my initial expectations were reasonable. However, under this new system, I had better refined and specific standards, and I controlled the 60 percent of the current course that was required to move forward and onward to the next course. Since I knew their needs for the subsequent units and courses, the result would be that the students would be more prepared for future success.

I have used this new organization and course grade conversion for a few years and have only made minor adjustments. The most empowering attribute of my system is that I can be flexible in converting to a traditional grade. I know what is best for my students and make adjustments to the seemingly hardline rubric and conversion system.

What's the Bottom Line?

- Grades should be based on learning goals (standards, expectations, outcomes, etc.), not assessment methods, so teachers should use gradebooks where the columns primarily represent the learning goals and secondarily represent assessment methods.

- Grades should be for standards, not subjects, at least through Grade 8, and preferably until after Grade 10.

- Teachers should have a clear understanding of what learning results are expected.

- Reporting should allow for focus on information on each learning goal.

- Credit should be granted only when students are proficient on all of the critical learning goals.

Guideline 1: Relate grading procedures to learning goals (i.e., standards).

Analyze Guideline 1 for grading by focusing on three questions:

Why use it?

Why not use it?

Are there points of uncertainty?

After careful thought about these points, answer these two questions:

Would I use Guideline 1 now?

Do I agree or disagree with Guideline 1, or am I unsure at this time?

See the following for one person's reflections on Guideline 1.

A REFLECTION ON GUIDELINE 1

Why Use It?

- Makes grades meaningful.

- Aligns with the base for curriculum, instruction, and assessment.

- Realistically reflects intentions of course/grade.

- Provides clear goal/focus.

- Students know why they received grades.

- Makes teachers accountable.

Why Not Use It?

- Contributes to loss of creativity.

- Requires too great a shift in thinking/practice.

- Learning goals are often vague and numerous.

- May engender negative community reaction.

- Requires a large amount of work to select learning goals, develop grading plan, etc.

Points of Uncertainty

- How many and what learning goals?

- Specificity of learning goals?

- Grade level specific or several grades?

- Subject grades or just grades for standards?

- Word choice—parent and student friendly?

- Learning goals weighted or not?

- Mastery or pass/fail?

CHAPTER 2

Using Performance Standards

Performance standards specify "how good is good enough." They are the indicators of quality that specify how adept or competent a student demonstration must be.

—Ohio State Department of Education (2017)

But five right and five wrong is batting .500. That's really good.

—*Family Circus;* 4/13/17, Baseballer Billy to Mom
who is not happy with his test score

Guideline 2

Use clearly described criterion-referenced performance standards

a. The meaning of grades (letters or numbers) should come from clear descriptions of a limited number of levels.

b. If they hit the goal, they get the grade (i.e., no bell curve)!

THE CASE OF . . .

Sally's Shocking Grade

Sally was a very capable mathematics student new to a small school in a high-income suburb. The school believed that the way to ensure maximum student effort was to have a rigorous curriculum and high expectations. Sally's junior math class was taught by Mrs. Jones, who was generally acknowledged to be an excellent teacher and who prided herself on her "high standards." Sally really enjoyed the class and believed she was learning effectively, but no matter how well she thought she did, all of her test and performance scores were no more than 73 percent. She was absolutely shocked when she received her first quarter report card, and her math grade was a D.

Her parents immediately called the school to inquire why their daughter had received "such a low grade." They were informed that the school and Mrs. Jones had high standards and that the school's grading scale required a D for grades between 70 and 76 percent. Sally

(Continued)

doubled her efforts in the second quarter, but she still received scores in the 70s and received another D. Her parents could not accept this and arranged for Sally to transfer to another school in the same district with a semester program. Sally enrolled in the same math course in the second semester and continued to perform at the same level as she had in her previous school. In this school, Sally's scores were almost all fours (on a scale where four meant "excelling"), and she received a grade of A. The difference in the two situations was not Sally's achievement but rather the "standards" applied by her teachers and the grading scales they used.

WHAT'S THE PURPOSE OF THE GUIDELINE?

This guideline supports learning and encourages student success by ensuring that grades depend on clear, public performance standards that are understood by teachers, students, and parents and that are consistently applied by teachers, especially teachers teaching the same grade level or course. Also, grades are based on the student's own achievement, not on how that achievement compares with that of other students. Under this guideline, the chance factors of getting the "easy" or the "hard" teacher or being in a high- or low-performing group are eliminated, and there is no artificial rationing of high (or low) grades as there is when relative standards (norm referencing or the bell curve) are used to distribute grades.

This guideline is critical because failure to describe performance standards clearly and making complicated conversions between levels and percentages and letter grades are two of the main reasons why standards-based grading has been challenged and, in some cases, rejected completely or partly. Moving to a limited number of levels is a huge change from the traditional use of points and percentages, so the why and the what has to be communicated often and effectively to students, parents, and the school community.

WHAT ARE THE KEY ELEMENTS OF THE GUIDELINE?

Everybody believes in standards, preferably high standards. But often, it is not clear what is meant by *standards*. The use of standards always involves comparison and judgment because we are trying to answer these questions: How good is it? Or how good is good enough? So the key question is this: What reference points should we use? It is often not acknowledged sufficiently that there are two components to standards: content standards and performance standards. Figure 0.2 in the Introduction illustrates this. Guideline 1 dealt with content standards; this guideline deals with performance standards. All standards-based jurisdictions have content standards, but many do not have appropriate performance standards. The result of this gap is that performance standards are sometimes left to the individual teacher to establish and apply. This is unsatisfactory and should be seen as unacceptable because if standards-based reform is to achieve its promise, there must be clear, agreed-upon performance standards so that judgments of quality made by every teacher are as consistent as possible.

Performance standards are clearly at the heart of assessment and grading, so teachers, schools, and districts must make sure that they get them right.

There are a number of aspects of performance standards that need to be addressed: how to develop performance standards; criterion or norm referenced; how many levels; labels for the levels; descriptors for the levels; level of specificity of performance standards in the classroom; achievement, growth, or progress; and when do the standards apply.

1. How to Develop Performance Standards

How good is it? How good is good enough? One might suggest that these questions are impossible to answer, but there are six ways of approaching performance standards and standard setting:

> ### Six Methods
>
> 1. Develop a norm.
> 2. Develop a criterion.
> 3. Use tacit knowledge.
> 4. Describe verbally.
> 5. Use exemplars.
> 6. Use a combination of methods.

This six-fold classification is helpful because it shows a variety of performance standards or standard-setting approaches. Let us review each method in more detail.

Standard Based on a Norm

A norm is usually a number (often a mean) that is used as a standard against which performance is measured or compared (e.g., IQ test scores). Norms always compare performance with performances of others and are used appropriately in competitions when ranking is necessary. The concept of norms is expressed most clearly in the bell curve, or "normal distribution." This concept holds that there will be an equal number of high and low performers and that, on any performance, a population will be spread as shown in Figure 2.1.

> In the real world, standards often involve combining several approaches.

FIGURE 2.1 Normal Distribution or Bell Curve

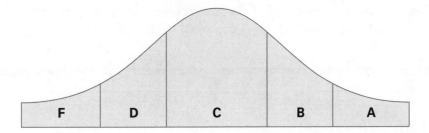

Standard Based on a Criterion

A *criterion* is a reference point, often a number, against which performance is measured—for example, words per minute in keyboarding. Criterion-referenced standards also compare, but the comparison is with a performance level, not the performance of others. For example, the world-class standard for the one hundred meters is ten seconds. Any runner near this time is a world-class sprinter, but we would not expect a twelve-year-old runner to perform at this level. We can, however, use the world-class time as a basis for criterion-referenced standards at various age groups.

Standard Based on Tacit Knowledge

Tacit knowledge belongs to the expert or connoisseur. These standards may begin as criterion-referenced standards but, in their highest form, reside only in the head of the expert. This level of knowledge comes only as a result of many years of study and/or practice. An example of this standard is judging Olympic diving or gymnastics.

Standard Based on Written Description

Written description involves statements that make a standard explicit, public, and accessible so that the standard is known and can be met because students know what is expected. Written description is probably most easily developed through the use of rubrics that provide descriptions of several levels of performance. Such descriptions provide the criteria that are used to judge the quality of student learning.

Standard Based on Exemplars

Exemplars of performance or behavior can be shown in various formats, including visual or text form, to help people recognize the standard when they see it. Exemplars are not standards but rather represent standards—for example, writing samples (sometimes called *anchor papers*) or videotaped performances of oral presentations or demonstrations of skills in music, drama, and physical education.

Standard Based on Combinations of Methods

In the real world, standards often involve combining several of these approaches. In figure skating, experts apply criteria, using their tacit knowledge to arrive at the presentation component of the score for each performance. It is also worth noting that the expert's tacit knowledge has been developed from verbal descriptions of the criteria, as well as from many hours of study of examples of either live or videotaped performances. A similar process should take place in the classroom—the teacher, as the expert on a subject or grade level, uses criterion-referenced descriptions of levels of performance and exemplars (when available) and his or her tacit knowledge to determine the level of the student performance. The problem in the past has been that such measurement has been very inconsistent because it has been individual and private, as verbal descriptions and exemplars have been lacking. Fortunately, over the last ten years, these have become more widely available, and teachers have been trained in their use so that teacher judgment has become more consistent. How performance standards were developed in one school is described in the following educator contribution.

Educator Contribution

Jake Dibbert, *Associate Principal, Middle School*
Michelle Kuhns, *Director of Learning*
Jennifer Mendes, *Associate Principal, High School*
Dr. Michelle Remington, *Associate Superintendent*
American School of Dubai

The Power of the Pyramid: A Protocol for Collaborative Drafting and Consensus Building

We developed the Power of the Pyramid protocol to "develop clear, rich criterion-referenced descriptions of a limited number of levels of achievement" (O'Connor, 2011, p. 67). The protocol took approximately two hours and thirty minutes, with relatively tight facilitation, and proved to be a great way to get initial input from our ninety middle and high school faculty members on the criteria for achievement levels.

Room Setup:

- Chairs for groupings set up around the room, each with either an easel or chart paper on a wall with a large pyramid drawn on it (see Figure 2.2). We grouped by department, to foster interdepartmental clarity, but mixed groups would also be fine. This works best with groups divisible by four, so preferably eight or twelve. Groups should be no larger than twelve.

- Essential Question displayed: How do we define levels of student performance?

- Only one person per department has a computer for recording the group's consensus responses.

- Sticky notes (large) and pens.

- Optional but powerful: A Google doc displayed for all to see that has a table prepared for achievement level description entries from each group (see Figure 2.3).

FIGURE 2.2 The Pyramid for Displaying Group Responses

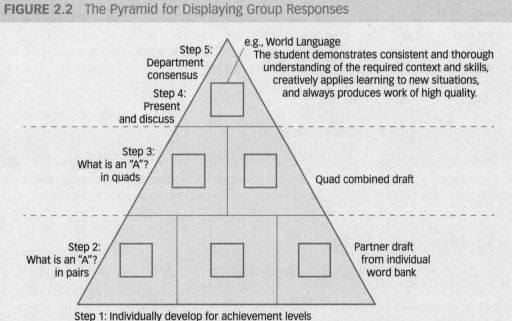

Facilitator Sets the Stage—Why do we need common achievement descriptions? (3–5 minutes)

Use the research arguments that best address your school context here. Consider speaking to grade subjectivity, consistency for students across their classes (so that an A is an A no matter which class they are in), and transparency, among other research-based reasoning.

Step 1: Generate an Individual Word Bank (5–7 minutes)

Have participants generate an individual word bank for each achievement level. To get them thinking, pose the following:

> If percentages were taken out of the equation in regards to grades, what words would you use to describe a student earning an A in your class? B? C?

(Continued)

(Continued)

Using the paper at each group's station, participants individually jot down descriptive words that describe A, B, C, D, and F achievement in their classes.

Encourage participants to keep in mind the following Helpful Considerations (Guskey & Bailey, 2009):

- Levels of understanding/quality

- Levels of mastery/proficiency

- Frequency of display

- Degree of effectiveness

- Evidence of accomplishment

- Think about achievement only, not growth or process this time

Step 2: Drafting an *A* Grade Descriptor (7–8 minutes)

With a partner from the same department and using their word banks, have pairs write a draft description of a top achievement level (an A grade). Each pair should come to consensus on their achievement description and place it on one of the spaces at the bottom of the department's pyramid. Once all drafts are on the pyramid, take a moment to read them quietly.

Step 3: Moving Up the Pyramid (5 minutes)

Have each partnership join forces with another pair. In quads, combine the ideas from the first two drafts, and come to consensus on a revised achievement description for an A. Place the new draft in one of the spaces in the middle of the consensus pyramid.

Step 4: Present and Discuss (5–7 minutes)

Have each quad present their description to the rest of their group, explaining any thinking or notable discussion that took place during the drafting. Allow time for the rest of the group to ask questions and discuss similarities they see in the drafts.

Step 5: Consensus (10 minutes)

Using the similarities and strengths from the mid-pyramid drafts, come to consensus on either one of the drafts or a combination of more than one as the larger group's final descriptor. Post this on the wall near the top of the pyramid. Have one member of the group write the final revision in the blank on the Google doc for the other groups in the room to see.

Step 6: Repeat Steps 1–5 for Another Achievement Level

Continue to post them for the faculty to see. The A takes the longest amount of time to draft. Allow groups to choose the next level for them to tackle. Subsequent descriptors will take a little less time for the groups to draft.

FIGURE 2.3 Performance Levels Descriptors for Five Subjects

Grade Descriptors: Achievement Levels MS/HS - Jan

	Creative Arts	English	Math	P.E.	Science
Rep					
A	Wow Factor! • Mastery of concepts and skills taught • Consistently applies knowledge creatively to new situations • Exhibits informed risk taking • Inspires their classmates	EXEMPLARY. The student demonstrates an extensive knowledge and understanding of the content and consistently applies this knowledge. In addition, the student has achieved a very high level of competence in the processes and skills, and can apply these skills to new situations.	Students can consistently and independently demonstrate proficiency and apply to new situations	Mastery is always demonstrated in subject matter. Knowledge and skills are regularly applied to a variety of situations. Consistently exceeds all performance indicators and standards. Creatively applies knowledge and skills in a variety of situations. Consistently communicates and articulates information and ideas with a high degree of clarity and with confidence.	An A student will demonstrate mastery of content with the ability to communicate, make connections and apply skills and knowledge to new situations. The student consistently demonstrates originality and insight and always produces the highest quality of work.
B	PROFICIENT•Understands concepts and skills taught • Often applies knowledge creatively to new situations	SKILLED. The student demonstrates a thorough knowledge and understanding of the content and a high level of competence in the processes and skills. In addition, the student is able to apply this knowledge and these skills to most situations.	Most of the time students can independently demonstrate proficiency and can apply to similar situations	Mastery is regularly demonstrated in subject matter. Knowledge and skills are sometimes applied in a variety of situations. Consistently meets all performance indicators and standards. Frequently communicates and articulates information and ideas with a considerable degree of clarity and with confidence.	A B student demonstrates a solid understanding of standards and considerable familiarity with concepts. There is appropriate evidence of skills of analysis, synthesis, and evaluation. The student is consistent with higher level processing and aplication, and produces high quality work.
C	BASIC•Basic understanding of concepts and skills taught • Sometimes applies knowledge creatively to new situations	SATISFACTORY. The student demonstrates a satisfactory knowledge and understanding of the main areas of content and has achieved a basic level of competence in the processes and skills.	Students occasionally demonstrates a basic level of proficiency with assistance	Proficient achievement is inconsistently demonstrated in subject matter. Knowledge and skills are rarely applied in a variety of situations. Sometimes meets performance indicators and standards. Sometimes communicates and articulates information and ideas with a moderate degree of clarity.	A C student demonstrates a general understanding of standards and basic familiarity with concepts. There is occasional evidence of skills of analysis, synthesis and evaluation but is inconsistent with higher level processing and application.
D	LIMITED• Limited understanding of concepts and skills taught • Limited engagement	EMERGING. The student demonstrates a limited knowledge and understanding of the content and has achieved a low level of	Students can sometimes apply skills in normal situations with support and demonstrates limited knowledge	Achievement is rarely demonstrated in subject matter. Students cannot apply knowledge and skills. Student rarely meets performance indicators	A D student demonstrates a limited understanding of standards, with some misconceptions. The student can sometimes complete tasks, with

2. Criterion or Norm Referenced

Using Norm Referencing

Traditionally, the bell curve has been used to assign marks and grades, especially at the college level. This approach has many problems, which are eloquently summarized by both Guskey and Bellanca:

> Because normative criteria and grading on the curve tell nothing about what students have learned or are able to do, they provide an inadequate description of student performance. Plus, they promote unhealthy competition, destroy perseverance and other (positive) motivational traits, and are generally unfair to students. At *all* [my emphasis] levels of education, teachers should identify what they want their students to learn, what evidence best reflects the learning, and what criteria they will use to judge that evidence. (Guskey, 2015, p. 58)

> Grades, especially those based on the competitive curve, create fearsome anxieties for students . . . as well as for teachers. In our highly individualistic society, the grading curve exacerbates the most negative aspects of competition. Because the grading curve brands winners and losers, it works against the goal of successful learning for all students. . . . For every student who wins with an A, there is one who loses with a B, C or F. As the top scorers become more enamored of their successes in school, one by one, the bottom dwellers give up and go elsewhere. (Bellanca, 1992, p. 299)

There are technical reasons why the use of the bell curve is inappropriate. To establish a normal distribution, the sample size must be large (at least several hundred, preferably thousands). It is simply wrong to grade on the curve if the population size is small. To be technically correct, one could use the curve at the classroom level but only for very large classes—for example, all freshman English students in a very large high school or college. Even in this situation, philosophical (and practical) considerations should lead teachers away from the bell curve. Consider this: The class whose marks/grades are curved may be the best—or worst—the school has ever had. If it is the best, many students receive much lower grades than they really deserve; if it is the worst, many students receive much higher grades than they really deserve. It is clear in this situation that grading on a curve tells very little about what students know or are able to do. Grades are meant to be vehicles of clear communication—grading on the curve does not meet this standard because it often produces grades that are almost meaningless as measures of achievement.

An argument often made for the use of norm referencing in classroom grades is that it maintains standards. As noted earlier, this is not always the case—if you have a very weak class, students who do not deserve A's will get them if the bell curve is used. An extreme example of this occurred in California immediately after World War II. Many returning servicemen (and they were almost all men!) enrolled in college as a result of the GI bill; at this time, virtually all colleges used the bell curve. Aware of this, some men had their wives enroll in the same courses as they did. Because the wives did no work and therefore got the F's on the curve, the husbands were guaranteed higher grades!

As Rick Stiggins said in a workshop presentation in Toronto, Canada, in May 1992—and nothing in this regard has changed since then—"There is no pedagogical, psychological, or scientific reason to assume in advance that achievement will be distributed in any way—whether normally or skewed in some direction—before instruction begins." Therefore, norm referencing, or the bell curve, is not appropriate at the classroom level.

It is also critical that there be no grade rationing in different years in school or college. It appears that some high school teachers—and particularly first-year college teachers—claim they have high standards because their class averages are low, many students fail, and few students receive A's. Bonstingl (1992) examines this view thoughtfully and somewhat humorously in a chapter titled "The Bell Curve Meets Kaizen" (*kaizen* means continuous improvement). He posed this question:

> Why does it seem the farther we get from first grade, the less likely we are to view education's central purpose as nurturing people's innate potential through the development of patterns of success, and the more likely we are to view education as a judgmental, gatekeeping function? (pp. 2–3)

Examples at the college level include Princeton University, which, from the fall term of 2004–2005 until 2014, required that in each undergraduate department, no more than 35 percent of students received a grade of A, and the University of Alberta, which publishes tables showing the distribution of grades, approximating the bell curve, that professors are expected to follow. For example, in first-year courses, the limit on grades of A is 24 percent of students, rising to 37 percent for fourth-year courses (University of Alberta, 2006). Such procedures are usually put in place on the grounds that they control grade inflation. I believe that such procedures are unjustifiable, as they imply that achievement is fixed and is not influenced by the quality of teaching and learning. They are also very unfair to students: If a student has a professor who is a very effective teacher and they learn well, still, no matter how many actually achieve at a high level, only a set percentage of them will receive A's. Rigid grade distributions also sets up a situation that is competitive rather than collaborative; one Princeton student was quoted in a *USA Today* article as saying, "It used to be that you'd let somebody copy your notes if they were sick. . . . Now, if someone misses classes, you'd probably still let them, but you're also thinking: Gee, you might get the A while I don't?" (Bruno, 2007, p. 9D).

Grade inflation occurs because no clear school-wide understanding exists about what grades mean. If a high percentage of students show, based on high-quality, rigorous assessment, that they excel in any class, then they all should get A's. Grades should be about quality, not distribution. Resorting to quotas and the bell curve shows that the administration and faculty are academically irresponsible and intellectually lazy because they are not prepared to go through the admittedly difficult exercise of defining performance standards. It was at least somewhat encouraging that the committee at Princeton that recommended that the numerical requirements for grades be ended said, "We have come to feel strongly that departments should spend their time developing clear and meaningful evaluative rubrics for work within their disciplines rather than aligning grades to meet specific numeric targets" (Princeton University, 2014, p. 4).

> It is difficult—if not impossible—to achieve complete agreement on what quality is. Decisions do have to be made, and the performance standards chosen will have much greater credibility if they are public.

Reflecting on . . . Sample Scenarios

Take a minute to consider these situations:

1. What do you think would happen in your school if you did an outstanding job; all of the students in your class were highly motivated, worked hard, and achieved at a high level; and all of the students received the highest possible grade?

2. What do you think would happen in your school if you did a good job; most of the students in your class were unmotivated, lacked basic knowledge and/or skills, did not work very hard, and achieved at a low level; and almost all of the students received failing grades?

If the school's objective for grades is to support learning and encourage success, Situation 1 needs to be celebrated. But Situation 2 needs to be carefully examined, and program decisions need to be made to try to ensure that it does not happen again.

Far too often, however, neither situation would be allowed. In Situation 1, administrators have lowered student grades or at least severely questioned the teacher about their "standards." As Juarez (1990) points out, "Normative grading forces the teacher into the absurd 'Catch 22' position of not being viewed as successful unless a percentage of his or her students are unsuccessful" (p. 37). In Situation 2, student grades would probably be raised and the teacher's competence doubted.

Neither of these administrative decisions is acceptable. If all students perform at a high—or at a low—level, then they should receive the appropriate marks and grades. There should be no artificial rationing of high or low marks or grades. This is particularly important in the so-called subjective subjects, such as English and history; students who show high achievement must be able to receive very high scores and grades in these subjects in the same way as students get very high scores and grades in the so-called objective subjects, such as mathematics and physics. Marks or scores of four on a four-point scale or of 100 percent do "not indicate perfection, but rather that the student has achieved all 'objectives' at the highest standard identified" (Pratt, 1980, p. 257).

> There should be no artificial rationing of high or low marks or grades.

Using Criterion Referencing

In standards-based systems, we must use criterion-referenced standards. At times, these standards involve numbers, but more often, they are verbal descriptions of various levels of performance developed from the tacit knowledge of experts (teachers, in collaboration with their students) supported by key exemplars of quality products, performances, or behaviors.

The more people involved in the discussions and decisions on these criterion-referenced standards, the better. Determining the performance standards, whether for Grade 1 visual arts, high school senior mathematics, or college biology, is not an easy task. Equally vital is that the criterion-referenced standards have credibility with the students, teachers, parents, and the community where they are used. It is extremely difficult—if not impossible—to achieve complete agreement on what quality is, but decisions do have to be made, and the performance standards chosen will have much greater credibility if they are public and if the process by which they were determined is open and accessible. This does not mean that there needs to be a public standard-setting process for each assessment used, but teachers need to be able to align the standards they are using with publicly available performance standards.

Marks and grades must reflect actual student performance based on publicly available, criterion-referenced standards, not artificially determined distributions. Cereal and car manufacturers strive to produce 100 percent of their products with a grade of A; educators must strive for this as well and not be satisfied with class averages of about 70 percent, which is often the case. Teachers must be careful that they do not have a bell curve lurking in the back of their minds; they must be prepared to give students the grades they deserve based on comparison with absolute (criterion-referenced), not relative (norm-referenced), standards.

3. How Many Levels?

Figure 2.4 provides some possibilities for establishing performance standards. Hitting safely in baseball field is extremely difficult, so a score that would be considered failing in most classrooms (40 percent) is superb—and there has only been one .400 hitter in modern baseball history! In the United States, grading scales have mostly linked a letter grade to a percentage range and brief descriptors (see Figure 2.5) while in Canada, the focus (sadly) is on percentage grades that are sometimes linked to letter grades. Around the world, a wide variety of grading scales are in use; according to Wikipedia (2017), a number of countries in Europe and Africa use a twenty-point scale in which twenty is considered perfect (and is rarely awarded), sixteen is excellent, and twelve is passable. Brazil, Argentina, and Indonesia use a ten-point scale while Russia and most of Eastern Europe use a five-point scale. In countries that use percentages, there is a wide range in conversion between percentages and letter grades; in the United States, the most common scale is a ten-point scale, with an A being 90–100 percent and an F being below 60 percent; in Canada, commonly 80–100 percent is an A, and an F is below 50 percent; in Tanzania, failing is 0–34 percent; in South Africa, 75–100 percent is an A, and in India, commonly 70 percent is "Distinction" (A), and 0–39 percent is failing. I list these to show that percentages on their own have no meaning.

One problem with many of these scales, especially the percentage scale, is that there are too many levels. The number of possible levels varies from two (competent/not competent, pass/fail) to five (A to F) through thirteen (A to F with + and – for A–D) to 101 (the percentage scale), which is used almost exclusively in Canada because of provincial policies. In his brilliant, must-read article titled "The Case Against Percentage Grades," Guskey (2013) notes that percentage grades were "relatively rare in U.S. schools until the early 1990's" and he blames the increased use of grading software and "the partialities of computer technicians" for "the resurgence of percentage grades" (p. 69). He notes that "percentages are . . . easy to calculate and easy for most people to understand" (p. 69). He then describes serious logistical and accuracy problems with percentage grades (pp. 70–71) and concludes that the solution to these problems is "to do away with percentage grades and use an integer grading system of 0–4 instead" (p. 71) as this will lead to grades that "are more meaningful and reliable" (p. 72).

This leads me to the conclusion that *the time has come to abandon percentage grades* and grading scales that link symbols (letters or numbers) to percentages and numeric scales. But

FIGURE 2.4 Establishing Performance Standards

When establishing performance standards, it is necessary to ask the following questions:

How good is good enough?
What reference points do we use?

Landing a Plane Safely

Anything less than 100 percent is unacceptable

Hitting Safely in Baseball

.400 (i.e., 4 times out of 10)   Superb
.300 (i.e., 3 times out of 10)   Excellent (salary $10 million+)
.200 (i.e., 2 times out of 10)   Minimally Proficient

Free Throws in Basketball/Success Rate in Curling

90%+   Excellent
80%–89%   Very good
Below 80%   Needs Improvement

Traditional School Approaches

90–100%   Outstanding   Excellent
80–89%   Above Average   Good
70–79%   Average   Satisfactory
60–69%   Below Average   Poor
>60%   Failing   Unacceptable

Standards-Based Approaches

(should be described by levels, should not be linked to percentages)

Advanced   Above standard
Proficient   Meets standard
Limited   Below but near standard
Basic   Well below standard

FIGURE 2.5 Grading Scales in North America

LETTER	ONTARIO	BRITISH COLUMBIA	MONTGOMERY COUNTY, MD*	LOUDON COUNTY, VA
A	80–100	86–100	90–100	94–100
B	70–79	73–85	80–89	85–92
C	60–69	50–72**	70–79	77–84
D	50–59		60–69	70–76
F	Below 50	Below 50	Below 60	Below 70

NOTE: 69 percent is a C in Ontario, C+ in British Columbia, D in Montgomery County, and F in Loudon County.

* This is by far the most common scale in use in North America. In many places, finer distinctions are made by adding a + and sometimes a – to each letter grade with percentage ranges for each.

** British Columbia uses C+, C, and C–; these have been combined here.

what is the right number of levels? I believe the answer is between two and seven. In a pure standards-based system, there would only be two levels—Proficient and Not (yet) Proficient—but I believe it is appropriate, at times, for those who are not yet proficient to distinguish between achievement that is close to proficient and that which still has a long way to go. I think a case can also be made that to encourage and acknowledge excellence that there needs to be one or more levels above proficiency. If we think in terms of four levels, these words (that I first saw used in Edmonton [Alberta] Catholic Schools) capture the basic idea very clearly:

Wow

Got it

Almost There

Oops; Oh No, Not Yet

I'm obviously not suggesting that we use those words in any official documents, but I think they help to come up with the formal language that is needed to make the differences between the levels clear.

4. Labels

There are a wide variety of labels for performance standard levels (see Figure 2.6), and there are important considerations as to what labels should be used because they are the words commonly used to identify levels on report cards, and they are the words most used by teachers and students. First, it is important that there be an obvious progression from highest to lowest, as there is in all the examples in Figure 2.6, even the humorous sets. Second, the concept base must be the same for all, as is the case for the first three; Column 1 and Column 2 qualitatively label achievement while Column 3 labels frequency. Columns 4 and 5 are problematic because they mix achievement as an absolute for the top two levels with progress that is relative for the bottom two levels. Third, it is necessary to avoid some words, such as *exceeding*[1] or *extending*, because what is necessary for students to do to exceed or extend is often unclear. It is particularly important that the highest level be attainable by students achieving at a grade level. For example, to receive the highest performance level at, say, Grade 4, it should not mean that students have to be achieving at a Grade 5 level. In the San Juan, California, School District's "Explanation of Markings" (Figure 2.7), the top level is labeled as "Advanced," and "exceeds" is used in the descriptor, but it is given a clear double meaning—"more depth/extension with grade-level work *and/or* performing at a higher grade level"—which makes it acceptable. The word "exemplary" should also not be used because it implies perfection, and the top level should be achievable

FIGURE 2.6 Possible Labels for Performance Standard Levels

Advanced/ Excels	Above standard	Consistently	Advanced	Exemplary/ Exceeds	Jedi Master	Bonfire
Proficient	At standard	Usually	Proficient	Proficient	Jedi	Torch
Partial/ Limited	Close to standard	Sometimes	Approaching	Progressing	Padawan	Candle
Minimal/ Basic	Well below standard	Seldom	Beginning	Beginning	Youngling	Match

---

[1] See Thomas Guskey, "Why the Label 'Exceeds Standard' Doesn't Work," *Finding Common Ground, Education Week* blog, October 17, 2014, http://blogs.edweek.org/edweek/finding_common_ground/2014/10/why_the_label_exceeds_standard_doesnt_work.html.

without perfection. Ideally, the labels are used on report cards, not letters or numbers, because the words are more affirming, especially for young children.

Standard Levels:

Advanced (4):

The student **consistently** meets and at times exceeds (*more depth/extension with grade-level work and/or performing at a higher grade level*) the standard as it is described by the grade level *key indicators*. The student, with relative ease, grasps, applies, and extends the key concepts, processes, and skills for the grade level. The student's work is comparable to the *student models* and *rubrics* that are labeled *advanced (4)*.

Proficient (3):

The student **regularly** meets the standard as it is described by the grade level *key indicators*. The student demonstrates proficiency in the vast majority of the grade-level *key indicators*. The student, with limited errors, grasps and applies the key concepts, processes, and skills for the grade level. The student's work is comparable to the *student models* and *rubrics* that are labeled *proficient (3)*.

Approaching (2):

The student is **beginning to**, and **occasionally** does, meet the standard as it is described by the grade-level *key indicators*. The student is beginning to grasp and apply the key concepts, processes, and skills for the grade level but produces work that contains many errors. The student's work is comparable to the *student models* and *rubrics* that are labeled *approaching (2)*.

Below (1):

The student is **not meeting** the standard as it is described by the *key indicators* for this grade level. The student is working on *key indicators* that are one or more years below grade level. The student's work is comparable to the *student models* and *rubrics* that are labeled *below (1)*.

SOURCE: San Juan School District, CA. Used with permission.

5. Descriptors for Performance Standards

While the labels provide a starting point, to be truly useful, there must be additional descriptive words to make the performance standards useful (see Figures 2.5, 2.6, and 2.7). These descriptors need to be clear and unambiguous and in language easily understood by students and parents (especially the double set of descriptors from the Anglo-American School of Moscow; see Figure 2.8), and they need to be reasonably brief—four or five sentences/phrases at the most. These descriptors of the performance standards should be based on what is necessary to be deemed competent or "proficient" or "meeting the standard" or "achieving mastery," as this should be the objective for all students. In the widely used four-level scale (see Figure 2.9 for an example), this is usually the second-highest level so that the highest level is above this standard while the lower levels are close to and well below this standard. For example, in Ontario, this performance level is called "the provincial standard" and is defined as being "well prepared for the next grade or course." This may seem a little vague, but I believe that it is a concept that the educational system in Ontario has always used and, thus, has real meaning for students, parents, and teachers. It has rarely

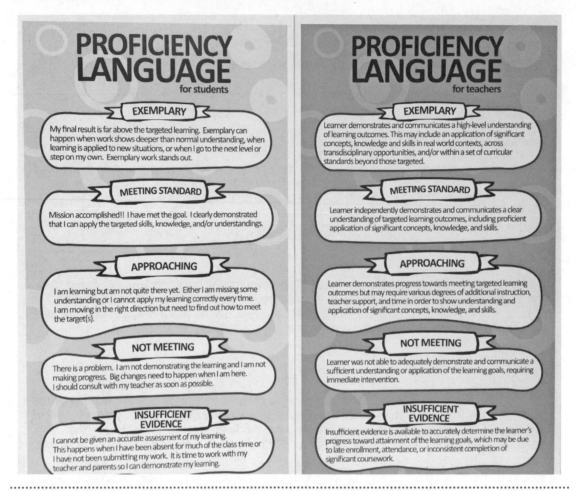

SOURCE: This graphic was developed by Noah Bohnen, Michael Johnson, Melissa Schaub, and Leigh Anne Toler. The Anglo American School Communications Department created the poster graphics.

[2] The descriptors are very good, but I would prefer to see the top level labeled as "Excels."

been suggested that grades just at the passing level mean a student is achieving well or even satisfactorily—these descriptors have been reserved for higher achievement levels.

To be really useful for students, parents, and teachers, performance standards should be described in even greater detail. One way to do this is with descriptive grading criteria, as in the example for high school English in Chapter 6 on page 193. Descriptors like these could be adapted for any grade or subject. Another approach is the one being used in the province of Ontario. Brief descriptors of five levels—one to four, plus failing—are provided, along with detailed achievement charts with descriptors for each of the four levels of achievement for a number of criteria within four categories of knowledge and skill (see Appendix F, page 325, for an example). These achievement charts provide fairly broad general descriptors, but when read horizontally, a relatively clear quality progression can be seen for each criterion. Their greatest value, however, is that when they are read vertically, one gets a real sense of performance at each level. Read this way, the charts can give students, parents, and teachers a real sense of each level of achievement. These achievement charts also form the base from which to develop classroom scoring tools, be they traditional marking schemes, checklists, or fully developed rubrics.

FIGURE 2.9 Pennsylvania Performance Standards

Advanced

Students achieving at the advanced level demonstrate superior academic performance. Advanced work indicates an in-depth understanding or exemplary display of the skills included in the Pennsylvania Academic Content Standards.

These students:

- demonstrate broad in-depth understanding of complex concepts and skills
- make abstract, insightful, complex connections among ideas beyond the obvious
- provide extensive evidence for inferences and justification of solutions
- demonstrate the ability to apply knowledge and skills effectively and independently by applying efficient, sophisticated strategies to solve complex problems
- communicate effectively and thoroughly, with sophistication

Proficient

Students achieving at the proficient level demonstrate satisfactory academic performance. Proficient work indicates a solid understanding or display of the skills included in the Pennsylvania Academic Content Standards. This is the accepted grade-level performance.

These students:

- can extend their understanding by making meaningful, multiple connections among important ideas or concepts and provide supporting evidence for inferences and justification of solutions
- apply concepts and skills to solve problems using appropriate strategies
- communicate effectively

Basic

Students achieving at the basic level demonstrate marginal academic performance. Basic work indicates a partial understanding or display of the skills included in the Pennsylvania Academic Content Standards. Students achieving at this level are approaching acceptable performance but have not achieved it.

These students:

- demonstrate partial understanding of basic concepts and skills
- make simple or basic connections among ideas, providing limited supporting evidence for inferences and solutions
- apply concepts and skills to routine problem-solving situations
- communicate in limited fashion

Below Basic

Students achieving at the below basic level demonstrate unacceptable academic performance. Below basic work indicates a need for additional instructional opportunities to achieve even a basic understanding or display of the skills included in the Pennsylvania Academic Content Standards.

These students:

- demonstrate minimal understanding of rudimentary concepts and skills
- occasionally make obvious connections among ideas, providing minimal evidence or support for inferences and solutions
- have difficulty applying basic knowledge and skills
- communicate in an ineffective manner

SOURCE: Used with permission by Jacques Gibble, Supervisor of Curriculum and Instruction, Donegal School District, Mount Joy, PA.

As it was with labels, there are some words or concepts that should not be used in descriptors. One concept that is often seen in descriptors is the degree of independence shown by students or the amount of help they receive. I strongly suggest that, except for students with IEPs, this concept should never be part of the descriptor because determining a student's level of achievement should always be based on what they can do independently. Independent performance is a given and isn't appropriate in the descriptor of levels.

What Do You Think?

1. What do you see as the strengths and areas for improvement in the performance standard descriptors in Figures 2.7, 2.8, and 2.9?

2. How would you change them to make them (a) higher quality and (b) user friendly, especially by students and parents?

6. Establishing Classroom Assessment Performance Standards—Level of Specificity

Figure 2.10 identifies the performance standards necessary for classroom assessments. It is essential to describe the generic, overall levels and labels and then use them as the base for developing the more specific task, subject, and/or grade-level performance standards. When grades are related to learning goals, it is essential that teachers mark each assessment on clear, pre-established criteria. The use of rubrics or scoring guides is essential, and it is ideal to have students involved in the development of the rubrics or scoring guides (see Chapter 8). These scoring guides must be based on the more general performance standards that have been established at the state/province, district, or school level (as shown in Figures 2.7, 2.8, and 2.9). If this link is missing, then teachers will develop scoring guides that are very

FIGURE 2.10 Performance Standards for Classroom Assessment

For classroom assessment,
performance standards

OVERALL   =
performance descriptors
(school, district, state, or provincial,
for e.g., A B C D; 4 3 2 1; E M N U)
that form the base for

TASK/   scoring tools (rubrics, points/marks, etc.)
GRADE/   +
SUBJECT   work samples (exemplars)
    +
SPECIFIC   commentaries on the work samples

SOURCE: Adapted from *New Standards Sampler*, National Center on Education and the Economy, www.ncee.org.

inconsistent, as different teachers or groups of teachers may have very different ideas about what constitutes *excels* or *proficient*.

As Stiggins says in almost every workshop he has ever presented, "Students can hit any target they can see and which stands still for them." But teachers have to provide this clarity and consistency in the form of rubrics or detailed scoring guides. Then, students know what is expected and have some chance of producing it.

Currently, how specific these classroom-level performance standards should be is probably the hottest issue related to standards-based grading, so I'm including two lengthy but important contributions from educators about how they believe these performance standards can be developed.

First, Nancy Bolton describes the whole process from deconstructing standards to the development of proficiency scales and then Tom Hierck and Garth Larson describe the process that they developed and advocate that they call "Target-Based Grading" (see Hierck & Larson, 2016).

It is important to note that the difference between proficiency scales and target-based grading is that target-based grading emphasizes solely what a student needs to be able to do in order to be considered proficient on the identified target and does not differentiate between levels within the target as the proficiency scales do.

Educator Contribution

Natalie Bolton, PhD
Associate Professor, University of Missouri–St. Louis

Using Criterion-Referenced Performance Standards as Reference Points to Determine Grades

Learning goals/standards are more useful when embedded in a proficiency scale or a performance scale to determine grades. Creating and using criterion-referenced performance scales aligned with standards is a high need for schools and districts today, especially as they transition to standards-based grading and reporting systems. Creating and using criterion-referenced performance scales involves a multistep process.

Step one is to deconstruct standards to identify learning targets. Deconstructing standards involves articulating a standard or learning goal into simpler explicit learning targets to guide daily classroom instruction.

Step two involves classifying the deconstructed learning targets. A taxonomy related to cognitive complexity should be used to classify deconstructed learning targets. J. Chappuis, Stiggins, S. Chappuis, and Arter (2012) use a hierarchical taxonomy that has four levels (knowledge, reasoning, performance skill, and product, as shown in Figure 7.2) to deconstruct standards. Identifying the thinking processes in the verb of the standard derives the cognitive complexity of a standard and learning target.

Step three is to take classified deconstructed learning targets and develop criterion-referenced performance scales. A well-designed performance scale, based on a taxonomy, can function as an effective communication tool between teachers, students, and parents, as it outlines the progression of learning toward the standard (Moore,

(Continued)

(Continued)

Garst, & Marzano, 2015). In Figure 2.11, three performance levels are articulated noting a progression in demonstrating mastery of the standard using performance levels (not meeting, partially meeting, meeting). In some cases, for product and skill targets or more complex reasoning targets, partially meeting a standard might be further distinguished and articulated into two levels (partially meeting high and partially meeting low).

FIGURE 2.11 Sample Performance Scale

LEVEL	PERFORMANCE DESCRIPTOR
Meets Standard	Targeted learning goal/standard (knowledge, reasoning, skill, or product) as written with accuracy and phrased as, "With accuracy, student will be able to . . ."
Partially Meeting Standard (high)	Meets targeted learning goal/standard with minor inaccuracies/misunderstandings. OR Foundational processes (provides detailed knowledge and application, if applicable) of the underpinning content of the standard with accuracy and phrased as, "With accuracy, student will be able to . . ."
Partially Meeting Standard (low)	Meets targeted learning goal/standard with major inaccuracies/misunderstandings. OR Limited or minimal knowledge of the underpinning content of the standard and phrased as, "With accuracy, student will be able to . . ."
Not Meeting Standard	Student has no success or major misconceptions with the targeted learning goal/standard.

Examples of standards, their deconstruction, and application of the prior performance scale using the Chappuis et al. (2012) taxonomy follows. Deconstruction of Common Core State Standards has been used in all examples and adapted from the Kentucky Department of Education (2011a, 2011b). Verbs are bolded within the performance descriptor language.

Models of work at each performance level should also be used to define and highlight content depth and accuracy expectations.

Example 1: English Language Arts Grade 3 Reading Reasoning Standard Using Performance Levels

Standard: (CCSS ELA Reading Literature/Key Ideas and Details/Grade 3/Standard 2)

Recount stories, including fables, folktales, and myths from diverse cultures; determine the central message, lesson, or moral; and explain how it is conveyed through key details in the text.

(Taxonomy: Reasoning)

(Continued)

(Continued)

Meets Standard	With accuracy, student will be able to do the following: **Determine** the moral of a fable, lesson of a folktale, and central message of a myth. **Determine** how the central message, lesson, or moral is conveyed through key details in the text.
Partially Meeting Standard	Meets targeted learning goal/standard with inaccuracies/ misunderstandings. *OR* With accuracy, student will be able to do the following: **Recognize** or **recall** specific vocabulary (**story, fable, folktale, myth, diverse cultures**). **Recount** stories from diverse cultures, fables from diverse cultures, folktales from diverse cultures, and myths from diverse cultures.
Not Meeting Standard	Student has no success or major misconceptions with the targeted learning goal/standard.

Example 2: Mathematics Grade 8 Expressions and Equations Reasoning Standard Using 0.0–2.0 Performance Levels

Standard: (CCSS Mathematics Grade K (K.CC.2)) Count forward beginning from a given number within the known sequence (instead of having to be at 1). (Taxonomy: Knowledge)	
Meets Standard	With accuracy, student will be able to do the following: **Count** forward by 1's beginning with another number other than 1 (verbal sequence only)
Not Meeting Standard	Student has no success or major misconceptions with the targeted learning goal/standard.

Step four is then to use the performance scales to determine grades. (See Chapter 6.)

Teachers should use the performance scales for the basis of instruction, feedback, assessment, and determining grades. Additionally, teachers should share performance scales with students that are written in student-friendly language that describe the levels of performance relative to the learning target. Models of work at different performance levels aligned with performance scales should also be shared with students. Students can use the performance scales and models to self-assess their work and develop and monitor student learning goals.

Educator Contribution

Tom Hierck, *Education Consultant*
Garth Larson, *Director of Learning, Winneconne School District, Wisconsin*

Target-Based Grading in Collaborative Teams

Grading Reform

Schools and districts looking to make their grading and reporting practices more meaningful and appropriate are challenged to ensure that any change positively impacts student learning. This struggle to transform to a more effective strategy has led educators to move from their traditional standards-based approach to grading to a target-based approach. In a target-based system, the most important tier of instruction (often referred to as Tier 1 or core instruction) is designed to reflect both the standards and specific academic and behavioral targets that clearly identify what all students must know and be able to do. We've created a guide titled *Target-Based Grading in Collaborative Teams: 13 Steps to Moving Beyond Standards* (Hierck & Larson, 2016) for implementing target-based grading and reporting that accurately reflects student learning. We believe this structure will help districts align their efforts from Grades K through 12 to ensure consistency and accuracy for students and parents.

What Is Target-Based Grading and Reporting?

Unlike traditional standards-based models of grading and reporting, target-based grading and reporting requires teachers to grade and report against specific learning targets, not the standard as a whole. This model allows parents and students to clearly understand what children are expected to learn in class and also provides them with feedback on progress toward specific targets.

The Thirteen Steps (to be completed in collaborative teams)

1. Review the standards in collaborative teams.

2. Rate the standards as priority or supporting.

3. Meet vertically with others, and make appropriate adjustments.

4. Analyze whether or not teams can adequately teach, assess, reteach, and reassess (if necessary) the priority standards (broken down into learning targets) within the given timeframe of the school year.

5. Complete final review in grade level and/or content level.

6. Write learning targets specifically aligned to the priority standards.

7. Create proficiency scales or Google documents that store the proficiency targets.

8. Build assessments aligned to proficiency scales or proficiency targets.

9. Design and deliver units of instruction that specifically address the identified learning targets.

10. Administer common formative and summative assessments.

11. Analyze the results of the assessments, and provide feedback within each target.

12. Allow students to be reassessed on targets with which they struggled.

13. Report proficiency levels against learning targets at different points in the school year using a summative scoring rubric or algorithm.

At this juncture, it may be helpful to clarify the difference that we see in focusing on academic standards versus focusing on learning targets and why we feel the need to move beyond standards. Academic standards are broad statements of what students should know and what they should be able to do in each content area at every grade level. Although standards tend to have a relatively high level of complexity, they are often too broad to truly emphasize the skills, knowledge, and reasoning necessary for today's learners. Academic standards should serve as the starting point for a conversation on what schools and districts should expect of their students. Learning targets are specific and clearly stated objectives for what students should know and be able to do within a broader academic standard. Some standards may encompass several targets while others may encompass very few. These targets can be organized from the least complex to the most complex within a given unit of study and should drive instruction and assessment. These two components of effective instruction are interdependent and become increasingly more so when assessment is used as evidence gathering.

Assessment as Evidence Gathering

The Winneconne Community School District (WI) has been working on becoming a target-based grading and reporting district for the past four years with a goal of making the final leap in the fall of 2017. Key steps the educators in this district have taken include organizing learning targets via Google to clearly understand what is expected of students in each grade level or course; writing assessments that are target specific for teachers to determine if their students are proficient (3), approaching proficient (2), or needs support (1);[3] and determining how the evidence of proficiency against all learning targets will be used to determine a student's summative grade.

As educators look at ways to make their grading and reporting practices more meaningful and appropriate, it is critical to ensure that the changes positively impact student learning. Some key ideas that emerge from a target-based approach that facilitate these positive outcomes are as follows:

- Teams of teachers break prioritized standards into specific learning targets, which become the basis for instruction and assessment.

- Units of instruction and assessments are designed to help students meet specific learning targets rather than the general standard. Teachers are able to identify the learning target(s) against which they are checking proficiency within every assessment they give.

- Reassessment becomes a much more manageable task as students are only reassessed on targets with which they struggled and are not required to retake the entire assessment.

- Teachers are able to utilize the information from assessments to determine the next best instructional steps.

As with any change in education, the initial steps will be messy and may require some letting go of past practice. As with the most effective changes educators have embarked on, this shift will be worth the gains made, and student learning will be the ultimate beneficiary.

---

[3] As noted previously, I have difficulty with this label because I think all demonstration of achievement, however strong or weak, should be independent, and support is an instructional, not an assessment, variable.

The Issue With Specificity

There is almost universal agreement that we need clear descriptions of a limited number of levels, but how specific they should be is the subject of much debate. The crux of the issue is, Do we need performance standards for every learning target, often referred to as *proficiency scales*? Or should they be developed just for standards or assessment tasks? For the learning phase when we are using the formative assessment process, very specific learning targets, like those advocated by Hierck and Larson (2016), are necessary, but I think that they don't have to be written in great detail for each target. One problem I see with the proficiency scales is that they often just provide learning progressions that are not performance standards, as students could do the required activities brilliantly, satisfactorily, or poorly; they may work well for right/wrong questions, but they don't work when it is about levels of quality because students could perform from Level 0 to Level 4 on the descriptors provided in proficiency scales for Levels 3.0 and 4.0. The other main problem is that providing proficiency scales for every learning target is a large, maybe too large, amount of work for teachers, and for students, "it risks reducing learning and 'proficiency' on that learning to a composite of countless factoids of knowledge, potentially with little or no deep understanding or ability to transfer" (personal communication from Damian Cooper, February 28, 2017).

I believe the best approach to the issue of the level of specificity for performance standards is that we develop overall performance level descriptors, and based on those descriptors, teachers develop learning targets somewhat informally, as needed, during the formative assessment process, and for summative assessments, they provide robust rubrics or other tools related specifically to the assessment task and the standards that it covers.

A good example of what I described in the previous paragraph is the organization of standards that was included in Chapter 1—the identification of four or five "Big Ideas" for each course. Cameron and Gregory (2014) describe the process they recommend and provide an example of what they call a *learning map* and the evidence that would be used (see Figure 2.12). Note that a variety of assessment tools are used, which include rubrics, checklists, and points based marking schemes.

Ideally, exemplars or anchor papers that enable students and teachers to see actual examples of performance at various levels should support rubrics and other scoring guides. Exemplars provide aiming points and then takeoff points for students as they deepen their understanding of what quality is and what level of achievement is possible. For teachers, exemplars provide a base for consistency in scoring; in fact, the more teachers can do collaborative scoring and discuss actual work samples in relation to exemplars, the more consistent scoring will become. In this connection, it is important to recognize that "teachers do not easily or automatically agree with each other on what student work is proficient. Such agreement takes intensive work over the course of time. Without it we are doomed to an unfair system" (Reeves, 2006, p. 114). Exemplars can really help teachers to reach agreement and make the system fair(er).

7. Achievement, Growth, or Progress

Another aspect of appropriately describing achievement involves communicating clearly whether the performance standard is about achievement (an absolute standard, achieve *at*), growth, or progress; growth requires comparing students' current achievement with their achievement in the past (growth *from*) while progress requires comparing where students are relative to proficiency (progress *to*). The differences between these for three students are illustrated in Figure 2.13. I believe that achievement should be seen as the grading variable, with growth and progress being seen as reporting variables.

FIGURE 2.12 Evidence for Each Big Idea Recorded on a Learning Map

ENGLISH LANGUAGE ARTS GRADE 7			
STUDENTS . . .	A	B	C
1. Read a wide variety of text using reading and thinking strategies to increase understanding.	Read a wide variety of challenging text independently and with ease. *Regularly use both reading and thinking strategies to arrive at a deep understanding of text.*	*Read a variety of grade-level text independently.* Typically use some reading and thinking strategies. Usually *show accurate understanding and with some text, move to a deeper level.*	Read short and direct text independently. May need support to use reading and thinking strategies. Often understand the gist of the text.
EVIDENCE: Annotated Reading Inventory ✓ Reading Strategy Grid ✓ +			
2. Respond to text as a way to increase understanding, enjoyment, and appreciation of language, literature, and story.	Respond by making a variety of insightful connections that deepen understanding. Show enjoyment and appreciation of the importance of language/literature/story in people's lives.	*Respond by making some meaningful connections that typically focus on self and others a way to increase understanding. Show enjoyment of language/literature/story and recognize its importance to self and others.*	Respond by making some connections to personal experiences as a way to strengthen understanding of text. Show some enjoyment of particular topics and texts and recognize particular aspects of language and story that are important to them.
EVIDENCE: Selected response (rubric score 2) Interview (teacher notes) Text Comparison (graphic representation) 15/20			
3. Communicate in written, visual, and digital media forms for different purposes and audiences.	*Communicate confidently and effectively in a variety of forms. Appropriately and creatively use the power of language to engage and impact audience. Consistently use conventions to clarify meaning and purpose.*	Communicate successfully in many forms. Experiment with some language techniques and show an increasing awareness of audience. Follow most conventions to clarify meaning and purpose.	Communicate in an increasing number of forms. May require teacher support to try out new forms and use language features. Need reminders to use conventions so meaning and purpose are clear.
EVIDENCE: Electronic portfolio Final draft of memoir (rubric score 3) Prezi: story/poem 9/10			
4. Use oral language to communicate ideas/information for different purposes and audiences.	Communicate effectively and with confidence in a wide variety of oral settings. Listen attentively and ask relevant questions to extend conversations. Use the power of language in different ways to increase clarity of purpose and impact audience. Consistently use conventions to improve oral communication.	*Communicate effectively in many different oral settings. Listen to others and use skills such as asking questions to sustain conversations. Use language in ways that hold the attention of audience and achieve purpose. Regularly use conventions to improve oral communication.*	Communicate with some success in familiar oral settings. Can listen to the ideas of others and offer ideas and opinions. With teacher support, may try out new ways to use language when expressing ideas/information. Often need reminders to use conventions to clarify purpose and meaning for audience.
EVIDENCE: Persuasive argument (rubric score 2) Poem presentation 7/10 Listening Observation (teacher notes)			

(Left side vertical label: **BIG IDEAS**)

SOURCE: Cameron and Gregory (2014, p. 19). Used with permission.

FIGURE 2.13 Achievement, Growth, and Progress

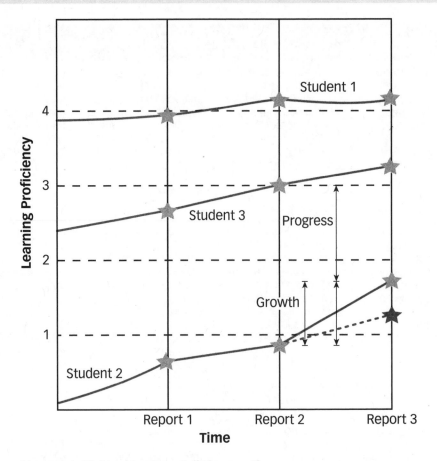

Student 1: High achievement, little growth
Student 2: Low achievement, great growth, some progress
Student 3: "Good" achievement, some growth, significant progress

Confusion between achievement and progress is evident when report cards with grades are called *progress reports* because if report cards have grades on them, they are achievement reports or *status reports*, as they are named in Hawaii. If they were truly progress reports, they would have a different symbol system and descriptors. (See O'Connor, 2013, p. 54, for an example of how a school district in California reports on both achievement and progress.) This distinction is important in all subjects, but it is critical in performance subjects such as physical education, where it must be absolutely clear whether the goal is mastery (achievement), improvement (progress), or some combination of the two. (See Melograno, 2007, pp. 47–48, for an interesting and useful example of how this could be done.)

8. When Do Performance Standards Apply?

One difficult aspect of performance standards that must be addressed is whether they refer to the time up to each report or whether they should be considered in relationship to year-end standards. There is no easy answer to this dilemma, but whichever approach is taken, it must be made very clear to all involved, especially parents of young children. Schools and districts have to choose between achievement at the time of the report or reporting on achievement relative to year-end grade-level proficiency on each report card.

Each alternative has advantages and disadvantages. Grades based on achievement at the time of the report card are clear about where students are on the learning opportunities students have had up to that point, but they are usually based on teachers estimating what is expected at that point because standards are usually written as year-end standards. Grades based on year-end proficiency show where students are relative to goal status, but they result in few students being identified as proficient until well into the school year, and this requires a lot of explaining to parents—and students, especially young students. An example of a school district that uses year-end standards throughout the year is the Eau Claire School District in Wisconsin.

I believe the most practical approach is to consider that reports are for the content standards introduced or developed in that reporting period and that grades reflect achievement relative to the level of performance expected at that point in the school year. I know that this approach may introduce an element of uncertainty or inconsistency, but it seems to be the fairest to students and clearest for parents. Probably the best approach is that used by school districts like Central Kitsap in Washington, which has developed—and published— rubrics and exemplars for each reporting period for its elementary schools. Another approach is to provide two scores or grades: one period-referenced score and one standards-referenced score. A way to do this would involve using a one-to-four scale for period-referenced scores and a plus-and-minus scale (++, +, –) for standards-referenced scores. Guskey and Bailey (2001, p. 99) provide an excellent example of a report card that used this approach in their thought-provoking book, *Developing Grading and Reporting Systems for Student Learning*.

The critical starting point for clear performance standards is to develop clear, rich descriptors of a limited number of performance levels, however they are labeled. These levels then need to be linked to the performance standards for marking and scoring. Performance standards will likely be applied consistently by teachers and understood by students and parents when this combination of clear overall descriptors is linked to rubrics, which, in turn, are supported by exemplars and commentaries on the exemplars explaining why the sample was chosen to be representative of the stated level of performance.

Performance Standards: What Is Needed Now

Putting all of these ideas on performance standards together leads me to the conclusion that we must acknowledge that traditional grading scales, which link letter grades to percentages and one- or two-word descriptors, are incompatible with a standards-based system. The basic problem with the percentage system is that it has too many levels. This implies a precision that simply does not exist because no one can describe the difference between 71 and 73 percent. It has also led to grading being seen—and practiced—as merely a mechanical exercise in which students earn points, and teachers calculate averages (sometimes to three decimal points!). Highly regarded programs, such as Advanced Placement (AP) and the International Baccalaureate (IB), use levels (five and seven, respectively), and it is time that this becomes the norm in K–12 education. Ideally, the decision about the number of levels and their meaning should be made at the same level as the decisions on content standards (usually, the state or provincial level), but if this is not done, then the decision on performance standards must be made at the district or school level. The number of levels may vary from two (proficient/not proficient) to no more than seven—preferably, four or five. As noted previously, these levels need to be clearly described, and then, they should be used for all marking and grading. Level scores are easy to do when a rubric is used (see Figure 2.12), but teachers will almost certainly continue to use points for scoring assessments, especially some tests and exams. In these situations, what teachers will need to do is decide the relationship between the points and the levels, score the assessment by points, and then record the level achieved in their gradebook. For example, if a test is scored out of 100, the cut score for excelling might be 92; for proficiency, it might be 84; and for approaching proficiency, it might be 72. It is important to emphasize that these cut scores are not fixed or arbitrary. One of the most serious problems with traditional grading scales is that they are based on the idea that 90 percent is always excellent, 80 percent is always proficient, and so on, but this is not true. The relationship depends on the difficulty of the concept or skill and the difficulty of the assessment.

Consider the examples from the world of sports identified in Figure 2.4. In Major League Baseball, minimal competency in hitting is 20 percent, but in the NBA, competency in free throws is about 80 percent; hitting a baseball is much more difficult than making a free throw. In the classroom, concepts and skills vary in difficulty, as does the difficulty of assessments.

Thus, when scoring assessments by points or percentages, teachers must decide, for each assessment, the cut scores for each level, and this information should be available to students before they begin the assessment. On difficult concepts or skills or a difficult assessment, as illustrated in Figure 2.14, the cut score for excelling might be 70 percent, but on easy concepts or skills, the cut score for excellence might be 95 percent. The score recorded in the gradebook is the level score, so at any time when there is sufficient information, a summary judgment of each student's level of proficiency can be made. How these scores can be combined formally into grades will be addressed in Chapter 6.

FIGURE 2.14 Determining Levels for Percentage- and Points-Based Assessments

LEVEL	EASY %	EASY __/20	MODERATE %	MODERATE __/20	DIFFICULT %	DIFFICULT __/20
4	95	18.5	85	16.5	70	14
3	85	16.5	70	14.0	50	10
2	75	14.5	55	11.0	30	6
1	Below 75	Below 14.5	Below 55	Below 11	Below 30	Below 6

Another advantage of moving away from percentage grading scales to levels is that it significantly reduces the concerns about different grading scales in different school districts. Parents, especially, express concern that students in districts with grading scales with high cutoffs, like 93 percent for an A, are at a disadvantage when it comes to GPA, college admission, and scholarships. In fact, this is probably not the case because apparently high grading scales often result in easy assessments, as teachers feel the need (and pressure) to have a certain number of students receiving A's. This concern is obviously reduced or eliminated if, instead of using traditional grading scales, all schools use a level system with clear definitions of the levels.

What's the Bottom Line?

What performance standards should be used? Teachers should stop using points and percentages and use clearly described, criterion-referenced (or absolute) performance standards based on proficiency, with a limited number of levels that are public, based on expert knowledge, clearly stated in words, and supported by exemplars or models.

Guideline 2: Use criterion-referenced performance standards as reference points to determine grades.

Analyze Guideline 2 for grading by focusing on three questions:

Why use it?

Why not use it?

Are there points of uncertainty?

After careful thought about these points, answer these two questions:

Would I use Guideline 2 now?

Do I agree or disagree with Guideline 2, or am I unsure at this time?

See the following for one person's reflections on Guideline 2.

A REFLECTION ON GUIDELINE 2

Why Use It?

- The standards are clear to all.

- Words have real meaning.

- Contributes to improved quality of work.

- All learners know what they need to do to be successful.

- Facilitates focus on self-assessment and growth, not competition.

- Makes marking/grading more consistent.

Why Not Use It?

- Developing criteria, rubrics, and the like is time consuming.

- Who says what quality, mastery, or proficiency is?

- Doesn't teach the competitiveness students will need in "real" world.

- Standards may be set too high or too low.

- May not allow for flexibility or creativity.

Points of Uncertainty

- What is proficiency/mastery?

- How many levels?

- How to label? How to describe? How specific?

- Achievement, growth, or progress?

- When do the standards apply?

- Linking levels to letter or number grades?

CHAPTER 3

Grading Individual Achievement

When anything other than the level of achievement on the stated learning goals is figured into a . . . grade, we lose the meaning of the grade.

—J. Chappuis and S. Chappuis (2002, p. 113)

Teachers add a little testing, a touch of homework, a pinch of participation, a sprinkle of attendance, and a handful of "secret ingredients" to create their own, individual grading recipes.

—Kelly (2016)

Forcing compliance through punitive measures and extrinsic rewards will not make struggling kids smarter or more capable.

—Christodoulou (2016, p. 69)

Guideline 3

Limit the valued attributes included in grades to individual achievement.

a. Grades should be based on achievement (i.e., demonstration of the knowledge and skill components of the standards). Effort, participation, attitude, and other behaviors should be reported separately.

b. Grades should be based on *individual* achievement.

THE CASE OF . . .

Rick's Mysterious Falling Grade

The report card mathematics grade that Rick received in December in Grade 8 was much lower than the grade he received in June at the end of Grade 7. His parents were very concerned because Rick had always enjoyed mathematics and achieved at a high level. They went to the parent–teacher conference wondering whether he needed a tutor. When they put this question to his teacher, she said that this was not necessary. She went on to say that his mathematics results were excellent; all of his test scores were at the highest level, but he had received low scores for participation, effort, group work, notebook, and homework. Rick's parents felt the grade was misleading because it did not indicate clearly Rick's level of mathematics achievement. Further discussion led Rick's parents to conclude that he was not being challenged as he already could do all of the math he was being asked to do, and his poor behaviors were occurring because he was bored in his math class.

WHAT'S THE PURPOSE OF THE GUIDELINE?

This guideline is critical because the primary purpose is communication—with students, parents, and many others—of the achievement status of each student. Thus, for communication to be clear and unambiguous, grades must be based only on achievement of the stated learning goals, and students should not be rewarded or penalized in their grades for behaviors. This doesn't mean that behaviors are unimportant; in fact, they are so important that a number of behaviors should be reported separately in an expanded format report card. (See Chapter 10, pages 265–268.)

WHAT ARE THE KEY ELEMENTS OF THE GUIDELINE?

Grading Achievement Only

For grades to have real meaning, they must be relatively pure measures of each student's achievement of the learning goals for each course/grade level. From a philosophical perspective, *achievement* may be defined narrowly as knowledge; somewhat more broadly as knowledge and skills; or most broadly as knowledge, skills, and behavior. The breadth of definition of achievement depends on the stated, clearly understood learning goals. For example, in a high school mathematics or science course, achievement may be defined quite narrowly, whereas in an elementary or middle school drama, environmental studies, or physical education course, achievement could and probably should be defined more broadly. The breadth of definition of achievement varies with the grade level and the nature of the course.

> For grades to have real meaning, they must be relatively pure measures of each student's achievement of the learning goals.

Practically speaking, this philosophical perspective is now virtually irrelevant in most jurisdictions because achievement is now defined by the standards that have been chosen or developed for each school or district, so achievement equals what is in the standards.

A number of viewpoints, new and old, relevant to this guideline can be found in the literature on grading. Guskey (2015) makes this interesting comparison—"If someone proposed combining measures of height, weight, diet and exercise into a single number or mark to represent a person's physical condition, we would consider it laughable. How could the combination of such diverse measures (that is, scales of inches, pounds, calorie intake per day, and number of minutes of exercise per day) yield anything meaningful?" (p. 74). He then points out that "teachers combine equally diverse measures of a student's performance" into what he calls a *hodgepodge grade* and states that this is "just as confounded and impossible to interpret as a physical condition grade that combined height, weight, diet, and exercise" (Guskey, 2015, p. 74).

Reeves (2016b) states that "student behavior matters, and it matters so much that we should not conflate behavior with academic performance" (p. 117). He suggests that supporters of traditional grading (that is, hodgepodge grading) believe that "traditional grading practices support personal responsibility and work ethic for students, while grading reform dismisses these qualities" (p. 111). He says, "Nothing could be further from the truth" and then asks these challenging questions:

- "Is homework completion at an all-time high?"

- "Is student evidence of personal responsibility and work ethic at an all-time high?"

- "Is cheating at an all-time low?" (Reeves, 2016b, p. 111)

He says that in 4 million miles of travel visiting schools that he has never found a school with traditional grading practices where the answer to the questions was yes.

Cizek (1996) found that teachers created what he calls "an uncertain mix." By *an uncertain mix*, he means that they combined the marks they had assigned to individual assignments and tests . . . with three other kinds of information:

- formal achievement-related measures (attendance, class participation);

- informal achievement-related measures (answers in class, one-on-one discussions); and

- other informal information (impressions of effort, conduct, teamwork, leadership and so on). (pp. 104–105)

He concludes that "this mix of factors is difficult to disentangle" (p. 105).

Gronlund and Linn (1990), in their classic book on educational measurement, state that

> letter grades are likely to be most meaningful and useful when they represent achievement only. If they are contaminated by such extraneous factors as effort, the amount of work completed (rather than the quality of the work), personal conduct and so on, their interpretation will be hopelessly confused. When letter grades combine various aspects of pupil development, not only do they lose their meaning as a measure of achievement, but they also suppress information concerning other important aspects of development. (p. 437)

> "Grades often reflect a combination of achievement, progress, and other factors. . . . This tendency to collapse several independent elements into a single grade may blur their meaning."
>
> —Bailey and McTighe (1996, p. 121)

Coates and Draves (2015) state, "There are no beneficial effects from including behavior in grading" and suggest that "the negative effects are numerous and troubling" (p. 32). They say "every day in every school and in every college . . . students are penalized for turning work in late, missing class or not doing the work. This results in millions of students being prevented from entering or graduating from college with disastrous consequences for society" (p. 34). They provide convincing evidence that one of those consequences is that we lose huge numbers of boys from education as they drop out of high school or are not accepted for college because including behavior in grades has a disproportionate impact on boys. The title of their book is *Smart Boys, Bad Grades!*

My twenty-three years in high school classrooms supports this because I taught many students, almost all boys, who were not good students and/or behaved badly in Grade 9 but who were good students and solid citizens by the time they were in Grade 11. These students received very low grades in the first two years of high school and very good grades in their last two years but, with the common use of four-year GPAs, these students wouldn't be able to recover enough to have an overall GPA that was considered acceptable for college entry. As a result, I consider four-year GPAs based on grades that include behavior to be gender discrimination against boys.

> Grades should be limited to individual achievement and not used as punishment.

The basic concepts embodied in this guideline are illustrated in Figure 0.12 in the Introduction. This diagram shows that teachers make some sort of assessment of everything that students do in the school or classroom (the outer rectangle), but from that entirety, they select a representative sampling of what students do to grade and/or to report. The *grading* variables should be achievement of the process and product learning goals, whereas attitude, learning skills, and effort should be seen as *reporting* variables. *Achievement* demonstrates knowledge, skills, and behaviors that are stated as learning goals for a course or unit of instruction, which, in most jurisdictions, means the standards. If a behavior is in the public, published document outlining the standards, it is achievement; if it is not in the standards, it is not achievement and is a reporting variable, not a grading variable. For example, in the Grade 9 curriculum in Ontario, teamwork or cooperation is mentioned in the "Expectations" (as the standards are called) for twelve subjects, including music and English, but it is not mentioned in the other nine subjects, including mathematics and geography. In the twelve subjects, then, it is legitimate for teamwork to be a (small) part of the grade, but in the other nine, the only place teamwork should be considered is for Collaboration in the Learning Skills part of the report card (see Figures 10.3 and 10.4).

This guideline does not imply that grading is simply a clinical, objective procedure. A great deal of professional judgment is involved in grading, as teachers develop an assessment plan and choose or develop the assessment instruments (Guideline 7), evaluate the process and product components of grades (Guidelines 4 and 5), and record the results after deciding how to organize the collection of evidence, and determine grades (Guidelines 1, 2, and 6). These aspects are considered in discussions of those guidelines.

A basic principle in Guideline 3 is this: Grades are limited to achievement and should not be used as punishment for poor attendance, inappropriate behavior, or lack of punctuality. These are discipline problems, and although they usually impact achievement, they should be dealt with as such. Schools have rules or student codes of behavior that set standards and penalties; penalties for rule or code infractions should not be academic penalties. Lowering grades simply because of poor attendance, misbehavior, or lateness distorts achievement; grades then do not have clear meaning. Bobby's C may reflect his consistent achievement at that level, whereas Ann's C, although she consistently achieves at an A level, may result from her many absences, frequent lateness, and misbehavior. This mixed result is inconsistent with this guideline; schools or districts that have such penalties in their grading policies need to move them to their discipline policies and ensure that their formal and informal communication vehicles allow them to report poor behavior, attendance, and lateness in an accurate and timely manner. An excellent example of this is provided by Eleanor Burkett (2002) in her book *Another Planet* (still a must read for high school teachers) in which she shares her observations of a year spent observing in a suburban Minneapolis high school. She follows the principal, several teachers, and a number of students and shares their "stories." One of the students is Nick Olson, who is brilliant but is continually on the verge of dropping out because he was "fed up with acing exams but getting Cs at the end of the trimester because he refused to do the worksheets assigned in order to help students study so they could ace exams" (p. 124).

> Students' grades appear on their personal report cards and therefore should not be contaminated by the achievement (or lack of achievement) of other students.

The practical implication of Guideline 3 is that schools/districts need to have an expanded format report card with information about behaviors. Many schools at all levels provide a single grade for "Citizenship" or "Effort" or other similar titles. It is important to state that this doesn't meet the requirements of Guideline 3. I would go as far as saying that I think such single grades are almost useless because either so much is packed into a single grade or the concept is not defined and is so vague that no one sees this grade as meaningful. What is needed is the following:

a. Agreement on separating achievement and behavior.

b. Agreement on what are the most valued three to six behaviors that are strongly valued by the school/district and its community (maybe up to eight but no more). If there is a mission or vision statement, the valued behaviors can be derived directly from those statements.

DMPS Citizenship and Employability Skills Rubric

		Academic Conduct	Work Completion	Working With Adults	Working With Students
Exceeding	4	**The student:** • Arrives on time prepared for class every day. • Participates every day, actions drive instruction forward. • Consistently does what's expected and helps others do the same.	**The student:** • Completes work as assigned every day. • Routinely submits work on time. • Takes full advantage of retake/redo opportunities and support.	**The student:** • Assumes responsibility for learning by seeking help and asking questions in a timely manner. • Consistently listens and follows suggestions given by adults. • Consistently demonstrates effective communication skills and willingness to work with adults.	**The student:** • Effectively leads a group of students. • Can help resolve most conflicts. • Seeks out different points of view. • Embraces diversity in others.
Meeting	3	**The student:** • Arrives on time prepared for class consistently. • Participates in class, actions benefit instruction. • Accepts responsibility for their actions, rarely requires redirection.	**The student:** • Consistently completes work as assigned. • Usually submits work on time. • Takes advantage of retake/redo opportunities and support.	**The student:** • Usually assumes responsibility for learning by seeking help and asking questions when needed. • Usually listens and follows suggestions given by adults. • Usually demonstrates effective communication skills and willingness to work with adults.	**The student:** • Effectively communicates with other students. • Does not participate in conflicts. • Accepts different points of view. • Accepts diversity in others.
Developing	2	**The student:** • Arrives on time prepared for class inconsistently. • Participates in class, actions at times distract from instruction. • Usually follows redirection and changes their actions.	**The student:** • Inconsistently completes work as assigned. • Inconsistently submits work on time. • Occasionally takes advantage of retake/redo opportunities and support.	**The student:** • Occasionally seeks help and asks questions when needed. • Inconsistently listens and follows suggestions given by adults. • Sometimes demonstrates effective communication skills and willingness to work with adults.	**The student:** • Occasionally communicates effectively with other students. • Does not escalate conflicts. • Occasionally accepts different points of view. • Occasionally accepts diversity in others.
Beginning or Insufficient Progress	1	**The student:** • Rarely brings materials to class, even with teacher coaching. • Rarely participates, comments often distract from instruction. • Does not follow redirection to change their actions.	**The student:** • Rarely completes work as assigned. • Rarely submits work on time. • Rarely takes advantage of retake/redo opportunities and support.	**The student:** • Rarely seeks help and asks questions when needed. • Rarely listens and follows suggestions given by adults. • Rarely demonstrates effective communication skills and willingness to work with adults.	**The student:** • Does not communicate effectively with other students. • Escalates conflicts. • Does not accept different points of view. • Does not accept diversity in others.
No Evidence	0	**Even with help, the student:** • Does not bring materials. • Does not participate. • Does not follow directions. • Escalates situation when given redirection.	**Even with help, the student:** • Does not complete work as assigned. • Does not submit work on time. • Does not take advantage of retake/redo opportunities and support.	**Even with help, the student:** • Does not seek help and ask questions. • Does not listen and follow suggestions given by adults. • Does not demonstrate effective communication skills nor a willingness to work with adults.	**The student:** • Initiates conflict. **Even with help, the student:** • Does not communicate effectively. • Does not accept different points of view. • Does not accept diversity.

Adapted with permission from Council Bluffs School District

*All bullet points are indicators for the level. Not all indicators must be met in order to score a student at a particular level in each category.

c. Agreement on the performance standards and the important characteristics of each behavior. Ideally these are published in a rubric, like the one for Des Moines Public Schools in Figure 3.1.

d. Design the expanded format part of the report card, and decide where it will be placed in the report card.

e. Communicate, communicate, communicate to parents and the community about the why and the what of reporting behaviors separately.

Examples of expanded format report cards can be seen in Figures 10.2, 10.3, and 10.5.

Behaviors That Must Be Addressed

Before discussing how to deal with the valued behaviors that have often inappropriately found their way into grades, it is important to state unequivocally that these behaviors must be consciously taught to students, especially if there are going to be grades for those behaviors/learning skills on report cards. Sackstein and Hamilton (2016) say, "Of course, we want students to be able to manage their time, meet deadlines, do quality work, and take ownership for their learning, but simply doling out assignments doesn't achieve those goals" (p. 37). They then state that "we should provide direct instruction and models of best behavior, teaching students how to keep track of deadlines and class materials; how to manage time efficiently; and how to be accountable for their work" (p. 39). Doing these things improves responsibility and organizational skills and Sackstein and Hamilton then suggest six ways to do it (pp. 40–43).

Attendance

Standards-based systems are about proficiency, not attendance or seat time, so attendance has no place in grades. Attendance is important, as most students need to be present and engaged in learning almost all the time to become proficient, but some students can achieve well without regular attendance, and their grades should not be lowered because of absences. Attendance or absence should be reported clearly on report cards and in parent portals on online student information systems.

School policies, especially for high schools, often go to great lengths to distinguish between excused and unexcused absences. This is legitimate and may be necessary for accountability or financial or legal purposes, but it is not appropriate for assessment and grading because our only concern should be this: Do they know or understand or can they do, regardless of absence or whether the reason for the absence is good, bad, or indifferent? Gathercoal (2004) makes this very clear when he states, "Excused and unexcused absences are not relevant to an achievement grade. There is no legitimate purpose for distinguishing between excused and unexcused absences. For educational purposes, therefore, there needs only to be recorded absences" (p. 163). He also describes an interesting exchange in a workshop he presented on this issue:

Teacher: "Are you telling me that if a student has been ill and another has been skipping, that they both should be able to make up the work missed?"

Gathercoal: "[Yes,] both needed an educator when they returned, perhaps the one who skipped more than the other."

Academic Dishonesty

Academic dishonesty is a particularly difficult aspect of misbehavior, again mainly in high schools, because it crosses the line between behavior and achievement, because it increasingly involves the use of technology that students often understand and use more effectively and appropriately than teachers, and because of the emotions involved in a breach of trust. Schools and districts need procedures to deal fairly and appropriately with academic dishonesty, including cheating and plagiarism. This can be achieved best by having a clear district or school policy on academic honesty. Many schools and districts have these policies available on their websites, and they typically have the components that you see here in the policy of the New Berlin (WI) School District at http://www.nbexcellence.org/parents/academic-honesty.cfm.

Academic Honesty

New Berlin students' primary responsibilities are to learn and achieve to the best of their abilities. In order to meet the needs of each student and assess progress, teachers expect that assignments and tests represent a true picture of that student's own performance. Administrators, faculty, students, and families are all important contributors to upholding academic integrity in our school community. These practices will provide a consistent framework to guide the learning process for staff and students.

Plagiarism

"Plagiarism" comes from the Greek root word "kidnapping" and is the theft of someone else's ideas, words, or other without clearly acknowledging the creator and using that material as one's own. Plagiarism includes an exact copying or rewording of another's work, paraphrasing, partial quotation, or summarization of another's work without properly acknowledging the creator of the original work. Plagiarism includes copying any of the following without limitation: tests, homework, research, speeches, presentations, programs, class assignments, lab reports, graphs, charts, essays, compositions, and term papers.

Plagiarism is a form of intellectual and academic dishonesty that can be done intentionally or unintentionally. Intentional plagiarism is the deliberate presentation of another's work or ideas as one's own. Unintentional plagiarism is the inadvertent presentation of another's work or ideas without proper acknowledgment because of poor or inadequate practices.

Unintentional plagiarism is a failure of scholarship; intentional plagiarism is an act of deceit.

Examples include but are not limited to the following:

- Downloading information from the Internet or other source and submitting it as one's own work, and/or

- Submitting as one's own work that which is copied or translated from another source.

Cheating

Cheating is the deliberate or attempted use of unauthorized materials, information, technology, and study aids, as well as giving or receiving improper assistance. The student is responsible for consulting the teacher regarding whether group work is permissible on assignments, projects, tests, or other academic exercises.

Representing or attempting to represent oneself as another or attempting to have oneself represented by another in an academic endeavor constitutes cheating. Forging of signatures and/or falsifying or altering grade-related documents, programs, or information is considered cheating.

(Continued)

(Continued)

School staff responsibilities are to do the following:

1. Use the Academic Integrity Practices to set classroom expectations.

2. Lead a discussion within the first week of each course identifying expectations with regard to academic honesty and include this information in the course syllabus.

3. Continue to educate students and offer guidance regarding acceptable and unacceptable behavior in areas that shall include but are not limited to test taking, researching, writing, and using library and computer resources.

4. Promote circumstances in the classroom that reinforce academic honor and promote self-expression.

5. Enforce the Academic Integrity Practices in a fair and consistent manner.

6. Use and continually revise forms of assessment that require active and creative thought and that promote learning opportunities for students.

7. Evaluate the effectiveness of efforts and make necessary changes to promote academic integrity.

Consequences of Academic Dishonesty

1st Incident:

1. The teacher will notify the student prior to contacting the parent.

2. The teacher will notify the counselor and grade-level administrator.

3. The counselor will arrange a meeting with the student and student's parent/guardian and notify administration.

4. The administration will record the incident in the school data system.

5. The administration and organization advisors will review the student's eligibility for honor societies and academic awards as well as his or her eligibility for student privileges.

6. The student will complete the assignment/assessment/work OR an alternate assessment/assignment, as assigned by the classroom teacher at a time arranged by the staff member.

7. The student will be administered at minimum an administrative detention yet allow for increases up to and including an in-school suspension dependent upon the severity of the situation (NOTE: a suspension would be reported to the Athletic/ Activities Director as a violation of the SDNB Co-Curricular Code of Conduct).

2nd Incident:

1. Steps 1 through 7 from the first incident will be followed.

2. The student will be issued a suspension from school, and attend a conference conducted by an administrator with the teacher, counselor, and student's parent/guardian.

3. The student will not be eligible for school-based scholarships.

4. If the student accrues two plagiarism offenses and is currently enrolled in an AP course or courses, that student will not be allowed to take the AP exam(s) for any AP courses of the current semester. The student will likewise incur a reduction in credit from the 5.0 scale to the 4.0 scale.

5. The offense will be reported to the Athletic/Activities Director as a violation of the SDNB Co-Curricular Code of Conduct.

6. Administration will notify the student and parent/guardian in writing that any future infraction in any class will result in loss of graduation/end-of-year privileges, as outlined in the 3rd incident.

3rd Incident:

1. Steps 1 through 4 from the second incident will be followed.

2. The school will report violations of academic honesty to scholarship committees.

3. High school students will not participate in graduation activities and ceremony. Middle school students will not be permitted to participate in end-of-year school-sponsored activities.

4. Administration will notify the student and parent/guardian in writing that any future infraction in any class will result in a referral for a pre-expulsion conference as outlined in the 4th incident.

4th and Any Subsequent Incidences:

1. Steps 1 through 4 of third incident will be followed.

2. Student will be referred for a pre-expulsion conference.

Academic Dishonesty Appeal

The student and his or her parent/guardian have recourse in the event that the individual's right to due process may not have been upheld.

Like most school and district policies, New Berlin's policy consists of a statement about the importance of academic honesty, definitions of plagiarism and cheating, school/staff responsibilities, consequences of academic dishonesty for first through fourth offenses and beyond, and an appeal process. There are two very important aspects of the New Berlin policy that are not typical and are very important. First, six of the seven school/staff responsibilities listed are about educating students about academic honesty and about using practices that reduce academic dishonesty. Second, the consequences for academic dishonesty don't include zeros or mark reduction or no credit for the academically dishonest "work." This is appropriate because academic dishonesty is primarily a discipline problem, so it should incur behavioral consequences. Instead, the academic consequence is that "the student will complete the assignment/assessment/work OR an alternate assessment/assignment, as assigned by the classroom teacher at a time arranged by the staff member." "Do it again honestly" is the appropriate academic consequence because what is needed is accurate evidence of the student's achievement, not tainted evidence or evidence that has been distorted by penalties or zeros. While teachers may have little difficulty with this philosophically, they frequently express concerns about the practical difficulty of creating comparable alternative assessments. One method that can frequently be used to deal with this is an oral test/exam—it does not take long to prepare several probing questions that will find out very quickly what a student knows or understands and on which academic dishonesty is impossible. Unfortunately, this way of dealing with academic dishonesty is still relatively rare, as I found out after a web search for "High School Academic Honesty Policies." There were over 2.5 million hits, and I spent forty-five minutes looking at fifteen policies, and New Berlin was the only one that didn't include no credit or mark penalties for this behavioral infraction. Hopefully, this will change as schools move away from assessment method–based grading to standards-based grading.

Think About This . . .

"Words such as *lying, dishonesty, misrepresenting, deception,* and *morality* appear in the literature on cheating and may be applied to situations in which students do not realize that they are 'wrong' in school terms. The line between helping (an ethical behavior) and cheating (an unethical behavior) is culturally inscribed and variable. Where the line is drawn is related to cultural differences in conceptions of the purposes of schooling, notions of how knowledge is constructed, the nature and meaning of assessment, and the relationship between the individual and the group."

—Rothstein-Fisch and Trumbull (2008, p. 158)

Useful information can be found at the website of Clemson University's Center for Academic Integrity (www.academicintegrity.org), where there are resources for high schools for developing a culture of integrity.

What Should Not Be in Grades?

Effort, participation, attitude, and other personal and social characteristics need to be reported separately from achievement. There is also no place for extra credit and bonus points. Figure 3.2 shows an *inappropriate grading plan* for a performance subject.

FIGURE 3.2 Sample Grading Inventory

In this extract from an actual high school grading inventory for a performance subject, the asterisked items should not be included in grades.

	% of grade
*Daily activities	40%
Major projects and performances	30%
*Journals (reflections on projects and performances)	10%
*Attendance and punctuality	20%

Attendance Scale	**Late (Tardiness) Scale**
20 marks—perfect attendance	Subtract 1/2 mark—first tardy
16 marks—3 absences	Subtract 1/2 mark—second tardy
12 marks—4 absences	Subtract 1 mark—tardies thereafter
8 marks—5 absences	
4 marks—6 absences	
0 marks—7 absences	

Reflecting on . . . Grading Plans

Consider the effects of the grading plan shown in Figure 3.2 on the following scenarios, in which a block schedule with seventy classes can be assumed:

Scenario 1—A student who missed 10 percent of the classes would be able to receive a grade of no more than 80 percent, even if he or she got perfect marks in all other aspects of the course.

Scenario 2—A student who missed 7 percent of the classes and who was late for 10 percent of the classes would be able to receive a maximum grade of 82 percent.

Are these accurate results?

- Does this inventory produce grades with clear meaning?
- Does a procedure like this promote attendance and punctuality?
- Does a procedure like this honor learning?

Effort, Participation, Attitude

Hard work (effort); frequent responses to teacher questions; intense involvement in class activities (participation); and a positive, encouraging, friendly, and happy demeanor (attitude) are all highly valued attributes. However, they should not be included directly in grades because they are very difficult to define, even more difficult to measure, and easy for students to manipulate.

Stiggins (1997) suggests that participation is often a personality issue—some students are naturally more assertive while others are naturally quieter. This is often related to gender and/or ethnicity, so we run the risk of perpetuating bias if we include effort and participation in grades. Another problem is that

> factoring effort into the grade may send the wrong message to students. In real life just trying hard to do a good job is virtually never enough. If we don't deliver relevant, practical results, we will not be deemed successful, regardless of how hard we try. (p. 418)

The inclusion of attitude presents similar problems; positive attitude has many dimensions, is very difficult to define, and is extremely difficult to measure. It is also very easy to manipulate—students can fake a positive attitude if they think or know it will help their grade.

> "Factoring effort into the grade may send the wrong message to students. In real life just trying hard to do a good job is virtually never enough."
>
> —Stiggins (1997, p. 418)

To a considerable extent, personal and social characteristics do contribute to achievement, but including a mark for attitude as part of a mark for a product blurs the assessment of achievement and the meaning of the grade. Also, including a mark for effort or any of these characteristics means a double benefit for successful students and double (or triple or quadruple) jeopardy for less successful students. This approach is clearly inaccurate and unfair.

One example of a school that does this is the International School Yangon, as described in this contribution from Laurie Ransom, the director of teaching and learning.

Educator Contribution

Laurie Ransom
Director of Teaching and Learning, International School Yangon

Grading Individual Achievement and Reporting Behavior, Effort, and Participation Separately

At the International School Yangon (ISY), as we began developing our standards-based report cards, we knew we had to create a format where nonacademic/achievement grades were separated from the traits that influenced learning but could and should not be factored into the academic achievement grade. In the elementary school, we created two sets of "Behaviors That Support Learning" grade descriptors: one for homeroom (core classes) and one for specialist classes (art, music, world languages, PE, and technology). For the homeroom classrooms, we created a list of behaviors that support learning that has been fine-tuned over the years through teacher feedback (Figure 3.3). Teachers grade these attributes based on a frequency scale—CUSR ("Consistently," "Usually," "Sometimes," and "Rarely")—and also provide comments on these (strengths and areas to improve). (Originally, we had chosen and "O" for "Often" instead of usually, but parents mistook the letter "O" for a zero on the report card.) Because specialist teachers would not assess students on each of the attributes, the homeroom teacher would assess her or his students on them. Given the shorter time homeroom teachers spend with students, we created a synthesis of behaviors that support learning for these classes so that one grade could represent a group of behaviors (Figure 3.4).

FIGURE 3.3 ISY Elementary School Behaviors That Support Learning and Grade Descriptors (Homeroom)

C = Consistently Evident U = Usually Evident S = Sometimes Evident R = Rarely Evident	• Stays focused and uses time effectively • Completes work and tasks • Demonstrates organizational skills • Resolves conflicts in appropriate ways • Follows directions • Works independently • Seeks help when needed • Actively participates in classroom activities • Exhibits qualities of a growth mindset

SOURCE: The International School Yangon Elementary School Report Card Guide; Deron Marvin and Laurie Ransom.

On the secondary school report card, the nonacademic attributes are called "Habits and Attitudes That Support Learning" and are divided into three categories: "Preparedness," "Engagement," and "Initiative." Within each of these overarching categories are elements of the IB Learner Profile and our school's Expected Schoolwide Learner Results (ESLRs).

FIGURE 3.4 ISY Elementary School Specialist Classes Behaviors That Support Learning Grade Descriptors

C = Consistently Evident U = Usually Evident S = Sometimes Evident R = Rarely Evident	• On task, engaged with, and focused on learning without teacher influence • Exhibits a positive and respectful attitude towards class guidelines, class expectations, and to classmates • Comes to class prepared in every way needed • On time for class and ready to begin learning

SOURCE: The International School Yangon Elementary School Report Card Guide; Deron Marvin and Laurie Ransom.

FIGURE 3.5 Habits and Attitudes That Support Learning

C = Consistently Evident U = Usually Evident S = Sometimes Evident R = Rarely Evident	**Preparedness**	• Is on time for class and ready to learn • Is prepared with needed materials and demonstrates organizational skills • Completes and submits assignments and homework on time
	Engagement	• Stays focused on learning and instruction during class • Is actively engaged in class discussions and learning • Places effort into work • Collaborates effectively • Is respectful to individuals, the class, and guidelines
	Initiative	• Reflects on learning and takes appropriate steps to improve • Listens and responds to instructions and feedback • Displays confidence to take on new challenges • Pursues inquiry and curiosity within learning • Demonstrates honesty and integrity in learning

SOURCE: The International School Yangon Elementary School Report Card Guide; Christina Powers and Laurie Ransom.

An excellent structure for teaching and assessing learning-related behaviors is provided by Costa and Kallick's (2000) *Assessing and Reporting Habits of Mind*. They have identified sixteen habits; this large number can be made manageable by focusing on three to five habits each grading period.

> Strong effort, active participation, and positive attitude are highly valued attributes, but they are reporting variables, not grading variables.

To summarize this issue, consider this statement by Reeves (2006): "We err gravely when we call compliance and politeness 'algebra' or 'English' or any other label that conflates proficiency with behavior" (p. 118).

Late Work

A major problem, especially in middle and high schools, is the issue of not submitting required assessment evidence ("work") on time. (See Figure 3.6.)

FIGURE 3.6 Dealing With Late Work

1. Make expectation of meeting timelines clear.

BUT when they don't meet the timelines

2. Provide support, not penalties.

3. Include lateness in behaviors/learning skills.

4. Communicate clearly about timelines and performance.

5. Use consequences—communication (parent contact) and time for time.

At the high school level in my former school district, penalties for handing work in late were as high as 10 percent per day to a maximum of 50 percent (including weekend days!). There are three problems with these approaches. First, the penalty that students receive distorts their achievement, thus contributing to a mark and ultimately to a grade that does not have clear meaning. Second, the punitive nature of the penalty provides a powerful disincentive for students to complete any work after it is more than one or two days late, so no intelligent student would bother completing the work after three days. Third, the penalties rarely change subsequent student behavior. The student who hands work in late in Week 2 frequently exhibits the same behavior in Week 8 and Week 15. Such policies are obviously opposed to a learning/success orientation—that the work is done and that learning occurs should hold more importance than when the work is done and when learning occurs. This does not mean that handing work in on time is not important—timeliness is very important—but as I once heard Joel Barker say, "It is best to do it right and on time, but it is better to do it right and late than the reverse."

> The intent is that tardiness be dealt with appropriately so grades have meaning and communicate clear, easily interpretable information about achievement and, second, that the procedures used are likely to assist students to eliminate the problem.

In the school or college situation, there are several important considerations about due dates for student work. One is that required work is sometimes part of an instructional sequence and needs to be submitted before marked work is returned. A second consideration is that teachers need to have a reasonable workload—they cannot be expected to mark huge amounts of work on the last day or two of a grading period.

In both situations, the concept of an absolute deadline after which no work will be accepted for inclusion in grades—in that grading period—may be appropriate and/or necessary. This does not mean that students automatically receive zeros or severe penalties. In the case of work in an instructional sequence, this type of work usually has a formative purpose and so should not be included in grades anyway (see Chapter 4); all the teacher needs to do is record that the work was not done or was handed in late. If there is a behavioral section on the report card, this information will be reported there. In the case of a lack of time for the teacher to grade, the most appropriate approach would be to record an incomplete and include the mark in the student's grade in the next grading period, when the teacher has had a reasonable amount of time to assess the student's work. When I was a classroom teacher, I would accept no assessments for marking in the week before grades were due as I refused to rush my marking or get little sleep in that week, but all that went in the gradebook was NS (Not Submitted). After grades and report cards were complete, I would then mark the late assessment, and it would become part of the ongoing body of evidence of achievement for the continuous process of accumulating evidence that can be used to determine grades when required.

Think About This . . .

"In the past I have been an absolute stickler for handing in work on-time with exceptions on a case-by-case basis. I had in my mind that I was promoting excellence by doing that. . . . Over time I realized I was sending the message that timeliness was more important than learning. There are many deadlines that I miss for paperwork and the like simply because I am too busy or something came up that needs to be attended to first. That is real life. While I push my students to hand work in on time, I'd rather have the work than not because the work I assign is designed to teach and practice important concepts we're working on. I (now) post [lists of] student missing work outside their homeroom doors, and they have done a far better job of turning it in—and getting current work handed in on time."

—Ellen Berg, secondary teacher, quoted in Wormeli (2006, p. 104)

A third consideration for due dates is that these are frequently quite arbitrary, especially for major performance assessments, such as term papers. In these—and, in fact, in all—situations, teachers should encourage and support students to submit work on time, but if they do not, teachers should not use penalties. I recognize that this will not be acceptable to some teachers, so if penalties are used (hopefully only in transition to true standards-based grading), they should be kept small. Think of your favorite author—let us call her Margaret. Imagine that when Margaret was in high school, she was a brilliant writer but always handed work in late. Using the punitive procedures described earlier, although receiving A's or 90 percent or more on each piece of writing, Margaret would probably have received relatively low grades because her marks would have been reduced one or two letter grades, or 20–30 percent. The final grade would give no idea of the high quality of her writing or of her tardiness problem. Far better that Margaret get the 90 percent or better that she deserved as marks and that the report card state A or 4 or 95 percent *and*, "Margaret is a brilliant writer, but she always hands her work in late." Now we have real information. If she is going to be a novelist or a playwright, it is not much of a problem—publishers have deadlines, but for novels and plays, the deadlines are often flexible. If, however, she aspires to be a journalist or an advertising copywriter, she will probably not be hired because in those occupations, the deadlines are as important as the quality of the writing.

It must be emphasized again that the intent here is not to encourage students to hand work in late. The first intent is that tardiness be dealt with appropriately, so grades have meaning and communicate clear, easily interpretable information about achievement. The second intent is that the procedures used are likely to assist students to eliminate the problem. Many years of teachers using penalties show that they do not work and that they basically give students excuses not to do the work.

A far more positive approach is one that has been developed in the York Region School District in Ontario. This approach, developed by Cathy Costello with assistance from Barry McKillop, is titled "Creating a Culture of Responsibility" (Costello & McKillop, 2000). Just the name itself indicates the orientation of this approach. An adapted version is provided as Figure 3.7. What is most important here is the support orientation: schools need to develop procedures for situations where students are not completing essential assessment evidence in

FIGURE 3.7 Getting Work in on Time

1. Set clear and reasonable timelines, with some student input.

2. Ensure that the expectations for the task/assignment are clearly established and understood.

3. Support the students who will predictably struggle with the task without intervention.

4. Find out why other students' work is late, and assist them.

5. Establish the consequences for late work, such as
   - afterschool follow-up;
   - makeup responsibility within a supervised setting;
   - parent contact;
   - notation in the mark book for each assignment that is late;
   - "grades" on a learning skills/work habits section of the report card; and
   - comments on the report card that reflect chronic lateness.

6. Provide the opportunity for students to extend timelines:
   - Student must communicate with the teacher in advance of the due date.
   - Students must choose situations carefully, as this extension may be limited to a fixed number of uses.

SOURCE: Adapted from "Creating a Culture of Responsibility" with permission from the York Region School District Board, Ontario, Canada.

a timely manner. This should involve school-wide collaboration and should include times and places where students will get assistance to get the assessments done. Depending on school structures (e.g., bussing) and the availability of educators to provide support, this may happen before school, at lunchtime, or at the end of the school day, after classes have ended. We provide support at these times for students who are having difficulty with learning, but our job is to provide support for all students who are having difficulties, so we should also provide support for students who don't submit assessment evidence on time.

It is important that providing support not be left to individual teachers; it should be based on school-wide collaboration that shows that all teachers are committed to helping all students—whether we like them or not and whether not they exhibit the behaviors we like (!!!)—to be successful. Maybe the best way to provide this type of support is to build a support period into the timetable. There are many schools that are doing this with an interesting array of acronyms and titles—SOAR, WIN, FAST, FLEX, Qu#SST, Callback, and Tiger PAWS. Schools and districts using this support mechanism are located widely across the United States and internationally, mostly in middle and high schools. Some of those schools/districts are Hillview MS (CA), Cherry Creek HS (CO), John Kennedy HS (IA), Jefferson City HS (MO), Holden MS and HS (MO), Viking MS (WI), Charlevoix M/HS (MI), Fairfax County middle and high schools (VA), Sanborn Regional HS (NH), Robert Thirsk HS in Calgary (AB), and the American School Foundation in Monterrey, Mexico.

> Flex Blocks at the secondary level in New England have taken off. Interventions, Extensions and Enrichment for all students during a school day instead of the "Hit or Miss" of after school help is timely and best practice. (posted by Brian Pickering on Facebook on the Standards Based Learning and Grading group on April 5, 2017)

An excellent approach is used at Sanborn Regional High School in Kingston, New Hampshire, as described by Brian Stack, the principal. He describes it for a competency-based education school, but I believe a similar approach would be effective in any school.

Educator Contribution

Brian Stack
Principal, Sanborn Regional High School, New Hampshire

Flexible Learning Time Provides a System Approach to Differentiation in a Competency Education School

One of the keys to the early success of our competency education model at Sanborn Regional High School has been the inclusion of a flexible grouping period that is built into our daily bell schedule. Since the 2010–2011 school year, our Freshman Learning Community teachers have benefited from having this flexible time to personalize instruction and provide students with support for intervention, extension, and enrichment as needed throughout the school year. One year later, we added this flexible time to our Sophomore Learning Community structure. In the 2014–2015 school year, this flexible time model was expanded to include all four grade levels in our high school.

Our flexible grouping period is known as the Focused Learning Period at Sanborn Regional High School, and it operates in a forty-minute time period each day. The Focused Learning Period is time for our students to engage in the following activities:

- **Intervention:** Small groups of students work with the teacher on content support, remediation, or proactive support.

- **Extensions:** Whole-class groups in which the teacher extends the current curriculum beyond what can be completed during a class period.

- **Enrichments:** Above-and-beyond activities that go outside of the curriculum to expand the experiences of our students.

The Focused Learning Period is not optional at our school. All students are expected to participate. Since the time is built into the school day, all teachers are available to students at the same time. Students are scheduled into a Focused Learning Period with approximately fifteen other students in the same grade level and/or career interest. A teacher is assigned to each group of students as an adviser.

Our school's bell schedule operates on a six-day (A–F) cycle (see Figure 3.8). A and D days are reserved for the students to engage in traditional advisory activities with their adviser, and B, C, E, and F days are reserved for focused learning activities. On the first day of the cycle (A day), students meet individually with their adviser to develop a schedule for where they will spend their focused learning time for the rest of the six-day cycle. For example, a student may be asked to spend B day getting math intervention with her math teacher and F day working on an extended project with her art teacher. On C and E days, the student may be able to choose where she would like to spend her time based on the availability of her teachers.

(Continued)

(*Continued*)

To make the scheduling of students run smoothly each day for the Focused Learning Period, this year, our school purchased customized software that allows each of our teachers to schedule the students in their advisory to all of the places they will need to go during the six-day cycle. The software allows teachers to preschedule students who need specific intervention or support. It also allows students to have a view-only ability to view their schedule at any time. The software has made a huge difference in our ability to run the period efficiently. Prior to purchasing the software, our teachers tried to accomplish the scheduling through homemade Google Doc forms and spreadsheets, but none proved to be as efficient as this web-based tool. Several companies offer such software. Our school uses the company Enriching Students, but this is not the only company out there.

To maximize the potential of our Focused Learning Period as a system-wide tool for differentiation and personalization, we put the control and power of monitoring the time into the hands of our Professional Learning Community (PLC) teams. We recognize that for our PLC teams to do this effectively, two things need to happen:

1. The teachers in our PLC teams must share students so that they can develop common performance assessments that are linked to competencies, administer those assessments to their students, analyze the data from those assessments together, and make changes and adjustments to their instruction and the curriculum as a result of what the data tells them about student learning. At our school, we have abandoned the traditional department structure of grouping teachers by their subject. At our school, teacher teams are grouped by grade level when possible so they share students and can have these important assessment discussions.

2. Our PLC teams have a tremendous amount of collaboration time. When we adopted a new bell schedule this year that includes the daily Focused Learning Period, we also built it in such a way so that each of the teachers in our PLC teams have a sixty-minute common planning time each day. Additionally, we gave back all of the time during which we had teachers performing duties such as monitoring the hallway and cafeteria to the teams so that teachers could use the time for PLC collaboration. The result is that on average, our PLC teams meet between two and three hours each week. Some meet more often because they choose to use much of their individual planning time for this collaboration. Creating this time in our master schedule was almost an impossible feat, but we found a way to make it happen. It makes all the difference in the world. If you are curious about what our bell schedule looks like, you can view it at http://www.sau17.org/images/stories/highschool/Lori/2014-2015/1415_bell_sched.pdf.

For us, developing a flexible time each day to provide intervention and enrichment to our students has been a key to allowing us to provide all of our students with the differentiation and personalization that they need to be successful in our competency-based system. I challenge each of you to look at the ways your school responds when students need that support or enrichment. Competency education doesn't create the need for differentiation. That has always existed. It does, however, highlight and expand upon the need for schools to be responding to all student learning needs on an ongoing and consistent basis.

SOURCE: Slightly adapted from the article published on September 8, 2014, in the Competency Works Newsletter. Retrieved April 4, 2017, from http://www.competencyworks.org/how-to/flexible-learning-time-provides-system-approach-to-differentiation-in-a-competency-education-school/

Figure 3.8 is the bell schedule for Grades 11 and 12; there are small variations for Grades 9 and 10.

FIGURE 3.8 Sanborn Regional High School Grades 11 and 12 Bell Schedule

GRADES 11 AND 12							
TIME	MINUTES	A DAY	B DAY	C DAY	D DAY	E DAY	F DAY
7:20–8:40	80	1	2	1	2	1	2
8:44–9:24	40	Advisory	FOCUSED LEARNING	FOCUSED LEARNING	Advisory	FOCUSED LEARNING	FOCUSED LEARNING
9:28–10:28	60	3	4	3	3	4	3
10:32–11:32	60	4	5	5	4	5	5
11:36–12:02	26	LUNCH	LUNCH	LUNCH	LUNCH	LUNCH	LUNCH
12:06–1:06	60	6	7	6	6	7	6
1:10–2:10	60	7	8	8	7	8	8

Details of another high school program at Vergennes Union High School in Vermont can be found at http://www.vuhs.org/about-us.

An interesting approach at a middle school is found at Hillview MS in the Menlo Park School District. They describe their approach this way:

> Qu3ST, which stands for Quiet Sustained & Supported Study Time, occurs during "Open Session"—the last period of the day (except for Thursdays)—and is available to all students in Grades 6–8. This important time provides students with essential academic support before the school day ends, allows busy students to get a jump-start on their homework or ask questions about difficult concepts, or gives more time to complete a task. This quiet, friendly, and supportive environment is also a great place to catch up on outside reading demands or study for an upcoming assessment. (retrieved April 4, 2017, from http://district.mpcsd.org/Page/499)

Scheduling students into support periods can be extremely complex, but it is happening sufficiently that commercial software has been developed specifically for this purpose. See flexisched.net and/or enrichingstudents.com. Also, two students at Fond du Lac High School, the largest high school in Wisconsin, developed the program that is being used there; an interesting blog about their software, *Rebentify Scheduling*, can be found at http://blogs.edweek.org/edweek/finding_common_ground/2017/06/two_students_one_master_schedule_and_a_big_solution.html.

Another author who illuminates this topic with clear logic and support for students is Forest Gathercoal in his wonderful book *Judicious Discipline* (2004), a must-read, at least for all school administrators with responsibility for discipline. He notes that "lowering achievement grades for misbehavior does not always teach responsibility, but it always does pass on misinformation" (p. 154). He also says that

> teachers who accept late work tell me that students are more likely to complete their assignments if they know it will not be graded down. It also communicates to students that all class assignments have a legitimate educational purpose that must be fulfilled. (p. 154)

Extra Credit and Bonus Questions

I have made the case that penalties should not be used for behavioral infractions because, among other reasons, they distort achievement, making it appear that students are achieving at a lower level than they actually are. It is, therefore, equally important that student achievement not be distorted upward by the use of extra credit or bonus points. There is a long tradition in middle schools and high schools, especially in the United States, of allowing students to boost their grades by doing things that have little or nothing to do with the learning goals. Consider this example provided by a high school mathematics teacher in Michigan.

> To illustrate the misuse of the point system, consider the food drive that my high school holds each fall. In a well-meaning attempt to encourage motivation for a good cause, some teachers offer extra credit to students who bring in cans of food to donate. Aside from the fact that not all students have an equal opportunity to boost their grade . . . think about the message that this practice sends to kids about the meaning of "points." It shifts their focus from demonstrating what they have learned and toward collecting as many points as possible. (Huhn, 2005, p. 81)

Over the years, I have heard of many examples of extra credit, ranging from bringing in tissues to attending basketball games. My favorite example is found in this quote from a letter to the editor written by a high school senior in central Pennsylvania:

> Recently it was "Dress like an Egyptian Day" at my school. If we dressed like an Egyptian, we got extra credit. When we didn't (which the majority of the kids didn't), our teacher got disappointed at us because we just "didn't make the effort." . . . One of the most frustrating things in my mind is that we get graded on something that has no educational value. I would very much like to discontinue these childish dress-up days. —Jennifer Starsinic, Hummelstown (Starsinic, 2003)

Grades are supposed to be measures of achievement, so it is appropriate that students have "extra" opportunities to improve their grades, but these opportunities must involve demonstration of the knowledge and skills in the standards, as the opportunities described previously did not. If these extra opportunities to improve grades are to be valid, it is equally important that the additional demonstration of knowledge and skill be at a higher level of achievement, not just more work earning more points. Thus, it is inappropriate to have bonus points on tests that simply make it appear that students' achievement is higher than it really is. It makes no sense for a student to be able to score seventy points on a test that has a maximum recorded value of fifty points. Furthermore, the bonus questions are usually those that allow teachers to distinguish between students who are competent and those who are excelling, so all students should be expected to attempt these questions.

It is worth noting that an Iowa state legislator thought that this was a sufficiently important issue that he introduced legislation that would prevent schools from giving extra credit for school supplies (Ryan, 2017).

Problems With Bonus Questions/Points

- Mathematical distortion inappropriately inflates student achievement (e.g., 70 out of 50).
- Bonus questions are usually conceptual, higher-order thinking questions.
- Bonus points hide weaknesses.

Grading Individuals

The other extremely important aspect of this guideline is the emphasis on grading individuals on their personal achievement rather than grading individuals on their group's achievement. With the increasing focus on the ability to work effectively with others in school and at work, this emphasis on individual achievement may seem strange. But remember that students' grades appear on their personal report cards and therefore should not be contaminated by the achievement (or lack of achievement) of other students.

FIGURE 3.9 Kagan's Critique of Group Grades

ARGUMENT		COUNTER ARGUMENT
The real-world argument—Preparing students for the real world requires that they develop cooperative learning skills; in the real world, teams are rewarded for their group effort.	BUT	"In the real world there are many unfair practices . . . that doesn't justify unfair practices in the classroom."
The employment skills argument—Grading the social skill of cooperation, which is highly desired by employers, shows students that it is important.	BUT	"Group grades don't necessarily foster social skills," and "group grades on academic projects do not fairly assess the cooperative skills of individuals because, for example, if most members of the group cooperate very well, everyone in the group—even the least cooperative student—receives a high grade. The reverse is also true and is probably a more serious problem."
The motivation argument—Students won't work together unless it counts in the grade.	BUT	"There are many better ways to motivate students."
The teachers' workload argument—Some teachers prefer marking groups because it is faster than marking many individual papers.	BUT	"This is not a legitimate short cut. Group grades tell us nothing reliable about individual performance."
The grades-are-subjective-anyway argument	BUT	"The sometimes subjective nature of grading does not justify using a method that is even less precise."
The grades-aren't-that-important argument	BUT	"Try explaining it to the parents of a student who, based on his or her grades [which included group marks for cooperation], has just narrowly missed being accepted to a desired college."
The credit-for-teamwork argument	BUT	"Individuals should be given credit for their individual work, not a free ride on the work of others."
The group-grades-are-a-small-factor argument—Some argue that it is all right to use group marks because they rarely have a significant impact on the final grade.	BUT	"Very occasionally is far too often if it means giving individual grades that do not reflect individual performances."

SOURCE: Adapted from Kagan (1995).

Concerns About Group Grades

It is unfortunate that group marks are one of the reasons why students and parents give group work a bad name. Cooperative learning—despite its importance for the development of capable citizens and productive employees and its value to learning, as shown by a significant body of research—has struggled against this legacy.

In an excellent article, Kagan (1995) provides strong criticism of eight arguments for group grades (Figure 3.9 on the previous page). He also gives seven reasons why he is "unequivocally opposed to group grades" (p. 69; see Figure 3.10). Then, he suggests "alternative ways to accomplish the same goals" (p. 71). (Please note that in most cases, Kagan uses *grade* to mean what this book calls *mark*.) Kagan also suggests that cooperative learning skills could be recognized through a variety of other approaches that are more effective than group marks. He says that it is preferable to give students a mark for "group skills" or marks for specific cooperative skills.

FIGURE 3.10 Kagan's Seven Reasons for Opposing Group Grades

1	**No fair**. Group grades are so blatantly unfair that on this basis alone, they should never be used.
2	**Group grades debase report cards.** If the grade a student gets "is a function of who the student happens to have as a teammate," then no one can use the grades in a meaningful way.
3	**Group grades undermine motivation.** There are two problems here: (1) group grades penalize students who work hard but have cooperative learning partners who don't, and (2) they reward students who don't work hard but have hardworking partners. Both scenarios have undesirable effects on student motivation.
4	**Group grades convey the wrong message.** Grading practices send students messages about what is valued. The basic point of the guidelines presented in this book is that grading should emphasize and support learning and success, but if grades "are partially a function of forces entirely out of their control," it sends entirely the wrong message to students.
5	**Group grades violate individual accountability.** This is a key principle of cooperative learning. If it is applied effectively and appropriately, students are likely to achieve more; if not, students will find ways to manipulate the situation to their personal advantage.
6	**Group grades are responsible for parents', teachers', and students' resistance to cooperative learning.**
7	**Group grades may be challenged in court.**

SOURCE: Adapted from Kagan (1995).

Marking Cooperative Learning

How then should cooperative learning be marked? Obviously, the key is to focus on assessing the skills of each student as an individual. One way to do this is to use an assessment sheet, such as the one shown in Figure 3.11.

> Bonus marks distort achievement grades because they mix other factors with achievement. It is better not to use them.

While students are working on a cooperative learning task, the teacher walks around the classroom and records information on each group. Observations may be made by the teacher, by students of other students, or by students of themselves but are restricted to two or three skills at one time. Feedback is given to individuals, to groups, and to the class as a whole. After students practice their cooperative skills and observation skills, then a sheet, patterned on Figure 3.8, can be used to summarize each student's achievement in this area. If—and it is a big if—teamwork or cooperative skills are part of standards, this summary can be

FIGURE 3.11 Group Cooperative Learning Assessment

Assessor:	Teacher ❑	Peer ❑	Self ❑	
	Put the appropriate symbol in the boxes for each student.			
	Evidence of skill observed ✔		Not observed yet ✘	

Names of students in the group / Cooperative learning skill	Student 1	Student 2	Student 3	Student 4
Stays focused on task				
Fulfills assigned role				
Contributes ideas and solutions				
Works well with others (listens, shares, and supports others)				
Shows interest and involvement				
Additional skills (developed by teachers and students)				

SOURCE: Reprinted with permission, © 1995 Toronto District School Board, Ontario, Canada.

converted to scores for inclusion in student grades. If, however, these characteristics are not specifically mentioned in your standards, then evidence of these skills should only be used in the comments or learning/social skills part of the report card.

Another way to focus on individual learning in cooperative learning situations is to have students document the processes they followed individually and collectively and to write a reflection about what they learned. An example of this is provided by educator contributor Denine Laberge.

Educator Contribution

Denine Laberge
Teacher, Collège Louis-Riel
Winnipeg, Manitoba

Facilitating Student Reflection on the Learning Process

When I have students working in groups for research projects, each earns an individual grade. To do this, I have students complete a "Process Paper" detailing the process they followed throughout the project. In this paper, they give particulars about their learning from the brainstorming stage to the final product. They list the questions they had that guided the research, the sources they used to find answers to their questions, new questions that arose from their reading, and the choices they made to create the final product. Finally, they have a reflection piece to add to this where they share their thinking about their learning experience.

(Continued)

One year, I had students researching the country of their choice, viewing it through a variety of lenses (political, geographical, cultural, religious . . .). Referring to the "one-child policy" in China, one student wrote a reflection about how strange it would be to have family gatherings with no cousins, no aunts and uncles . . . I remember thinking, "No, no, they would have extended family," but the more I thought about it, the more I realized she was right. I had just never thought about it that deeply before. This made me aware of the thinking that was occurring in these projects. She had been invested in her work and in the learning that had taken place. She couldn't copy or fake that. The process paper allowed me to assess with much more precision what grade each student had earned, even if they all worked on the same project.

In conclusion, note that "a carefully constructed cooperative environment that offers challenging learning tasks, that allows students to make key decisions about how they perform, and that emphasizes the value (and skills) of helping each other to learn" (Kohn, 1991, p. 86) is far more important than coming up with the perfect way to mark cooperative learning. The various aspects of cooperative learning (see Figure 3.11) can then be included in grades or learning skills, depending on whether they are part of the standards or not. This can be a challenging aspect of marking and grading. The ideas to keep in mind are that (1) cooperative learning is an instructional strategy, and (2) we must assess individual achievement within the cooperative learning setting.

Think About This . . .

"It is essential to emphasize that cooperative learning is an *instructional strategy*, **not** an *assessment strategy*. If teachers want to evaluate students while working on a cooperative task, then the evaluation must be clearly outlined in the role expectations for each student. It must be very clear to students exactly on what they are going to be evaluated. The evaluation of each student should be based on what he/she accomplishes. There should not be a group mark. We cannot stress this enough. Further, teachers must develop the evaluation strategy as they design the assessment. Students should not have to guess what they are expected to do nor how their mark will be calculated."

—Stephens and
Davis (2001, p. 25)

Brookhart (2013) provides a number of suggestions for how to assess individual achievement in cooperative learning that meet Stephens and Davis's requirements in "Grading and Group Work," pages 13–36.

Not a No-Fail Policy

In a column in the *Toronto Globe and Mail* on the first day of the 2014–2015 school year, Margaret Wente stated, "In Canada, the godfather of . . . no-fail assessment policies is Toronto consultant, Ken O'Connor." She said this because of my advocacy of the practices required by Guideline 3—separating behavior from achievement and not using mark penalties for "late work, skipped assignments, absence, missed exams or even cheating." She labels this as "fashionable pedagogy" and states that "parents, taxpayers and governments are demanding more rigour and accountability and higher standards from the education system, while (school districts) and consultants are pushing for less." Nothing could be further from the truth—Guideline 3 is not a no-fail policy; in fact, it holds students to higher standards because it says your grade will be based only on your academic achievement, and it will not be inflated by compliance and completion. Students will be held truly accountable because regardless of the reason for absence or the failure to submit or late submission of required assessment evidence or academic dishonesty, they will be required to do the work and to do it honestly, and they will be evaluated solely on the quality of their individual academic performance. Guideline 3 is not "no-fail," and it is not soft; it is hard!

What's the Bottom Line?

What should be in grades?

- Grades should include individual achievement only, based on the published learning goals for the school/district.

What should not be in grades?

- Mark penalties or bonuses

- Effort, attitude, behavior, attendance, punctuality, tardiness, and group work, unless they are specifically stated in the standards for a grade or course. These should be assessed and reported separately. (See also Chapter 10.)

Guideline 3: Limit the valued attributes included in grades to individual achievement.

Analyze Guideline 3 for grading by focusing on three questions:

Why use it?

Why not use it?

Are there points of uncertainty?

After careful thought about these points, answer these two questions:

Would I use Guideline 3 now?

Do I agree or disagree with Guideline 3, or am I unsure at this time?

See the following for one person's reflections on Guideline 3.

Why Use It?

- Gives "pure" grades.

- Gives a clear picture of student achievement, whereas mixing achievement and effort gives a muddy picture of both.

- It is based on standards.

- It is very clear, concrete, and specific.

- Clarifies priorities.

- Creates more accountability for really knowing student strengths and weaknesses.

Why Not Use It?

- Attitude and effort are important in student's future.

- Clear definition of achievement is lacking.

- Participation and achievement are closely linked.

- Report card does not allow separation of achievement and effort.

- School and district policy preclude its use.

Points of Uncertainty

- Where do participation and effort fit?

- How to include critical employability skills?

- How to report in a manageable way?

- Students need to see the consequences of their behavior in an obvious way.

- How do I get students and parents to value the behavioral part of the report card?

CHAPTER 4

Sampling Student Performance

The standards movement . . . precipitated a renewed interest in what might be the most favorable course of action to prepare students to meet the expected standards. . . . What emerged was an almost unified belief that formative assessment practices were the most effective and efficient way to increase student achievement.

—Schimmer (2016, p. 10)

You must learn to fail intelligently . . . one fails forward towards success.

—Thomas Alva Edison, as quoted in Fullan (2005, p. 22)

Ever tried. Ever failed. No matter. Try again. Fail again. Fail better.

—Stan Wawrinka, professional tennis player
—Samuel Beckett phrase on his left forearm

Guideline 4
Sample student performance—do not include all scores in grades.
a. Do not include assessments used for *formative* purposes in grades—provide feedback using words, rubrics, or checklists, *not* scores.
b. Include information primarily from a variety of *summative* assessments in grades.

THE CASE OF . . .

Heather's Grim Grade

Heather is a very capable student who generally achieves at a very high level. She has always liked and done well in English. On her first report card in Grade 11 English, she gets a C; both her parents and Heather are shocked and upset by the low (for her) grade. They express their concern to her teacher, who provides them with a computer printout showing how Heather's C was calculated. What is revealed is that the marks for virtually every piece of work that was done were included in the letter grade. First drafts, experimental pieces, quizzes on spelling and grammar—marks for all of these were included. Heather did not do well on any of these, but her unit tests, final drafts, and a major project all received scores at the highest level. Heather likes to experiment and to take risks on creative tasks; she also needs a lot of practice to understand concepts and detail. By including all of the scores from the formative assessments in her grade, her teacher had emphasized Heather's process as a learner rather than the strength of her achievement.

WHAT IS FORMATIVE ASSESSMENT?

> Formative assessment is a planned process in which assessment-elicited evidence of students' status is used by teachers to adjust their ongoing instructional procedures or by students to adjust their current learning tactics. (Popham, 2017, p. 95)

WHAT'S THE PURPOSE OF THE GUIDELINE?

This guideline requires that teachers have a clear understanding of the *purpose* of each assessment and the need for a variety of assessment strategies. It is essential that teachers distinguish clearly between the more formal assessments that take place during the *formative assessment process* and *summative assessment* and that they recognize that different assessment strategies will reveal evidence of students' strengths and weaknesses. (The issue of variety in assessment will be dealt with in Chapter 7.)

The major focus of this chapter is the need for appropriate use of the formative assessment process and summative assessment. The formative assessment process is used to give feedback to students and teachers during the learning process about "how it is going" so that they can make appropriate adjustments in learning and teaching, whereas summative assessments are used to make judgments about the quality of learning at a point in time and so are included in the determination of grades. This approach deals with two serious problems: (1) the "does-this-count?" syndrome exhibited by students and (2) the "I-have-too-much-marking" syndrome exhibited by teachers. In high schools, this may be the single most important guideline because secondary teachers especially have a strong tendency toward putting a number on everything students do and putting everything into the grade.

This guideline is ultimately about making it clear that school is not just about the accumulation of points that become grades; it is about learning—a process that requires students to understand that it is alright to make risk-free mistakes early in the learning because those early attempts will not "count." As McTighe (1996/1997) points out,

> We know that students will rarely perform at high levels on challenging learning tasks at their first attempt. Deep understanding or high levels of proficiency are achieved only as a result of trial, practice, adjustments based on feedback, and more practice. (p. 11)

WHAT ARE THE KEY ELEMENTS OF THE GUIDELINE?

Formative and Summative Assessment

It is essential that educators clearly understand the concepts of formative and summative assessment. (See Figure 4.1 and the glossary in Appendix I for more definitions of terms used.)

> Formative—The formative assessment process is designed to provide information for improvement and/or adjustment to a program for individual students or for a whole class (i.e., informal conversations and questions and observations and more formal quizzes, initial drafts/attempts, homework, and questions during instruction). (Often referred to as assessment *for* learning.) In relation to his definition quoted earlier, Popham (2017) says that his emphasis on process is

done "to disabuse readers from thinking that certain kinds of tests are *themselves* either formative or summative" (p. 96).

Summative—Assessment/evaluation designed to provide information to be used in making judgments about a student's achievement at or toward the end of a period of instruction (i.e., tests, exams, final drafts/attempts, assignments, projects, and performances). (Often referred to as assessment *of* learning.)

Teachers need a very clear vision of their purpose for each assessment. If assessment is principally to inform learners about their strengths and weaknesses, as well as to inform teachers about how successful instruction is as it proceeds, then assessment is formative. On the other hand, if assessment is primarily to inform about the achievement status of the learner, then it is summative. This is not an absolute distinction—note the use of the word *primarily* in the previous sentence. Some overlap occurs (e.g., summative assessments can also provide formative feedback if students receive more than scores).

FIGURE 4.1 Comparison of the Formative Assessment Process and Summative Assessments

	FORMATIVE ASSESSMENT PROCESS	SUMMATIVE ASSESSMENTS
Purpose	To monitor and guide learning while it is still in progress	To judge the success of a process/product at the end (however arbitrarily defined)
Time of assessment	During the process or development of learning	At or toward the end of the process or when the product is complete
Types of assessment techniques	Informal observation, on a minute-to-minute, day-to-day basis Formal assessments—quizzes, homework, teacher questions, and worksheets	Formal assessments—tests, projects, term papers, exhibitions, and observation
Uses of assessment information	To improve and change learning while it is still going on or being developed	Judge the quality of a process/product; grade, rank, and promote
How it is shared with students	Words	Symbols

SOURCE: Adapted from Airasian (1994, p. 136).

It is increasingly important that this distinction be clear, as "in mid-2006, when formative assessment was first starting to attract the interest of many educators . . . A number of commercial measurement companies were, at that time, (and subsequently) trying to peddle their tests because those tests were supposedly 'formative' and, therefore, should be seen as more relevant to teachers' instructional decision making" (Popham, 2017, p. 95). Popham goes on to say that the formative label was being used "in a fairly fast-and-loose fashion" (p. 95) because the tests themselves are not formative: it is how the results are used that determines whether an assessment is formative or summative.

It is worth noting that the entire December 2007/January 2008 issue of *Educational Leadership*, titled "Informative Assessment," had many excellent articles on the formative uses of assessment that are still useful in 2017.

Assessing Process and Product

It is also extremely important that teachers do not equate process with formative assessment and products with summative assessment. Processes like scientific inquiry may and should be assessed both formatively and summatively; similarly, products may be assessed both formatively and summatively. Furthermore, summative assessments are not only tests and exams; a large variety of assessment methods can be used summatively (see Figure 7.4 on page 206).

A good example of a process that can be assessed formatively and summatively is student use of safety skills in a laboratory or vocational program. Starting on the first day, the teacher introduces students to critical safety skills. Students are given or develop clear criteria indicating levels of performance, possibly in the form of a rubric that describes various levels of quality. Students practice their safety skills daily as the teacher observes and feeds back to them information as to their strengths and weaknesses. The students are also encouraged to self-assess and reflect on the development of their safety skills. The teacher should keep track of these observations, but these records should be in words, not scores as points or percentages. This process continues over a number of weeks. Near the end of the first grading period, the teacher announces that, for several specific days, the same criteria and the same observations will be used to assess students' safety skills and that the scores will be included in their grades. This period of observation becomes the summative assessment of their process skills. There are no scores from the practice weeks, so that cannot be included in the grade. The observations made during the practice weeks are used to provide valuable reporting information about growth and progress.

> "Too often, educational tests, grades, and report cards are treated by teachers as autopsies when they should be viewed as physicals."
>
> —Reeves (2000, p. 10)

Another example of a performance that can be assessed both formatively and summatively is a student seminar presentation (individual or group). Usually, these major projects are scheduled far in advance, so students need periodic guidance to keep them on track. The teacher may provide students with a schedule for checking such things as hypothesis, first draft, audiovisual needs, and second draft. Students might also have a practice presentation. For each of these steps and for the presentation, students have clear criteria indicating various levels of performance. As with the safety skills, the teacher provides students with descriptive feedback on each step to help them develop their performance. The teacher keeps records of these process steps, preferably as narrative using words that may be "Going well," "OK," and "Not going well" or "Done" and "Not done." (Teachers could use symbols for these words like *, +, and – or ☑ and ×.) None of these will be included in students' grades; instead, they will be used for dialogue with students and parent communication when necessary. The only marks included in a student grade are marks for each of standards included in the actual seminar presentation—the summative assessment of the product. Most students need to follow the process steps, and the quality of their final performance depends to a great extent on how diligent they have been in following them. However, some students may be able to present a high-quality seminar without following some—or even all—of the recommended process steps. Because it is the seminar presentation that counts in grades, students do not suffer lower grades if they do not follow the suggested steps.

The strong messages here are that formative assessment shouldn't be included in grades and that formative assessments should get descriptive feedback, not scores. Given the following real example from a high school history course in 2017 of including formative assessment scores in grades inappropriately (Figure 4.2), these messages can't be stated strongly enough.

FIGURE 4.2 High School History Gradebook

TESTS/QUIZZES (WEIGHT: 60.0)

NAME	DUE DATE	ASSIGNED DATE	PTS. POSS.	SCORE	%
Chapter 16 Section 2 Quiz	3/13/2017	3/13/2017	24	16	66.66
Chapter 16 Section 4 Quiz	3/14/2017	3/14/2017	16	16	100
Chapter 17 Section 1 Quiz	3/15/2017	3/15/2017	18	18	100
Chapter 17 Section 2 Quiz	3/16/2017	3/16/2017	18	4	22.22
Chapter 17 Section 3 Quiz	3/17/2017	3/17/2017	12	4	33.33
Chapter 17 Section 4 Quiz	3/27/2017	3/27/2017	12	6	50
Chapter 18 Section 1 Quiz	3/28/2017	3/28/2017	16	2	12.5
Unit 6 TEST World War 2 TEST	3/29/2017	3/29/2017	100	76	76
Unit 6 TEST World War 2 Study Guide	3/29/2017	3/29/2017	20	18	90
Chapter 18 Section 2 Quiz	3/30/2017	3/30/2017	12	8	66.66
Chapter 18 Section 3 Quiz	3/31/2017	3/31/2017	16	12	75
Chapter 18 Section 4 Quiz	4/3/2017	4/3/2017	20	14	70
Chapter 20 Section 1 Quiz	4/4/2017	4/4/2017	20	10	50
Chapter 22 Section 1 Quiz	4/5/2017	4/5/2017	22	18	81.81
Chapter 22 Section 2 Quiz	4/6/2017	4/6/2017	16	4	25
Chapter 22 Section 3 Quiz	4/7/2017	4/7/2017	12	10	83.33
Chapter 22 Section 4 Quiz	4/10/2017	4/10/2017	12	5	41.66
Chapter 22 Section 5 Quiz	4/11/2017	4/11/2017	20	20	100
Unit 7 TEST New Balance of Power	4/13/2017	4/13/2017	150	120	80
Chapter 19 Section 2 Quiz	4/14/2017	4/14/2017	16	14	87.5
Infinite Campus Displaying Tests/Quizzes Totals			**562**	**399**	**70.99%**

HOMEWORK/CLASSWORK (WEIGHT: 30.0)

NAME	DUE DATE	ASSIGNED DATE	PTS. POSS.	SCORE	%
WW2 Project Part 1 Map	3/17/2017	3/17/2017	45	29	64.44
Chapter 17 Worksheets	3/28/2017	3/28/2017	5	5	100
WW2 Project Part 2 People	3/29/2017	3/29/2017	105	59	56.19

Event Project Rough Draft 1	4/7/2017	4/7/2017	15	15	100
ELO Wkst Unit 7	4/13/2017	4/13/2017	20	17	85
Event Project Rough Draft 2	4/18/2017	4/18/2017	15	13	86.66
Infinite Campus Displaying Homework/Classwork Totals			**205**	**138**	**67.31**
SUM of Entries			**205**	**138**	**67.32**
Term T4 Term Grade Totals				**D+**	**68.93**

In just over a month, unbelievably, there are *twenty-one* entries in Tests/Quizzes that count for 60 percent of the grade and six entries in Homework/Classwork that count for 30 percent of the grade. (I have no idea how a teacher could do this amount of marking and have time to eat or sleep.) As a result of that "recipe," the student's current grade is 68.93 percent. I believe that everything except for the two tests should not be part of the grade, so the student's current grade, just applying Guideline 4, should be 78.00 percent, a rather significant difference!

> Many assessments are designed to provide information so that teachers can adjust instruction and students can improve performance. This should be the prime purpose of quizzes.

The Role of Formative Assessment

Identifying the role of formative assessment as "for learning" is not new. Way back in 1969, Benjamin Bloom wrote that "we see much more effective use of formative evaluation if it is separated from the grading process and used primarily as an aid to teaching" (quoted in Wiliam, 2011, p. 33).

Unfortunately, it is or has been "new" to many experienced teachers because it wasn't part of their experience as students or when they were learning to be teachers. For example, I began teaching in 1967 (yes, I'm old), and I knew nothing about formative assessment until I attended a compulsory professional development session in my school in 1988. In his contribution, Hugh O'Donnell, a now retired teacher from Oregon, describes how he learned about formative assessment, how he implemented it in his classroom, and the impact it had on him and his students.

Educator Contribution

Hugh O'Donnell
Retired Middle School Social Studies Teacher
Hillsboro School District, Oregon

The Impact of Understanding the Real Purpose of Formative Assessment

In the fall of 2000, just about six months before I met Ken O'Connor at his professional-life-changing 2001 ASCD Institute in Albuquerque, New Mexico, based on the first edition of *How to Grade for Learning*, I was privileged to attend what I believed was the best

(Continued)

(*Continued*)

back-to-school teacher in-service held by the Hillsboro School District since I joined the district in 1982. Nadine Zimmerlund, executive director of curriculum and instruction for Hillsboro School District 1J, and two of her curriculum and instruction administrators had attended the Assessment Training Institute (Portland, OR) Summer Conference in July 2000 and brought back to our district the insights of "assessment literacy," researched and popularized by Rick Stiggins and his ATI colleagues. It was the first time I had heard of classroom assessment being divided between summative assessments and formative assessments. The concepts that Nadine and her colleagues presented made sense, especially with regard to facilitating and grading student achievement.

This was an era during which most teachers, including myself, measured student achievement with regard to how well students satisfied our class rules and idiosyncratic grading guidelines. Points earned or forfeited and then generalized by the mean average were the name of the grading game, and zeros were handed out for all manner of failures to satisfy teacher expectations. I struggled with how to accurately report student achievement and also be cognizant of the effect of grading practices on student achievement and the feelings of students. Fortunately, for the students, I had studied statistics for three quarters as an undergraduate sociology major and therefore rejected the idea that zeros (outliers) could be included in a mean average. Additionally, including zeros in a grade would be illogical because zeros are not assessment.

But besides learning about the need to measure student achievement accurately, the distinction between formative assessment (practice) and summative assessment ("showtime!") turned out to be—for me—the heart of the whole grading/assessment matter.

In a 1998 *Kappan* article, "Inside the Black Box: Raising Standards Through Classroom Assessment," Paul Black and Dylan Wiliam made a research-backed argument that formative assessment—essentially, the feedback loop between teacher and student that informs the teacher of the effectiveness of his or her instruction and informs the student of his or her academic achievement—is our most valuable instructional tool. And it functions best with verbal or written feedback to the student rather than a letter or numeric score.

I took these ideas to heart and ceased to include practice (formative assessment) in my grading averages. From that point on, only summative assessments figured into my averages that were determined by the median, not the mean.

The result of this change produced some gratifying and sometimes unexpected positive results.

My students began to concentrate on learning from mistakes; they found no need to engage in cheating or avoidance of difficult tasks; they no longer had to dread grading abuses like zeros being included in their report card grade or "docking" for late work; they felt that I was "fair," became more engaged in learning, and performed better on summative assessments; they reported that they endured less anxiety about "work that counts," and the more likely other teachers were to cease grading formative assessments, the less likely students were to compare teacher grading systems unfavorably.

As a teacher, I found that student-involved formative classroom assessment multiplied my instructional effectiveness because I had thirty "assistant teachers," and student record-keeping of formative assignment feedback relieved me of a significant portion of gradebook work.

Hugh O'Donnell's Reasons for Not Including Formative Assessment in Grades

1. Students concentrate on learning from mistakes instead of suffering the disappointments of lowered grades.

2. Students endure less anxiety about "work" that "counts."

3. Students engage in less cheating or avoidance.

4. The stage is no longer set for other grading abuses like giving zeros or "docking" for late work.

5. Student–teacher relationships improve.

6. Students learn more and perform better on summative assessments.

7. Student comparisons of teacher grading systems vanish.

Feedback: The Main Product

Many assessments are designed to provide information so that teachers can adjust instruction, and students can improve performance. For example, this is—or should be—the prime purpose of quizzes. Teachers give a quiz during the instructional process to see how students are doing with their learning. If every student in the class is achieving well, the teacher knows to move on rapidly, but if some or all students are not achieving well, reteaching using different teaching/learning strategies is called for.

Similarly, individual students are informed about how they are doing and so can act appropriately. The teacher, of course, also uses information about individual students for remediation or enrichment. The same considerations apply to teacher questions, most homework, worksheets, and teacher observations during initial student attempts at any activity, such as writing, constructing a map, or completing lab reports. All of these are *learning activities* and should not be identified as *assessments*. Figure 4.3 identifies the similarities and differences between teaching/learning activities and summative assessment. Figure 4.4 shows the relationships involved clearly: After initial instruction and formative assessment, all students receive further instruction. Those who were successful receive enrichment while those who need improvement participate in correctives (i.e., reinstruction in a different way—not just slower or louder!) and may take more formative assessment. When they are ready, students take the summative assessment(s) and either move on to new instruction or to further correctives.

It should be clear that peer and self-assessment should be taught, facilitated, and used often. Both primarily provide information that improves learning and, thus, are part of the formative assessment process. Peer assessment and/or self-assessment should be included in grades only rarely, when such assessment is a stated learning goal and when students have had many opportunities to practice it. Then, we know that the likelihood is high that the assessment will be of sufficient quality.

The importance of feedback and the role of formative assessment have been highlighted by Black and Wiliam (1998) in their iconic article "Inside the Black Box." These two researchers looked at a large number of studies done over a ten-year period and discovered strong evidence that improving formative assessment leads to huge gains in student achievement. They found that this was true for all students, but they also found "that improved formative assessment helps low achievers more than other students and so reduces the range of

FIGURE 4.3 A Comparison of Teaching/Learning and Summative Assessment Activities

Common Elements

- Focused on standards, learning targets, and expectations
- Engaging for students
- Enhance students' knowledge and skills

Teaching/Learning Activities	Summative Assessment Activities
• Introduction, instruction, or practice for students learning knowledge and/or skills	• Students demonstrate knowledge/skills on which they have had opportunity to practice
• Introduce criteria; allow for feedback, self-assessment, and guided practice	• Are based on known criteria
• Focus on individual or group learning	• Focus primarily on individual student performance
• May be narrow in focus—introduce or provide practice for specific skills and knowledge	• Usually broader—integrate important skills and knowledge
• Information for communication with students and parents and information on growth and progress and/or learning skills/ work habits on report cards	• Used to determine report card grades and provide information for comments

FIGURE 4.4 The Role of Formative and Summative Assessment

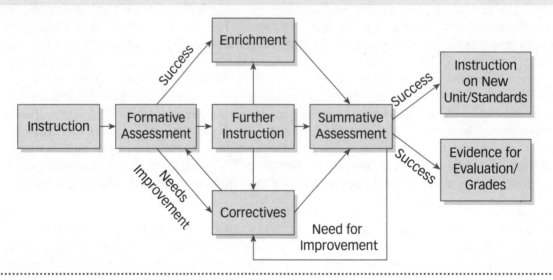

SOURCE: Adapted from Guskey and Bailey (2001, p. 98).

achievement while raising achievement overall" (p. 141). Another important finding was that "the giving of marks and the grading function were overemphasized, while the giving of advice and the learning function are underemphasized" (p. 142). They suggest that these deficiencies could be reduced by a "culture of success," "advice on what (each student) can do to improve," and "self-assessment by pupils" involving "thoughtful reflection in which all pupils can be encouraged to take part" (pp. 142–143). All of this means that if teachers want students to be successful, they must do more to involve students in the assessment process so that they understand when assessment is part of the formative process so they can benefit from feedback and ultimately achieve at a much higher level. This will only happen if formative assessment is risk-free (i.e., it is not part of grades).

It is important to note that writing thirteen years after "Inside the Black Box," Wiliam (2011) says that there are five "key strategies" of formative assessment:

1. clarifying, sharing, and understanding learning intentions and criteria for success [Guidelines 1 and 2],

2. engineering effective classroom discussions, activities, and learning tasks that elicit evidence of learning [Guideline 7],

3. providing feedback that moves the learning forward [Guideline 4],

4. activating learners as instructional resources for one another [Guideline 8], and

5. activating learners as the owners of their own learning [Guideline 8]. (p. 46)

(Detailed explanations of each of the strategies can be found in Wiliam, 2011, pp. 151–158.)

Discussing the critical role of feedback, Tomlinson and McTighe (2006) quote legendary football coach Vince Lombardi as summing it up this way: "Feedback is the breakfast of champions" (p. 77). They note that "all types of learning, whether on the practice field or in the classroom, require feedback," and that "the high-quality feedback systems necessary to enhance learning are limited in our schools, at least in academic classrooms" (p. 77). They suggest that "four qualities characterize an effective feedback system. The feedback must (1) be timely, (2) be specific, (3) be understandable to the receiver, and (4) allow for adjustment" (p. 77).

Think About This . . .

The Effectiveness of Feedback

"At least 12 previous meta-analyses have included specific information about feedback in classrooms. These meta-analyses included 196 studies and 6.972 effect sizes. The average effect size was 0.79 (twice the average effect). To place this average of 0.79 into perspective, it fell into the top 5 to 10 highest influences on achievement in Hattie's (1999) synthesis, along with direct instruction (0.93), reciprocal teaching (0.86), students' prior cognitive ability (0.71), and also can be contrasted with other influences such as acceleration (0.47), socioeconomic influences (0.44), homework (0.41), the use of calculators (0.24), reducing class size (0.12) and retention back 1 year (–0.12)."

—Hattie and Timperley (2007, p. 83)

In a very comprehensive review of the research on feedback, Hattie and Timperley (2007) note that the greatest benefits (effect sizes) from feedback occurred when students were "receiving information feedback about a task and how to do it more effectively. Lower effect sizes were related to praise, rewards, and punishment" (p. 84). They conclude that "feedback is more effective when it provides information on correct rather than incorrect responses and when it builds on previous trials" (p. 85). They also caution that

> providing and receiving feedback requires much skill by teachers and students. . . . [It] does not merely invoke a stimulus-and-response routine but requires high proficiency in developing a classroom climate, the ability to deal with the complexities of multiple judgments and deep understanding of subject matter to be ready to provide feedback about tasks or the relationship between ideas, willingness to encourage self-regulation, and having exquisite timing to provide feedback before frustration takes over. (p. 103)

It is clear that a large amount of research has been done on the impact of feedback, and three things stand out to me as the results of that research:

- the quality of the feedback is critical,

- descriptive criterion-based feedback is much more effective than numerical scoring or letter grades, and

- feedback on learning goals leads to more positive results than feedback that just makes the learner feel good (e.g., praise).

All of these research findings have significant implications for teachers, especially the second point. Common practice has been for teachers to put scores and comments on student assessments, but "the research shows that when students receive a 'grade' and a comment, they ignore the comment" (Leahy, Lyon, Thompson, & Wiliam, 2005, p. 22). Wiliam (2011) provides descriptions of three studies (pp. 107–111) that show that "the effect of giving both scores and comments was the same as the effect of giving scores alone. . . . giving scores alongside comments completely washed out the benefits of the comments." I wish I had known this 40 years ago because it would have saved me countless hours of writing comments. The research shows that we have to make a choice: *We either put a score or a comment on student work but not both, and if we want to advance student learning, we choose the comment!*

Brookhart (2007/2008) summarizes the research and makes many helpful suggestions; issues she discusses include when to give feedback, how much feedback, what mode is best, and the best content for feedback. She suggests that teachers should focus on work and process, try for description rather than judgment, and be positive and specific. She says that teachers should "take as many opportunities as you can to give students positive messages about how they are doing relative to learning tasks and what might be useful to do next" (p. 59).

Another useful view of feedback is provided by the late great Grant Wiggins (2008) when he states,

> Feedback is . . . not . . . praise or blame, approval or disapproval. . . . Feedback is not evaluation, the act of placing value. Feedback is value-neutral help on worthy tasks. It describes what the learner did and did not do in relation to her goals. It is actionable information, and it empowers the student to make intelligent adjustments when she applies it to her next attempt to perform. (p. 5)

J. Chappuis (2015) concludes that "the ultimate goal of formative assessment . . . is that both the teacher and the student know what actions to take to keep learning on a successful track" (p. 10) and that for students, this means that students should be able to answer three questions:

- Where am I going?

- Where am I now? and

- How can I close the gap? (J. Chappuis, 2015, p. 10)

The power of formative assessment comes from being clear about its purpose and the use made of the results. White (2017) points out that "formative assessment and feedback go hand in hand. Formative assessment allows us to gather information about our learners and their engagement in the learning goals so we can make instructional decisions. . . . Feedback allows us to enter into a *dialogue* [my emphasis] with our learners about the decisions they make, their understanding of the content, and their developing skills" (White, 2017, p. 81). The idea of feedback and formative assessment being about *conversation* is powerful and almost suggests the ongoing discussions that take place about whether formative assessments should be scored, and whether they should be included in grades is, at the very least, misguided, but probably it is foolish. White helpfully suggests, "There is a series of steps to help guide us as we design formative assessments that lead to feedback: (1) commit to the process; (2) utilize the learning continuum, (3) determine the purpose, (4) identify the method, (5) capture artifacts, (6) plan how to use the data and take action, and (7) ensure accuracy and reliability" (White, 2017, pp. 81–82). In the following pages, she expands and provides useful suggestions on each of these steps (pp. 82–88). As this is such a critical aspect of grading for learning and as one of my strongest beliefs is that learners—students and teachers—must be reflective, I would like to draw your attention to the comprehensive set of reflection questions that is provided on pages 97 and 98 (White, 2017).

Richard Cash, who focuses his work on self-regulation in the classroom, has varied experience as an educator. He sees the role of descriptive feedback as being a key to students exhibiting the Type I behaviors identified by Daniel Pink (2009) in the following educator contribution. For more about Pink's ideas on motivation, see pages 9–11 in the Introduction.

Educator Contribution

Richard M. Cash, EdD
Educator, Author, and Consultant
Former Classroom Teacher, Saint Paul Public Schools, Saint Paul, Minnesota
Former Director of Gifted Programs, Bloomington Public Schools, Bloomington, Minnesota

Using Descriptive Feedback to Develop Self-Regulation for Learning

An issue I encountered as a teacher was that many of my students were highly extrinsically motivated. My students would ask, "What do I need to do to get an A?" or "How many points is this worth?" This need for the extrinsic reward of a grade told me that students weren't doing the work for the desire to learn.

One of the ways I found for shifting my students from extrinsic to intrinsic learners was through the use of descriptive feedback. Descriptive feedback is the ongoing process of keeping students informed as to what they are doing well, where they need to focus attention, and how to get to the goal. No grade or number is given. I often used the "sandwich" model for giving this type of feedback: the first comment is positive, the second comment

(Continued)

is where effort needs to be applied or what needs to be addressed, and the third comment is overall what the student is doing well. (Example: "You are using the correct method to solve this problem. You should use your graphing calculator to check your answer. Keeping your focus on accuracy will get you to your goal.")

At first, my students struggled with feedback only, but after a period, they got used to the idea and desired it over just a grade. Additionally, I saw an increase in their personal self-regulation, the ability to manage themselves to learn. They were more focused on the process over the product. In my work with gifted students, who often possess a "fixed mindset" ("I'm only as smart as my last grade"), descriptive feedback helped to move them from fearing failure to desiring the challenge through the learning process.

Here are tips I've learned about descriptive feedback to develop self-regulated learners:

- Limit the feedback—focus on the learning objectives, strategy development, and/or the standard

- Keep statements succinct; too much information is just as confusing as too little information.

- Be specific in your comments—avoid comingling too many different ideas.

- Be direct about what needs improvement—don't keep your students guessing.

- Use affirmative language in your remarks—positive framing is more powerful than the negative.

- Never, ever, compare students—keep the comments on the individual student.

- Focus statements on effort over achievement—this will develop a growth mindset.

The Role of Coaching

In activities such as band and basketball, students understand that practice counts, not directly but indirectly. It is practice that makes the spring concert great or enables the team to make the playoffs. When we put a mark that counts directly on everything students do in the classroom, we contradict the value that practice represents to students. Coaching of the type that we see in band and basketball is needed in the classroom. It may not be easy, but through an educative process, students may be helped to understand that participating fully in learning activities, doing relevant and meaningful homework, and trying their best on quizzes that do not count directly toward their grade are practice and will usually lead to much better performance on the summative assessments that do count in grades. (Note: For those students who do well on formative assessments and not as well on summative assessments, teachers must carefully consider the concerns addressed in Chapters 5, 6, and 7.)

Feedback as Motivation

Feedback in the form of words can be very motivational. After a score of 7 out of 10 has been put on a small assignment, not much more can be said. If, however, teachers indicate a strength and an area of improvement, they have the basis for discussions with individual students to help them improve their work. The basic principle at work here is that words open up communication, whereas numbers close it down—prematurely at that.

It is also important to distinguish between feedback and guidance; *feedback* provides descriptive information about what the student did while *guidance* provides information about what the student should do to improve. Students need both, but the sequence in which they are provided is very important. We should always provide feedback before guidance, but I believe that as educators (and parents), we often provide guidance before feedback. The problem with giving guidance first is that the learner may have a defensive reaction and not really hear the feedback, but if we give descriptive feedback first, the learner is much more likely to be open to—and act upon—the guidance.

Quantity of Marking

A very common complaint of teachers at all levels is that they have to do too much marking. This is often true—because they mark too much! It is not necessary, from a measurement point of view, to mark everything students do. Assessment can be reliable as long as there are several pieces of assessment evidence for each learning goal from each student.

Marking everything is also not necessary from an educational point of view. Many teachers claim they must mark everything so that students will do the work. But as has been indicated, this does not provide good information to students and, according to many experiments, damages motivation. A much better approach, thus, is for teachers to check students' learning evidence regularly without providing marks. This lightens a teacher's workload in a number of ways:

> Words open up communication, whereas numbers close it down.

- Some evidence can simply be recorded as done or not done.

- Some evidence—for example, first drafts in creative writing—can be skimmed for a general overall impression rather than examined for the detail that is necessary to arrive at a score.

- Some evidence can be assessed by focusing on one or two key characteristics rather than everything. Strengths and weaknesses in essential aspects can be described clearly in this approach by providing comments only, not marks or scores.

- Some assessment evidence can be assessed by peers, which gives students important practice in identifying strengths and weaknesses while appropriately reducing a teacher's marking burden.

Compared with marking everything, each of these approaches saves time and is more beneficial to students because most teachers are very conscientious when marking work that will be included in student grades.

Technology has also come to help teachers in this regard, as there are now a number of products that teachers can use to more rapidly and effectively communicate feedback to students and engage in dialogue outside of the classroom and school hours. Several of the educator contributions describe the use of Seesaw (https://web.seesaw.me), which can capture student learning in a variety of forms and allows teachers to provide feedback online.

Matt Miller (2017), of *Ditch That Textbook* fame, provides the following variety of both high-tech and low-tech approaches in his blog titled "10 Strategies for Lightning Quick Feedback That Students Can Really Use."

Educator Contribution

Matt Miller
Author, Ditch That Textbook

10 Strategies for Lightning Quick Feedback That Students Can Really Use

1. **Play a quick formative assessment game**. There are lots of great techy options here: Kahoot! (http://getkahoot.com), Quizizz (http://quizizz.com), and Quizlet Live (http://live.quizlet.com). The list goes on and on. If we want kids to get meaningful repetitions with instant feedback, they're a great option.

2. **Use digital assignment tools.** These tools let you create an assignment and send it out to students digitally. As students work, they can get instant feedback. Some options including the following:

   Google Forms quizzes (forms.google.com)—Create simple quizzes using Google Forms. Then, click the settings gear button in the top right corner, and choose "Quizzes." Add instant feedback for students once they're done with the quiz. They won't have to wait on you to grade it!

   Formative (goformative.com)—Create digital assignments with questions, teacher-created drawings, videos, and more. (I LOVE the draw-your-answer option called the "show your work" question.) Watch in real time as students answer and give them instant . . . comments.

   ClassKick (classkick.com)—The brilliance of this one is that students can give each other anonymous help. Who says the teacher has to give all of the feedback? Create an assignment. Let students work. They can digitally raise their hands for help. The teacher can help—or students who are finished can help. Everyone is invested in everyone else's learning.

3. **Comments in Google Slides, Docs, etc.** I'm a HUGE proponent of Google Apps/ G Suite for its instant collaboration. I love creating a slide presentation and sharing it with students (giving everyone editing rights with the "Share" button). Each student gets a slide for his or her work. Students and the teacher can leave comments for each other. Plus, those comments are "nested"—you can reply to specific comments and keep that "conversation" separate from other comments.

4. **The paper version of #3.** Tech isn't a necessity for instant feedback! Have students complete a task on paper. Then, have them pass their papers to the student behind them. That student provides some pointed feedback (positive, constructive, or both). Then, pass to the student to the right. Then, pass again. Return papers to their owners.

5. **Post to social media.** Looking for a bigger audience than the classroom? Have students copy sentences from their work (or take a photo of a paragraph) and post it to

---

social media. Use hashtags to reach a larger audience. They can get feedback from whomever sees it. (Note: Know that this opens them up to a broad audience that could abuse that privilege. But also know that people are generally good, and inappropriate comments rarely happen.)

6. **Provide online flashcards.** There's something to be said about flashcards, even in a digital age. They still provide instant feedback. Using a tool like Quizlet lets students create their own flashcards—even for classes where the teacher might ask, "What's a Quizlet???" Students can share flashcards with each other.

7. **Do speed dating.** Not real matchmaking in the classroom. The academic version. The way I've done it is to arrange chairs/desks in two circles: an inner circle facing out and an outer circle facing in. Give each pair of students a minute or so to talk and provide feedback. Then rotate.

8. **Communicate in a backchannel, like TodaysMeet.** TodaysMeet (http://todaysmeet .com) creates what's essentially a private chat room for you and your students. Just making one of these available for students to use gives them a place to ask questions and trade ideas. Participate and monitor as the teacher as little or much as you decide.

9. **Use Voxer for group or individual feedback.** Voxer (http://voxer.com) is a digital walkie-talkie app. (And more!) Voice feedback is often the fastest and easiest. Have students download the app and create an account. You can create a whole-class, large-group Voxer group or engage in one-on-one, private feedback with personal Voxer chats.

10. **Bellringers, exit tickets, and class polls.** They're a classroom staple—and for a reason! They still work. Do them on little slips of paper. Do a hands-up poll. Or find a digital tool to conduct them. The important part is that you ACT ON THEM. When you get data from them, make the feedback instant. Don't wait until tomorrow.

The Role of Mistakes

A very important concept that is also honored by this guideline is the idea that mistakes are our friends. Robert Sternberg, a past president of the American Psychological Association, says, "If you're afraid of making mistakes, you'll never learn on the job, and your whole approach becomes defensive" (Krakovsky, 2007, p. 28). Spady (1987) notes that mistakes are "inherent elements in the journey toward learning competence" (p. 11). The problem with including everything, Spady states, is that grades "label those mistakes failures and make their consequences *irreversible*, [which] is counter to the notion of human growth and our inherent potential for change and improvement" (p. 11). North Americans, in particular, need to change their beliefs about errors and develop strategies that allow errors to be used effectively. In their research into the results of Trends in International Mathematics and Science Study (TIMSS) 3, Stigler and Stevenson (1991) found that

> for Americans, errors tend to be interpreted as an indication of failure in learning the lesson. For Chinese and Japanese, they are an index of what still needs to be learned. These divergent interpretations result in very different reactions to the display of errors—embarrassment on the part of American children, calm acceptance by Asian children. They also result in differences in the manner in which teachers utilize errors as effective means of instruction. (p. 44)

Clearly a large step in the right direction would be using formative and summative assessment appropriately.

Homework

Many teachers inappropriately include homework as a specific part of grades. Most of the time, homework is formative and therefore should not be part of a grade. There are, however, bigger issues than just whether homework should be part of grades. Boaler (2016) states,

> PISA, the international assessment group, with a data set of 13 million students, recently made a major announcement. After studying the relationships among homework, achievement, and equity, they announced that *homework perpetuates inequities in education* [my emphasis] (Program for International Student Assessment [PISA], 2015). Additionally, they questioned whether homework has any academic value at all, as it does not seem to raise achievement for students. This is not an isolated finding: academic research has consistently found homework to either negatively affect or not affect achievement. (p. 107)

She also says, "When we assign homework to students, we provide barriers to the students who most need our support. This fact, alone, *makes homework indefensible* (Boaler, 2016, p. 107, my italics).

Sackstein and Hamilton (2016), in their wonderful book *Hacking Homework: 10 Strategies That Inspire Learning Outside the Classroom*, concur with Boaler, in that they state that "homework is one of the most misused tools in education," and they pose this question: "Shouldn't we spend less time assigning and grading homework for the sole purpose of marking a grade in the grade book and devote our energy to improving students' learning experiences?" They note that teachers are "often expected to give homework assignments every night" (Sackstein & Hamilton, 2016, p. 16) because of district policies or parental pressure, so rather than advocating for the elimination of homework, they believe that we should "reimagine it in a way that makes more sense for teachers, parents and students" (Sackstein & Hamilton, 2016, p. 19). They then provide ten "hacks" to the traditional arguments that homework is essential. Some of the hacks are as follows:

1. Break up with daily homework; work around policies (pp. 23–35).

2. Teach organization and responsibility in class; ramp up accountability and time management skills (pp. 37–54).

3. Customize to meet student needs; be flexible with assignments and timelines (pp. 71–84).

4. Amplify student voice; incorporate choice in how students learn at home (pp. 127–139).

5. Display growth; empower students to track their improvement and display progress (pp. 157–170).

I see all of the hacks mentioned—and the others not listed—as being applicable to more than just homework, as they are also best practices in teaching to inspire learning *in* the classroom.

As an educator contributor to this book, Connie Hamilton identifies strategies to use when students don't do homework and common homework scenarios and suggests why they are problematic and possible approaches that are much more "friendly" to learning—and learners.

Educator Contribution

Connie Hamilton, EdD
Curriculum Director, Educational Consultant, and Author
Michigan

Homework and Responsibility

Common perceptions that many teachers have around homework are that it teaches responsibility and measures learning. However, there are a variety of problems in everyday scenarios (see Figures 4.5 and 4.6).

FIGURE 4.5 Strategies to Use When Students Don't Do Homework

IF STUDENTS DON'T DO HOMEWORK	
BECAUSE THEY . . .	**CONSIDER . . .**
Are active in many extracurricular activities	What learning benefits they receive as a result and determine if homework is really more important
Don't know how to do it	Making it at an independent level
Poorly manage their time	Instructional strategies to help them learn time management
Can't keep track of assignments	Helping them develop an organizational system
Don't have support at home	How feasible is it for them to do it independently; what other options exist?
Don't see the point	Making the purpose clear and ensuring it's relevant and not just busy work
Don't have resources	How tools and supports can be made accessible

If you don't know why, ask them.

Then, make the necessary adjustments, including reconsidering if it's given at all.

FIGURE 4.6 Homework Scenarios—Problems and Solutions

SCENARIO	PROBLEM	LEARNING-FRIENDLY APPROACH
During class, the lesson runs long, and the time to apply new learning is cut short. An activity is planned for the end of class, but students don't have enough time to complete it, so the teacher asks students to take it home and finish it as homework.	New learning often requires scaffolding and support that cannot be assumed is provided at home.	• Reserve homework for content in which students can engage at the independent level. • When assessing student mastery of new concepts, provide those assessment opportunities in class, not as homework.
	Grading students on their practice with a new skill or concept is premature.	

(Continued)

(Continued)

SCENARIO	PROBLEM	LEARNING-FRIENDLY APPROACH
Homework is assigned, but some students don't complete it.	It is often assumed that when a student doesn't complete an assignment, she or he should be punished with a zero in order to encourage her or him to be more responsible in the future.	• When students don't complete homework assignments, determine why (see Figure 4.5). • Respond to the cause for students not doing homework with a solution that fits the reason.
	A quantitative piece of data is factored into a student's overall grade (see Chapter 6 for more information about zeros), but there is no evidence that the student didn't learn.	
A responsibility grade is collected and included in the overall grade if students make an effort to complete homework.	Responsibility is a character trait and a life skill but not a standard.	• Separate assessment data by standard, content, or skill. Keep in mind that while student effort can certainly influence the result of student learning, responsibility as a stand-alone doesn't indicate mastery of content. • If students lack employability skills, teach them directly. • When behavior grades are collected, that should be independent of academic reporting.
	When grades around effort are included in an overall grade, but lessons are around content, not behavior, there is no system or support to improve a learner's work habits. Instruction ≠ Assessment	
An assignment or task is given to a student, and it's returned to school accurate. The teacher uses the homework as evidence that the student has learned the content and grades it as proficient.	There are many unknowns about how the homework was completed. Intensive parent, peer, or Google support may have played a factor in the end result.	• Include an option for students to self-report how much and what type of support they needed in order to complete homework. Example: I was able to complete the assignment ○ Based solely on my own knowledge ○ With help from the book, notes, a class video, etc. ○ With help from someone at home ○ In collaboration with a peer ○ After searching the Internet
	Even if homework is used as a formative assessment, it can be misleading regarding what students are actually capable of doing independently.	• Collect multiple measures of student learning—don't rely on homework as a reliable source of data.

FIGURE 4.7 Ensuring Quality Homework

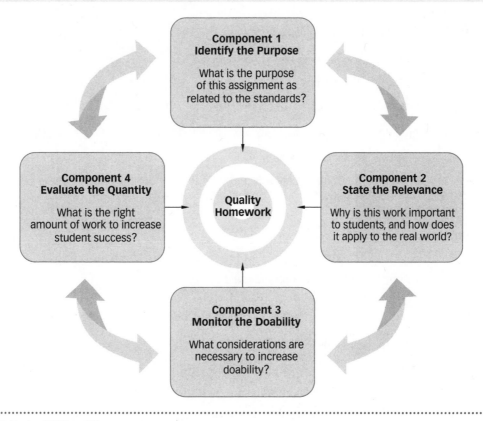

SOURCE: Depka (2015, p. 32).

Depka (2015) stresses the importance of being clear about purpose and says, "Student work should be classified by purpose, not location" (p. 16). She identifies four purposes of "work"—diagnostic, introductory, formative, and summative (p. 17). With regard to homework, when the purpose has been clearly identified and communicated, Depka says that "a quality approach to homework design is essential" (p. 22). She provides a useful graphic (Figure 4.7) and detailed explanations of the four components for quality.

Depka also addresses the issue of grading and homework. She states strongly, "Because formative work is either preparation or practice (or in her categories, introductory), students are not yet expected to have the knowledge and skills necessary to perform. Grading them during this period of learning would be premature and could negatively skew the grade. . ." (p. 71). "Students need the time to practice new skills to successfully demonstrate acquisition. The report will be *inaccurate* if practice attempts are used as part of a summative grade" (p. 72).

> Excluding formative assessment scores from grades does not mean that they are unimportant.

A helpful approach to homework was developed by the Elmbrook School District in Wisconsin; homework is classified as practice, preparation, or integration with descriptions of the desirable characteristics and examples of each type (see Figure 4.8).

FIGURE 4.8 Three Types of Homework Assignments

Practice Assignments

- Must be related to instructional objectives

- Review and reinforce newly acquired skills or knowledge

- Give independent practice for a new concept/skill

- Should have an allowance for mistakes as part of the learning process

- Should be commented on or spot-checked but not counted as a part of the academic grade

- Demonstrate effort, not mastery of concept

Examples: Ten math problems using the algorithm taught in class; writing a paragraph with a strong lead after a lesson on leads in writing; rehearsing foreign language verb tenses that have been introduced this week

Preparation Assignments

- Provide background information for upcoming lessons

- Indicate with completion effort, not outcome mastery

Examples: Reading the description of an experiment prior to the date of the experiment; bringing in a newspaper article related to a current event being studied; selecting a favorite poem to share with the class the following day; using the textbook to label a map of an area, which will then be discussed in class the following day

Integration Assignments

- Are frequently long-term, continuing projects that parallel classwork

- Enrich classroom experiences and deepen the student's understanding

- Provide opportunities for problem solving and critical thinking

- Integrate skills, applying many different skills and knowledge sets to a task

- Require students to apply previous learning to complete these assignments

- Require students to be provided support and materials if needed

- Require project expectations and grading procedures for the assignment to be clear to students and parents

SOURCE: Used with permission from the School District of Elmbrook, Wisconsin.

Concern About Excluding Formative Assessment Scores

It is very important to emphasize that excluding formative assessment scores from grades does not mean that they are unimportant. Formative assessments are critical to the learning process because they provide information to students and teachers (and parents) while the learning is going on. Teachers must emphasize this to students and to parents to develop a new understanding of what counts. The somewhat trite message I would give is that "everything counts, some as practice, some as performance." I think that we can make this clear when we use analogies from sports and the arts. There is no evaluation for the dress rehearsals for plays and no scores for practice, for example, for teams in the week between games in the National Football League. Also, many teachers have found that when students understand how practice "counts" and how feedback helps them to get better, getting students to do meaningful, relevant, engaging homework is no longer a problem. Following is a sampling from the #sblchat (standards-based learning Twitter chat) on April 19, 2017.

SOURCE: Retrieved April 23, 2017, from https://storify.com/garnet_hillman/sblchat-4-19-17-facing-the-hurdles-of-sbg

Further anecdotal evidence of this is provided by the experience of the modern language department at Rutherford High School in Panama City, Florida. Led by department head Sandy Wilson, all teachers in this department made a clear distinction between formative and summative assessment. They found (and I have heard students attest) that their students discovered that this approach is very beneficial to their understanding of language and that they approach summative assessments with great confidence. Students said things like, "The test is less stressful because we have practiced the material till we know it and we know we know it before the test," "We have more fun in class because there is no grade attached to formative exercises. We are expected to make mistakes to help us learn," and the real kicker—"It is obvious that the teacher wants us to learn" (personal communication, June 2003). It is essential that teachers know which students are doing well and which are not. This knowledge allows all concerned to build on the strengths and correct the weaknesses of individual students.

Taking into account all of the above, it is clear that teachers need to keep information about formative assessment, sometimes just "done" and "not done" or sometimes "done well," "done OK," and "done poorly," and that the most constructive approach is *no-mark, comment-only* formative assessment.

> What does count for grades is the performances that students give to demonstrate the knowledge, skills, and behaviors they have acquired as the result of instruction and practice.

The Role of Summative Assessment

Summative assessment should be designed to provide information for specific purposes and carried out only when progress needs to be summarized and evaluated. At other times teachers should focus on the formative use of assessment.

—Assessment Reform Group (2003, p. 12)

Performance: Data Source for Grades

What does count for grades are the performances that students give to demonstrate the knowledge, skills, and behaviors they have acquired as the result of instruction and practice. These demonstrations usually occur at or toward the end (however arbitrarily *the end* is defined) of a unit, a course, or a grading period. "Teachers[, however,] should present the summative performance assessments tasks to students at the beginning of a new unit or course" (McTighe & O'Connor, 2005, p. 12). McTighe and O'Connor suggest that

> this practice has three virtues. First, the summative assessments clarify the targeted standards and benchmarks for teachers and learners. . . . Second, the performance tasks yield evidence that reveals understanding. . . . Third, presenting the authentic performance tasks at the beginning of a new unit or course provides a meaningful learning goal for students. (p. 12)

Variety of Summative Assessments

This guideline does not emphasize just exams and unit tests. There are many possible summative assessments, especially if teachers use performance assessment (see Figure 7.4). For most subjects, teachers should use a combination of assessment types:

- Paper-and-pencil tests—Primarily for knowledge

- Performance assessment—Primarily for skills, application of knowledge, and behaviors

- Personal communication—To evaluate aspects of all types of learning goals

Good examples of varied summative assessments are those that drivers complete before they can obtain a driver's license. First, the driver must usually take a written test on the rules of the road and common driving situations. This is sometimes followed by an eye test, and finally, a performance assessment of the critical skill—driving. Student drivers must pass all three tests to obtain a license. This model can be applied in the classroom when we want students to demonstrate their knowledge, skills, and behaviors.

Also note that most people take lessons and practice for a long time before they try the driving test. While they are doing this, the instructor provides them with feedback. Instructors do not give each lesson a mark to be factored in with the score on the driving test that determines if the license will be issued!

It must be emphasized again that Guideline 4 supports learning and encourages student success by giving students opportunities to practice before undertaking assessments that count directly in grades. In this regard, there are two critical points. First, not only must students have opportunities to practice their knowledge, skills, and behaviors, but they also must have opportunities to practice the type of assessment that is to be used summatively before a summative assessment is made. Second, educators must use more than one assessment method.

> Give students opportunities to practice before undertaking assessments that count directly in grades.

Below, from McColskey and McMunn (2000), is a valuable set of questions that teachers should think about:

- If students' work is graded on a daily basis, can they relax and really think and learn, or do they have to constantly worry about getting a bad grade?

- Of what value to students is the feedback they receive from practice tests?

- Does an overemphasis on grading increase or decrease the motivation of those most likely to be struggling with the topic or skill?

- When students are just beginning to learn a new skill or topic, do grades on homework or assignments designed to help them explore a topic make some of them fearful and anxious?

- How important is it to help students learn how to assess and improve their work? (p. 118)

Teachers need to plan carefully the summative assessments that will provide sufficient evidence for evaluating student achievement of a group of learning goals, say in a unit, and plan equally carefully the formative assessments that will help the students to be successful on the summative assessments. This planning should also include who is the assessor. For an example, see Figure 4.9.

FIGURE 4.9 A Unit Assessment Plan

PURPOSE	ASSESSMENT TASK/STANDARDS	ASSESSOR
Summative	Map—3 standards	Teacher
	Supported opinion short essay—4 standards	Teacher
	Test—2 standards	Teacher
Formative	Map draft 1	Self
	Map near final	Peer
	Supported opinion draft	Peer/Self
	Quiz(zes)	Teacher/Self

It should now be clear that formative and summative assessment both have important roles to play in the teaching/learning process; although they overlap somewhat, the purpose of each is fundamentally different. This is highlighted by J. Chappuis et al. (2012). "We . . . call formative assessment by another term—assessment *FOR* learning [. . . We call summative assessment] assessment *OF* learning [summative]" (p. 25). They go on to say, "Understanding the distinction between assessment *for* learning . . . and assessment *of* learning is pivotal to realizing gains in student achievement." (A detailed comparison of assessment of and for learning can be found in J. Chappuis et al., 2012, p. 25.)

Figure 4.10 summarizes Guidelines 3 and 4 and shows what evidence should be tracked, what should be tracked and reported, and what should be scored to determine grades.

FIGURE 4.10 What to Keep Track of, What to Report, and How to Report It

SUM TOTAL OF EVERYTHING STUDENTS DO IN SCHOOL/CLASSROOM

Diagnostic and practice events
- In-class work: exercises, problems, tasks
- Homework that is for practice
- Trial, feedback, and revision
- Quizzes and other formative assessments

Track (Teacher and/or Student)

SELECTION OF MOST VALUED ITEMS FOR REPORTING PURPOSES

Academic progress
- Learning gains
- Improvement over time
- Specific strengths and areas needing work

Skills of independence and cooperation
- Work habits
- Attendance
- Cooperation/group skills
- Homework completion
- Organization skills
- Behavior
- Academic honesty

Track and Report

SELECTION OF ACHIEVEMENT ITEMS FOR GRADING PURPOSES
- Periodic assessments
- Final exams and papers
- Reports/projects
- Culminating demonstrations of learning

Record and Grade

SOURCE: Adapted from Chappuis et al. (2012, p. 300).

What's the Bottom Line?

What should be included in grades? Scores from summative assessments should be included. *What should not be included in grades?* There should be no scores available from the formative assessment process, so there shouldn't be any scores from formative assessments.

What Is the Practical Implication of Guideline 4?

1. Teachers who use hard-copy gradebooks should have a page in their gradebooks for tracking purposes—the formative page—and a page for grading—the summative page—or they should clearly identify scored assessments in their online gradebooks as either formative or summative. The notations for formative assessment could be *, +, and – or ☑ and × or something similar.

2. Homework, if it is used, has little or no place in grades.

Guideline 4: Sample student performance—do not include all scores in grades.

Analyze Guideline 4 for grading by focusing on three questions:

Why use it?

Why not use it?

Are there points of uncertainty?

After careful thought about these points, answer these two questions:

Would I use Guideline 4 now?

Do I agree or disagree with Guideline 4, or am I unsure at this time?

See the following for one person's reflections on Guideline 4.

A REFLECTION ON GUIDELINE 4

Why Use It?

- Feedback allows students to improve performance.

- Reduces marking load for teachers.

- Encourages learning through practice, risk taking, and not fearing mistakes.

- Allows for reteaching and relearning and self- and peer assessment.

- Says school is about learning, not just accumulating points.

- Research supports importance and role of formative assessment.

Why Not Use It?

- Some students, if not rewarded by grades, will not work.

- If fewer marks are factored into grades, it may make grades less accurate.

- May have a negative effect on motivation.

- Students may not understand enough to value feedback without marks/grades.

Points of Uncertainty

- How to select what goes into a grade and what doesn't?

- How are formative and summative assessment balanced?

- Can students get over the "does-it-count" syndrome?

- What is the role/place of quizzes?

- Students want "pay" in the forms of grades to feel motivated to work.

CHAPTER 5

Emphasizing More Recent Evidence

We say we want them all to learn; we don't say we want them all to learn fast or the first time. If some students have to work harder and take longer before they demonstrate proficiency, so be it. In the final analysis, if they demonstrate proficiency, we give them the grade that reflects that.

—DuFour (2007, p. 263)

My driver's license doesn't have stamped on it "Passed on the second attempt." It looks the same as everybody who passed the first time.

—Ken O'Connor, who failed his driving test once

Guideline 5

Grade in pencil—keep records so they can be updated easily.

a. Use the most consistent level of achievement with special consideration for the more recent information.

b. Provide several assessment opportunities (varying in method and number).

THE CASE OF . . .

Sandeep's Amazing Improvement

Sandeep was ten years old when he registered for a Red Cross swimming class. He had recently emigrated from a landlocked country where opportunities to learn to swim were very limited, and he had never done anything more than try to swim a few strokes in shallow water. He chose to register for the swimming class because he realized that in his new country, there were many lakes, and in his new city, he would have many opportunities to go swimming with his new friends. He was fortunate that he had been assigned to Mr. Smith's class. Mr. Smith was an excellent teacher who had great ability in identifying student strengths and weaknesses in swimming and in providing appropriate activities to maximize student progress.

As would be expected, Sandeep did not swim very well in the first few weeks. His technique was poor, and he struggled to swim more than a few feet at a time. Most of Sandeep's assessments in the first four weeks were well below proficient, but he could see that he was getting better, so he persevered. In the second four weeks, Sandeep improved significantly, so most of his assessments on different aspects of swimming were approaching proficient, and one or two were proficient. In the final four weeks, it all came together for Sandeep—the combination of Mr. Smith's excellent teaching and Sandeep's perseverance resulted in him being judged proficient on every aspect. If Red Cross procedures required that the assessments for the whole twelve weeks be simply averaged, as is often done in schools, Sandeep would have been evaluated as below proficient. Sandeep had clearly mastered the Level 3 swimming proficiencies at the end of the twelve weeks, and on that basis, Mr. Smith awarded him with his Level 3 certification.

WHAT'S THE PURPOSE OF THE GUIDELINE?

This guideline supports learning by acknowledging that learning is an ongoing process and that what matters is how much learning occurs, not when it occurs. We take courses to learn, and what we did not know at the beginning should not be held against us. We also need to honor individual differences by recognizing that students learn at different rates and do not always perform at their real level on their first attempt, in a set time, or on one method of assessment.

To illustrate this, consider a study for the Bill and Melinda Gates Foundation, *The Silent Epidemic: Perspectives of High School Dropouts* (Azzam, 2007). This study lists the reasons students give for leaving school. Two of the top-five reasons were "missed too many days and could not catch up" and "was failing." I believe that traditional grading practices make a significant contribution to both of these reasons because when students fall behind in systems where all scores are averaged to determine grades, students who fall behind have no chance of recovery and frequently drop out of school. The report suggests five actions that could improve a student's likelihood of completing school. None of these included changes in grading practices, but if emphasis was placed on more recent achievement, with multiple opportunities to demonstrate competence, students would know that "it is never over till it's over" and be far less likely to drop out of school.

> What matters is how much learning occurs, not when it occurs.

WHAT ARE THE KEY ELEMENTS OF THE GUIDELINE?

Think About This . . .

"If students demonstrate achievement at any time that, in effect, renders past assessment information inaccurate, then you must drop the former assessment from the record and replace it with the new. To do otherwise is to misrepresent that achievement."

—Stiggins (2001, p. 431)

The process by which new drivers are accredited can effectively illustrate the principles involved in this guideline. Driving competence requires both knowledge and skills, and these are usually assessed, respectively, by a selected response test and a performance assessment. The process is multiphase. First, students learn about the rules of the road and other aspects of driving on their own. When they believe they are ready, they present themselves for the written test. If they do not pass the written test, they may study more and take the test again (and again and again, if necessary!). There are costs associated with this—certainly time and usually money—but each test experience is separate. Their efforts on second (or later) tests are not averaged with their previous scores.

Second, after passing the written test, aspiring drivers move on to driving lessons. Most struggle at the beginning, but with good instruction and good feedback (formative assessment), they progress. They do not, however, receive marks for each lesson! When their instructor believes they are ready for the driving test, they present themselves at the test center. (As the instructor has no marks for each student, these cannot be provided to the assessor to average with their performance on the exam.) The student then attempts the driving test. Many pass on their first attempt, but many (including me) fail on their first attempt. When this happens, most aspiring drivers practice very hard on their deficiencies (parallel parking for me) and, when ready, attempt the test again. When they present themselves at the test center, the assessor, who does not know—or care—that they failed the first (or previous) time(s), does not average their performances with previous attempts. If student drivers meet the requirements of the test this time, they pass and receive their license.

> For knowledge or skills that are in any way cumulative or repetitive, teachers need to look particularly at the more recent information to determine grades.

In both the written and performance assessments, the assessor uses the most recent information, and the opportunity exists for more than one attempt at each assessment. It is important to note that the fact that a driver made more than one attempt at either part of the test does not appear on the license! What matters is *whether* the competency was demonstrated, not *when* it was demonstrated!

There are obvious differences between obtaining a driver's license and what happens in schools. Time is the most significant difference: Schooling is generally defined by the calendar, whereas obtaining a driver's license is not. There are, however, many similarities, especially the emphasis on combining knowledge and skills to demonstrate competence. Thus, the principles involved in testing new drivers are applicable, to a considerable extent, to classroom assessment.

Use the More Recent Information

If a kid falls head over heels in love and flunks the first math chapter test (getting 15 out of 100), and gradually over the term comes up to 95 out of 100, the grade the kid gets is going to be a C–. How long is he or she going to pay for that 15? And does the C– really show what the kid knows? (Hart, 1996, p. 60)

[A district administrator said,] "I was meeting with our high school Advanced Placement Teachers, who were expressing concerns about our open enrollment process and the high failure rate. One math teacher said that while a particular student was now making grades in the 80s, she had made a 12 on an initial test,

'so there is no way she is going to make a passing grade for the first nine weeks.'"
(Wiggins, 2004, p. 9)

These quotes demonstrate very clearly the reasons why teachers should *keep records so they may be updated easily*. The suggestion that teachers should grade in pencil is somewhat symbolic, but it *is* easier to use the more recent information and do the necessary updating of written records if the records are entered using a pencil—ideally one with an eraser! When using a computer grading program, it is easy to replace an old score with a new one and make the appropriate alteration in the grade. What is really important is not the method of recording but the mindset that, for knowledge or skills that are in any way cumulative or repetitive, teachers need to look particularly at the more recent information to determine grades.

> Teachers should base grades on the most consistent level of performance, not the whole range of performance.

Suitability for Different Grade Levels

Another way to say this is that teachers should base grades on the most recent level of performance, not the whole range of performance. This obviously applies in the previous examples—swimming and driving—but it has broad application in elementary schools, especially in the early grades, where we often see rapid development in student knowledge and skills over the course of the school year. Using the more recent information is essential because of the varied and often significant improvement of skills and abilities in young learners. Teachers sometimes attach first-month and last-month writing samples to final report cards; for most early year students, the differences are immense. When rapid development is taking place, to base final grades in any way on assessments in the first grading period is obviously wrong.

In middle school, high school, and college, basing grades on recent performance applies to a considerable extent in most subjects but is probably most obvious in modern languages, mathematics, writing, drama, career technical subjects, and other courses that emphasize skill development and/or performance. At a policy level, this concept has been included in the provincial policy in Ontario, where, at both the elementary and secondary levels, teachers are required to look for evidence of the most consistent achievement. At the secondary level, teachers are also instructed to give special consideration to the more recent evidence of achievement.

This Is Not Improvement Grading

Some may see this guideline as an endorsement for what is often called *improvement grading*. It very definitely is not. First, improvement grades distort achievement by factoring in scores for improvement rather than just achievement. The distortion is particularly severe for students at the top and bottom ends of the achievement scale. Those at the top end find it very difficult to obtain improvement points because they have little room to improve, whereas those at the bottom end may obtain many improvement points, which have the effect of communicating that their achievement is much greater than it really is.

Second, it is much better simply to use the more recent information; students then get a full credit for their improvement rather than a score based on artificial manipulation of numbers. We are able to focus on grading as an exercise in professional judgment, rather than as an exercise in mechanical number crunching.

Improvement is best considered as a reporting variable and not primarily as a grading variable. Grades then are based on the students' most consistent level of achievement with special consideration for more recent achievement.

Reflecting on . . . Grading Plans

Consider the grading plans in Figure 5.1, which were found on (nameless) high school websites in the United States. After reviewing the plans, ask yourself the following questions:

- What problems do you see with these grading plans?

- What changes would you make to each grading plan to make it consistent with Guideline 5?

FIGURE 5.1 High School Grading Plans

The following uniform process is used to calculate student grades:

Courses on 4-by-4 schedule:

(first-quarter average × 40%) + (second-quarter average × 40%) + (comprehensive final exam × 20%)

Courses on an A/B schedule:

(first-semester average × 40%) + (second-semester average × 40%) + (comprehensive final exam × 20%)

Semester Grading System
Most classes will have final examinations each semester.

The grading system for those classes, which have finals to determine a final grade, is as follows:

LETTER GRADE	POINT VALUE
A+	12
A	11
A–	10
B+	9
B	8
B–	7
C+	6
C	5
C–	4
D+	3
D	2
D–	1
F	0

Final examination counts one-fifth of the semester grade. The nine-weeks grades count double value. The nine-weeks grades are assigned a numerical value from the above scale and doubled. The three values are added and divided by five. Only on a rare occasion would a student receive a passing grade for a course after receiving two (2) failing grades out of the three (3) grades issued (two nine-week grades and one semester exam).

It is very important to state clearly that grading plans like these have to be seen as unacceptable if the development of skills, knowledge, and understanding in a course or at a grade level is cumulative in any way, yet I still see many schools that use grading procedures identical to those in Figure 5.1. The only situation in which that approach would be acceptable is if all of the learning goals in each quarter or semester are completely discrete.

A much better approach is to eliminate grading periods (quarters, terms, trimesters, etc.) as part of the determination of grades. They may be kept for administrative and communication purposes, but they have no place in standards-based grading, where we look at the pattern of a student's performance over a full year or course. An excellent rationale for ending marking periods is provided by Mike Kelly, principal of Eyer Middle School in Macungie, Pennsylvania.

Educator Contribution

Mike Kelly, Principal
Eyer Middle School, Macungie, Pennsylvania

The End of Marking Periods

In many schools, including the one in which I work, teachers have adopted great practices, such as ongoing formative assessment, reteaching, retesting, and allowing students to redo assignments. However, even with the implementation of these successful grading and instructional practices, the old "learning clock" still counts down to the end of the marking period. It's like trying to beat the sand timer in a board game. All learning must be complete before all the sand gets to the bottom on the hourglass, or it's too late. So why?

Why do we have a system that encourages teachers to race against the clock to jam in one last project or test before the end of the marking period? I would argue we no longer need these arbitrary time limits for learning in our current system.

With instructional approaches such as standards-based grading, grading for mastery, objective-aligned assessments, retakes, and redos, do marking periods create arbitrary time constraints on opportunities for learning? When marking periods are removed, we promote a growth mindset approach to learning, and students can continue to strive toward mastery, being exposed to multiple ways of learning, as well as being given multiple attempts/methods to demonstrate their learning.

With the ability for parents to check grades online at any time, the need to periodically update parents via report cards no longer exists. I know some will argue that not all parents have access to grades online. However, for the sake of this blog post, I am focusing on the majority. After all, more people own a cell phone than a toothbrush. Another argument against the removal of marking periods is that a new marking period gives students a fresh start, or a clean slate. However, by implementing some of the practices I mentioned before (retesting and redos), students are constantly and continually given a fresh start and a new chance at learning.

Another flaw in traditional marking periods is their equal weight. In our system, each of the four forty-six-day marking periods ends in a grade that is weighted equally. But any teacher will tell you that not all marking periods are created equal. When ten days in the

(Continued)

third marking period (22 percent) are taken up by standardized tests, how can teachers and students accomplish the same amount of learning as in the second marking period? However, our current system weights all marking periods the same when calculating a student's final grade.

There is much more to consider when it comes to evaluating grading and assessment practices; however, the removal of marking periods is something worth more consideration.

What thoughts or ideas do you have about traditional grading practices that should be reevaluated?

Update: Our school is currently (2015–2016 school year) piloting a continual, yearlong grading period for all of our sixth-grade courses. We have removed the traditional four marking periods and have one ongoing grading period. So far, so good! More updates to come in future posts.

....

SOURCE: This was originally published as a post on Principal MKelly's EduMic on April 26, 2015. Retrieved April 26, 2017, from https://principalmkelly.com/2015/04/26/the-end-of-marking-periods.

NOTE: In one of those updates, Principal Kelly wrote that they evaluated all of the feedback and decided to not only continue our continual grading period in sixth grade but also expand into seventh grade. "With the support from our district, we plan to continue implementation during the 2016–2017 school year. I am confident we will learn more in our second year of implementation and continue to make improvements."

Provide Several Assessment Opportunities

This guideline acknowledges individual differences in many aspects of education, especially in planning teaching/learning strategies, and recognizes that life is full of second chances. The practical application of these principles is that, as much as possible, we must offer students multiple and varied assessment opportunities to support learning and encourage student success.

Individual Differences

Students learn at different rates and are able to demonstrate their knowledge and skills in different ways and at different speeds. This is part of our acknowledgment of individual differences, which encompass learning styles and multiple intelligences, as well as a more general understanding that students are different in many ways and that fairness requires equity of opportunity, not uniformity. As we acknowledge differences in learning, it is logical—and critical—that we provide opportunities with a flexible time frame for students to demonstrate their knowledge and skills.

> Offer students varied assessment opportunities to support learning and encourage student success.

Multiple and Varied Opportunities

In the real world, very little of consequence, including writing this book, depends on a single opportunity for performance. Most performances are practiced several times before they become real—think about writing, theater, and film, to name a few. In each of these fields and many others, there is a great deal of assessment and redoing before a final product is released. Also, individuals are not evaluated on one piece of writing or one film;

judgment of their quality as a performer is made over a body of work. This is also true in sports; individuals get many chances within each game to improve their performance, and teams have multiple opportunities to improve their performance because they play many games over the course of a season. The idea of second chances is taken even further in learning to be a surgeon or a pilot; aspiring surgeons practice on cadavers while those learning to fly practice for hours in simulators before practicing in a real plane.

As life provides second (and more) chances, so should school. There are many reasons why students do not perform at their best on the day designated by a teacher for a test or performance. These may relate to learning, physical, or emotional factors. The objective of teachers is to accurately identify the level of performance of students. To do this, teachers need to vary assessment in many ways, including the number of opportunities, time available, and the methods used. (See Chapter 7.)

Assessing the same concepts and skills using different questions and/or tasks can provide a number of opportunities for students to demonstrate achievement. One potential problem, however, is unreasonable extra work for teachers; to avoid this, teachers may use computers to collect banks of items and tasks. This can be done at the school, district, and/or state level.

As schools move to provide second—or more—opportunities for students to demonstrate competency, limitations are often put on these opportunities. It is important to state clearly that these opportunities must be available to *all* students, and there must be no limitation on the contribution that the reassessment makes to the student's grade. Nolen and Christopher, as quoted in Wormeli (2006), state the case for the latter very clearly. "Policies that give only partial credit for revisions are little better than no-revision policies—why should the student spend time and effort revising if the best they can hope for is a slight improvement in the grade, despite the fact that he now understands the work" (p. 115).

Practical Considerations

Having provided a number of suggestions for how students can be provided with flexible assessments, it is now time for a qualifier. Second or multiple assessments do not mean an endless set of opportunities for students. This would be unrealistic and would place far too great a burden on teachers. As Ebert (1992) said, "Second chances do not just appear, nor do they naturally work out without some evidence [of students] using past mistakes to enhance future success. Therefore, reassessment is the opportunity and students learn the responsibility" (p. 32).

> "The consequence for a student who fails to meet a standard is not a low grade but rather the opportunity—indeed, the requirement—to resubmit his or her work."
>
> —Reeves (2000, p. 11)

There are practical implications from Ebert's remark:

- Any reteaching, review, or reassessment is done at the teacher's convenience.

- Students should be required to provide evidence that they have completed some *correctives* before they are allowed a reassessment opportunity. Correctives may include personal study/practice, peer tutoring, worksheets, review classes, and so forth. For example, when I failed my driving license test because of poor parallel parking, I practiced parking every day in the week leading up to my second test. If I had not applied this "corrective," I probably would have failed a second time.

- It is quite reasonable for an "opportunity cost" to be attached to reassessment so that students will recognize that their self-interest is served by doing well the first time. The opportunity cost attached to my second driving test was the time I put into practicing, the time for the second test, and the fee for the test. I would have much rather passed the first time!

Correctives and reassessment opportunities can be organized somewhat informally, but if teachers want to provide these opportunities with a clear structure, Figure 5.2 on page 162 suggests a way to do it. Whatever approach teachers use, it is critical that reassessment opportunities be available to *all* students. Although the main purpose of second-chance assessment is to help students who have not performed well, to be fair and to be seen to be fair, it must be available to all students.

Guideline 5 is designed to support learning and encourage student success by focusing on more recent information and by having considerable flexibility in assessment with regard to the number of opportunities and the methods by which students can demonstrate their knowledge and skills. Two contributions from educators provide the philosophical and pedagogical reasons for reassessments (Rick Wormeli) and a practical "how to" (Denine Laberge).

Educator Contribution

Rick Wormeli
Author/Consultant
Herndon, Virginia

Thoughts on Relearning and Reassessing for Full Credit

I once asked a colleague what he thought he was teaching his students who expressed remorse when failing a test or a project and requested a chance to learn the material properly and redo the assessment but was denied doing so because of his "No Redos" policy. He said that he was teaching them to meet deadlines, thus preparing them for the working world.

I asked him, "Did the student learn the content you were hired to teach him?"

My colleague shook his head, "No." So I continued, "When did incompetence become acceptable to us?"

My colleague pushed back: "He needs to learn time management."

"Show me the research," I countered, "that says F's and zeros build executive function, time management, and self-discipline—the skills you're seeking for this student."

He had nothing. The simple truth is that redoing work and assessments is far more demanding and maturing, both personally and academically, than receiving an unrecoverable F for a failed, initial attempt ever could be. Letting a student escape with incompetence, caving in to his immaturity or lack of development, is abdicating our adult role in the teaching/learning dynamic. We tell him instead to get back on the bicycle and try again and again until he rides all the way to the park. Recording unrecoverable F's at the top of students' tests is a cop-out.

Teachers claim that they are trying to get students competent with the standards of their discipline, but they often resort to simplistic teacher algorithms: a few lectures, a video, a vocabulary activity, students complete an online practice module, and then a test on

Friday. This is not the stuff of long-term retention. Competence comes with meaningful learning and multiple iterations and experiences. Even before the time of Benjamin Bloom's compelling mastery learning research on the topic, we've known the power of reteaching and reteaching until students finally master content.

Can pilots redo landings? They do so hundreds of times before real passengers are on board so they learn how to handle every emergency swiftly and safely. How do architects learn to design buildings, writers learn to write successfully, or surgeons learn their proper procedures? How do programmers learn to code and teachers learn to teach? They do so by doing the skills of their craft repeatedly, listening to the helpful critique from practiced mentors after each attempt, and then revising their efforts to incorporate those new insights in the next attempt. Why would any of us take this away from today's students? It's how all of us became the professional workers and leaders we are. Every single hero in every field we lift up as exemplars to students—sports, medicine, technology, dance, engineering, gaming, graphic design, politics, law, literature, music, and math—excelled for having engaged in their discipline over and over and over, getting better each time. Reiteration is one of the most effective teaching practices of all time. To prohibit its use in a misguided attempt to build character is close to malpractice.

So, what's the best approach?

First, choose the most pivotal standards to emphasize and focus redo, feedback, and reassessment energies on them. We really can't do it for all standards, but we can for those that matter most.

Second, set up a list of options for students to use as they design their plan of relearning that must be completed prior to reassessing, and impress upon students that there must be demonstrable shifts in learning in order to warrant the reassessment. Include mandatory student reflections, too: *What is different between the first and subsequent attempts? What new decisions did they make in their learning this time that they did not make first time? What did they learn about themselves as students?*

Third, walk the journey with them; don't just wag an admonishing finger from afar. "You-should-have-dones" turn into the Charlie Brown teacher's "Wa-Wa-Wa's" in the blink of an eye. This is not to say you're going to do the work for the student; it merely means you'll be there, through the easy and the difficult parts, as a resource. You'll ask guiding questions, do status checks, be a listening ear when the student needs to vent, and sometimes sit with him as he does his work. You'll also hold up the bigger picture of his progress so he can see the patterns that being too close to the work prevented him from seeing. You'll make hope visible.

Fourth, feel free to offer alternative assessments, if the first one would be too easily copied.

Fifth and finally, whatever you do, record full credit for the evidence of mastery presented. As teachers, we have no moral authority or right to knowingly falsify a grade, nor would we ever want our own, hesitant first steps with something we were learning to count in the report of our final competence. This means all of those measures we used for decades in mistaken attempts at fairness are now void. These include giving only half a point for corrected items, limiting the reassessment score to only a 70 percent, averaging the new score with the former score, and allowing only low-scoring students to redo.

And what if the grade levels next in line for our students don't allow redos—won't students be overly dependent on redos and thus disabled by such a practice? No. The two

(Continued)

(*Continued*)

biggest preparations for the next grade level are personal maturation and real competence in the subjects they are learning now. Maturity and tenacity come from walking through the relearning/reassessing process, not from the F recorded at the top of the test. Recovery from failure teaches students far more than the label for failure ever could. It's hard to imagine student incompetence being helpful in the next level of our disciplines because it's not. Students knowing their stuff is.

And what about professional certification exams for lawyers, pilots, mechanics, doctors, teachers, accountants, architects, real estate agents, EMTs, FBI agents, nurses, police officers, and every profession with a specialized field of training? These exams can be redone; if the initial attempt is less than passing, they can be done in the year we are ready to take them, not always in the same year as age-equivalent classmates. More importantly, however, how will these individuals perform well on these exams? By being thoroughly competent in their field. So would the alternative to relearning/reassessing (i.e., one and done, with no hope for improvement, thereby assuring incompetence) be helpful? Not even close.

John Hattie, Benjamin Bloom, Susan Brookhart, Rick DuFour, Tom Guskey, and many others have research on the positive effects of relearning/reassessing in K–12 classrooms, but we don't really need it to make our point. Our ten-month-old wobbles on his first step, then bounces to the floor in a happy collapse. We don't declare him a nonwalker at that point and shake our heads in disappointment, thinking that he's now learned an important life lesson. Instead, we recognize the power and freedom of being able to walk on your own, and we wish it for our child. So we smile, gently take his hand, help him up, and declare, "Almost! Let's try it again."

NOTE: A more detailed article on this topic by Rick Wormeli titled "The Right Way to Do Redo's" can be found on Middleweb at https://www.middleweb.com/31398/rick-wormeli-the-right-way-to-do-redos. Accessed on April 7, 2017.

Educator Contribution

Denine Laberge, Teacher
Collège Louis-Riel, Winnipeg, Manitoba

Emphasizing More Recent Evidence

Every test or assessment my students complete can be considered formative to a certain extent. When I give a math test, for example, students who wish to have a rewrite can do so. Of course, everything is discussed with me, and there are limits, and this is decided on an individual basis.

Some teachers will complain that this is unfair and that other students got it right the first time—that they shouldn't have more time or opportunity than the others. The issue of fair to me is that every student gets what he or she needs to succeed. If that means a second chance, then that's what they get.

As the year progresses, the number of rewrites decreases considerably for two reasons. First, the rewrite is not free. They have to pay with time and effort, valuable commodities in high school. Second, as they work for the reassessments, they develop study habits that help them in future assessments, and they, like many others, get it right the first time. At the beginning of the semester, it is not unusual to have ten to twelve requests for the first test. By the second or third test on, there are about two or three. These are the students that just need more opportunity to learn the material and master the concepts.

Students must reflect on their results and take responsibility for them. (This is done using the Reassessment Request Form, Figure 5.2.) For example, a student must write the grade obtained and give the reason for this grade. If the reason is, "I didn't understand it," then his or her responsibility is to come see me or to ask questions or to get help from a friend, among other possible solutions. If they don't do any of these things, then they do not take responsibility for their part in the process, and the conversation we have about this is eye opening for some of them.

They must also complete three tasks; two I assign, and the third they choose.

First, they must arrange a time to come see me to go over the assessment. We look at their analysis form (see Figure 5.2) and go over their errors. They confirm understanding, or they state the work they will do to solidify it. The point is that they must talk about their learning. It is through talking to them that I become aware of what the problem is, and they are made aware of where they are. Sometimes, they understand more than they realize, and their confidence (or lack thereof) is what gets in the way. Being aware of this helps.

Second, they must correct the first assessment to show that they understand all of the concepts targeted in that assessment. I can see in the processes used that the understanding is clear or if there are misunderstandings that still need to be addressed.

Third, they choose a final activity to complete. For example, if they struggled with the problem-solving component of the test, then they may want to practice with extra problems from the textbooks available in class.

The request form must be signed by the student, by the parent, and by me. This keeps the parent informed, and the student knows that we are all working together to help him or her succeed.

For those who struggle regularly in math, this is a comforting process. They take the time they need to learn and do not get discouraged because they know they are not alone and that we are, in fact, interested and working toward their academic success.

In order to write the reassessment, students must present their evidence of new work (their corrected first assessment and the extra work they have done to confirm understanding). If they do not present it at the time of reassessment, they do not write until they present the work done to rewrite.

For students who think a reassessment is a laziness failsafe, they realize very quickly that it is not free. They will work hard to be entitled to rewrite, and working hard the first time is a lot less time consuming than the reassessment process. For teachers who refuse to give rewrites because they do not want the extra work, they start to see that the student is the one who does the majority of the work. I usually have more than one version of my math tests anyway, so there is no need to write a new one. If I do need to write a new one, then I use the original as a template, and it does not take very long.

Reassessment is often not very time consuming. For example, if a student did well on most of the test but struggled in the problem-solving questions, then he or she rewrites the problem-solving questions only. I already know he or she understands the rest of it.

Finally, the mark they get on the rewrite is the one that stands. If the new mark is lower, then it tells me that it wasn't completely understood the first time. This is rare, but it does happen. The more recent score tells me where they really are in their learning.

FIGURE 5.2 Reassessment Request

Reassessment Request

Personal Information

Name: _____ Date: _____

Subject: _____ Concept: _____

Reflection

Grade obtained: _____

Reason: _____

_____

_____

Three things I have done to improve my understanding of these concepts

1. See teacher at lunch or at arranged time (date: _____)

2. Assessment analysis and correction

3. Choice: (Please specify) _____

Date of reassessment: I will be ready by this date: _____

Request

I request the opportunity to resubmit this assessment in order to confirm understanding of the concepts covered. I have worked hard and have completed all of the required steps to improve my understanding.

Signatures

_____   _____   _____

Student   Parent   Teacher

Please attach

• The first assessment (test, quiz, project, . . .)

• Evidence of completed tasks

The Power Law

One way to implement this guideline is to use the power law of learning, which, according to Stuart (2003), has been identified by researchers in the fields of measurement and psychology. She notes that the power law "validates what good classroom observers have known all along" (p. 198) and what this chapter is about: Learning is a process that moves from limited to greater understanding over time, and this should be acknowledged when we summarize achievement. The power law of learning quantifies this process and has "demonstrated more accurate final indicators of student performance than are provided by averaged scores" (Stuart, 2003, p. 198). The power law can be built into formulas used to calculate grades and has been incorporated into some computer grading software, such as the Rediker Teacher Plus Gradebook Version 1.37.0 and 1.38.0.

Three Reasons to Reassess

1. The student has truly and legitimately grown their learning after a summative assessment (through further practice, recursive teaching) and is willing and able to demonstrate this growth.

2. Conflicting assessment information is preventing the teacher from making a professional judgment about proficiency.

3. External circumstances are interfering with validity (poor assessment prompts, unexpected events, etc.) (Katie White, posted on #ATAssess on January 11, 2017)

Two Important Considerations

What Should Happen Before Formal Reassessment Opportunities?

Scott Habeeb addresses this issue very clearly in a blog titled "Redo's and Retakes? Sure. But Don't Forget to Loop!" originally published on October 6, 2016, with this statement about R/R (i.e., redos/retakes):

> Let's remember that R/R is not the ONLY way—and often not the best way—to implement standards-based philosophies.

He is not suggesting that R/R practices should stop but that we should do what he calls *looping*—teachers regularly assessing students to gauge the level of student learning that leads to individual standards being assessed multiple times and, more than likely, through multiple measures. He says, "The problem with typical R/R practices is that they have a tendency to cause all of us—educators, students, and parents—to think and communicate in terms of grades rather than learning." Habeeb then states that "the power of assessment is greatly enhanced when, rather than after-the-fact, . . . teaching and assessment practices—such as looping—are interwoven into the fabric of the learning process."

Vatterott (2015) also addresses this issue with this question, "How do I make sure students are ready for (summative) assessments?" (p. 76). Her answer is "more pre-test/less retest" (Vatterott, 2015, p. 76) because as she says, "What seems to make sense is to have more and better formative assessments" (Vatterott, 2015, p. 76). In other words, if we provide lots of feedback—and especially if students don't take summative assessments until they have demonstrated readiness—then the focus is on learning.

Doing what Habeeb and Vatterott recommend significantly reduces the number of students who need or want formal reassessments and is certainly preferable to just emphasizing or providing reassessment opportunities. It requires that teachers and students be focused on learning proficiency, not grades, points, or percentages.

Another way to reduce the need for separate reassessments is to spiral the assessment of standards as part of an assessment plan. Principal Nathan Wear describes how this is done at Solon High School in the following educator contribution.

Educator Contribution

Nathan Wear, Principal
Solon High School, Iowa

Multiple-Opportunity Assessment

Teachers should consider utilizing multiple ways of assessing the same standard for different students, as well as important communication techniques.

Spiralling

A challenge at Solon High School was getting teachers to think about time spent on instruction in a different way. Our school utilizes an eighty-four-minute block, and teachers were used to spending most of the time on direct instruction, guided practice, and independent practice. Through the introduction of standards-based grading, teachers began to spiral curriculum throughout the course to better utilize instructional time in a block. One way teachers did this was to reteach students who struggled on previous assessments at the end of each block. Another example was to embed previous assessment items on future assessments. Not only did this allow for the teacher to use this information as a built-in reassessment, but it also provided a way to spiral the curriculum to check for retention of important standards.

Solon High School teacher Karry Putzy used spiraling in her Spanish class as a way to use multiple assessments throughout the week. Most often, she gave quizzes on Monday, Wednesday, and Friday. A student score later in the week would replace a previous score. Here is language from her class syllabus on how spiraling worked in her classroom.

> Assessments of individual learning targets most often will be quizzes. The most recent/representative score from evidence on quizzes will replace any previous learning target score. Learning targets may be quizzed more than once. . . . Reassessments are to be completed within two weeks of the original assessment receipt/return. Learning targets will reappear on exams; thus, learning the material for that learning target is our goal.

Keeping a Log

As you progress through implementing standards-based grading in your school or classroom, you will want to be sure to keep track of how many times a student has reassessed. First, this will help inform your instruction as to whether you are making an impact on the student's learning. Think about a student in your class that you have taught multiple times how to do something and he or she still doesn't get it. A reflective teacher will think about the ways that future instruction can be modified to better help this student understand the standard. Secondly, this may be a sign that a student has a learning disability that a child study team should address. Lastly, this can be a great point of data for teachers to share with parents at conference time. This data can show how some students choose to persevere with learning.

There are two ways teachers at Solon High School have found success in tracking the number of times a student has reassessed. One is the old-fashioned checklist. Teachers will list assessments in some type of notebook or spreadsheet and keep track of how often students reassess. Another way is to capture this data in a student management system. For example, a teacher can include notes about how often the student reassessed a particular learning target in the comment section for students and parents to see.

Recognizing and Dealing With Opposition to Reassessment

There are a number of examples of school districts where there has been significant opposition to reassessment from parents and teachers. In some cases, it has unfortunately led school districts to dramatically change the use of reassessments and other aspects of grading reform.

Opposition is based on comments like this:

Parents	Teachers
"Reassessment creates a confusing system where students expect second chances. How long before a motivated student learns that he can earn the same grade with a lot less work?"	"I feel that this policy has damaged our student population. We are doing a disservice to them when it comes to their future jobs. Our students show no responsibility, and I get on a daily basis, 'I haven't studied. . . . When is the reassessment?'"
"I like the overall goal. But I don't want children to always think they can redo things so they don't try their best the first time. We are not preparing our children for the 'real world.'"	"Students aren't reassessing to further their learning. The students and the parents just want the better grade. Reassessment is an opportunity to master the standard and further their understanding. Students THINK they should be given a reassessment without going through the requirements to do so. Students want an extension on the reassessment whenever they would like. Our culture and the community has not taken reassessment as an opportunity to grow."

These comments reveal problems with the fidelity of implementation of formal reassessment procedures, but they also raise concerns that must be addressed through the creation of a culture of learning, professional development, and frequent communication about the why and what of reassessment and other, more effective grading practices to students, parents, teachers, and the community. There are, however, many testimonials from students, parents, and teachers about how important reassessment is in promoting a culture of learning. The following is an example:

At Parent–Teacher Conferences this week nearly every parent made a point to mention how much their child loved my grading system (SBG) because the availability of retakes took the pressure off performance and allowed the kids to focus on learning. I can't tell you how many times I heard "I wish every teacher graded the way you do." That's how I know we're doing the right thing.

—Barry Fuller, physics teacher at Byram Hills High School, Armonk, New York, posted on the Standards Based Learning and Grading Facebook Group page, December 16, 2016

What's the Bottom Line?

Teachers should focus on reteaching and reassessing proficiency on learning goals as a normal classroom practice. However, when appropriate, students should be given second (or more) chances to demonstrate what they know, understand, and can do on varied methods of assessment.

Grades should be determined by the student's most consistent level of achievement, with emphasis on more recent evidence. This means that final grades should almost never be determined by simply averaging the grades from several grading periods (e.g., adding the grades from Terms 1 through 3 and then dividing by 3). More recent information almost always provides a more accurate picture of student achievement.

The practical implication of this guideline is that teachers need to keep their records—on paper or on a computer—in ways that can easily be changed or updated. "Grade in pencil" may not always be literal advice, but it needs to be the mindset that teachers have about recording grades.

Guideline 5: Grade in pencil—keep records so they can be updated easily.

Analyze Guideline 5 for grading by focusing on three questions:

Why use it?

Why not use it?

Are there points of uncertainty?

After careful thought about these points, answer these two questions:

Would I use Guideline 5 now?

Do I agree or disagree with Guideline 5, or am I unsure at this time?

See the following for one person's reflections on Guideline 5.

Why Use It?

- Achievement at the end is what counts.

- Promotes and recognizes progress.

- Supports and helps to develop perseverance and growth mindset.

- Learning is not a race.

- Computer grading programs make it easy to "grade in pencil."

- Extent to which learning goal is achieved is more important than when it is achieved.

- Supports the results of effective teaching.

Why Not Use It?

- Encourages "slackers" to wait until the last minute.

- Time constraints make reassessment difficult.

- Those who do best the first time often do best later as well.

- Average of several attempts is fairer than best score.

- Students can manipulate—play the system.

Points of Uncertainty

- Emphasis on formal reassessments or "looped" assessment opportunities throughout the course or year or both?

- Effect on student motivation.

- Transition into real world—second chances?

- Is one student's third attempt a fair comparison with another's first attempt?

- Reliability/validity of test items on second or third test.

CHAPTER 6

Determining Grades

Data should inform, not determine, decisions.

—Consultant, The Hay Group, International Management Consultants

Students never fail to turn in an assessment or drop out of school because they kept forgetting their pencil.

—Hill and Nave (2009, p. 106)

Guideline 6
Determine, don't just calculate, grades. a. Crunch numbers carefully—if at all. b. Think "body of evidence" and professional judgment.

THE CASE OF . . .

Charlene's Inaccurate Grades

Charlene was a brilliant Grade 11 student who received almost perfect marks on every summative assessment (tests, products, demonstrations, etc.) for which she was present—and she usually was present to take major tests/exams and to submit major assignments on the due dates. Charlene, however, missed many classes and often did not hand in required work (homework, first drafts, etc.). She also did not complete her notebook, and because of her absences and shy personality, her participation in class discussions was infrequent. As a result of these circumstances, there were always many zeros in teachers' gradebooks for Charlene—for missed quizzes, lab reports, small assignments, notebook, attendance, participation, and so forth. Charlene received a D in most subjects, and because of her lack of success, she was considering dropping out. Charlene's low grades resulted from averaging her many zeros with her 90+ percent scores and clearly did not reflect her achievement. She was penalized over and over again for her poor attendance—which was caused by her single-parent father frequently requiring her to stay at home to look after her younger siblings!

he comment that opens this chapter was made by a consultant for the Hay Group, a large international management consultancy, who was sitting next to me on a flight from Philadelphia to Toronto in late January 2001. I know that was a long time ago, but it had a powerful impact on me then and still does over sixteen years later. He was describing the most difficult aspect of his job—namely, convincing his clients of the truth of this statement. We talked about this for a while, and then it struck me that this is exactly the message I have been trying to get across about grades. To have grades that have real, not just symbolic, meaning and to enable us to focus on learning, not just accumulation of points, grading must be seen not as a numerical, mechanical exercise but as an exercise in professional judgment. In other words, we must use the evidence we collect—numbers or words, separate or combined—to determine grades in such a way that any measures of central tendency (mean, median, or mode) are just part of the evidence, not the determinant of the grade.

Warning

Most—but not all—of this chapter assumes that teachers are *not* implementing Guideline 2—the use of levels instead of points and percentages—and Guideline 5—emphasizing more recent achievement. If these two guidelines are fully implemented, Guideline 6 becomes virtually unnecessary. It is, however, realistic to recognize that some teachers will continue to see grading as primarily a number-crunching exercise, and some will have to continue significant number crunching to fulfill the responsibilities imposed on them by state/provincial policies and/or school/district assessment and grading procedures that include grading scales based on points and percentages. Thus, many of the examples in this chapter are based on traditional approaches to collecting data on student achievement.

WHAT'S THE PURPOSE OF THE GUIDELINE?

This guideline supports learning and encourages student success by having teachers question the widely accepted but seriously flawed practice of simply averaging marks to arrive at final grades. This questioning leads teachers, first, to examine all aspects of number crunching, such as measures of central tendency weighting, the use of zeros, and how to include level/rubric scores that are involved in the calculation of grades, and, second, to consider whether grading is—or should be—merely a numerical, mechanical exercise or whether it is—or should be—an exercise in professional judgment. For teachers who ignore or cannot implement Guidelines 2 and 5, this guideline is critical because, at the very least, they need to examine their number-crunching practices. For teachers who move toward grading as an exercise in professional judgment and apply one or more of the other guidelines, especially Guidelines 2 and 5, there will possibly be some degree of involvement with number crunching, so this guideline remains important for them as well.

WHAT ARE THE KEY ELEMENTS OF THE GUIDELINE?

Number crunching has been part of teachers' lives from the time grades were introduced. This guideline is about how grades are determined and requires that teachers

1. recognize that averaging should have no place in the determination of grades and that grades should be determined by the use of logic rules;

2. understand the limitations of the mean and, for any required number-crunching, examine the appropriateness of each of the measures of central tendency;

3. consider whether and, if necessary, how various components included in grades should be weighted;

4. (re)consider the use of zeros; and

5. consider how to include level/rubric scores in grades.

Discussion of each of these issues should lead to the conclusion that for grades to be accurate, grading must be an exercise in professional judgment, rather than simply a mechanical, numerical exercise.

Over the last few years, I have had a clear indication of how serious this issue is by the questions posted on the "Ask the Grade Doctor" section on my website (www .oconnorgrading.com) from 2009 to 2015. In December 2015, I felt I had to post this statement:

> In the six plus years that "Ask the Grade Doctor" has been "open" about 3,700 questions have been posted and I have answered many of them. Although there was a clear statement asking that questions that were only about the calculation of grades not be submitted, the majority of the questions posted have been in that category. In each year at obvious times in the school year I have been inundated with questions of that type. This year has been by far the worst and so I have reluctantly decided to shut down this part of my website.

Here is a small sample of those questions that I think clearly shows why this guideline must be implemented if we want accurate, meaningful grades.

> "If I have a c in my class and I got 15 extra credit points how much of my c will go up?? (My c is 85%) plus we have an end of the quarter project that will give us 200 points in my science class. So how much will I go up?"

> "I have a 52 in an English class. I have 4 zeros, all homework grades. I completed two over-due essays and let's say i made a 60 on both of them, leaving me with only two zeros. What would my new average be?"

> "I have a 62% in PE if i get a 75%-100% every day for 21 days how much will my grade go up?"

> "I have a 16 average in english i have 2 weeks left of the 6 weeks what will be my final grade??"

AND this is my all-time "favorite"!!!

> "I need help calculating what I need to get in the final to pass
>
> - 1st exam 38/54, which is worth 19.05%;
>
> - 2nd exam 37/54, which is worth 19.05%
>
> - 3rd exam 35/51, which is worth 19.05%
>
> - and I have finals, which is worth 21.43%
>
> - and a lab, which is worth 21.42%
>
> I need overall 75 or above to pass this class so far I have 69.17% what do you think I need to get in my finals to pass this class? Please help."

1. Measures of Central Tendency

> Grades based on averaging have meaning only when averaging repeated measures of similar content. Teachers average marks on fractions, word problems, geometry, and addition with marks for attendance, homework, and notebooks—and call it mathematics. In mathematics we teach that you cannot average apples, oranges, and bananas, but we do it in our grade books!
>
> —Canady, during a presentation in Toronto, 1993

Reflecting on . . . Problems With the Mean

Study the information in Figure 6.1. Assume that these are the marks four students have received for ten summative assessments in a school subject—elementary, secondary, or college—*on a similar set of learning goals.*

FIGURE 6.1   Issues With the Mean

ASSESSMENTS IN ORDER	KAREN %	KAREN Level	ALEX %	ALEX Level	JENNIFER %	JENNIFER Level	STEPHEN %	STEPHEN Level
Assessment #1	0	0	63	2	0	0	0	0
Assessment #2	0	0	63	2	10	1	0	0
Assessment #3	0	0	63	2	10	1	62	2
Assessment #4	90	4	63	2	10	1	62	2
Assessment #5	90	4	63	2	100	4	63	2
Assessment #6	90	4	63	2	100	4	63	2
Assessment #7	90	4	63	2	100	4	90	4
Assessment #8	90	4	63	2	100	4	90	4
Assessment #9	90	4	63	2	100	4	100	4
Assessment #10	90	4	63	2	100	4	100	4
Total	**630**	28	**630**	20	**630**	27	**630**	24
Mean	63%	2.8	63%	2.0	63%	2.7	63%	2.4
Median	90%	4.0	63%	2.0	100%	4.0	63%	2.0
Mode	90%	4.0	63%	2.0	100%	4.0	?	??

NOTE: Only for the purposes of this figure 85–100% = 4, 70–84% = 3, 60–69% = 2, 50–59% = 1, and 0 is for no evidence. *There really is no equivalence between the percentage scale and the ordinal scale.*

- What grade should each student receive based on the percentages? Why?

- Is it accurate to use the same approach with each student?

- What additional information would help you make this decision?

- How does the use of levels rather than percentages change your view of the grade each student should receive and the role of number crunching in the determination of grades?

Most fifth-grade students learn the difference between mean, median, and mode, and thus gain the insight that the arithmetic mean, or average, may not be the best representation of a set of data. Yet the teachers of those students remain stubbornly allegiant to the average.

—Reeves (2007, p. 230)

The average does not have to be the mean; teachers should consider using the median or the mode. These are the accepted measures of central tendency taught in mathematics classes, usually starting about Grade 5! The *mean* is the total of the values divided by the number of values. The *median* is the middle value of the data listed in numerical order. The *mode* is the most frequently occurring number. This aspect of Guideline 6 asks teachers to consider two dimensions of importance: (1) quantity or quality and (2) all or some evidence.

Note that using percentages, all students in Figure 6.1 received the same mean scores but that the median and mode scores for Karen and Jennifer are much higher. In schools using traditional grading schemes, such as the one illustrated in Figure 6.2, all four students would receive a grade of 63 percent, which would vary from a C to an F, depending on the grading scale in use.

FIGURE 6.2 Number Crunching With Percentages in Traditional Grading

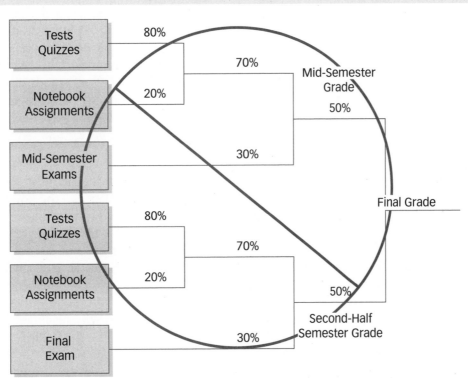

The traditional approach emphasizes quantity over quality and completing all assessments, rather than doing some superbly and missing some. It also ignores any consideration of more recent achievement (Guideline 5). It is clear, however, that the achievement of each student is very different. Karen generally produced high-quality evidence, but for some reason, she did not submit three of the ten summative assessments. Alex produced consistently mediocre results but submitted all of the summative assessments. Jennifer produced superb evidence on six of the assessments but did very poorly on three of the assessments and did not submit one of the assessments.

Stephen's performance was very inconsistent—four assessments were excellent, four were mediocre, and two were not submitted. The mean and median are the same for Stephen, and it is not possible to calculate a mode; clearly 63 percent is not an accurate summary of his achievement, so none of the measures of central tendency provides an accurate grade. This example illustrates that the more inconsistent a student's performance is, the more *none* of the measures of central tendency works. Teachers then must use the numbers to inform but not determine the grade—in other words, they have to use their professional judgment. For a distribution of scores like Stephen's, professional judgment should lead to a grade that recognizes that although it took a long time, at the end of the grading period, Stephen really had a high level of understanding and should get a high grade—almost certainly an A.

> Medians "provide more opportunities for success by diminishing the impact of a few stumbles and rewarding hard work."
>
> —Wright (1994, p. 723)

These scores were from assessments on a similar set of knowledge and skills, so learning is incremental. Determining a grade should, therefore, be based on the trend in the student's performance, with considerable emphasis on the more recent assessments (as described in Chapter 5).

In deciding grades for the students in Figure 6.1, consider the following:

> Averaging falls far short of providing an accurate description of what students have learned. For example, students often say, "I have to get a B on the final to pass this course." But does this make sense? If a final examination is truly comprehensive and students' scores accurately reflect what they have learned, should a B level of performance translate to a D for the course grade? If the purpose of grading and reporting is to provide an accurate description of what students have learned, then *averaging must be considered inadequate and inappropriate* [emphasis added]. (Guskey, 1996, p. 21)

Guskey's statement clearly identifies the problem with using the mean, the most commonly used measure of central tendency: The mean always lets the bad overtake the good so that for every low mark earned, a student needs many good marks to return to his or her real level. This is evident in the grades of Karen and Jennifer—most of their work is of a very high quality, but for some reason(s), they either did poorly on or did not submit some of the assessments. This problem is compounded when teachers include zeros for behavioral reasons (attendance, tardiness, misconduct, etc.).

Doug Reeves provides a powerful statement on the next page as to why teachers shouldn't be mean.

The Median Alternative

An alternative to using the mean is to use the median. Wright (1994) states that teachers' marks are ordinal data (numbers on a scale whose intervals are uncertain or inconsistent) and that "the median is the statistically correct measure of central tendency for ordinal data" (p. 724). This is the technical argument for using medians, but an equal or more important argument is the philosophical one. Wright advocates medians and uses them in his college courses because they "provide more opportunities for success by diminishing the

Educator Contribution

Douglas Reeves
Founder, Creative Leadership Solutions
Boston, Massachusetts

Rejecting the Average

In schools around the world, students learn about the differences among the average (the arithmetic mean), median (the middle point), and the mode (the most frequent point) in a data set. Why? Because ten- and eleven-year-old children know intuitively that politicians and marketers can mislead the public with statistics. "The average"—whether it's income, unemployment, or performance in hockey, baseball, or soccer—doesn't tell the whole story. They all know of individuals and teams that struggled early on and then succeeded. They read heroic stories of people who succeeded against the odds and triumphed after a series of failures. They have personally experienced the exhilaration of success after a series of disappointments. In other words, they know that how they finish—the latest and best evidence—is more important than how they started. If students understand the limitations of the average, why do adults persist in using it?

I have found two illustrations useful in persuading teachers to reject the average and embrace the use of the latest and best evidence. First, consider the annual student concerts. These are joyful events in which students sing and play, and parents cheer and applaud. But only the heroic music teachers recall the dreadful practices in the months that preceded the concert. Students were out of tune and rhythmically impaired. Their voices, strings, and reeds yielded a cacophony of sound that was, to put it charitably, not ready for the concert. And yet, over time, the feedback of the teacher and the diligent practice of the students yielded the performance that led parents to stand and cheer at the concert. So consider this: if the concert audience were to judge students on the average of their work, they would sit on their hands and refuse to applaud because the errors of the beginning of the year would be averaged into the performance at the end of the year. However silly that sounds, that is precisely the logic that the use of the average demands.

The second illustration hits close to home for most teachers. The majority of teachers have a graduate degree, and most graduate degrees require a course in statistics and research. It is fair to say that these courses, which I have taught, are not the favorite of most educators and school administrators. "I'm teaching social studies—why do I need to learn statistics? I'm an English teacher—why do I need to pass a research course? I didn't like algebra when I had it in high school—why do I need it now?" These and many less charitable comments characterize the early weeks of a graduate class in statistics and research. But as the semester progresses, the same students gain an understanding of the purpose of the class—to make them critical consumers of research. By the end of the semester, they achieve the "Now I get it!" stage of learning and are in the professor's office explaining why they should be evaluated not based on their average performance but rather on the "Now I get it!" stage of learning. They are quite correct and should apply the same standard to their own students once they return to their classrooms.

impact of a few stumbles and rewarding hard work" (p. 723). Wright notes that all students have days on which they do not produce their best evidence and that not every student is good at everything, but neither of these failings suggests that most of the time students do not produce high-quality evidence of achievement. The use of the mean emphasizes variability, whereas the use of the median reduces the impact of variability dramatically.

Assuming the use of Guideline 1, to use the median, teachers must convert all scores to a common scale (ideally, level scores). Then, they calculate a median for all the scores on each standard from the summative assessments used in a course (which, ideally, would not be more than 10—and preferably less for each standard). Next, if necessary, they calculate a median among the standards grades to arrive at the final subject grade. (For a teacher not using Guideline 1, the categories would be assessment methods, not standards.)

> The median has the greatest impact when performance is highly variable.

The use of the median has the greatest impact when performance is highly variable. Thus, students who perform at a consistently high level or at a consistently low level would see little or no difference in their final grades, regardless of which method of central tendency is used.

The problem with the use of the median for many teachers is their fear that it encourages students to play games and manipulate the system to their advantage by making minimal or no effort on some assessments. If this is (or becomes) a problem, it may be necessary to require that students submit/complete a certain number of assessments with a required minimal level of performance. It also may be necessary to designate some assessments as essential: If a critical assessment is not submitted, it should be recorded as missing (a blank space in the gradebook) or not submitted (NS), and the summary judgment would be "incomplete" (an I grade), regardless of the quality of other assessment evidence submitted by that student. However, if the median is used in association with the other guidelines, if students have a clear understanding of the supportive success orientation of the grading procedures being used, and if the students are presented with course material and assessments that are interesting and engaging, lack of effort should not be a problem.

The primary purpose of grades is to communicate achievement. Regardless of which measure of central tendency is used, grades (symbols) need to be supplemented by as much information as possible. If the median is chosen, it is particularly important that some form of narrative reporting be used so that teachers can provide a clear picture of achievement.

It is important to note that Guideline 6 suggests only to *consider* using the median. Given that grades should be based on each student's most consistent achievement, teachers should also consider the use of the *mode*—the most frequently occurring number in a series of numbers. To use the mode, marks/scores would have to be recorded by level—4, 3, 2, 1 or A, B, C, D, F. Changing from the use of the mean is a giant step for many teachers and many communities—but it is a step that must be taken.

2. Weighting Marks—if Necessary

A second aspect of Guideline 6 that educators may need to consider is weighting components carefully to achieve intent in final grades. The way in which marks are combined sometimes involves varying the importance or weighting of the different learning goals and/or assessment methods. Chapter 1 suggested that grading plans need to be based primarily on learning goals rather than assessment methods. Regardless of which approach teachers use, it is very important that weighting reflect the intent and emphasis on different learning goals/assessments in the final grade. *The rule of thumb should be that unless differential weighting is absolutely necessary, all categories are of equal weight.* In Ontario, for example, in many subjects, the four achievement chart categories (Appendix F) are of almost equal weight, but the subject association for physical and health education recommends that 60–65 percent of a student's grade should come from the Application category because that is the focus of PHE courses.

The Issue of Variability of Scores

Technically, variability of scores on each assessment also needs to be taken into account; a test with a range of scores from 40 to 80 percent has a different impact than a performance assessment for which the scores vary from 10 to 100 percent. It would be ideal if scores were equated through the use of standard scores before being weighted. See Thayer (1991) for a detailed description of these procedures.

Because there is enough in this guideline (let alone the other seven!) for teachers to consider without dealing with these highly technical issues, not much detail is provided here about standardizing scores. The issue of variability of scores, however, is something that teachers need to be aware of, especially when class rank, scholarships, and awards are being determined, as illustrated in Figure 6.3. Note also that the significance of this issue is greatly reduced when level scores are used instead of percentages.

Reflecting on . . . Simple Averaging

Consider the situation shown in Figure 6.3.

Each student stood first or had equal first grades in five subjects, but Michael was second in calculus with 97 percent, whereas Megan was first in music with 89 percent. If these grades are simply averaged, Michael will be ranked first even though Megan had a slightly higher average on the five subjects that they each studied. Is this fair?

FIGURE 6.3 Simple Averaging

	MICHAEL	MEGAN	HIGHEST GRADE IN SCHOOL
English	96%	96%	96%
Chemistry	97%	96%	97%
Biology	96%	100%	100%
Physics	97%	97%	99%
Algebra	92%	92%	94%
Calculus	97%	n/a	99%
Music	n/a	89%	89%

3. The Use of Zeros on the Hundred-Point Scale

Mathematically and ethically this is unacceptable. (Wormeli, 2006, p. 138)

> Teachers need to devise better ways of dealing with work that is late, missing, or neglected other than simply assigning zeros.

Reeves, Jung, and O'Connor (2017) identified the use of zeros as one of the four grading practices that "result in inaccurate measures and encourage students to see school as being about compliance and point accumulation rather than learning" (p. 43). The first was dealt with earlier in this chapter, and the second was dealt with primarily in Chapter 3. Now it is time to deal with the issue of the big *0*.

Teachers often use zeros when students fail to submit required assessment evidence and for academic dishonesty because teachers feel that if nothing has been submitted or if students have behaved badly, the score should reflect this and that the zero will lead to more responsible actions in the future. However, a number of serious problems arise with the use of zeros:

- The effect of such extreme scores, especially when coupled with the practice of averaging

- The lack of proportionality between 0 and 50–70 percent as the passing score compared with the much smaller differentials between the other score points in the grading scale

- The inaccurate communication that results from the use of zeros

- The ineffectiveness of zeros as responsibility-creating mechanisms

Consider the following real example I observed in the spring of 2001. In a high school that issues report cards after four-and-a-half weeks, grades in one subject were based on five scores. One student, whom I shall call Janice, received scores of 90, 0, 82, 72, and 76. The mean score was 64 percent, and the passing grade in the state is 70 percent, so Janice received an F. Imagine if we did this in calculating the average weekly temperature. Let's say the high temperature in Phoenix, Arizona, each day for five days in July was 105°F, but we forgot to record it for two days and recorded zeros. The average would appear to be 75°F! Janice failed the class both because the extreme score of 0 had a disproportionate impact on the average and because of the 70-point differential between the D/F cut point and 0, compared with a 10-point differential between each of the other cut points (D/C, C/B, and B/A).

A parent's view of this issue was provided by Susan Hedges (Mathews, 2005). Commenting on the requirement that no grade below 50 percent be given in the schools attended by her children, she wrote,

> I am the parent of two children who have passed through the school system with learning disabilities (dyslexia in one, Attention Deficit Hyperactivity Disorder in the other), and I applaud the change to a new baseline for grades. It is a lot fairer to students who struggle to complete assignments. Both my children have been in the position of not turning in assignments, getting zeros and then being unable to recover no matter how hard they worked for the rest of the semester. On the classic 100-point grading scale, it is very hard to recover when a zero has to be averaged with grades of 60 or better to pass. It is a long way down to zero. (p. GZ06)

> If incompletes are used, mechanisms must be in place that support students and make it possible for them to complete the missing work.

In the interest of mathematical accuracy, the lowest possible score should be no more than the differential between the other cut points. If this approach had been used, the 0 would have become a 60, and Janice's grade would have been 76 percent (a C or D). "Recognizing this some schools have responded with the *minimum 50* (or 63 if the pass/fail cut is 70%) grading policy. . . . But this inevitably leads to the retort that students are 'getting 50 points for doing nothing,' and school administrators often beat a hasty retreat" (Reeves, Jung, and O'Connor, 2017, p. 44). The more appropriate and more direct way to solve this problem is to use a level score scale with an equal numerical difference between each point on the scale. Using this method, Janice's scores might become 4, 0, 3, 2, and 2, resulting in a mean, median, and mode of 2; her letter grade would probably be a C. This is a minimally acceptable solution to the use of zeros when grades are just calculated.

The inclusion of the zero in a percentage scale in the grade for Janice led to a serious miscommunication of her achievement. She clearly was not a failing student, as four of her five scores were above or well above the pass/fail level, but because of the one zero and the mean, she received an F. The F in no way communicated the quality of most of her achievement or the fact that one piece of assessment evidence was missing. The teacher expects that the F will cause Janice to make greater effort in the next grading period. Guskey (2000), however, disagrees: "No studies support low grades or marks as punishments. Instead of prompting greater effort, low grades more often cause students to withdraw from learning" (p. 25). It is far more appropriate to have Janice take responsibility for her learning and be held accountable for the missing work.

What, then, should be done about "work not submitted" (which is what late work becomes after a hard deadline has passed)? The use of a strictly numerical approach to grade determination, the median or mode rather than the mean, and/or a more appropriate point differential (e.g., where if 70 is the pass/fail cut point, 63 is given for missing work instead of 0) would help overcome some of the worst effects of traditional approaches. The other acceptable numerical approach, noted earlier, is to use a level score scale with equal numerical difference between each point on the scale. These numerical alternatives are illustrated in Figure 6.4, where the student received marks of 95, 85, 75, and 65 on four assessments but did not submit one of five required assessments.

FIGURE 6.4 Alternatives to Zeros

STUDENT SCORES	101-POINT SCALE	EQUAL DIFFERENCE SCALES	
		5-POINT SCALE	50-POINT SCALE
95	90–100 (A)	4	95
85	80–89 (B)	3	85
75	70–79 (C)	2	75
65	60–69 (D)	1	65
0	< 60 (F)	0	50
Mean	64 (D)	2 (C)	74 (C)
Median	75 (C)	2 (C)	75 (C)

SOURCE: O'Connor (2011, p. 98).

These changes from traditional practice are minimally acceptable alternatives to the use of zeros, but they are not the best approaches. If, for example, the missing assessment evidence was a major task essential to valid and reliable assessment of Janice's achievement or if the teacher takes a more holistic approach to grade determination, then the question that needs to be asked is this: Do I have enough evidence to make a valid and reliable judgment of the student's achievement?

- If the answer is yes, the grade should be determined without the missing piece, which is recorded in the grade book as "M" for "Missing" or "NS" for "Not Submitted." The fact that the evidence was not submitted should be reported in the work habits/learning skill section and/or in the comment section of a report card.

- If the answer is no, then the grade should be recorded as "I" for "Incomplete" or "Insufficient evidence." This symbol communicates accurately that, while the student's grade could be anywhere from an A to an F, at the point in time when the grade had to be determined, there was insufficient evidence to make an accurate judgment. If the grade "I" appears on an interim report, then corrective action can be taken during the next grading period. If the I is on the final report card, it has the same effect as an F, but the student should still have the opportunity to submit the missing assessment by an agreed-upon date.

Think About This . . .

"I never give zeros. If an assignment is forever missing, it goes in my book as a fifty. That's an F, punishment enough. Entering a zero has devastating mathematical consequences on grade averages, often putting students in an irrecoverable position. Why bother to keep working when you know nothing you can do will bring that average up to passing? I want them working, not shut down.

"If we entered grades as forty/A, thirty/B, twenty/C, ten/D, zeros would be OK. But if ninety/A, eighty/B, seventy/C, sixty/D, fifty/F, entering a zero in the gradebook is the equivalent of giving a kid a K. For that reason, if a kid miserably fails a test—for example, a score of 35 percent—I put it in as fifty/F.

"Fifty/F is low enough. If kids never turn in work, or consistently fail tests, they will still average an F and fail. But, if they have just a few bad days, they can raise their average with quality work and pass."

—Susan Bischoff, secondary teacher, as quoted in Wormeli (2006, p. 138)

If I's are used, mechanisms must be in place that support students and make it possible for them to complete the missing assessment evidence. This means that schools or districts must be prepared to devote human and financial resources to make this possible. A number of schools in have adopted an approach they call ZAP—zeros aren't permitted. This has a double meaning: Teachers are not permitted to put zeros in their gradebooks, and students are not permitted just to "take" a zero. During scheduled makeup time, called *ZAP time*, students are given support to complete missing evidence of achievement. To make it clear that it is better not to have to attend ZAP, one school scheduled the ZAP time from 4:00 p.m. to 6:00 p.m. on Fridays—except on Fridays before a holiday!

A very comprehensive approach to the issue of missing assignments developed by Tennessee middle school principals Danny Hill and Jayson Nave is called the *Power of ICU*. Educator contributor Sherri Nelson provides a description of how this works at Huron (SD) Middle School and educator contributor Cory Strasser provides the details of how ICU is used at Pipestone M/HS in Minnesota.

Educator Contribution

Sherri Nelson
Director of Curriculum, Instruction and Assessment
Huron School District, South Dakota

The Consequence for Not Doing Your Work . . . Is Doing Your Work

The Power of ICU is an academic support system for students built around a school-wide list of missing assignments. All students completing all quality assignments is the focus of this approach. This proven formula for student success, developed by Danny Hill and Jayson Nave, requires school leaders to assemble armies of support (teachers, parents, paraprofessionals, counselors, and administrators) and challenges staff to create multiple intervention opportunities to help all students experience real academic success.

Students with missing or poor-quality assignments have their names placed on an electronic ICU list that can be viewed by all staff members. Parents immediately receive automated texts and/or e-mail messages when their children's names are added to the ICU list. Students are asked by a variety of staff members: *"Whom do you owe?" "What do you owe?" "What is your plan?" "What do you need?"* and *"How can I help?"* Staff members reteach concepts and provide students with extra assistance to complete their work: before school, during lunch, during intervention time, and after school. Once students produce quality work, their names are removed from the ICU list and follow-up messages inform parents the work has been completed.

Making a Difference

Middle school teachers in Huron, South Dakota, have successfully redefined accountability by eliminating zeros and holding students accountable for learning. Since implementing the Power of ICU formula (completion + quality assignments + healthy grading practices), students in Grades 6–8 (for four consecutive years) have exceeded NWEA MAP growth projections in math and reading, and state assessments confirm the school has substantially narrowed the achievement gap in both areas of academic study. This improvement in student achievement is a result of Huron Middle School staff working collaboratively to ensure all learners experience academic success; most transformative was their focus on redefining accountability and implementing, with fidelity, an academic support system for struggling students to complete and improve the quality of their work.

Huron Middle School—Power of ICU Goals

1. Equip all students with the knowledge and skills they need to be successful in high school.

2. Redefine accountability by holding all students accountable for learning.

3. Improve communication between parents, staff, and students.

4. Provide extra support (time and assistance) to students before, during, and after school to help all students experience real academic success.

Educator Contribution

Cory Strasser
Principal, Pipestone M/HS, Pipestone, Minnesota

A Common Approach to Building the Brickhouse Culture–Power of ICU Assignments

1. The assignments we give have a value for learning and are attached to learning goals and standards.

2. Assignments that have the greatest value for learning go on the list. These assignments may not always be graded.

3. Grading/marking—We only grade assignments that have value for learning and are connected to learning goals and standards. We expect students to complete practice work that may or may not count toward a grade.

4. Extra practice—The practice we send home is relevant to improve, practice, or review learning and can be done by the student at home. (autonomy, mastery, purpose)

5. Late assignments—full credit or reduction up to 10% of the grade—teacher discretion.

Consistent Practices for Using the ICU List

1. Ask the four questions: Who do you owe? What do you owe? What do you need? How can I help? Start by saying, *Can you tell me what is on your list?*

2. Start your day with the ICU list. When you start your computer, pull up the ICU list (bookmark it on your Web browser), and check it frequently. That way, when a student brings in an assignment, you can check it and remove it from the list in a timely manner.

3. There is a difference between correcting assignments and a student turning the assignment in. If a student hands the assignment in, skim it, move it to "Pending" on the ICU list, and correct it later when you are ready. If, when correcting, the work is not done to your expectations, give it back, and put him or her back on the list. Emphasize quality work.

4. Every assignment is e-mailed/texted to the parent. Attach assignments as necessary. Likewise, when assignments are taken off, the parent receives a follow-up text.

5. Update your list before going home at 3:45 p.m. each day when possible. Updating the list before 7:00 p.m. has been effective. Communicate to students that this is the time frame when you update it consistently.

6. Use Schoology/Google Classroom/other LMS to post assignments and so forth, allowing those to be readily available for all students, teachers, and staff. Updating the LMS serves as a communication tool and reduces the excuses students can give: "I don't have access to that assignment!"

7. Give students a visual with motivation. Write student names on the board, and have them take their name off when the assignment is completed.

8. When a student who is not in your class has completed an assignment, take it right away, and give it to the teacher or put it in their box. Even send them an e-mail reminder.

9. Take two minutes at the end of the class/lesson in order to review the list and remind students of their missing assignments. This is especially effective prior to lunch and at the end of the school day. Even put the list on the board.

10. Coaches/supervisors—Use the list to check students' missing assignments. Give students extra time and support (before or after school, in study hall, etc.) instead of practice or contests.

11. Study hall/ISD teachers—Students on the ICU list are *not allowed* to use the library or other privileges.

12. Advisory—Connect with kids and ask the four questions. Tell stories. Provide support.

13. No sarcasm.

How We Do ICU: Providing Supports

- **Parent meetings**—Recommendations come from grade-level team meetings. Counselor-arranged meetings to discuss assignments and academic progress. This is done when students are becoming chronic on the list or have a high number of missing assignments.

- **Classroom Blitz**—Individual teacher blitz of students who have several missing assignments.

- **Paraprofessionals**—Serve as lifeguards, providing another layer of support.

- **Learning Center**—High School and Middle School Learning Center available—especially on Wednesdays during PLCs and for Power Hour or extra time and support after school.

- **Study hall/ISD teacher**—It is imperative you are checking the lists and requiring students to stay in your study hall for extra help and not go to the library. Remember, they are not being punished; we are just providing extra help.

- **Blitz Days**—Random and unassigned time frames to reward students while providing extra time for students to receive support from teachers.

- **Homecoming and Snow Week**—Students who do not have missing assignments participate. Others work with teachers to complete assignments.

Head Lifeguard

Role—pull kids from study hall, pull kids from lunch, assist teachers with phone calls, track the list, and so on.

Wednesday

End-of-Day Approach—25-minute study sessions

1. Teacher grade-level teams will meet on Tuesday after school to review the ICU list for their grade level.

(Continued)

a. Grade-level team determines which students should be the focus for the Wednesday study session.

b. The focus is on a small group of students (depending on the size of the list) with similar assignments. This helps paraprofessionals supervise and narrow the learning focus for this time.

c. The grade-level team leader will put his or her list into an e-mail and send it to the head lifeguard.

2. Head lifeguard will compile the list and send one e-mail to all staff by Wednesday morning.

3. Teachers utilize advisory to talk to students about being on the list.

4. At the beginning of seventh period, teachers should remind students who are on the list. At the 2:50 p.m. bell, teachers will walk designated students to study rooms.

You may not agree with every aspect of both of the ICU approaches described previously, so you could make adjustments if you choose to implement this program or one like it. You might even prefer an approach suggested by Dave Nagel—Amnesty Days.

Educator Contribution

Dave Nagel
Author/Consultant
Indianapolis, Indiana

Amnesty Days

Amnesty Days are basically school wide makeup days. Amnesty Days, or periods, are scheduled instructional time devoted to supporting students who are behind or for students to make up missing work (regardless of the reason) without penalty. The word *amnesty* comes from the Greek amnēstía, meaning *forgetting*. Granting someone amnesty means obliterating the ramifications of his or her offense. The implementation of Amnesty Days as a support practice, by definition, prohibits teachers from including any penalty or point deduction for student work submitted late (Nagel, 2015, p. 113). Teachers and school leaders who implement Amnesty Days periodically can significantly reduce the negative impact of two root causes of course failure: students missing multiple assignments and students getting too far behind in content understanding. Amnesty Days also serve as a buffer day in the curriculum that provides teachers time to reteach focused lessons for students that need more time and practice to grasp specific content.

··

NOTE: Further suggestions about ways to support students can be found in Nagel (2015, pp. 110–115), where he provides more details about Amnesty Days and what he calls MEAEC IT Happen—*Missing Essential Assignments or Assessments Extended Chance.*

Appropriate language for "Incomplete" in a school policy or student handbook can be found in Figure 6.5.

FIGURE 6.5 Statement About Incomplete in Student or Teacher Handbook

(Note: Where text appears in italics below, schools/districts would replace it with what they consider to be an acceptable time frame or learning support or the appropriate words.)

It is each student's responsibility to provide required evidence of achievement in a timely manner. If students have not met this responsibility (late or missing evidence), they will have additional opportunities to complete all major assessments and performance tasks. For a *period of time*, these opportunities will be provided by the student's teacher and will be voluntary; after a *period of time*, students will be required to attend *study hall*, where they will receive support.

Students need to understand that a teacher's professional judgment near the end of each grading period regarding their body of evidence will determine their grade at that point, so it is important that students complete sufficient assessment evidence to the best of their ability. Teachers will record an M in their gradebook for such missing work. If sufficient evidence has not been provided near the end of a grading period, the grade shall be reported as I for Incomplete. If this is on the final report card, it is a failing grade and means no credit.

Students will have *a period of time* past the end of the grading period to complete any "major assessments" (with no late penalty) that are required for teachers to be able to determine a grade for a student. When the assessment has been marked, an appropriate adjustment will be made in the student's grade.

At the beginning of each course/semester, teachers will provide students with an assessment plan (see Figure 6.6, Assessment Plan and Template) that lists all "major assessments" and the minimum requirement for sufficient evidence (e.g., "There will be these seven major assessments [listed with approximate dates]. A minimum of five, including the third and fifth, must be completed. If a student's performance is inconsistent, the student may be required to complete more than five assessments.").

FIGURE 6.6 Assessment Plan and Template

An ASSESSMENT PLAN should start with the

- desired results (learning goals, standards, etc.), then the summative assessments that are going to be used to determine whether the student "knows and can do"; next should be the

- diagnostic assessment(s) that are going to help to determine the what and how for teaching and learning; then should come the

- formative assessments that are going to help students achieve the learning goals and that are going to cause the teacher to adjust teaching and learning activities; and

- homework,

- quizzes that provide practice for tests,

- practices that prepare for performances, and

- first drafts and second drafts that provide practice for (final) product(s).

(Continued)

FIGURE 6.6 (Continued)

A vital part of the ASSESSMENT PLAN is

- *how much* evidence and
- *which* assessments
- are critical to being able to determine student achievement/grades (e.g., there will be *nine summative assessment* opportunities, of which *at least six* [including the *third, fifth and ninth*] must be done).

Not using zeros for assessment evidence not submitted is a difficult and often emotional issue for teachers. The approach suggested here is educative and supportive but "hard" on students because it requires students to be truly accountable and complete all essential assessments. It is also an attempt to acknowledge that although we work in a calendar-driven system, learning is or should be time independent.

Additional ideas about the use of zeros can be found in Reeves (2004) and Guskey (2004).

4. Including Level/Rubric Scores in Grades

Rubric scores don't convert directly to grades. (Arter & Chappuis, 2006, p. 111)

If a teacher uses rubrics and level scores instead of points or percentages (out of 10, or 100), another aspect of number crunching needs to be considered: how to determine grades from rubric scores.

The Wrong Way

One approach that should *not* be used is shown in Figure 6.7. It illustrates a strictly numerical approach, which results in an inaccurate grade. Ideally, the learning goals are not weighted, but if the importance of the learning goals varies significantly, then they could be weighted as in Figure 6.7. Marilyn received a total of thirty scores on five assessments for six learning goals. All were scored on four-point rubrics, so the total unweighted possible

FIGURE 6.7 Marilyn's Scores in Grade 5 Social Studies

LEARNING GOAL	SUMMATIVE ASSESSMENT #1	S.A.#2	S.A.#3	S.A.#4	S.A.#5	TOTAL	WEIGHT	ADJUSTED TOTAL
L.G. 1	3	3	3	4	4	17	2	34
L.G. 2	4	4	4	1	4	17	3	51
L.G. 3	1	2	3	4	4	14	2	28
L.G. 4	3	2	1	3	3	12	1	12
L.G. 5	4	3	4	3	4	18	3	54
L.G. 6	1	2	2	3	3	11	1	11
Total						**89/120**		**190/240**
Percentage						**74.2**		**79.1**

NOTE: Based on four-point rubric

points are 120. Marilyn received 89 points, which, if calculated as a percentage, provides a grade of 74 percent. Grades should also be determined for each learning goal. If the teacher's judgment leads to the conclusion that weighting is necessary, total weighted points would be used. In Figure 6.7, weights are provided and applied in the last two right-hand columns. As a result, Marilyn receives a weighted score of 190/240, giving her a calculated final grade of 79 percent.

This appears to be straightforward, but it isn't accurate. Twenty-two of the thirty scores Marilyn received are 3s or 4s, which, if linked to grades, would be A's and B's. In many jurisdictions, however, Marilyn's 74 percent or 79 percent would be a C, so clearly, something is wrong with the conversion. The problem is the lack of an appropriate relationship between the four-point scale and the percentage grading scale. If Marilyn had received scores of 3 for every learning goal on every assessment, she would have a grade of 75 percent (weighted or unweighted), which, in most jurisdictions, would be a C, but the intent—the second-highest category—is clearly that she receives a B.

None of the numerical conversion approaches is satisfactory, largely because rubric scoring has an entirely different basis than scoring by points. With rubrics, there really is not just a numerical step between each level; there is a qualitative difference between each level, which is described in words and assigned a number simply as a label. It is mathematically acceptable to reduce data, but it is mathematically incorrect to expand data, so points or percentages may be converted to levels, but levels should not be converted to points or percentages.

The Right Way

The following educator contribution describes how and why a school for high-achieving students moved to a leveled system. Conversion to percentages is mathematically incorrect but must be done because it is required by provincial policy—and as a private school, it would lose accreditation if it didn't follow policy.

Educator Contribution

Rosemary Evans
Principal, University of Toronto Schools

Leveled Assessment and Grading at University of Toronto Schools

University of Toronto Schools (UTS) is a school for high-achieving students affiliated with the University of Toronto. Students are admitted on the basis of merit. The admission process includes use of the Secondary School Admission Test (SSAT) supplemented by a modified version of the Multiple Mini Interview, developed at McMaster Medical School, a bias-free interview format. Competitive entry had resulted in a competitive atmosphere in the school and a tendency for students to reference their performance against others. To moderate this atmosphere and to encourage students to focus on individual growth in relationship to criteria, the school implemented leveled grading. Percentage grading as required by the Ministry of Education was seen to be exacerbating this competitive tendency. Detailed level descriptors were developed for each discipline under each of the four Ontario assessment categories: knowledge, thinking, application, and communication. Department members used Ministry of Education Achievement Charts (an example of which can be found in Appendix F) matched to Overall Expectations from Ministry Curriculum documents for each subject area to develop achievement level descriptors. Five levels of achievement were described for every subject (see table on next page).

(Continued)

(Continued)

Achievement Level Descriptors—Canadian and World Studies

LEVEL	KNOWLEDGE AND UNDERSTANDING	THINKING	COMMUNICATION	APPLICATION
	Knowledge of content (e.g., facts, terms, definitions) Understanding of content (e.g., concepts, ideas, theories, interrelationships, procedures, processes, methodologies, spatial technologies)	**Use of planning skills** (e.g., organizing an inquiry; formulating questions; gathering and organizing data, evidence, and information; setting goals; focusing research) **Use of processing skills** (e.g., interpreting, analyzing, synthesizing, and evaluating data, evidence, and information; analyzing maps; detecting point of view and bias; formulating conclusions) **Use of critical/creative thinking processes, skills, and strategies** (e.g., applying concepts of disciplinary thinking; using inquiry, problem-solving, and decision-making processes)	**Expression and organization of ideas and information** (e.g., clear expression, logical organization) in oral, visual, and written forms **Communication for different audiences** (e.g., peers, adults) and purposes (e.g., to inform, to persuade) in oral, visual, and written forms **Use of conventions** (e.g., mapping and graphing conventions, communication conventions), vocabulary, and terminology of the discipline in oral, visual, and written forms	**Manipulation of knowledge and skills** (e.g., concepts, procedures, spatial skills, processes, technologies) in familiar contexts **Transfer of knowledge and skills** (e.g., concepts of thinking, procedures, spatial skills, methodologies, technologies) to new contexts **Making connections within and between various contexts** (e.g., between topics/issues being studied and everyday life; between disciplines; between past, present, and future contexts; in different spatial, cultural, or environmental contexts; in making predictions)
5	*The student:* Demonstrates thorough knowledge of all content as expressed in the overall expectations consistently and independently. Demonstrates a deep and thorough understanding of all concepts (e.g., historical, geographic) as expressed in the overall expectations consistently and independently.	*The student:* Uses planning skills with a very high degree of effectiveness (e.g., organizing an inquiry, formulating questions, gathering and organizing data and evidence, and information; setting goals; focusing research) consistently and independently. Uses processing skills with a very high degree of effectiveness (e.g., interpreting, analyzing, synthesizing, and evaluating data, evidence and information; analyzing maps; detecting point of view and bias; formulating conclusions) in a wide variety of contexts consistently and independently. Uses critical/creative thinking processes with a very high degree of effectiveness (e.g., applying concepts of disciplinary thinking; using inquiry, problem-solving, and decision making processes) consistently and independently.	*The student:* Expresses and organizes ideas and information with a very high degree of effectiveness (e.g., in a clear and concise manner) in a wide variety of contexts consistently and independently (e.g., without prompting or support). Communicates for different audiences and purposes with a very high degree of effectiveness consistently and independently (e.g., without prompting or support). Uses appropriate conventions, vocabulary, and terminology of the discipline with a very high degree of effectiveness consistently and independently (e.g., without prompting or support).	*The student:* Applies knowledge and skills in a wide variety of familiar contexts, including sophisticated contexts, with a very high degree of effectiveness consistently and independently. Transfers knowledge and skills to a wide variety of new contexts, including novel contexts, with a very high degree of effectiveness consistently and independently. Makes connections within and between various contexts, including novel contexts, with a very high degree of effectiveness consistently and independently.

LEVEL	KNOWLEDGE AND UNDERSTANDING	THINKING	COMMUNICATION	APPLICATION
4	Demonstrates thorough knowledge of most content as expressed in the overall expectations consistently with little or no support. Demonstrates a thorough understanding of most concepts (e.g., historical, geographic) as expressed in the overall expectations consistently and independently, with little or no support.	Uses planning skills with a high degree of effectiveness (e.g., organizing an inquiry, formulating questions, gathering and organizing data and evidence, and information; setting goals; focusing research) consistently with little or no support. Uses processing skills with a high degree of effectiveness (e.g., interpreting, analyzing, synthesizing, and evaluating data, evidence and information; analyzing maps; detecting point of view and bias; formulating conclusions) in a wide variety of contexts consistently with little or no support. Uses critical/creative thinking processes with a high degree of effectiveness (e.g., applying concepts of disciplinary thinking; using inquiry, problem-solving, and decision making processes) consistently with little or no support.	Expresses and organizes ideas and information with a very high degree of effectiveness (e.g., in a clear and concise manner) in a variety of contexts consistently and independently, with little or no support. Communicates for different audiences and purposes with a very high degree of effectiveness consistently and independently, with little or no support. Uses appropriate conventions, vocabulary, and terminology of the discipline with a very high degree of effectiveness consistently and independently, with little or no support.	Applies knowledge and skills in a variety of familiar contexts, with a high degree of effectiveness consistently, with little or no support. Transfers knowledge and skills to a variety of new contexts, with a high degree of effectiveness consistently, with little or no support. Makes connections within and between various contexts, with a high degree of effectiveness, consistently with little or no support.
3	Demonstrates considerable knowledge of most content as expressed in the overall expectations consistently with occasional support. Demonstrates considerable understanding of most mathematical concepts as expressed in the overall expectations consistently with occasional support.	Uses planning skills with considerable effectiveness (e.g., organizing an inquiry, formulating questions, gathering and organizing data and evidence, and information; setting goals; focusing research) consistently with occasional support. Uses processing skills with considerable effectiveness (e.g., interpreting, analyzing, synthesizing, and evaluating data, evidence and information; analyzing maps; detecting point of view and bias; formulating conclusions) in a wide variety of contexts consistently with occasional support. Uses critical/creative thinking processes with considerable effectiveness (e.g., applying concepts of disciplinary thinking; using inquiry, problem-solving, and decision making processes) consistently with occasional support.	Expresses and organizes ideas and information with considerable effectiveness (e.g., in a clear and concise manner) in a wide variety of contexts consistently and independently, with occasional support. Communicates for different audiences and purposes with considerable effectiveness consistently and independently, with occasional support. Uses appropriate conventions, vocabulary, and terminology of the discipline with considerable effectiveness consistently and independently, with occasional support.	Applies knowledge and skills in most familiar contexts, with considerable effectiveness consistently with occasional support. Transfers knowledge and skills to some new contexts, with considerable effectiveness consistently and with occasional support. Makes connections within and between some contexts, with considerable effectiveness consistently with occasional support.

(Continued)

(Continued)

LEVEL	KNOWLEDGE AND UNDERSTANDING	THINKING	COMMUNICATION	APPLICATION
2	Demonstrates some knowledge of content as expressed in the overall expectations often/mostly with support. Demonstrates some understanding of some concepts as expressed in the overall expectations often/mostly with support.	Uses planning skills with some effectiveness (e.g., organizing an inquiry, formulating questions, gathering and organizing data and evidence, and information; setting goals; focusing research) often/mostly with support. Uses processing skills with some effectiveness (e.g., interpreting, analyzing, synthesizing, and evaluating data, evidence and information; analyzing maps; detecting point of view and bias; formulating conclusions) in a variety of contexts often/mostly with support. Uses critical/creative thinking processes with some effectiveness (e.g., applying concepts of disciplinary thinking; using inquiry, problem-solving, and decision making processes) often/mostly with support.	Expresses and organizes ideas and information with some effectiveness (e.g., in a clear and concise manner) in a wide variety of contexts often/mostly with support. Communicates for different audiences and purposes with some effectiveness often/mostly with support. Uses appropriate conventions, vocabulary, and terminology of the discipline with some effectiveness often/mostly, with support.	Applies knowledge and skills in some familiar contexts, with limited effectiveness, often/mostly with support. Transfers knowledge and skills to some new contexts, often/mostly with support. Makes connections within and between some contexts, with some effectiveness often/mostly with support.
1	Demonstrates limited knowledge of content as expressed in the overall expectations. Has difficulty demonstrating knowledge, even with support. Demonstrates limited understanding of concepts as expressed in the overall expectations. Has difficulty demonstrating understanding, even with support.	Uses planning skills with limited effectiveness (e.g., organizing an inquiry, formulating questions, gathering and organizing data and evidence, and information; setting goals; focusing research) even with support. Uses processing skills with limited effectiveness (e.g., interpreting, analyzing, synthesizing, and evaluating data, evidence and information; analyzing maps; detecting point of view and bias; formulating conclusions) even with support. Uses critical/creative thinking processes with limited effectiveness (e.g., applying concepts of disciplinary thinking; using inquiry, problem-solving, and decision making processes) even with support.	Expresses and organizes ideas and information with limited effectiveness even with support. Communicates for different audiences and purposes with limited effectiveness even with support. Uses appropriate conventions, vocabulary, and terminology of the discipline with limited effectiveness even with support.	Applies knowledge and skills in some familiar contexts, with limited effectiveness even with support. Has difficulty transferring knowledge and skills to new contexts even with support. Has difficulty making connections within and between contexts, even with support.

From the CWS Curriculum Document:

"'Descriptors' indicate the characteristics of the student's performance, with respect to a particular criterion, on which assessment or evaluation is focused. *Effectiveness* is the descriptor used for each of the criteria in the Thinking, Communication, and Application categories. What constitutes effectiveness in any given performance task will vary with the particular criterion being considered. Assessment of effectiveness may therefore focus on a quality such as appropriateness, clarity, accuracy, precision, logic, relevance, significance, fluency, flexibility, depth, or breadth, as appropriate for the particular criterion." (Ontario Ministry of Education, 2010, p. 18)

Level Grading Process

In collaboratively developing the descriptors, staff talked together about the grading criteria. Exemplar tasks were examined, and moderation sessions using selected samples of student work helped teachers to clarify and coordinate their understanding of the descriptors.

To determine a leveled grade at the conclusion of a grading period, our teachers examine the full portfolio of student summative assessments. They consider them using their professional judgment to assess student performance against each criteria and apply the guiding principle "most consistent performance with an eye to most recent." Teachers hold moderation sessions for grade reporting. They collectively look at a few students' assessment data to determine the level of performance to report at the end of the grading period. On the actual report card, parents and students see a level grade. (Our Information Technology Team converts the levels into an Ontario percentage grade as required for University grade reporting and for official transcripts.)

These detailed level descriptors similarly are helpful in establishing rubrics for grading culminating tasks. The result is a framework for interpreting achievement and, more importantly, for describing for and with students areas of strength and areas for improvement. Students are encouraged to predict their own levels of achievement and to establish their own goals, a strategy that John Hattie has identified as among the most powerful for improving student achievement.

5. Using Logic Rules to Determine Subject Grades

As I stated before, I believe subject grades add nothing of value and often detract from the primary purpose of grades, but as it is almost certain that most 9–16 schools and some, hopefully not many, K–8 schools will continue to have subject grades for the foreseeable future, we need to be clear about what is the best way to determine such grades. The best approach is to use a *logic rule*—that is, a series of statements that describe how grades for standards will be converted into subject grades. There are many different logic rules currently in use in schools. A good one comes from the Arts and Technology High School in Beaverton, Oregon (Figure 6.8). It shows how grades for standards should be determined by looking at the most consistent level of achievement.

Figure 1.4 provides an example of how a subject grade would be determined using this logic rule. The student is consistent on three of the standards that have a grade and inconsistent on the fourth but with a pattern of continuous improvement, so there are three 4s and one 2 as grades for the standards. The teacher didn't provide enough assessment opportunities for "Properties and Periodicity" for a standard grade to be determined, and on "Explaining Reaction Rates," the student failed to submit sufficient evidence, so the grade for that standard is I for Incomplete. When there is an I for any standard, the overall grade must be an I, as a subject grade can only be determined meaningfully in the absence of incompletes. So for a grade other than I to be determined, the student would need to produce sufficient evidence on "Explaining Reaction Rates" for the teacher to determine a grade for that standard. After the student produces sufficient evidence, the subject grade should be determined by a logic rule. When the student produces sufficient evidence for "Explaining Reaction Rates," regardless of the student's grade for that standard, the student's science grade would be a C because of the 2 for "Structure and Properties of Matter." If the student received a 3 or 4 for "Explaining Reaction Rates" and raised the grade for "Structure and Properties of Matter" to a 3, the subject grade would be an A. This sets a high bar, but the basic principle is that a student cannot get an A or a B if any standard grade is below proficient (B).

Another example is provided by Marilyn's scores in Figure 6.7. Using the most consistent level with emphasis on the more recent, the appropriate learning goal grades for Marilyn would be L.G. 1 = 4; L.G. 2 = 4; L.G. 3 = 4; L.G. 4 = 3; L.G. 5 = 4; L.G. 6 = 3, and using the logic rule in Figure 6.8, her subject grade would be an A.

FIGURE 6.8 Arts and Technology High School, Beaverton, Oregon, Logic Rule

	ATHS LETTER GRADE CONVERSION
A	• An **A** in a course is determined by the student presenting sufficient examples of work and assessments demonstrating level 3 and 4 for each long-term learning target, with a majority of 4s. • The student may not have any level 0, 1, or 2 for a long-term learning target.
B	• A **B** in a course is determined by student presenting sufficient examples of work and assessments demonstrating a mix of level 3 and 4 for each long-term learning target, with a majority of 3s. • The student may not have any level 0, 1, or 2 for a long-term learning target.
C	• A **C** in a course is determined student by student presenting sufficient examples of work and assessments demonstrating level 3 and 2 for each long-term learning target, with a majority of 3s. • The student may not have any level 0 or 1 for a long-term learning target.
NP	Not Proficient • If a student has not earned a C or higher in the class at the endpoint of the term, an **NP** will be reported on the progress report and online. When the student demonstrates proficiency for all targets at level 2 or 3 at a later date, the **NP** will change to the appropriate letter grade, and credit will be awarded as appropriate. The **NP** will remain on the student's transcript until proficiency is demonstrated. **NPs** that remain on a student's transcript at graduation or at the time of transfer to another school will be automatically converted to an **F**.
F	• An **F** is only reported on the transcript when a student abandons the opportunity to show proficiency.

SOURCE: West Linn-Wilsonville School District (2017).

6. Using Student Involvement to Determine Subject Grades

A different approach to determining grades is advocated by teachers under the acronym TTOG, which means "teachers throwing out grades." TTOG actually means "throwing out scores" because these teachers provide only descriptive feedback to students, and at the end of each grading period, students review their body of evidence with the teacher and decide the grade that should be on their report card. Most of these teachers would prefer to not have grades but are required to do so by district/state or provincial policies. An example of how one teacher does this is provided by Arthur Chiaravalli, an English teacher at Haslett High School in Michigan.

When making these types of decisions, it is important to note that teachers provide opportunities for students to discuss how assessments will be chosen, scored, and combined, but I believe that the decision about each issue rests with the teachers. This is how it should be—teachers apply their professional judgment and consider student suggestions, along with district, school, state, or provincial procedures and policies.

Educator Contribution

Arthur Chiaravalli
English Teacher, Haslett High School, Michigan

Determining Grades

A change I have adopted is involving students in the process of assigning a term grade. Since students receive very few scores over the course of a term, there actually isn't much to calculate—mean, median, or mode! This seemed to present an opportunity to further empower students by letting them have a say in the grade they think they earned.

Before the end of each term, I usually scale back the workload to allow students an opportunity to evaluate their overall performance using statements from my Descriptive Grading Criteria (https://goo.gl/jL7Zr7), adapted from Ken O'Connor's *How to Grade for Learning* (2009, p. 76). Students read over and listen to feedback they've received and identify examples of where they've met or exceeded learning targets. They note any instances where they exhibited exceptional insight or creativity in demonstrating their learning. Finally, they point out any evidence of growth, places they were able to turn weaknesses into strengths.

When they complete this process, they either sign up to conference with me personally or complete a linked letter (https://goo.gl/PNVUXV) or video (https://goo.gl/rmH1ed) explaining the grade they believe they deserve. Usually, I agree with the student's determination. Occasionally, I need to push back, asking the student to make sure their evidence supports statements from the Descriptive Grading Criteria.

Descriptive Grading Criteria

You must use phrasing from the Descriptive Grading Criteria throughout your grading letter, video, or conference, supporting it with concrete evidence from your work. Please feel free to ask for feedback at any point during the term if you want my opinion on your current grade and how you can improve it.

A **Outstanding**	• Quiz and test scores indicate a high level of understanding of concepts/ mastery of skills (A's) • Exhibits novel, insightful, and/or creative ways to show learning • All learning objectives are fully or consistently met and extended • Shows frequent evidence of growth, turning weaknesses to strengths
B **Good**	• Quiz and test scores indicate a good grasp of concepts and skills (B's) • Exhibits a combination of standard and novel/insightful/creative ways to show learning • Most of the learning goals are fully or consistently met • Shows some evidence of growth, with certain weaknesses remaining unaddressed
C **Satisfactory**	• Quiz and test scores indicate satisfactory acquisition of skills and concepts (C's) • Exhibits standard ways to show learning • More than half of the learning goals are fully or consistently met • Shows a few instances of growth, with several weaknesses remaining unaddressed
Incomplete	• Quiz and test scores do not show satisfactory acquisition of skills and concepts (< C) • Less than half of the learning goals are fully or consistently met • Provides too little evidence of learning to make a determination • Shows little or no growth

What's the Bottom Line?

How should teachers crunch numbers? They should reject the use of the average and crunch numbers very carefully, if at all!

Teachers should consider the following:

- The advantages of using level scores, instead of percentages or points

- The use of logic rules based on level grades for standards to determine subject grades

- The effect of various ways of calculating central tendency

- The effect of extreme marks, especially zeros

- Whether assessment tasks and/or learning goals should be weighted

- The effect of mark distribution

- The use of I grades, or "incompletes"

The practical implication of Guideline 6 is that teachers need to exercise their professional judgment, not just use mechanical, numerical calculations when assigning grades. The real bottom line is, if Guidelines 2 and 5 are consistently applied, Guideline 6 is almost not needed!

Guideline 6: Crunch numbers carefully—if at all.

Analyze Guideline 6 for grading by focusing on three questions:

Why use it?

Why not use it?

Are there points of uncertainty?

After careful thought about these points, answer these two questions:

Would I use Guideline 6 now?

Do I agree or disagree with Guideline 6, or am I unsure at this time?

See the following for one person's reflections on Guideline 6.

Why Use It?

- Logic rules produce consistent, defensible grades.

- The mean is mean to students.

- Median is fairer than mean—allows for a stumble or two.

- Median reduces impact of low marks, especially zeros.

- Rewards improvement and growth.

Why Not Use It?

- Encourages students not to do every assignment.

- Mean is common in colleges and universities.

- Median is too difficult to calculate.

- Often there are good reasons for a zero—it should count.

Points of Uncertainty

- Totally new idea—not sure students/parents would understand.

- What do grades mean when different procedures are used?

- What do zeros represent?

- Parent reaction.

CHAPTER 7

Quality Assessment and Keeping Records

An assessment-literate professional educator knows how to gather dependable evidence of student learning using high-quality assessments and how to use the assessment process and its results either to promote student learning or to certify it, depending on the context.

—Stiggins (2017, p. 64)

Guideline 7

Use accurate assessment(s), and properly record evidence of achievement.

a. Meet standards for accurate assessment: clear targets, clear purpose, and sound design (which requires that assessments be well written, use appropriate target–method match, use appropriate sampling, and avoid bias and distortion).

b. Record and maintain evidence of achievement (e.g., tracking sheets, spreadsheets, gradebooks—hard copy and electronic—portfolios—hard copy and electronic—etc.).

THE CASE OF . . .

Rob's "Bad" Grade

Rob was a high-quality critical thinker with good writing skills, but he was a reflective learner who had to take time to understand new concepts and skills and to think before he answered questions orally or on a test. He showed high levels of proficiency on summative assessments, although he often didn't complete them because he wrote slowly. He performed poorly on initial formative assessments. He also didn't do well on the quizzes based on prereading that took place before instruction.

Rob's history teacher had a very traditional approach to assessment, so he included all of the scores in his determination of grades with middle- and end-of-course paper-and-pencil exams. Grades in the history course were based partly on the students' essays and projects and partly on the quizzes and exams. Rob received almost perfect marks on the products, but he did poorly on the quizzes and exams. At the middle and end of the semester, his teacher assigned a mark for attitude and participation that was a holistic judgment with no criteria, and it came just from the teacher's memory. Robert wasn't interested in playing the game of school, so he got low marks in that category also. His final grade was a D.

WHAT'S THE PURPOSE OF THE GUIDELINE?

This guideline supports learning and encourages student success by ensuring that each student's grade comes from accurate assessments, the results of which have been recorded in a timely manner. The issue is that all involved understand the critical dimensions of quality assessment. Rob's teacher neither followed quality assessment principles nor recorded some evidence that he used in determining grades throughout the semester. Robert received a deflated grade—assuming that the main learning goals were to demonstrate knowledge and understanding of history.

WHAT ARE THE KEY ELEMENTS OF THE GUIDELINE?

Components of Accurate Assessment

Marks and grades are accurate and meaningful when—and only when—they are based on accurate assessment. Thus, it is essential that teachers know, understand, and apply quality standards when they plan and implement assessment in their classrooms. I have yet to come across a more straightforward, easy-to-apply set of conditions for quality assessment than what I heard Rick Stiggins describe in the early 1990s and which has been the basis of his work and books since then. (See Stiggins, Arter, J. Chappuis, & S. Chappuis, 2004, and J. Chappuis, Stiggins, S. Chappuis, & Arter, 2012.)

According to Stiggins, here are three quality standards:

1. clear purpose(s),

2. clear and appropriate targets, and

3. sound design.

Sound design requires well-written assessments, well-chosen assessments that match target to method, appropriate samples of the learning goals, and controlling bias or distortion.

> Marks and grades are accurate and meaningful when—and only when—they are based on quality assessment.

Stiggins sums up the conditions of quality assessment as "Doing It Right, Using It Well" and illustrates it with the helpful graphic in Figure 7.1.

Relating this to the guidelines in this book, Key 1 is Guideline 4; Key 2 involves Guidelines 1 and 2; Key 3 is Guideline 7; Key 4 requires Guidelines 3, 5, and 6; and Key 5 is Guideline 8.

Stating a Clear Purpose

Clear purpose comes from understanding *why* the assessment is being conducted and *what use* will be made of the assessment results by the many potential users—at the classroom level (students, teachers, and parents), at the instructional support level (remedial teachers, school building administrators, and central office support personnel), and at the policy level (district administrators, school board trustees, and state/provincial department personnel). All of these users have different needs, but as Stiggins wrote in 1997—and still asserts twenty years later—"There is no single assessment capable of meeting all these different needs. Thus, the developer of any assessment must start with a clear sense of whose needs the assessment will meet" (p. 16).

At the classroom level, which is the focus of this book, this quality standard means that the teacher needs a very clear understanding of purpose—that is, whether the assessment

FIGURE 7.1 Keys to Quality Classroom Assessment

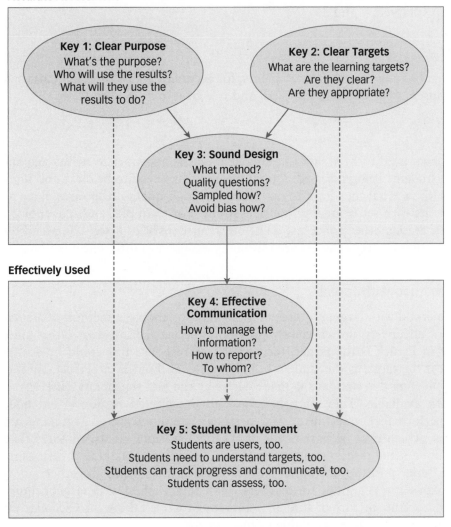

Accurate Assessment

Key 1: Clear Purpose
What's the purpose?
Who will use the results?
What will they use the results to do?

Key 2: Clear Targets
What are the learning targets?
Are they clear?
Are they appropriate?

Key 3: Sound Design
What method?
Quality questions?
Sampled how?
Avoid bias how?

Effectively Used

Key 4: Effective Communication
How to manage the information?
How to report?
To whom?

Key 5: Student Involvement
Students are users, too.
Students need to understand targets, too.
Students can track progress and communicate, too.
Students can assess, too.

SOURCE: S. Chappuis et al. (2017, p. 5).

is for diagnosis or for a formative or summative purpose and whether and how the results will be included in student grades. Detailed consideration of these issues is found in Chapter 4.

Setting Clear and Appropriate Targets

The importance of clear and appropriate targets cannot be overstated. If we do not know where we want to go, then we do not need a map to get there. But if we want to know how to get from point A to point B, we need a map. In the classroom, the "map" is provided by the content and performance standards that have been prescribed or established for each grade or course. In most courses, targets can be classified as follows:

- Knowledge (what students are to know)—from memory or retrieval from appropriate sources

- Application of knowledge (reasoning and skills)—what students are able to do

- Values/attitudes—what students are like—that is, how they behave

To meet the requirements of this guideline, teachers—and students—must understand what is being assessed—the learning goals (Guideline 1)—and what constitutes quality—the performance standards (Guideline 2). Suggestions about how these requirements can be met are found in Chapters 1 and 2.

Sound Design

Sound design has a number of requirements; for accuracy, all assessments must be well written, well chosen, appropriately sampled, and free from bias or distortion.

Well Written

All assessments need to be written in language that is appropriate to the age and reading level of the students being assessed. Questions and tasks need to be clear and unambiguous so students know what they have to do to produce high-quality responses. Each assessment strategy has its own set of quality considerations. For example, multiple-choice questions require that, among other concerns, question stems consist of a self-contained question or problem and that correct answers are randomly assigned to different positions.

Matching Method With Target

Matching method with target requires that the assessor choose a method of assessment that is capable of effectively and efficiently providing the needed information. If knowledge of vocabulary in French is the target, then a selected-response test could be an appropriate choice. But if the target is the student's ability to speak French, a performance assessment is needed. Meeting this standard is made easier by the fact that many different assessment methods are available. They may be classified as selected response, extended written response, performance assessment, and personal communication. Matching assessments with targets, which may be part or all of specified learning goals, requires that teachers know and understand targets and learning goals, know and understand various methods of assessment, and put the methods and targets/learning goals together appropriately. Figure 7.2 can serve as a guide for teachers. Matching method with target requires choices that give an accurate picture of student achievement while taking into account the human, material, and time resources available in the classroom.

Selecting Appropriate Samples for the Learning Domain

Assessment is a sampling procedure; sample selection is necessary because, in all assessment situations, only part of the learning domain can be chosen and because there are practical time and length considerations. Returning to the French example introduced earlier, in a vocabulary test, a representative sample of the words a student is supposed to know is used, whereas in a speaking ability performance, students speak long enough for teachers to make an accurate assessment of their ability.

Careful planning is the key to sample selection for all assessment methods. All require that teachers think carefully about what will be included so that valid inferences can be made about student achievement. For example, for paper-and-pencil tests, teachers may use some form of test specification chart in which they check that each learning goal is sufficiently sampled. Planning of this type should lead to teachers being able to draw confident conclusions about student achievement.

Ultimately, appropriate sampling for grading is about having enough of varied types of assessment information to make high-quality decisions when summarizing student

FIGURE 7.2 Matching Assessment and Learning Goals (Template)

Target to Be Assessed	Assessment Method			
	Selected Response/ Fill-In: Multiple-Choice, True/False, Matching, Fill-In	**Written Response**	**Performance Assessment**	**Personal Communication**
Knowledge	**Good**—can assess isolated elements of knowledge and some relationships among them	**Strong**—can assess elements of knowledge and relationships among them	**Partial**—can assess elements of knowledge and relationships among them in the context of certain tasks	**Strong**—can assess elements of knowledge and relationships among them
Reasoning	**Good**—can assess many— but not all— reasoning targets	**Strong**—can assess all reasoning targets	**Good**—can assess reasoning targets in the context of certain tasks	**Strong**—can assess all reasoning targets
Performance Skill	**Poor**—cannot assess skill level; can only assess prerequisite knowledge and reasoning targets		**Strong**—can observe and assess skills as they are being performed	**Poor**—cannot assess skill level; can only assess prerequisite knowledge and reasoning targets
Product	**Poor**—cannot assess the quality of the product; can only assess prerequisite knowledge and reasoning targets		**Strong**—can directly assess the attributes of quality products	**Poor**—cannot assess the quality of the product; can only assess prerequisite knowledge and reasoning targets

SOURCE: Stiggins and Chappuis (2012, p. 78).

achievement. This requires a base amount of information about the achievement of each learning goal. Measurement experts usually suggest that the right number of samples is a minimum of three because the first may be the result of luck, chance, or measurement error in one direction, and the second may involve the same factors in the other direction while the third will tend to confirm the first or the second. Two things are important to note about this:

1. If three is the minimum number of pieces of evidence, the desirable number may be five, *not* the fifteen or twenty-five pieces of evidence teachers have often thought they had to have in their gradebook. I must emphasize in the strongest possible way that this means that school/district policies requiring a set number of scores per week/ month are inappropriate and show that assessment literacy is lacking in the school and/or district leadership.

2. We do not need the same amount of information about each student. The more consistent a student's performance, the less evidence we need, whereas the more inconsistent a student's performance, the more evidence we need. The rule of thumb is, "If in doubt, you need another piece of evidence."

Another aspect of sampling that is very important is that we collect a variety of evidence and not just rely on one type of evidence. We can gather evidence of student achievement from *observing* students "performing," from the *products* students create, and from *conversations* with students. Unless the learning goal clearly indicates only one mode (e.g., writing), evidence should be collected from all three sources. So, for example, a student who knows and understands well but doesn't write well will be able to demonstrate his or her knowledge through performance or conversation. This process is called triangulation.

Controlling Bias and Distortion

> Bias or distortion from all sources must be controlled as much as possible in all assessment situations.

Bias or distortion from all sources must be controlled as much as possible in all assessment situations. How often have we heard teachers say things like, "Dexter's grade doesn't represent what he knows and can do because he doesn't test well"? In this situation, the teacher should adjust for Dexter's test problems by providing him with an alternative method or more time to demonstrate his real achievement.

Bias or distortion can occur in a number of circumstances:

- With all methods of assessments for all students (e.g., physical conditions such as noise, lighting, or seating; poorly worded directions or questions)

- With all methods of assessments for some students (e.g., emotional or physical health, motivation, assessment anxiety, reading/language ability, test-taking skill)

- With specific methods of assessment (e.g., multiple choice where there is more than one correct response; performance assessment, including essay questions, where criteria are inappropriate or lacking)

Further detail on sources of bias can be found in J. Chappuis et al. (2012).

Time   One of the most common sources of distortion in the assessment of student achievement is time—or the lack of it—because most assessments are time limited. Students who know and can achieve the learning goal(s) but who work slowly and need a lot of time to process and demonstrate their achievement have their achievement misrepresented when they are forced to rush their work or when they are unable to complete an assessment activity. Some skills do need to be demonstrated in a timed manner—for example, words per minute in keyboarding and air traffic control—but for most other knowledge and skills, the critical dimension is—or should be—quality, not speed.

Many students who achieve at high levels need considerable time to reflect and analyze before they are able to produce quality work. Other students are simply methodical and slow in their approach, and some just write slowly. Teachers need to take these personal differences into account and be flexible with time limits. This problem is usually most obvious in tests and exams. Teachers may help students by always testing in the period before a break and by providing some flexibility in the time allowed for students to complete examinations.

The complexity of this issue and the problem of trying to give students challenging tasks on exams are described very clearly by Manon (1995):

> Trying to crowd together several important tasks into one fretful hour makes no sense at all. . . . That our students ever complete a finished product on a timed mathematics test is indeed quite remarkable. Asking them to do their best work under such constraints is neither productive nor fair. Even the most accomplished of mathematicians would not wait until an hour before publication to begin work on *someone else's* hard problem. (p. 140)

One of the most common sources of distortion in the assessment of student achievement is time—or the lack of it.

Boaler (2016) says, "For about one-third of students, the onset of timed testing is the beginning of math anxiety" (p. 38). Math facts are held in the working memory part of the brain, "but when students are stressed, such as when they are taking math questions under time pressure, the working memory becomes blocked, and students cannot access math facts they know" (Boaler, 2016, p. 38). Boaler believes that teachers should set classroom norms by telling students what they value and don't value; one of her norms is *"I don't value students working quickly; I value (them) working in depth"* (p. 172). She goes on to say, "One thing we need to change in mathematics classrooms around the world is the idea that in mathematics speed is more important than depth" (p. 190). Powerfully, she notes that "our world's top mathematicians—people such as Maryam Mirzakhani, Steven Strogarz, Keith Devlin and Laurent Schwartz, who have all won the highest honors for their work—all talk about working slowly and deeply and not being fast" (Boaler, 2016, p. 190).

Both Manon and Boaler focus on mathematics, but I believe what they say applies almost equally to all subjects.

The time available for students on any assessment, especially high-stakes summative assessments, needs to be flexible. Very few aspects of knowledge and skill need to be demonstrated in a time-limited manner. In-class tests and formal examinations need to be conducted in a way that allows students considerable flexibility. Teachers recognize that different students process knowledge and skills at different rates; thus, it is important to measure the quality, not the speed, of the performance. Also, when assessments involve on-demand writing, the speed at which individuals write is an important factor. Some students can fill a page in quickly, whereas other students who know and understand just as well may take much longer.

Although a school's schedule or exam timetable may present logistical difficulties, there are many ways to provide flexibility. Teachers can plan in-class tests for significantly less time than the length of the class. One math teacher I know used this approach in a seventy-six-minute period: ten minutes to review, fifty minutes to take the test, and sixteen minutes for flex-time, during which students may continue working on the test or do other work.

Another approach can be used if a school has a rotating timetable. Teachers can schedule tests when the class occurs in the period immediately before lunch or in the last period of the day, thus providing automatic flex-time. For formal examinations, when there is a school-wide schedule, exam lengths could be set with a plus or minus factor of, say, one third. For example, for ninety-minute exams, students would have up to two hours, whereas for two-hour exams, students would have an additional forty minutes available to them.

This approach not only provides some flexibility but also allows an exam schedule with two or three exams per day. Both examples allow exams to be held at 9:00 a.m. and 1:00 p.m. Although it is not a desirable practice, if high schools need to have three exams per day, most exams would be ninety minutes, with the longer exams scheduled for the last time period. For example, exams would start at 9:00 a.m., 11:30 a.m., and 2:00 p.m., with any two-hour exams starting at 2:00 p.m.

For high schools on a block schedule, a very educationally appropriate but rather radical approach is to have a four-day exam schedule, with one day designated for each period. In this type of schedule, no time limit needs to be set on any exam, as each teacher has the whole day to assess students. This type of schedule eliminates common exams—for all Grade 9 math classes, for example—but it also means that teachers have great flexibility with regard to their methods of assessment. These can range from traditional paper-and-pencil exams to individual oral exams or performance assessments. If teachers/schools believe strongly in the need for common exams, modify the above schedule so that the designated-day schedule is used for common exams in the mornings, with the afternoons being set aside with extended time available for the designated-day schedule.

It is very important to emphasize that in all these situations, flexible time is provided to allow all students to demonstrate what they know and are able to do. Teachers professionally plan tests/exams for the stated time, not for the flexible time. A teacher should plan a ninety-minute exam in the belief that most students will be able to complete the exam comfortably in that time. The flex-time is not designed as a safety net for teachers who create exams that are too long; it is designed to assist those students who need extra time to show what they know and can do.

> It is very important to emphasize that flexible time is provided to allow all students to demonstrate what they know and are able to do.

Another important point about flexible time is that it must be available to all students, not just to those who have been identified as having special needs in one or more areas.

In conclusion on the issue of time, Howard Gardner (2002), the eminent Harvard cognitive psychologist and developer of the concept of multiple intelligences, wrote the following (note that although he speaks specifically to college learning, his words apply equally well to any academic setting):

> *Nothing of consequence would be lost by getting rid of timed tests* [emphasis added] by the College Board or, indeed, by universities in general. Few tasks in life—and very few tasks in scholarship—actually depend on being able to read passages or solve math problems rapidly. As a teacher, I want my students to read, write and think well; I don't care how much time they spend on their assignments. For those few jobs where speed is important, timed tests may be useful. (p. 7)

If teachers know that student marks and grades are not a true reflection of their achievement, it is almost certainly because one or more of the quality standards has been breached. In such situations, teachers must remember that grading is (or should be) an exercise in professional judgment, not just a mechanical, numerical exercise.

> Records need to be as individualized as possible.

S. Chappuis et al. (2017) state, "Policy drives practice. If school leaders want quality assessment practices in every classroom (and they should) then district and school policies must support the implementation and continued use of such practices. . . . It is part of the school leader's assessment responsibilities to revise policies so they provide a framework for sound practice and act in unison with each other" (p. 89).

Keeping Records

The second part of Guideline 7 requires teachers to keep careful and timely records of student achievement. The key point here is that records must be kept somewhere—on paper or on a computer—not just held in a teacher's head.

There are, of course, myriad ways for teachers to keep appropriate records. Records need to be as individualized as possible, so the best approach for the gradebook is to have a separate page for each student (see Figures 1.4 and 1.5). As discussed in Chapter 1, it is important that the records are organized by learning goals, not methods of assessment.

This may be manageable when teachers have a homeroom or core group, but it is very difficult for teachers in a rotary system, who will probably see one hundred to two hundred students each day. In these situations, teachers need to adapt the individual student sheets or forms to whole-class use by using spreadsheets or computer gradebooks. These can accommodate many students, and records can be kept for a number of learning goals.

Figure 7.3 summarizes the variety of assessment methods available and suggests a variety of recording approaches, and Figure 7.4 shows the variety of performances that may be chosen. Use of these assessment methods and recording approaches will provide teachers with a rich variety of achievement information—a student profile—on which to base grading decisions. Depending on grade level and subject, teachers decide which of the recording approaches are practical and appropriate for them and their students. However, as was suggested in Chapter 2, it is best to record only level scores in the gradebook.

FIGURE 7.3 Assessment Methods

ASSESSMENT METHOD	STRATEGY	RECORDING APPROACHES
Personal Communication	Observation Conversation	• ✓ or ✗ (done or not done) • Rubric score • Letter or number mark (x/10, %, A, B) • Symbol (G = good; S = satisfactory; NI = needs improvement)
Performance Assessment	Product Performance Process	• Notes—written or digital • Digital recording
Paper-and-Pencil Tests	Constructed response Selected response	• Score: Number or proportion • Correct marking scheme • Level score

What's the Bottom Line?

Accurate assessment and written or electronic record-keeping are essential if grades are to reflect real student achievement. The following are the practical implications of Guideline 7:

- Teachers need to be aware of and apply each standard of accurate assessment.
- Schools/districts should have assessment policies that affirm a commitment to quality assessment.
- Teachers need to keep records on paper or on the computer—not in their heads.

FIGURE 7.4 A Performance May Be . . .

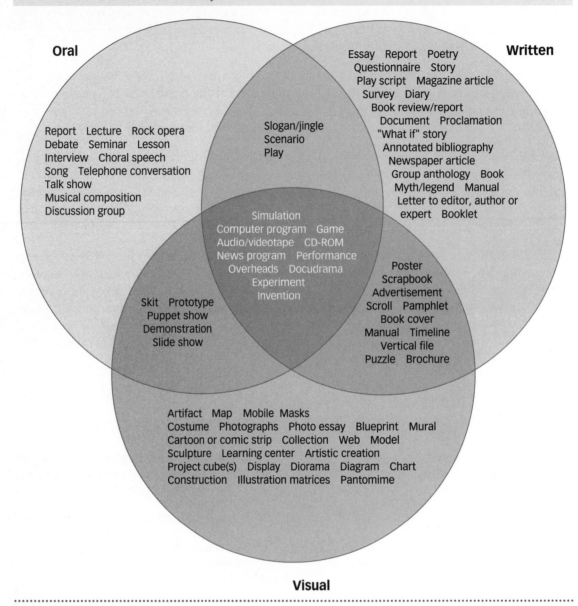

Oral

Report   Lecture   Rock opera
Debate   Seminar   Lesson
Interview   Choral speech
Song   Telephone conversation
Talk show
Musical composition
Discussion group

Slogan/jingle
Scenario
Play

Written

Essay   Report   Poetry
Questionnaire   Story
Play script   Magazine article
Survey   Diary
Book review/report
Document   Proclamation
"What if" story
Annotated bibliography
Newspaper article
Group anthology   Book
Myth/legend   Manual
Letter to editor, author or
expert   Booklet

Simulation
Computer program   Game
Audio/videotape   CD-ROM
News program   Performance
Overheads   Docudrama
Experiment
Invention

Skit   Prototype
Puppet show
Demonstration
Slide show

Poster
Scrapbook
Advertisement
Scroll   Pamphlet
Book cover
Manual   Timeline
Vertical file
Puzzle   Brochure

Artifact   Map   Mobile Masks
Costume   Photographs   Photo essay   Blueprint   Mural
Cartoon or comic strip   Collection   Web   Model
Sculpture   Learning center   Artistic creation
Project cube(s)   Display   Diorama   Diagram   Chart
Construction   Illustration matrices   Pantomime

Visual

SOURCE: Toronto District School Board, Ontario, Canada.

Guideline 7: Use accurate assessment(s) and properly recorded evidence of achievement.

Analyze Guideline 7 for grading by focusing on three questions:

Why use it?

Why not use it?

Are there points of uncertainty?

After careful thought about these points, answer these two questions:

Would I use Guideline 7 now?

Do I agree or disagree with Guideline 7, or am I unsure at this time?

See the following for one person's reflections on Guideline 7.

A REFLECTION ON GUIDELINE 7

Why Use It?

- Provides accurate measure of achievement.

- Ensures varied and appropriate assessment.

- Aligns with professional responsibility.

- Inspires greater confidence from students and parents.

- Accessible to all (not just in the teacher's head).

Why Not Use It?

- Amount of paper needed to record everything is too great.

- Amount of time needed to record everything is too great.

- Time needed to ensure quality is too great.

- Assessment literacy is insufficient.

- Tracking learning goals is much more difficult than recording marks.

Points of Uncertainty

- Consistency of teacher judgments.

- Who determines validity and reliability?

- Level of assessment literacy.

- Who determines quality?

- Political agenda.

CHAPTER 8

Involving Students in Grading and Assessment

We must constantly remind ourselves that the ultimate purpose of education is to have students become self-evaluating. If students graduate from our schools still dependent on others to tell them when they are adequate, good, or excellent, then we have missed the whole point of what education is about.

—Costa and Kallick (1992, p. 280)

Guideline 8

Discuss and involve students in assessment, including grading, throughout the teaching/learning process.

a. Ensure (age appropriately) that students *understand* how their achievement will be assessed and how their grades will be determined.

b. *Involve* students in the assessment process, through self-assessment, reflection, and goal setting, and in communicating about their achievement and progress.

THE CASE OF . . .

Huang's Lunchtime Surprise

It was November, fall sports had just finished, and it was almost time for mid-semester exams and reports. The junior varsity boys' volleyball team was having a pizza lunch to celebrate their season; they had won only one game, but most of the team were first-year players and had greatly improved over the course of the season. In addition to their skill development and their improved understanding of game strategy, they had also developed a very strong team spirit. Thus, the time and effort they put in was fun and worthwhile, even if their team record did not suggest a successful season. About fifteen minutes into the luncheon, the coach noted that Huang, their best defensive player, who had never missed a practice or a game, was absent. He asked about this and was told that Huang and several other students had stayed behind in English class to discuss their grades with Ms. Hector. A few minutes later, Huang arrived at the luncheon; it was obvious that he was upset as he joined in the celebration halfheartedly.

(Continued)

At the end of the luncheon, the coach asked Huang to stay and talk. Huang explained that his first-quarter English grade was much lower than he expected. Ms. Hector had included a number of scores that Huang and other students thought were not going to be included. Most of these were for what they thought were practice activities in the first three weeks of class.

Whether or not these scores should have been included relates to other grading guidelines (see Chapters 4 and 5). The issue here is that Huang and other students did not know what was included in the grade for their English class. This was in contrast to the assessment approach used on the volleyball team. For the team, the coach had stressed that the measure of the season would not be their win/loss record but their growth in skills and strategy and their enjoyment of practices, games, and the team experience. Throughout the season, he gave feedback to individuals and the team on their achievement, progress, and growth in these areas; their league matches and the final luncheon were the summative assessments!

WHAT'S THE PURPOSE OF THE GUIDELINE?

This guideline requires that the assessment plan and how grades will be determined are discussed age appropriately with students throughout the learning process in each class. When students know how they will be assessed—and especially when they have been involved in assessment decisions—the likelihood of student success is increased greatly. Students should be involved throughout the assessment process through self-assessment, reflection, and goal setting and by communicating to others about their achievement.

> When students know how they will be assessed—and especially when they have been involved in assessment decisions—the likelihood of student success is increased greatly.

WHAT ARE THE KEY ELEMENTS OF THE GUIDELINE?

There are two key elements: student understanding of and student involvement in (1) the assessment and (2) grading process. There is obviously overlap between these elements, but for the consideration of this guideline, I will discuss them separately.

Guideline 8, Part A: Student Understanding of How They Will Be Assessed and How Grades Will Be Determined

Several factors are involved in this discussion of student understanding, including the following:

- Strategies that improve student understanding

- Age appropriateness

- The amount of detail provided students about assessment

- What is meant by "the beginning of instruction"

Improving Student Understanding

Giving students real opportunities to understand how they are assessed and graded through discussion rather than announcement does not mean that students take over the teacher's professional responsibility to decide about assessment and to determine grades. Several decisions can be discussed with students. One is how they will demonstrate their competence on the learning goals of a course.

Armstrong (2000) provided an example of this by designing a form for students to indicate the type of performance assessment they would like to use to show their knowledge and skills. Armstrong provided a list of possible assessment activities from which students might choose, but students also were allowed to add their own suggestions to the list. Teachers could adapt this form to match their students' learning goals and provide a customized form for each of the major groupings of learning goals/standards. A similar approach is recommended by Tomlinson and McTighe (2006), who suggest that teachers develop tic-tac-toe cards with columns for written, visual, and oral products and performances. Some products or performances may be required, but there should also be choices for students.

A second type of decision that helps students understand assessment concerns how each assessment is marked or scored. Most commonly, teachers have set the criteria, but a powerful way to get deeper understanding is what is sometimes called coconstruction. Criteria development may involve a marking scheme, a checklist, or a fully developed rubric. An example from my personal experience was Grade 9 summer school students in a credit recovery class, in collaboration with their teachers (including me), developing the rubric shown in Figure 8.1. The students brainstormed the characteristics of an oral presentation, the teachers provided the categories, the students classified the characteristics, and the teachers provided the measurement scale (which is not very good!). The total class time to develop this rubric was about twenty-five minutes. This was time well spent, both in principle and in practice, because in the class in which the rubric was first used, twenty-two of twenty-three students performed in the top two levels. Even more significant was that all twenty-three students said they enjoyed doing the oral presentation, when previously they had hated doing it. They said they enjoyed it and performed better because they had a better understanding of what was expected.

A third approach to improving student understanding of assessment is involving them in scoring samples of student work (e.g., writing), which develops their understanding of what good writing is, and then developing a checklist or rubric.

A fourth way to improve understanding is by discussing openly how teachers will determine grades. Teachers may review some of the difficult issues, such as what ingredients will be included (e.g., how cooperative learning will be assessed); which activities will be marked for grades and which will not; and how performance over a semester, term, or year will be dealt with, especially if work shows marked improvement.

Age Appropriateness

The amount and nature of an assessment discussion with students will obviously vary with their age. It is, however, important that students understand assessment from an early age. This will help them to develop an assessment vocabulary and improve the likelihood that they will see assessment as something that is being done *with* them, not *to* them. Students who have such opportunities in the primary grades will likely develop a sophisticated understanding of assessment in high school.

FIGURE 8.1 Oral Presentation Criteria—Independent Research Project

Topic: _____ Name: _____			
A. Content • complete information • details • interesting/exciting • visual aid(s)	Unsatisfactory	Satisfactory	Very Good
B. Organization • intro, body, conclusion • stayed on topic • emphasized main points • asked question(s) at end	Weak	OK	Good
C. Delivery • spoke clearly • talked loudly enough • talked at a normal pace	Unclear	Clear	Very Clear
D. Nonverbal • eye contact • body posture • hand gestures • energetic/enthusiastic	Out of Touch	Some "Touch"	In "Touch"
E. Length • 5–7 minutes	3 minutes	4 minutes	5 minutes

SOURCE: Adapted from Toronto District School Board, Ontario, Canada.

> Timing is critical so that students see that assessment is integral, not just an add-on, to learning.

Students' ages will influence the way in which teachers share information with them. When most students in a class can read, it is not sufficient simply to tell students how they will be assessed; it is appropriate to provide assessment information in writing—to students and parents.

Amount of Detail

Students must be able to manage and understand the details about assessment of a whole course or an individual assessment. Information, especially about how teachers will determine grades, needs to be clear and concise. Ideally, teachers use uncomplicated methods to determine grades.

Students should be involved in discussion about assessment throughout the learning process, beginning the first week of class. Teachers generally preview course content and learning goals in the first day or two of each term; at about the same time, teachers should also inform students about assessment, especially about the nature of final or culminating assessment(s), because this information gives students an understanding of essential questions embedded in the course. Timing is critical so that students see that assessment is integral, not just an add-on, to learning. In addition to the "big picture" described earlier—how assessment will be used for the course as a whole—it is equally important that students are provided with this view throughout the learning process. We could call this the "small picture" (i.e., how assessment of each unit will be done and what summative assessments will be used). Myron Dueck describes how he did this and what he saw as the benefits in the following contribution.

Educator Contribution

Myron Dueck
Summerland, British Columbia

Helping Students Understand the Assessment and Grading Process

The decision whether or not to help students understand the grading and assessment process largely hinges on a few broader questions. Before diving into the structure, educators are encouraged to contemplate the following questions:

- Do I want to increase student engagement?

- Do I want students to reflect on their own learning?

- Do I want to create a learning environment that is welcoming to all students?

When we answer "yes" to any of these questions, we have begun to establish the *purpose* for involving students in grading and assessment throughout the learning process. Ultimately, educators should also ask themselves if these questions are accurate concerning their own learning journey. In my experience, most human beings appreciate having a voice when being assessed—this is no more apparent than educators themselves.

The first and most important step I ever took was to share with students the learning outcomes at the start of the learning process. At the outset of a unit of study, I would distribute unit plans that were separated into the categories of *knowledge, reasoning, skill,* and *product* (J. Chappuis, Stiggins, S. Chappuis, & Arter, 2012) (see Figure 8.2). By using the phrase "I can . . ." preceding each outcome, I wanted to encourage student ownership over the learning target. In recent years, I have come to recognize the power and importance of the command terms selected for each learning outcome. Command terms such as *define, describe, justify,* and *argue* are used to both determine the category the learning outcome fits into on the unit plan and to inform the educator as to the extent to which all levels of Bloom's Taxonomy or Webb's DOK are being represented (Dueck, 2014).

Once students are aware of the "destination," it is important to establish the map to getting there. With the help of Susan Brookhart, I established rubrics to assist in letting students know the success criteria for reasoning questions, performance tasks, and products

FIGURE 8.2 Unit Plan

Grade 8   History   **ATASCOCITA MIDDLE SCHOOL**   **Mr. Dueck**

Unit 4 – American Revolution – Targets 8.4 A-D (History)

Student Name: _____

STUDENT-FRIENDLY LEARNING TARGET STATEMENTS	
Knowledge Targets *"What I need to know!"*	❏ I know the definition of these terms and how they relate to the shaping of North America: **Treaty of Paris (1763) Seven Years War/French and Indian War** **Royal Proclamation** ❏ I know the basic areas of North American land ownership following the Treaty of Paris. ❏ I know the geographical location of the following political and physical features: **13 colonies (Connecticut, Delaware . . .)** **Appalachian Mountains** **Ohio Valley** **Battle locations (Lexington, Concord, Saratoga, Yorktown)** ❏ I know the definition of these terms and how they relate to the causes of the American Revolution: **Intolerable Acts Quebec Act Quartering Act** **Sugar Act Stamp Act Townsend Act** **"No taxation without representation" mercantilism** **Continental Army liberty Declaration of Independence** **Loyalists Patriots** ❏ I can briefly describe each of the following people AND explain what role each played in the American Revolution. **Samuel Adams Benjamin Franklin King George III** **Thomas Jefferson the Marquis de Lafayette Thomas Paine** **George Washington Molly Pitcher Penelope Barker** **Esther Reed Patience Wright Abigail Adams** ❏ I can list and describe the main terms AND issues of the Philadelphia Convention of 1787. **Articles of Confederation Second Continental Congress** **ratification Rhode Island boycott Virginia Plan** **Charles Pickney Plan New Jersey Plan Hamilton Plan** **slavery issue Connecticut Compromise**

Reasoning Targets *"What I can do with what I know."*	❑ I can **describe** the events that most contributed to or caused the American Revolution. ❑ I can **compare** the major battles of the American Revolution AND give my **opinion** as to which one was most significant. ❑ I can **evaluate** which people (major figures) played the most significant role(s) in the American Revolution (who had the biggest impact on the events of the American Revolution). ❑ I can **explain to what extent** the actions of the patriots against the British government were justified. ❑ I can **list** some of the main issues at the Philadelphia Conventions AND argue to what extent the decisions reached were good for all Americans.
Skill Targets *"What I can demonstrate."*	❑ I can arrange the 13 colonies in the correct geographic order. ❑ I can bring in three items that represent one of the key figures in the American Revolution AND explain to a group of my classmates why I chose these items.
Product Targets *"What I can make to show my learning."*	❑ I can produce a letter, newspaper article, monologue, or cartoon* that reflects the experiences of a young person living in the 13 colonies at the time of the American Revolution. Your project should include: ▶ **Fears** and **concerns** of a young person in the late 1700s ▶ At least two main **figures** and two key **events** discussed in class ▶ Evidence that you have **researched** the day-to-day life of a person living at this time (historical accuracy) (include a list of sources you used to find information—see rubric) *If you have a proposal for another way to show your knowledge, please consult Mr. Dueck.

(Brookhart, 2013). This past year, I found myself frustrated that my Grade 9 and 10 leadership students delivered journals that lacked immensely in detail and quality. As it turned out, the students reported to not understanding what made up a strong journal. The solution to this issue ultimately came once my students and I coconstructed rubrics focused on what elements constituted a strong journal entry and the performance criteria associated with each element (see Figure 8.3). These rubrics not only served as a guide for students writing better journal entries, but they were invaluable as tools to assist in student self-assessment and evaluation by the teacher. My students are required to use the rubric to self-assess prior to submitting the journal to the teacher.

The unit test process provided yet another opportunity to involve students in the assessment process. By rearranging the unit tests by learning outcome (see Figure 8.4), students were able to quickly and efficiently determine their strengths and challenges once the graded tests were returned. By tracking their scores on a customized sheet that corresponded to the test sections (Figure 8.5), students determined if the initial assessment results were summative or formative. If the student was satisfied with the results on the test, sections were summative,

FIGURE 8.3 Leadership Journal Rubric

	Expert 6/5	Apprentice 4/3	Novice 2/1
Inclusion of topics	All assigned topics are addressed. If absent, there is an effort to catch up on the topic in another way.	Most topics are addressed. Very few missed topics.	Journal is missing numerous/many of the assigned topics.
Quality of journal entries	All entries are thorough, and nearly all include instances of extended thought and additional items.	Most journal entries have evidence of further thought and interesting additional items.	Journal entries cover the basics only and seldom involve evidence of extended thought.
Evidence of including leadership concepts	Journal entries show a definite attempt to blend in the leadership concepts discussed in class.	Journal entries show a few instances of the student's attempt to blend in the leadership concepts discussed in class.	Journal entries show very few/no instances where student attempted to blend in the leadership concepts discussed in class.
Comments:			

whereas sections that were reviewed, studied, and reassessed were formative. As Wiliam (2011) argues, whether an assessment is formative or summative depends on our reaction to the data. With assessments separated by learning outcomes, students can also track previous quiz scores that correspond to the individual test sections. If evidence suggests that learning has improved since the quiz score, the more recent evidence can result in a more accurate summative grade. Asking students to monitor these changes and inform the teacher is a way to encourage student responsibility, voice, and advocacy.

In the end, I found that unit plans, cocreated rubrics, and tests separated by learning outcomes were vital to involving students in the entire assessment process. Though I began the journey focused on structures and systems, I ultimately came to realize that I had increased student engagement, harnessed the power of student reflection, and created a classroom environment that fostered confidence, positivity, and stronger relationships.

Ideally, teachers discuss assessment with students and provide a written assessment plan, including grading for each course, but these assessment plans are not carved in stone. If teachers believe a change is needed, they are flexible and make the change. It would be ideal to discuss the proposed change with students; at the very least, students must be informed of any change. This principle also applies to marking schemes or rubrics used to score assessments. If it becomes obvious during the scoring process that something is wrong with the scoring approach, then the teacher changes the rubric. The teacher informs students about the why and what of the change, and the amended scoring approach is, of course, applied to the work of all students.

FIGURE 8.4 Test Organized by Learning Outcomes

Paris Peace Conference Unit Test—History 12

General "ISM" definitions	8
Map section	11
The PPC "losers"	5
The PPC "winners"	3
Point-of-view	3
The PPC "hopeful"	3
Underlying problems	3
Document/evidence	8
Comprehensive paragraph A	8
Comprehensive paragraph B	8

Name: _____

Block: _____

Date: _____

PHOTO SOURCE: Library of Congress Prints and Photographs Division.

FIGURE 8.5 Student Test Tracking Sheet

Paris Peace Conference Unit Test Tracking Sheet   **History 12**

Name: _____   Test value: 60 points   Test score: _____

Topic	Value		Score	%	Retest?
General "ISM" definitions	8				
Map section	11				
The PPC "losers"	5				
The PPC "winners"	3				
Point of view	3				
The PPC "hopeful"	3				
Underlying problems	3				
Document/evidence	8				
Comprehensive paragraph A topic: _____	8				
Comprehensive paragraph B topic: _____	8				

UNIT TERMS: _____   Total: _____

❑ I DID complete all of the terms for this unit on either cards or sheets.

❑ I DID NOT complete either the cards or the term list for this unit.

Reason: _____

PREPARATION:

What **overall grade** (percentage or letter) am I hoping to achieve in this course? _____%

❑ I did all that I could to achieve my goal in preparing for this test.

❑ I can make the following adjustments to increase my grade:

✓ _____

✓ _____

Here is another example from an educator contributor about how he informs students about assessment and discusses it with them. Unlike with other contributions, I'm not going to reveal his identity until after you have read his contribution.

Educator Contribution

Talk About Assessment With Your Students . . . Often

I think it is critical to continuously talk about the assessment process with students. It is the teacher's responsibility to assist students in making connections between learning and assessment. I, very purposely, keep the conversation on grading in front of them. I want to make sure they understand the "rules of the game" because once they clearly understand how to be successful in this grading system, the odds are far greater that they will show proficiency in their work.

During the first few weeks of class, I take about five minutes per class and ask questions along these lines:

- What are some of the best grading practices you've encountered in other classes?

- Why, would you say, they were effective for you as the learner?

- Tell me about a time when a grade wasn't reflective of your learning?

- As a teacher, what can I do to best understand how you are doing in this class?

As the class progresses, I ask questions along these lines (maybe one or two per class, five minutes per class) to continue a dialogue on assessment for learning:

- Why do you think I give separate grades for professional habits (behaviors) and academics? What are the advantages of doing this? Disadvantages?

- Can you think of other times in life where someone may have multiple opportunities to accomplish a goal?

- What is challenging for you, as a student, when I don't give grades on every piece of homework in the class?

- Why do you think formative assessment is so important to this class?

- Your first opportunity to show your progress is coming up. What could I do to help you understand if you are "on track"?

- The project is due in two weeks. What are some ways in which you are using the rubric to help create a proficient piece of evidence?

I want to be clear with my students that "we are on the same team." Talking about the various grading and assessment processes on a regular basis (because they can't read my mind) helps them develop strategies to meet the academic and behavior goals of the class. And I use these discussions to better understand ways in which I can help them brainstorm strategies for success.

What grade level do you think this describes?

The contribution is from **Tom Buckmiller,** a **professor** in the **School of Education** at **Drake University** in **Des Moines, Iowa,** who says he has "had great success in using SBG in both my *graduate-* and *freshman-level university classes.* The student feedback consistently says students appreciate the clear learning targets and the focus on learning as opposed to point accumulation."

Another way to improve student understanding is through the development of a grading bill of rights. The following example cleverly captures what should be happening with assessment and grading and what students should know and understand.

Grading Bill of Rights

Just like our country has a Bill of Rights, you, as students in this classroom, have Grading Rights.

First—You have the right to know what you are being graded on—that is, your third-grade standards.

Second—You have the right to have practice time, or formative assessments, before game time, the summative assessments.

Third—You have the right to know your stars [what you did well] and stairs [what you need to improve] without embarrassment.

Fourth—You have the right to make up any missed work.

Fifth—You have the right not to have any grade penalty for being absent.

Sixth—You have the freedom to ask questions about a standard or grade.

Seventh—You have the right to know the standard, or target, before the lesson begins.

Eighth—You have the right to a fair hearing if, at any time, you disagree with a grade.

Ninth—You have the right to receive detailed feedback on your practice, or formative, assessments.

Tenth—You have the freedom to progress toward the standards, or targets, at your own pace!

SOURCE: Developed by Kathryn Burnett-Klebart, third-grade teacher, Allen Frear Elementary. Caesar Rodney School District, DE. Reprinted with permission.

Guideline 8, Part B: Student Involvement in Assessment and Grading

Why involve students in the assessment and grading process? Because to become successful learners they have to be able to answer three questions:

1. Where am I going?
2. Where am I now?
3. How can I close the gap (or get better if I'm already there)?

Question 1 is largely answered by improved student understanding using the strategies described in Part A, and it is the sine qua non for Questions 2 and 3 that require students to self-assess, reflect, and set goals. In other words, it is about promoting metacognition.

Tomlinson and McTighe (2006) state, "The most effective learners are metacognitive, that is, they are mindful of how they learn, set personal learning goals, regularly self-assess and adjust their performance and use productive strategies to assist their learning" (p. 79). It is the responsibility of teachers, therefore, to teach metacognitive strategies and to provide frequent opportunities for students to use these strategies. Some writers now call this "assessment *as* learning," and as one of the originators of the term, Lorna Earl describes how and why she developed this view of assessment in the following educator contribution.

Educator Contribution

Dr. Lorna Earl
Retired School District Research Director and Associate Professor
Ontario Institute for Studies in Education
Toronto, Ontario, and Waiheke Island, New Zealand

Assessment As Learning: What? Why? How?[1]

Background

Since the groundbreaking work of Terry Crooks (1988), Black and Wiliam (1998b), and the Assessment Reform Group (2002), assessment for learning has taken hold worldwide as a high-leverage approach to school improvement. In assessment for learning, we have a pedagogical approach that has the potential, at least, to influence student learning. From then on, a groundswell of educators and researchers were increasingly thinking about assessment for learning (AfL). Assessment for learning quickly became a pillar of school improvement approaches, billed as a pedagogical approach that had the potential for direct influence on student learning.

Assessment for learning was defined as follows:

> Practice in a classroom is formative to the extent that evidence about student achievement is elicited, interpreted, and used by teachers, learners, or their peers, to make decisions about the next steps in instruction that are likely to be better, or better founded, than the decisions they would have taken in the absence of the evidence that was elicited. (Black & Wiliam, 2009, p. 9)

As I studied and was actively engaged in a wide range of AfL projects in classrooms, I noticed something. The teachers were questioning, observing, probing, reframing, and investigating the learning of individual students in their classes. When I asked about what they were doing and why, the response was, "Figuring out what is going on in her head." "Trying to understand why he didn't get it. I thought the lesson was really clear." This was AfL in action. But there was a missing piece. The Black and Wiliam definition included "learners or their peers." In the classes that I was watching, it was teachers who were soliciting the evidence and using it but not the students.

What Is Assessment as Learning?

These observations moved me to thinking about assessment as learning—the kind of assessment that recognizes students as active, engaged, and critical assessors who make sense of information, relate it to prior knowledge, and use it for new learning.

> [In assessment as learning,] students are not only contributors to the assessment and learning process. They are the critical connector between them. The student is the link. Students as active, engaged and critical assessors can make sense of information, relate it to prior knowledge and master the skills involved. This is the regulatory process in metacognition, in which students personally

---

[1] Some of this material is excerpted (with references) from other writing by the author.

(Continued)

(*Continued*)

monitor what they are learning and use the feedback from this monitoring to make adjustments, adaptations and even major changes in what they understand. (Earl, 2003, p. 25)

When teachers focus on assessment *as* learning, they use classroom assessment as the vehicle for helping pupils develop, practice, and become comfortable with reflection and with critical analysis of their own learning. Viewed this way, self-assessment and meaningful learning are inextricably linked (Earl, 2003).

Why Assessment as Learning?[2]

Before teachers can plan for targeted teaching and classroom activities, they need to have a sense of what it is that pupils are thinking. What is it that they believe to be true? This process involves much more than, "Do they have the right or wrong answer?" It means making pupils' thinking visible and understanding the images and patterns that they have constructed in order to make sense of the world from their perspective (Earl, 2003). It means using this information to provide scaffolding for the learner to create new connections and attach these connections to a conceptual framework that allows efficient and effective retrieval and use of the new information.

The following anecdote gives a vivid description of how this learning process happens and the critical role that assessment plays in the learning process. When she was about five years old, my niece Joanna (Jojo to the family) came up to me and announced that "all cats are girls and all dogs are boys."

When I asked her why she believed cats were girls and dogs were boys, she responded, "Your cat Molly is a girl, and she's little and smooth; girls are little and smooth, too. Cats are girls. The dog next door is a boy, and he's big and rough, just like boys are big and rough. Dogs are boys." Clearly, she had identified a problem, surveyed her environment, gathered data, and formulated a hypothesis, and when she tested it, it held. Pretty sophisticated logic for a five-year-old.

I pulled a book about dogs from my bookshelf and showed her a picture of a Chihuahua, a dog that was little and smooth.

"What's this?" I asked.

"Dog," she replied.

"Girl or boy?"

"It's a boy; dogs are boys."

"But it's little and smooth," I pointed out.

"Sometimes, they can be little and smooth," said Jojo.

I turned to a picture of an Irish setter, surrounded by puppies. She was perturbed.

"What's this?"

---

[2] Partially excerpted from Earl (2003).

"Dog," she replied, with some hesitation.

"Boy or girl?"

After a long pause, she said, "Maybe it's the dad." But she didn't look convinced, and she quickly asked, "Can dogs be girls, Aunt Lorna?"

This anecdote is a simple but vivid demonstration of the process of assessment, feedback, reflection, and self-monitoring that we all use when we are trying to make sense of the world around us. Jojo had a conception (or hypothesis) about something in her world (the gender of cats and dogs). She had come to a conclusion based on her initial investigation that held with her experience. With the intervention of a teacher (Aunt Lorna) who used assessment (How do you know?) and created the conditions (the picture book) for her to compare her conceptions with other examples in the real world, she was able to see the gap between her understanding and other evidence. Once she had the new knowledge, she moved quickly to adjust her view and consider alternative perspectives.

This kind of assessment is at the core of helping students become aware of and take control of their own learning. And it is this kind of assessment that supports the type of learning that psychologists describe as conceptual change. Rather than transforming evidence that exists in the world to fit established mental structures (conceptions), the mental structures themselves shift (or accommodate) to take new evidence into account. Classroom assessment, in this view, promotes the learner's accommodation process. It is something best—and necessarily—accomplished by the learner herself since it is she who holds privileged access to the relevant beliefs, though as we saw before, the teacher's role is to help make them public (Katz, 2000).

Assessment as Learning: How?

Assessment *as* learning is not a series of tips and tricks. It requires changes in how teachers interact with their pupils, how they think about the material they teach, and, most importantly, how they use assessment in their daily work. Black and Wiliam said it best years ago:

> It is hard to see how any innovation in formative assessment can be treated as a marginal change in classroom work. All such work involves some degree of feedback between those taught and the teacher, and this is entailed in the quality of their interactions that is at the heart of pedagogy. (Black & Wiliam, 1998b, p. 16)

And as Michael Absolum in New Zealand reminds us,

> Learning-focused relationships are about using the considerable potential in the relationship between teacher and student to maximize the student's engagement with learning; about enabling the student to play a meaningful role in deciding what to learn and how to learn it; and about enabling the student to become a confident, resilient, active, self-regulating learner. (Absolum, 2006, p. 43)

A challenging but worthy goal.

Dr. Earl provides the theoretical and research base for involving students as assessors of their own learning. John Kerr, a self-described "teacher of students through English," in the following contribution, describes how this works in practice.

Educator Contribution

John Kerr
Balmoral Hall School
Winnipeg, Manitoba

Students Assessing Their Own Learning

It's probably best to start by saying that any classroom activity begins with the relationship between the people in the room, and some people may say that I teach English or that I am an English teacher or that I teach English to my students. When I get asked what I teach, my quick reply is, "Students." I care about my subject, but I am no "academic rationalist." I try not to teach English to my students but rather teach my students through the subject of English. This is significant in a few ways. In one way, it lets me engage the students that I work with in an open and honest way. Most of them are quick to see that I care about them and what we engage with while we're together. The other is that it allows the emphasis to be placed on the learning and the process. When I encounter students who seem to be "overly" concerned about their marks and their grades (which is most of the students who have ever worked with me), I strive to point out that if you concern yourself with the learning, the grades will take care of themselves—that the grades should be secondary to the learning. You will only use a grade once or twice, but you may use the learning over the course of a lifetime. Once this becomes real to the students, the rest falls more easily into place. When the students engage with this premise, with the work, learning, and process, they become the proverbial fish in the sea; they only consider what it means to be wet if they get taken out of the water.

Meaningful Assessment

It is important that any assessment task be related to curricular outcomes, learning objectives, and the students' own lives. Arguably, authentic assessment tasks are the most desirable but also difficult to arrange in every instance. In order to get a body of evidence and to give students an opportunity to develop their skills in any subject area, a variety of assessment tasks will need to be employed. I think it's important that students are given a variety of types and opportunities, but I also feel it's important to ask them about what types of things they could do with a particular learning sequence. At the beginning of any sequence, I identify the final assessment task and discuss what it will entail. We then revisit it at a "checkpoint" to see if it's still the "thing" we are going to do. I am willing to be flexible. It may be that the students are able to identify a more meaningful and authentic assessment task than I am, and because that represents the very best possible scenario, I willingly entertain good ideas.

Mentor Texts

Mentor texts provide students with a clearly defined assessment target. They ensure that all interested parties are on the same page when it comes to expectations. Mentor texts can take on a variety of forms, from professional performance to previous student work, but what is key is that they represent the highest quality and not the only way. Students should feel free to create and experiment with their own ideas and not be locked into "copying" or "parroting" the mentor text. At the same time, they provide a clear entry point and, in many cases, the necessary reassurance many students need to begin considering how they can best represent their own learning.

Rubric Creation

When creating rubrics, it is the teacher's responsibility to ensure that the rubric and the assessment task jibe. The curricular outcomes and learning objectives can be indicated for teacher use, but a student-friendly version should also be accessible to students as they create or prepare for their summative task. A good way to get students to think about their learning is to ask them what a specific outcome looks like in their own work. Using a term like *possible characteristics* allows them to see what the work can look like at a variety of learning levels. Providing students ownership of the process also ensures that most students are clear on what level is represented by their work. I like to revisit the rubric as we near the due date and ask them, "So where did you work the hardest? What do you want me to be sure to recognize about how you dealt with, let's say, *language use*?" I always try to use the common language we work to create as we build the assessment and rubric together.

Formative Feedback

As students work on a large-scale project or as they prepare for an in-class test, it is important that we dialogue about what is working and what isn't. This can look like a quick pop-in two-minute discussion, or it can be working through sample responses and the drafting process. Getting students to ask meaningful questions of their own process and their own work helps to build the skill of self-assessment. This, for me, is one of the primary reasons to include students from beginning to end. Accurate self-assessment is a necessary skill that needs to be developed through opportunity. It also gets them paying closer attention to the process and the learning that goes into it, as opposed to just focusing on the end product and the grade.

Reflection

After major assignments and at various checkpoints throughout the year, I have my students reflect. I pose three to five reflective prompts related to process and product and ask students to provide me with their own perspective. At no point do I ask them what grade they think they deserve. Instead, I encourage them to use specific examples and "detailed" thinking to support their claims. This takes practice, but again, it helps to develop the necessary skill of self-assessment. I clearly state to my students that my goal is that they should be able to get to a place where they don't need me telling them what they "got" on any project or assignment—they'll know.

Summative Feedback

At this point, there should be no surprises. Students often achieve the top level because of the previous steps. If there is an area where this is not the case, minimal feedback can quickly clarify how the correction or adjustment can be made. I work to echo or challenge students on their own reflections and will often use their language as I provide my final thoughts and, where necessary, a grade.

Application

The AP Language class had been reading *Othello*, and because the primary objective of the course was to help develop a synthesis between their reading, writing, and thinking, they had

(Continued)

(*Continued*)

been working at developing a "big" idea from the play and turning it into a seven-paragraph paper. The idea for the assessment was introduced along with the play. We spoke together as much about writing and "big" ideas as we did about Shakespeare and Iago. The paper was to include an introduction, conclusion, and a quote from each of the five acts as a supporting or jumping-off point for the "big" idea, the thread, that would give their paper symmetry and structure. As we worked through each act, students had the opportunity to consider their ideas and the ideas of others and to mine the text for that perfect quote from each of the acts. As we concluded each act, the students wrote on a potential quote and then shared their thinking with each other and the larger group. At the end of the play (and after concluding we didn't like Iago very much), we spoke together about what I would be looking for in their paper and what skills/objectives the class felt they were focusing on during its creation. The rubric was done, and all that was left was to set a tentative due date and a work trajectory for completion. I didn't even need to create an assignment sheet.

Self-Assessment, Reflection, and Goal Setting

We cannot learn anything well without being able to self-assess how we are progressing or achieving as a writer or as a pickleball player, but self-assessment is a learned skill, and so, teachers must teach students how to self-assess and reflect on their learning and provide them with lots of opportunities to practice and improve as self-assessors. A student saying, "It looks good to me," when it isn't good or, "I suck," when it isn't really bad is not effective self-assessment. The starting point for effective self-assessment is that teachers must make the intended learning targets clear to students and must provide them with descriptive feedback (Guidelines 1, 2, and 4). Teachers providing descriptive feedback models for students the type of thinking they need to do to self-assess.

There are also a variety of strategies that teachers can use that build and use students' ability to self-assess accurately. These include the famous three colored cups or traffic lights strategies where students identify that they are confident they have achieved the intended learning and/or they could teach it to another student (green) or that they're not completely confident about their learning (yellow) or that they don't understand the intended learning (red). Teachers may then get the students who chose green to help the students who identified as red while the teacher helps the students who identified as yellow. One variation of this is a teacher saying that the greens help the yellows, and the teacher helps the reds (Wiliam, 2011, pp. 154–158). Jan Chappuis (2015) also describes many useful strategies to build self-assessment skills in Chapter 4 of her excellent book *Seven Strategies of Assessment for Learning*.

Educator contributors provide other strategies as follows.

Educator Contribution

Matt Townsley
Former Math Teacher, now District Administrator
Solon School District, Iowa

Checking for Student Understanding

As a math teacher, I used mid-unit quizzes as a formal check for understanding. There were no scores, so nothing went into the gradebook. Instead, students completed a check of their own understanding in pencil using a Likert scale (see Figure 8.6) prior to turning in the quiz. I would write narrative comments on the quiz problems themselves . . . and then return the quiz with feedback, along with my red circles on their Likert scale. This was Metacognition 101 . . . getting kids to think about their thinking! When returning the quizzes to students, I would strategically match up kids with relative strengths and weaknesses that complemented one another (for example Johnny did well on Target 1 but not on Target 2. Suzie did not yet understand Target 1 but did well on Target 2) for the sake of a quick student-to-student conference. By requiring students to think about their thinking . . . and then conference with a classmate, they were involved deeply in their own assessment.

FIGURE 8.6   Checking for Understanding of Learning Targets on a Quiz

"Learning Targets" are the important concepts and ideas taught that you are trying to understand and apply.

Here were the learning targets assessed on this quiz and how well you are doing at meeting each one:

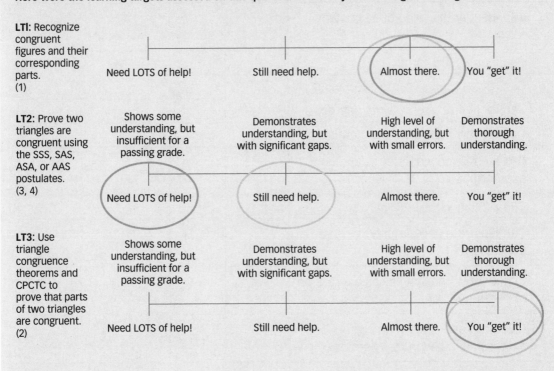

Educator Contribution

Denine Laberge
Teacher, College Louis Real
Winnipeg, Manitoba

Student Test Analysis

TEST ANALYSIS: ADDING AND SUBTRACTING POLYNOMIALS

Name: _____ Date: _____

Look at your corrected test, and indicate if your solutions are correct or if you have missed something. (This will count as an error.) If you have made an error, decide whether it is a simple error (you know how to correct it on your own) or a lack of understanding (you need help to understand how to solve it). On the reverse side of this page, explain and correct your errors. If there are questions you cannot do on your own, we will review them together.

Question	Learning Outcome	Correct	Error	Simple Error	I'm Not Sure What to Do
1	Can identify the number of terms and the degree of a polynomial				
2	Can identify the value of a constant term				
3	Can identify like terms				
4	Can recognize and name a trinomial				
5	Can recognize a term by its degree				
6	Can identify equivalent polynomials				
7	Can identify opposite terms and expressions				
8	Can simplify an expression				
9	Can illustrate and simplify polynomials				
10	Can identify and simplify an expression of perimeter				
11	Can write and simplify an algebraic expression in a word problem				
12	Can write and simplify an algebraic expression in a word problem				

Question	Learning Outcome	Correct	Error	Simple Error	I'm Not Sure What to Do
13a	Can write a formula described in a word problem				
13b	Can solve a problem with an algebraic equation and substitution				

CORRECTIONS

Question	Explain Your Error	Correct Your Error

A more detailed test analysis strategy was originally popularized by Rick Stiggins and the Assessment Training Institute. This version comes from Denine Laberge. The basic idea is that students identify whether their solutions were correct or not and then decide whether it was just a simple error that they know how to correct or involves something on which they need more help.

Engaging in self-assessment and reflection isn't just for academic achievement, as it can (and should) be used with the learning skills that a school expects of its students. International School of Yangon world studies and IB history teacher Nick Sturmey created a student self-reflection form for the "Habits and Attitudes That Support Learning" for use in the high school. The reflection form on the next page facilitates student self-assessment of their performance in this aspect and provides space for teachers to give them feedback. This type of reflection and feedback places these important attributes at the forefront of learning in the classroom.

THE INTERNATIONAL SCHOOL YANGON
Habits and Attitudes That Support Learning Self-Reflection

HABIT OR ATTITUDE	FOR EACH HABIT OR ATTITUDE FOR LEARNING, I . . . (PLACE A CHECK IN THE APPROPRIATE BOXES BELOW)			
	C—CONSISTENTLY	U—USUALLY	S—SOMETIMES	R—RARELY
Preparedness				
Am on time for class and ready to learn				
Am prepared with needed materials and demonstrate organizational skills				
Complete and submit assignments and homework on time				
Engagement				
Stay focused on learning and instruction during class				
Am actively engaged in class discussions and learning				
Place effort into work				
Collaborate effectively				
Am respectful to individuals, the class, and guidelines				
Initiative				
Reflect on learning and take appropriate steps to improve				
Listen and respond to instruction and feedback				
Display confidence to take on new challenges				
Pursue inquiry and curiosity within learning				
Demonstrate honesty and integrity in learning				

Comments and student declaration:

The teacher and student have discussed the student's performance in each of the above categories. The student understands what steps are needed to improve his or her performance.

Class/grade: _____   Date: _____

Name of student: _____   Signature of student: _____

Name of student: _____   Signature of student: _____

How to Use This Form

1. At the start of the reporting period, each student is given/sent a copy of this form.

2. The teacher goes through expectations for "Habits and Attitudes" and explains how students' performance will be recorded and reported.

3. During the quarter, the teacher makes notes on each student's performance. These notes may be amended/updated during the quarter. (The teacher can fill in the boxes in pencil or on a digital form.)

4. At the end of the reporting period, the student assesses his or her own performance. (The student can either fill in his or her own blank form or add to the teacher's form.)

5. The teacher and student discuss the student's performance and reach consensus on comments/checked boxes.

6. If necessary, a programme for improved student performance is devised. (This must be included in the "comments" box.)

7. Both the teacher and the student sign the form.

Providing opportunities for students to self-assess and reflect on their learning can also be done as part of a larger change in classroom practices and the communication of student learning. Below, Arthur Chiaravalli describes how he changed from scoring student work to just providing descriptive feedback, and how he now incorporates it into an online digital portfolio.

Educator Contribution

Arthur Chiaravalli
English Teacher, Haslett High School, Michigan

Using an Online Portfolio Platform to Enhance Self-Assessment

After years of practicing standards-based learning and grading with what I thought was increasing fidelity, I encountered two findings that radically changed my perspective on assessment, grading, and reporting.

The first finding comes from Ruth Butler (1988, as cited in Wiliam, 2011) regarding feedback. Butler examined three types of feedback: scores alone, comments alone, and scores with comments. Her study showed that depending on how well they did, scores alone make students complacent or unmotivated. Scores with comments are just as ineffective in that students focus entirely on the score and ignore the comments. Surprisingly, it was the students who received comments alone that demonstrated the most improvement.

The second finding comes from John Hattie (2012), whose synthesis of eight hundred meta-studies showed that *student self-assessment/self-grading* topped the list of educational interventions with the highest effect size. By teaching students how to accurately

(Continued)

(Continued)

self-assess based on clear criteria, teachers empower them to become *self-regulated learners* able to monitor, regulate, and guide their own learning. The reason students never develop these traits is that our monopoly on assessment, feedback, and grading has trained them to adopt an attitude of total passivity in the learning process.

Assessment

In spite of the many positive changes brought about by the standards-based mindset, my assessment practices were still bogged down by an overemphasis on scores and my total monopoly on assessment and grading.

I intuitively understood how feedback might be more powerful when unaccompanied by scores. When I returned papers to students, they would often flip immediately to the rubric stapled on back to view their scores, ignoring any feedback I'd painstakingly provided.

I also saw that my students were apparently mystified by assessment criteria, evidenced by the fact that from September to June, many continued to commit the same writing errors. How was this possible after all of the clear targets I provided, after all of the detailed feedback I gave? Part of it had to do with the fact that my assessments were all *scored*. If accompanying scores caused students to ignore my comments, then it made sense they wouldn't show much growth.

Additionally, I wasn't providing students with any opportunity to *internalize* standards through self-assessment. Feedback was *my* job. But as Terry Doyle puts it, "The one who does the work does the learning." I realized that, after years of providing feedback on thousands of papers, I had truly become an expert in writing criteria I taught. The problem was that I wasn't allowing my students to gain that same expertise by letting them use those criteria to assess themselves and one another.

As a result of these epiphanies, I began to see new ways to improve my assessment practices. First, I eliminated scores from as many assessments as possible, instead commenting on what they did well and what they could improve. Second, I insisted students start assessing themselves and others based on clear criteria.

Coming to the aid of these new priorities was the online digital portfolio, Seesaw. This platform allows students to independently document their learning by uploading it to the platform and filing it in folders associated with one or more standards. For each item uploaded, students add a comment (text or audio) self-assessing their work, making reference to general criteria, prior feedback, and, as time goes on, personalized goals. Usually, I then respond to this self-assessment, citing strengths and identifying one or more areas for further growth.

Most importantly, however, is what students do with the feedback once they've received it. As Dylan Wiliam points out, "No matter how well the feedback is designed, if students do not use the feedback to move their own learning forward, it's a waste of time." To this end, I continually have students access prior feedback in their portfolios, jotting down goals for subsequent attempts.

For example, students often complete short in-class "conclusions" analyzing how a certain literary element (a character, setting, symbol, motif, or theme) contributes to the meanings of the work as a whole. One frequent comment I make to students is to catalog more instances of that element's appearance in the work. So if water functions as a symbol in

Shakespeare's *Hamlet*, students should first of all spend time pointing out the various places where water seems to play a central role. Upon attempting another such writing with Camus's *The Stranger*, students will access this feedback from *Hamlet* and jot it down at the top of their paper. This time, they will make a more conscious effort to catalog several instances of a symbol—in this case, perhaps light—before attempting to analyze its significance. When logging this new attempt, students comment on how they demonstrated growth based on that earlier feedback.

All of these strategies develop students' self-assessment capabilities and help them to become the reflective, self-directed learners they need to be to be successful beyond K–12 education. Starr Sackstein (2015) states, "*Reflection* is an essential tool that enables students to decode what they know and what challenges them—and, most important to distinguish between the two" (p. 3). She suggests a number of ways in which teachers can make reflection effective and a natural part of what happens in the classroom:

- explicitly teach students what reflection is and allow them to practice during class time;

- teach students to question everything;

- avoid treating reflection as an add-on;

- make reflection more about actual learning than about how much the students like the content or learning activity;

- differentiate how students reflect;

- ask students to share their reflections with others; and

- model reflection. (pp. 4–5)

Self-assessment and reflection are essential for students to be able to answer, "Where am I now?" and "How can I close the gap (or get better if I'm already there)?" However, to really get better, it is necessary for students to set goals and to become good at it. Simply saying, "I want to improve X," or, "I want to get a better grade," is not sufficient. Teachers need to "explicitly teach students what an actionable goal is and how to set one" (p. 9). She suggests that students should set measurable long-term and short-term goals and that students should track how they are doing on the short-term goals. This fits well with Pink's suggestion that being able to see yourself getting better is a key to intrinsic motivation. (See page 10 in the Introduction.)

Nicole Vagle and Richard Cash are two authors who have helped me to bring this all together and extend my thinking about how and why we involve students in assessment and grading.

Vagle (2015) writes about fostering student *investment* in learning. She says she "deliberately (uses) the word *investment* instead of involvement to signal a reciprocal relationship between student and teacher, one that leads to the student taking the reins and beginning to own and value his or her own learning" (p. 11). She then provides a list what students do or have when they are invested. "They

- Have language to describe their learning

- Have a clear idea of quality and not-so-quality work

- Take action on descriptive feedback

- Revise their work

- Self-reflect on what the assessment means in terms of their learning

- Set goals based on assessment information

- Make an action plan in partnership with teachers to achieve their goals and improve

- Share their work and plans to improve, and

- Share their thoughts on what helps them learn and what gets in the way of their learning." (Vagle, 2015, p. 11)

Everything on her list is based on self-assessment, reflection, and/or goal setting, but when these occur as part of a reciprocal relationship they are more likely to be valued by students and to be used successfully in creating self-directed reflective learners.

Cash's 2016 book is titled *Self-Regulation in the Classroom* and is subtitled *Helping Students Learn How to Learn*. He defines self-regulated learning (SRL) as "a process in which the learner manages and controls his or her capacities of affect (feelings), behavior, and cognition (thinking)—the ABCs—to engage in learning, and improve achievement and performance" (p. 6). This is a broader concept than my focus on self-assessment, reflection, and goal setting as ways to improve engagement in learning and achievement, but clearly, in the big picture, all of the ABCs are important. The book is a comprehensive guide to SRL, and it has useful sections on reflection and goal setting, and I recommend it highly.

What's the Bottom Line?

Student understanding about how teachers will assess their academic achievement, including how teachers will determine grades, and student involvement in the assessment process through self-assessment, reflection, and goal setting are essential to support learning and encourage student success. It is critical that students see assessment not as something that is done *to* them separate and apart from instruction; assessment must be—and must be seen to be—something that is done *with* and *for* students as an integral part of the learning process.

Guideline 8: Discuss and involve students in assessment, including grading, throughout the teaching/learning process.

Analyze Guideline 8 by focusing on three questions:

Why use it?

Why not use it?

Are there points of uncertainty?

After careful thought about these points, answer these two questions:

Would I use Guideline 8 now?

Do I agree or disagree with Guideline 8, or am I unsure at this time?

See the following for one person's reflections on Guideline 8.

Why Use It?

- Students learn better and engage more when they understand how they will be assessed and graded.

- Students learn better and engage more when they self-assess, reflect, and set goals.

- Student and parent buy-in is greater.

- There are no secrets or mystery to assessment and grading.

- Stops any game playing or favoritism.

Why Not Use It?

- Student understanding of assessment is too limited.

- Puts teacher in a straitjacket—too restrictive.

- Sets up false idea that life is fair.

- Does not allow sufficiently for individual differences in students.

- Teacher should be in control.

Points of Uncertainty

- Degree of student involvement.

- Variation with student age/grade level.

- Amount of time needed to do this effectively.

- Amount of teacher collaboration needed.

CHAPTER 9

Grading Issues

Are our education policies designed for the convenience of adults or for the education of our children?

—Daniel Pink in Azzam (2014, p. 15)

Many grading issues have not been dealt with or are only touched upon in the detailed consideration of the grading guidelines. This chapter examines these issues: grading exceptional students, legal issues related to grading, competency-based learning/grading, and a number of external factors that impact grading—computer grading programs, grade point averages (GPAs), college grading and admission, and athletic eligibility.

GRADING EXCEPTIONAL STUDENTS

This is one of the most difficult grading issues for teachers, especially in school districts that have traditional approaches to grading. It is preferable *not* to grade special education students using letter or numerical grades. Checklists or rating scales that focus on improvement or learning gain are more appropriate. However, if district policy or parental expectations require traditional grades, teachers should remember that each of the grading guidelines is relevant to this issue and should pay particular attention to Guidelines 1 and 2 for exceptional students.

Applying Guideline 1

Grading should always be related to learning goals. If these have been modified to meet the needs/abilities of exceptional students, then grading should be based on the modified goals, not those that apply to regular students. Reporting of grades based on modified learning goals should clearly indicate that such modification has been made and ideally should indicate what the modifications are.

Applying Guideline 2

Grading should always be based on criterion-referenced standards, not norms. In a gifted class, if all student results meet the predetermined standard for an A, then all should receive A's. If some students' performances are also well above that standard, this becomes a reporting variable, but it is not a grading variable. The bottom line here is that being the weakest student in a high-achieving group should not disadvantage a student, nor should any student be advantaged by being the strongest student in a low-achieving group.

Relevant to both Guidelines 1 and 2 and the grading of exceptional students is the need for clarity and understanding of *accommodations* and *modifications*. The foremost authority on inclusion and grading exceptional students that I know of is Dr. Lee Ann Jung, and she provided the following definitions and the educator contribution on how to grade students who are behind grade level. The examples are from the Madison (WI) Metropolitan School District.

Educator Contribution

Lee Ann Jung, PhD
Chief Academic Officer and Cofounder
ASCD Student Growth Center

Differentiated Assessment and Grading Model: DiAGraM

For students who are behind grade level, determining the method for grading can pose a significant challenge for teachers. On the one hand, it seems unfair for a student with a disability to fail *because* of a disability. But on the other hand, it may seem equally unfair to hold students who are behind grade level to a completely different standard.

Leading up to the past decade, there has been relatively little in the special education research and practice journals to guide schools in how to approach grading for students who are behind grade level, particularly for those who qualify for an individualized education program, or IEP. Because of the sparseness of suggestions from the field, most teachers have made informal adaptations to the grading process for students with IEPs (Gottlieb, 2006; Polloway et al., 1994; Silva, Munk, & Bursuck, 2005). In middle- and upper-grade divisions, this has often led to inflated grades but still grades that were low, passing grades. This practice of inflating grades, unfortunately, leads to a disguising of true academic achievement status and, perhaps, to a lessening of a sense of urgency to intervene and support growth in key academic and social skill areas.

Through an iterative process of working with teachers in schools on issues of both practicality and fairness, an examination of the requirements of IDEA, and in response to the movement toward criterion-referenced or standards-based grades, I developed a model in 2007 as a recommendation for assigning grades to any student who is behind grade level (e.g., Jung, 2009). This model hinged upon educators' understanding clearly the distinction between accommodations and modifications and how they affect our measurement of learning (Jung, 2017b). This work was presented in tandem with Guskey's existing work on standards-based grading to make comprehensive recommendations for teachers, leaders, and school policy makers (e.g., Jung, 2009; Jung & Guskey, 2007, 2012).

A Differentiated Assessment and Grading Model (DiAGraM)

The four-step *Differentiated Assessment and Grading Model* (DiAGraM) (Jung 2017a) in Figure 9.1 is an adaptation of the earlier model and is an approach to grading any student who is behind grade level that leads to meaningful communication of students' performance. This is not the "special education grading model," as it also applies to those students who are behind grade level but do not qualify for special education services. In what follows, I will describe the five steps of the model that teams should take in making grading decisions for students who are behind grade level. Three of the steps are straightforward, one is more complicated, and one poses additional questions for school leaders and administrators to address.

FIGURE 9.1   Differentiated Assessment and Grading Model (DiAGraM)

Support Needed	Expectation Used	Assessment Strategy	Reporting Procedure
Accommodation	Use the grade-level criterion.	Assess the student's performance using the accommodation with no additional changes.	No change is needed to the report card or transcript grades.
Modification	Determine a modified, achievable, *comparably rigorous* expectation.	Determine the intervention and specific scale of measure for use on classroom assessment tasks. Everyone on the team uses the same intervention and scale of measure for this skill.	Grades reflect performance on the modified expectation. Note the grade was based on a modified expectation on report card and transcript.

SOURCE: Used with permission from Jung (2017a).

Step One: Determine the type of support that is needed.

In order to implement the Differentiated Assessment and Grading Model, we first must determine the type of support that is needed. Does the student need an accommodation or modification for this skill? Accommodations are support of a skill other than the skill measured in the standard. For example, if a student requires a person reading the material in social studies in order to demonstrate a social studies standard, this is an accommodation. If an accommodation is needed, again, grade the student as you grade every other student, with no penalty for the accommodation, even if the student has a disability. What

(Continued)

the team is saying is that the student's disability is not manifested in the social studies standard once the reading accommodation is provided (Jung, 2017b). Hold the student to the same expectation as every other student.

Step Two: Determine the expectation for standards requiring modification.

For skills that require accommodation, we apply the accommodation and hold the student to the grade-level expectation. When a standard requires modification, the team is saying that the student is behind grade level on the skill that is being measured. The team must identify the grade-level expectation and then the criterion that is expected for this student. The new criterion should be comparably rigorous to the grade-level standard. Modifications should only be used when the student's classroom assessment data indicate clearly that the student is behind grade level.

Step Three: Use the appropriate assessment strategy.

For skills that require only accommodations, this step is simple. We apply the accommodation and score the student's performance in the usual way. For skills that require modifications, though, we determine the specific scale we will use to measure performance. Once the scale is determined, we measure the student's performance on the *modified expectation*, not the grade-level expectation. There is no need to grade on the grade-level expectation because the team has already agreed that this is not a reasonable expectation for the student. To say the student failed the grade-level expectation is not new information. Instead, we take the "ruler" we use for the skill and move it to the student's level to see progress. It is important to know that this only works in grading scales that are qualitative in nature. That is, it works when schools have words that describe each of the letters or numbers used in the grading scale, and it does not work when schools use percentage-based grades.

Step Four: Report accurately.

For skills requiring only accommodation, no change to the reporting is needed. However the student performed with accommodation is reported as the accurate score or grade. When a student receives a grade that is based on a modified expectation, we must be clear, through the use of a symbol or other notation, that this was the case. Without this last step, the model only leads to inflated grades that do not communicate meaningfully. We want to be able to show that a student is doing well and meeting expectations but that the expectations the team set were based on below-grade-level standards. It is important (from both legal and best-practice reasons) that the notation apply to all students who need support, not only those who have IEPs. At the high school level, this leads to many questions about course credit and GPA that must be addressed up front by school leaders and the board.

Figure 9.2 provides examples of the process of using the Differentiated Assessment and Grading Model. This model can be an effective way to meaningfully communicate how a student who is behind grade level is performing. Without a clear procedure in place, teachers are left on their own to informally make decisions about grades for those students who require support. This leads to miscommunication about student performance, often for 20 percent of the school population or more. In a move to healthy grading practices, it is essential that schools not leave this conversation until later but rather incorporate discussion and move to policies and procedures for this population early in the process.

FIGURE 9.2 Examples of the Differentiated Assessment and Grading Model in Practice

SUPPORT NEEDED	EXPECTATION USED	ASSESSMENT STRATEGY	REPORTING PROCEDURE
Accommodation	Use the grade-level criteria.	Assess the student's performance using the accommodation with no additional chances.	No change is needed to the report card or transcript grades.
Example: Student needs to complete social studies assignments orally instead of in writing.	*Grade-level criteria are used for all assignments.*	*The student completes the social studies assignments orally, but the responses are assessed and scored according to the same criteria used for students who completed the assignment in writing.*	*The student's social studies grade is reported without any change or notation on the report card and transcript.*
Modification	Determine a modified, achievable, **comparably rigorous** expectation.	Determine the intervention and specific scale of measure for use on classroom assessment tasks. Everyone on the team uses the same intervention and scale of measure for this skill.	Grades reflect performance on the modified expectation. Note the grade was based on a modified expectation on report card and transcript.
Example: Student is behind in reading fluency and needs a lower-level reading requirement.	*Team determines that reading at eighty words per minute on second-grade material (rather than 150 words per minute on fourth-grade material) is achievable and comparably rigorous.*	*The student receives reading fluency intervention and is assessed on words per minute reading of second-grade content. Everyone on the team uses the same reading intervention strategies and assesses words per minute read of second-grade material. If the student achieves eighty words per minute, the student receives the score that coincides with mastering the expectation.*	*The student's reading fluency grade is reported according to the modified expectation, and an asterisk or other notation is added to the report card and transcript to denote the grade was based on a modified expectation. If the school uses a four-point scale, and the student achieved eighty words per minute by the end of the year, the student would receive a 4 on the report card and transcript.*

SOURCE: Used with permission from Jung (2017a).

If teachers follow all of these practices, exceptional students will receive grades that are meaningful and that support their learning. The key is that grades are based on public learning goals/standards and reflect real achievement, not some vague perception of their effort and their achievement relative to their ability.

LEGAL ISSUES RELATED TO GRADING

Legal Considerations for Exceptional Students

The practices just described constitute what I believe is the educative approach to grading and reporting for exceptional students. This is reflected in the check boxes for individualized education plan (IEP), English as a second language (ESL), and English skill development (ESD) on the Ontario provincial report cards (see Figures 10.3 and 10.4 in Chapter 10). My understanding now is that this type of notation could be used on report cards in the United States but cannot be used on transcripts.

This interpretation was based on the "Letter to Runkel," a letter written by David Dunbar (1996), chief regional attorney for the Office for Civil Rights Education, to Robert Runkel, state director of special education for the state of Montana. The Office for Civil Rights (OCR) is the enforcement branch of the Department of Education assigned to investigate violations of civil rights statutes. Runkel had written to the OCR to find out what criteria apply to a variety of aspects of grading for students with disabilities. The letter covers a wide range of issues, including class rank, honor roll, graduation, and the issuance of diplomas. From a grading and reporting point of view, the key consideration is the distinction between report cards and transcripts. The "Letter to Runkel" has been superseded by a letter and a series of questions and answers from Stephanie J. Monroe, the assistant secretary of civil rights, dated October 17, 2008.

Monroe makes the distinction between report cards and transcripts based on to whom they are available. She identifies report cards as being directed to parents and transcripts being available for postsecondary institutions and prospective employers. The letter states,

> the general principle is that *report cards* may contain information about a student's disability, including whether the student received special education or related services, as long as the report card informs parents about their child's progress or level of achievement in specific classes, course content, or curriculum, consistent with the underlying purpose of the report card. (p. 2)

She further states,

> transcripts may not contain information disclosing student's disabilities. . . . Information about a student's disability, including whether the student received special education or related services due to having a disability, is not information about a student's academic credentials and achievements. Therefore, *transcripts may not provide information on a student's disability.* (p. 2) [My emphasis]

This requirement is clear but may create a dilemma for educators, since educators want communication to be fair and to indicate honestly the level at which each student has achieved. The law and its interpretation must be followed; therefore, teachers must exercise great care. There is apparently little case law to help, but there are many legal opinions on the subject on the Internet.

Other Legal Issues

Teachers, especially in the United States, need to be aware that grading is or can become a legal minefield. Obviously, if this is a major personal concern, a lawyer should be consulted, but here are a few general comments on two aspects of grading that have attracted legal attention: lowering grades for nonacademic misconduct and due process (or the lack of it). Some of the legal issues involved in special education were discussed earlier in this chapter.

Lowering Grades for Nonacademic Misconduct

Hobbs (1992) reports on several cases in which school officials were ordered to reinstate students' grades that had been lowered because of students' absences, some of which were due to suspension. In these cases, the principle that the courts usually applied is that lowering grades as a disciplinary matter is illegal because it causes academic achievement to be misrepresented. He notes, however, that "the courts do not always decide for the plaintiff in challenges to academic practices or policies that deal with student grades" (p. 205). The key issue appears to be due process: If school officials have notified students of their rights and responsibilities and if there is an appeal process within the school or school district, then the courts are much more likely to rule in favor of the school. If, on the other hand, actions taken by teachers or schools are seen as being arbitrary, capricious, or in bad faith, then the courts are willing to intervene and rule in favor of students who have been denied due process.

It appears that the legality of grades is established when academic and nonacademic factors are kept separate and when students are accorded due process. All of the grading guidelines have a part to play in ensuring that grades can stand up to scrutiny by the courts. In particular, following Guidelines 3 and 8 should help teachers protect themselves against legal challenges to their grading practices.

Changing Grades

An interesting (and unfortunate) case in West Virginia highlighted one important legal consideration: When does anyone other than the teacher who assigned the grade have the right to change the grade. The West Virginia law (quoted in Karmasek, 2007) states that

> no teacher may be required by a principal or any other person to change a student's grade on either an individual assignment or a report card unless there is clear and convincing evidence that there was a mathematical error in calculating the student's grade. (p. 12)

> What is the effect of the use of GPAs? The main effect is to turn the whole high school experience into a four-year competition that emphasizes points rather than learning.

> The principle that the U.S. courts applied is that lowering grades as a disciplinary matter is illegal because it causes academic achievement to be misrepresented.

This very narrow law, which perpetuates the idea that grades are only calculated, was used as the basis for a ruling by a judge that a student's severely reduced score on a leaf collection and classification project, which was handed in late as the result of a student being out of school on an approved student council activity on the day it was due, should not be changed. The teacher was quoted as saying, "We . . . must have the professional latitude to establish our own policies and enforce them" (p. 7). She is clearly wrong, as teachers must follow state/provincial law and district/school policy (which she did not). Fortunately, in most jurisdictions, the law is not as narrow as West Virginia's and allows for grades to be changed by principals and others when it is clear that teachers have abused their authority.

COMPETENCY- OR PROFICIENCY-BASED EDUCATION

There is a strong movement, particularly in the New England states, that takes grading even further away from traditional grading than the guidelines for standards-based grading described in this book, and that is what is generally referred to as competency- or proficiency-based education. It is important to recognize that sometimes *competency-based*, *proficiency-based*, *performance-based*, and *mastery-based* just mean what is labeled here as *learning goals–based* or *standards-based*. There are, however, "five essential elements of competency-based (education) . . .

- Students advance upon mastery;

- Competencies include explicit, measurable transferable learning objectives that empower students;

- Assessment is meaningful and a positive learning experience for students;

- Students receive timely, differentiated support based on their individual learning needs; and

- Learning outcomes emphasize competencies that include application and creation of knowledge, along with the development of important skills and dispositions." (Sturgis, 2014) (An expanded description of these elements can be found in Townsley, 2014, pp. 2–4.)

All except the first element are generally part of standards-based grading, although the fifth element sees competencies as cross-curricular while standards-based focuses on standards by subjects or courses. It is therefore possible to have standards-based grading without being competency-based, but it is not possible to have competency-based education without standards- or competency-based grading, as the two main differences between standards-based grading and traditional grading are that standards-based grading is based on standards, learning goals, or competencies, not assessment methods, and with standards-based grading, achievement is separated from behaviors.

Townsley (2014) explains the differences between standards-based grading by noting that in competency-based education, students advance to higher-level work and can earn credit at their own pace, but this is not necessarily what happens in standards-based classrooms. Also, in CBE, "Learning expands beyond the classroom. This may or may not take place in a standards-based system. In a competency-based system, . . . students are encouraged to learn (and provide evidence of competencies) outside the classroom so that they can demonstrate competencies at their own . . . rate" (pp. 4–5).

As one example of this approach, consider the competencies and standards required for graduation in Maine:

A. Clear and Effective Communicator

Standard A: Understands the attributes and techniques that positively impact constructing and conveying meaning for a variety of purposes and through a variety of modes.

B. A Self-Directed and Lifelong Learner

Standard B: Understands the importance of embracing and nurturing a growth mindset.

These competencies can be demonstrated in any subject or course in the curriculum, so in all subjects, these should be the categories in the gradebook and on the report card, with or without the specific standards for each subject. Student transcripts could also be based on these competencies, with data drawn from each course taken by the student. (See an example in Chapter 12, pages 310–311.)

The move to competency-, proficiency-, or mastery-based education has been strongest in New Hampshire, Maine, Vermont, and Rhode Island, where there has been supportive legislation (Dorfman, 2016). There have also been significant moves in this direction in Oregon, Iowa, and Michigan. In Michigan, a commission set up by the governor came to this conclusion:

> Over the next decade, Michigan should move its P-20 education system toward a competency-based learning model, an approach that focuses on the student's demonstration of desired learning outcomes as central to the learning process. The focus of learning should be shifted toward a student's progression through the curriculum at his or her own pace, depth, etc. As competencies are proven, students will advance academically. (Michigan 21st Education Commission, 2017, p. 8)

This is the logical next step from a standards-based system, and it will be interesting to see whether this model becomes widespread across North America and internationally.

Many excellent resources about competency-based education can be found in the publications of iNACOL (inacol.org) and Competency Works (competencyworks.org).

EXTERNAL INFLUENCES ON GRADING PRACTICES

"We can't do that because we have to use or provide . . ." has been the reason given to justify ineffective and harmful grading practices for decades, and some of those influences continue to have considerable impact, especially at the high school level. Fortunately, some of these influences are declining because of improvements in, for example, computer grading programs and some college grading and admission procedures, but others like GPAs and athletic eligibility still drive aspects of grading procedures, even in schools/districts that have moved to generally more effective grading practices.

1. Computer Grading Programs

"We can't do that because our computer grading program won't let us."

Why Use a Grading Program?

If teachers follow the guidelines discussed in this book, record-keeping is a complex endeavor for the following reasons:

- Grades need to be related to learning goals (Guideline 1).

- Grades need to be related to clear descriptors of performance standards (Guideline 2).

- Teachers need to separate achievement data from other information, such as effort and participation (Guideline 3).

- Teachers need to separate formative assessments from summative assessments (Guideline 4).

- More recent information takes the place of older information, and teachers need to record second—or more—chance assessment scores (Guideline 5).

- The body of evidence for each student needs to be organized in such a way that it is accessible and helpful to teachers when they determine grades (Guideline 6).

Unless teachers rely completely on the more recent information and their professional judgment, this complexity means that most teachers will do at least some number crunching. If number crunching is done manually or by using a calculator, it takes a great deal of time. This time can be reduced by using a grading software program to enter, calculate, store, retrieve, summarize, and publish achievement data more efficiently. If teachers are very competent computer users, they can develop their own systems using spreadsheets, but most teachers will probably use a commercially produced program, either as part of a comprehensive student information system or as a stand-alone program. Over the last twenty years, the number and type of these programs has multiplied rapidly. An article published in *Education World* on April 15, 2017, lists twelve grading programs for Windows and four for both Windows and Macs (Steele-Carlin, 2000). G2 Crowd (2017) lists sixty student information systems, many of which have a grading component. Stand-alone programs like FreshGrade and JumpRope have been developed just for standards-based grading and reporting. There are also programs that have been developed for specific educational programs like ManageBac for the International Baccalaureate.

Inclusion on the lists in the articles or mentioned here is not intended as endorsement of any product but is simply information for those who may wish to investigate one or more of these products. (In the interest of full disclosure, readers should know that I am a consultant for PowerSchool and that I endorse PowerSchool's PowerTeacher Pro.)

Potential Problems

Teachers need to be aware of one major potential problem with computer grading programs: They vary considerably in what they can and cannot do. When I started using a computer grading program in the mid-1980s, the program completely controlled me, as there was nothing that could be changed. This no longer applies, as most programs now have considerable flexibility. Before deciding on a particular program, the district/school/teacher must check that the program has the flexibility to determine grades in a way that aligns with district or school procedures. The teacher must be able to control the program and have flexibility in determining grades for standards and overall subject grades (if required) by having the ability to override the computer. PowerTeacher Pro, for example, for any set of (standards) scores, calculates six metrics—mean, weighted mean, median, mode, highest, and more recent (2 to 20); the default is the average of the more recent three scores, but the teacher can override this if, in her or his judgment, it is not the best representation of the student's achievement. To follow Guidelines 3, 4, and 5, the grading program must allow a nil value or no mark for data the teacher wants available to students and parents but does not want included in the grade (e.g., formative assessment scores, such as quizzes and first drafts).

Another problem that teachers must be aware of is "garbage in, garbage out." Put less colorfully, if incorrect information is entered into the computer, incorrect grades will be calculated. Teachers must check for errors in the same manner that they check manually calculated grades.

As long as the potential shortcomings are avoided, teachers are encouraged to use quality computer grading programs to save time and as a support for their professional judgment. They are excellent *tools* for manipulating data, and the varied reports that can be printed provide valuable information to students and teachers. However, I must state again—the teacher, *not the* grading program, must make the decision about a grade.

> The teacher must be able to control the program; the program should not control how the grades are determined.

2. Grade Point Averages

"We have to have four-year GPAs, so we have to have lots of numbers."

Grade point averages (GPAs) are traditionally used by many schools to determine standing on the honor roll; class rank; and, in some places, eligibility for cocurricular activities. Also, many colleges use GPAs as all or part of acceptance decisions. Thus, they are very important for students and parents. How they are calculated should be a matter of great concern for colleges, school board members, administrators, and teachers.

Mathematical Calculation Systems
The Five-Point Scale

Traditionally, grade point averages have been calculated over the four years of high school on the following basis: A = 4 points; B = 3; C = 2; D = 1; and F = 0.

Weighted Scales

Some school districts assign different weights to some courses. Weighting is applied to more difficult courses, such as honors and advanced placement classes, so that for these courses, a higher value is assigned to grades (e.g., A = 5.2, A– = 4.77, B+ = 4.33, B = 3.9, and so on).

Problems With GPA Systems

Weighting is done to overcome one of the most serious criticisms of GPAs, which is that unweighted systems encourage students to take easy courses to inflate their GPAs. Weighted GPAs are intended to encourage students to take the more difficult courses without penalizing them when they receive lower grades. For example, a student would get more points for a B+ in a weighted course than for an A in an unweighted course.

One of the major problems with weighted systems is that they may cause conflict between teachers who are teaching courses that are weighted and those who are teaching unweighted courses. Partly for this reason and partly because of community attachment to existing systems, it is often very difficult to change how GPAs are calculated.

The Effect of Using GPAs—Time for Change

Even more basic than concern for the mathematical system used to calculate GPAs is the need for schools, school communities, and colleges to examine the whole GPA process and its effects. The first question educators need to consider is this: What is the effect of the use of GPAs? Clearly, the main effect is to turn the whole high school experience into a four-year competition that emphasizes points rather than learning. This is obviously inconsistent with the philosophy expressed in this book—and the mission statements and goals of many school districts. Because many colleges don't use the GPA provided by the school and either use their own formula or minimize the role of GPA in admission decisions, the necessity for this mathematical, noneducational process needs to be seriously debated.

If, however, after debating the issue of whether to calculate GPAs, a school/district decides in favor of GPAs, then a second question arises: Over how many years should a GPA be calculated? There is no reason that I can think of for GPAs in K–8 schools, so this should only be applicable to high schools.

As was pointed out in Chapter 3, many students, mostly boys, change quite dramatically over their high school years; very frequently, underachieving freshmen become high-achieving seniors. Why should their first-year performance be held against them at the end of high school? Guideline 5 states that for grading decisions, we should use the more recent information. The same principle applies to GPA calculation: *If GPAs are used, calculate them only on an annual basis and not cumulatively.* For college admission, ideally, the only GPA that should count is that of the senior year, but more *realistically*, two years could be included. Furthermore, schools should refuse to provide class rank data to anyone outside the school because it has no validity outside of the individual school—and limited validity within the school!

The third question that arises is whether every course a student takes should be included in the GPA. This is most commonly how it is done in American schools, but why does a student have to be good at everything? Wouldn't it make more sense to use a selection of the courses taken—for example, compulsory course, not electives—or the courses most relevant to the student's post high school destination or a selected number of each student's best courses.

I admit a bias on this issue because where I live, in Ontario, Canada, the equivalent of GPA is the average of the student's best six subjects in their senior—and sometimes also their junior—year. To illustrate how this works, I'll now describe what happened to my daughter in her last year of high school and first year of college. When my daughter, Bronwyn, started her Grade 12 year, she already had three Grade 12 credits, and she was taking six more Grade 12 courses that year. So she knew that only her best six would "count" toward gaining acceptance in her first choice of college. At that point, she was planning to take a general arts degree, including courses in psychology and economics. She knew that knowledge of mathematics would be helpful in those courses, and although her track record in math wasn't great, she took a Grade 12 math course. She passed that course, but she had many better grades that got her into her first choice, the University of Guelph. At the end of her successful first year, she acknowledged that the Grade 12 math course was very helpful in psychology and economics, but if she had been in most U.S.

high schools, she wouldn't have taken the math course and then had a more difficult freshman year in college.

3. College Grading and Admission

"Yes, but we have to do this to prepare students for the grading procedures they will experience in college."

"Yes, but we have to do this to ensure that our students get into college."

Over the more than twenty years that I have advocated for change in traditional grading and reporting procedures, the most persistent "Yes, buts" have been the two statements above. And to that I have always said (sometimes with much stronger words), "Balderdash."

There are a number of general reasons why those statements are wrong. The first is that they assume that all colleges are the same, and as I'll illustrate, that is not the case. The second is suggesting that we have to do now to students what (we perceive) will happen later to prepare them for the next level is false. What may be appropriate for eighteen- to twenty-one-year-olds is not necessarily appropriate for fourteen- to seventeen-year-olds, what may be appropriate for fourteen- to seventeen-year-olds is not necessarily appropriate for twelve- and thirteen-year-olds, and so on and so on. Furthermore, it is educational malpractice to use the bad assessment and grading practices prevalent at a higher level to prepare students for that level. The best preparation for the next level is to age-appropriately develop students as self-directed learners, and they will be able to adapt to whatever is thrown at them at the next level.

College Grading

High school teachers (and parents) often remember the horrendous assessment and grading procedures that they suffered from in college and assume that all colleges are the same and that none have changed. Unfortunately, there are still colleges that are in the dark ages when it comes to assessment and grading, but there are many where more enlightened procedures are being used. Very often these are colleges that have established "Offices of Teaching and Learning" to provide professional development on instruction and assessment. There is also a newsletter published ten times a year titled "The Teaching Professor" that provides articles for college educators about how to improve instruction and assessment. The company that publishes the journal also organizes an annual conference, and more than 1,000 educators attended the Teaching Professor Conference in Washington, D.C. in June 2016. It also publishes other professional development resources with titles including "What ethical issues lurk in my grading policy?" and "How can grading policy options influence student learning?"

There are also colleges that have developed principles for more effective assessment and grading and have implemented innovative approaches, and to illustrate this I will provide information about MIT, Wellesley, and Drake University.

Massachusetts Institute of Technology (MIT)

(2017 Best Colleges in America, ranked #2)

MIT states clearly that grades are not just a matter of calculation and that they shouldn't be norm referenced.

> In determining a student's grade, consideration is given for elegance of presentation, creativity, imagination, and originality where these may appropriately be

called for. Grades at MIT are not rigidly related to any numerical scores or distribution function, that is, grades are not awarded solely according to predetermined percentages. A student's grade in a subject is related more directly to the student's mastery of the material than to the relative performance of his or her peers. (MIT, 2016–2017)

MIT allows for incomplete grades and very long periods of time for completion of required evidence as long as everything is complete by graduation. The policy says that the completion date for outstanding work is normally before the date that grades have to be entered for the next term but "the instructor, in negotiation with the student, has the right to set an earlier or later date for pedagogical reasons or extenuating circumstances" (http://web.mit.edu/registrar/reg/grades/incompletes.html, accessed on April 17, 2017). This is much more flexible than most high schools!

MIT also has a very enlightened freshman grading policy, "designed to ease the transition from high school by giving students time to adjust to factors like increased workloads and variations in academic preparation." It includes the following, which can be found at http://web.mit.edu/registrar/reg/grades/freshmangrading.html (accessed on April 17, 2017):

> In the first semester and the January Independent Activities Period (IAP) freshmen are graded on a Pass or No Record basis in all subjects they take, where P (passing) means C– or better performance.
>
> In the second semester, freshmen are graded on an A, B, C or No Record basis.
>
> Subjects with a grade of P, A, B or C appear on both the student's grade report and transcript.
>
> Subjects with a grade of D, F, O (absent from final exam) or OX (absence satisfactorily explained) are only reported internally. They appear on the grade report but do not appear on the transcript. On the grade report these grades are followed by an N indicating no external record.
>
> A grade point average (GPA) is calculated for freshmen starting in the second semester.

There is also flexibility in later years through graduate school, where students can designate one or more subjects to receive pass/fail grading in place of A–F. For example, for sophomores there is an *exploratory option* that allows "sophomores (to) designate one subject as Exploratory in each of their fall and spring semesters. An Exploratory subject is one in which the student may either accept the grade awarded or change the subject to Listener status" (http://web.mit.edu/registrar/reg/grades/exploratory.html, accessed on April 17, 2017).

Wellesley College

Wellesley College, considered to be one of the best women's colleges, has a policy for freshmen that they call *shadow grading*. The website has the following statement. Note, in particular, the last sentence.

> Wellesley has instituted a shadow-grading policy for first years beginning with students entering in the fall of 2014. These students will receive pass/no pass grades in all of their courses for the first semester of their first year. The students themselves will be given a report of the letter grades that they would have received—"shadow grades"—but these will not appear on their official

transcripts and will not be released outside the College. This policy provides first-year students with the opportunity to learn about the standards for academic achievement at Wellesley and to assess the quality of their work in relation to these standards. *It further enables them to use their first semester to refocus attention from grades to intellectual engagement and inspiration and to learn how to grow as a learner in college.* [My emphasis] http://www.wellesley .edu/registrar/grading/grading_policy/shadow_grading_policy/node/42290, accessed on April 17, 2017)

Wellesley also allows students to choose whether to take each course on a letter grade or pass/fail basis. It should be noted that these enlightened policies are somewhat spoiled by a policy that requires a mean grade of no more than B+ for courses that have more than ten students. This is unfortunate, as it is bad practice and seems to contradict aspects of its mission statement.

Drake University, Des Moines, Iowa

As an institution, Drake University has mostly traditional grading procedures, but Professors Buckmiller, Peters, and Kruse in the School of Education are using—and researching—standards-based grading. In an article published in *College Teaching* in March 2017, they describe the impact of using standards-based grading in an educational technology course taught by Professor Kruse. "The purpose of the study was to evaluate perceptions of students enrolled in a university course employing standards-based grading" (Buckmiller, Peters, & Kruse, 2017, p. 3). Dr. Kruse's "goal was to provide rich, individual feedback as to how/why a student met, or did not meet a standard. Students would have the opportunity to revise and resubmit their lesson plan or else use the feedback to meet the standard(s) on a different assignment" (p. 4). The final grade was to be based only on student understanding of each standard at the end of the course. "The authors found that, while students were initially anxious about the paradigm shift and the additional work it would entail, they nevertheless viewed the model as clearer and more fair. As the study progressed, students reported moving beyond 'playing the game' of earning points for a grade and actually engaging more substantively with course content" (Buckmiller et al., 2017, p. 1).

Other examples of standards-based grading at the college level can be found in Owens (2015), where the author describes implementing standards-based grading in a college calculus course, and Beatty (2013), who describes implementation in two college introductory physics courses.

The developments at MIT, Wellesley, and Drake are very encouraging and hold out hope that there will be significant improvements and changes in college grading, and college grading will no longer be able to be used as an excuse for maintaining traditional grading in K–12 schools.

College Admission

It is understandable that grades are a significant concern for students—and parents—anxious to gain admission to the college of their choice, but this concern frequently leads to an overemphasis on the minutiae of points and percentages to the exclusion of concern about learning. This has been exacerbated by the use of class rank and four-year GPAs, but many high schools have eliminated class rank, and there is strong evidence that for many colleges, overall GPA is not the most important factor in admission decisions. According to the annual survey done by the National Association of College Admission Counseling, "The top admission decision factors for first-time freshmen have been consistent for decades.

The No. 1 factor—rated as considerably important by 79 percent of colleges—was grades in college prep courses, followed by strength of curriculum and grades in all courses (each 60 percent), and admission test scores (53 percent)" (Clinedinst, Koranteng, & Nicola, 2015, p. 16). It is very important that students and parents understand that the rigor of a student's program is extremely important. Generally speaking, small, elite colleges pay more attention to personal characteristics while large, public state university systems tend to rely more on the numbers/grades.

A student's grades in college-preparatory classes remain the most significant factor in college admission decisions.

Highly selective colleges look for students who:

- Complete core academic requirements.

- Take more challenging classes, even though they may have slightly lower grades than they'd achieve in lower-level courses.

- Enroll in several college-prep or college-level courses (such as AP®) and perform well.

- Take four years of a world language, showing evidence of academic discipline and challenge. (College Board, 2017)

The New England Secondary School Consortium, which promotes competency-based education, realized that it needed to alleviate the concerns of students and parents about college admission for students with competency-based grades/transcripts, so it has had extensive conversations with institutions of higher education in the region. According to the consortium, the following themes that have widespread application have emerged:

1. Admissions offices receive a huge variety of transcripts, including transcripts from international schools, home-schooled students, and a wide variety of alternative educational institutions and programs that do not have traditional academic programs, grading practices, or transcripts.

2. *Students with non-traditional transcripts—including "proficiency-based" or "competency-based" transcripts—will not be disadvantaged in any way during the admissions process.* (My italics) Colleges and universities simply do not discriminate against students based on the academic program and policies of the sending school, as long as those program and policies are accurately presented and clearly described.

3. As long as the school profile is comprehensive and understandable, and it clearly explains the rigor of the academic program, the technicalities of the school's assessment and grading system, and the characteristics of the graduating class, the admissions office will be able to understand the transcript and properly evaluate the strength of a student's academic record and accomplishments. (New England Secondary School Consortium, 2017)

It is very encouraging that sixty-nine public and private institutions of higher education from across New England (including Harvard, MIT, and Wellesley) provided statements and letters stating—unequivocally—that students with proficiency-based grades and transcripts will not be disadvantaged in any way. This will help change perceptions and will help all schools reduce the fears of students and parents that only traditional grading and reports are acceptable for college admission.

It is also interesting that the Making Caring Common project at the Harvard Graduate School of Education has started a process with representatives from many prestigious colleges to consider how to improve the role of the college admissions process in promoting and assessing ethical and intellectual engagement. The report makes recommendations about how and what to include with regard to (1) community engagement and service, (2) ethical engagement and contributions to others across race, culture, and class, and (3) reducing undue achievement pressure, redefining achievement, and leveling the playing field for economically diverse students. The recommendations in the last category are as follows: (1) Prioritizing Quality—Not Quantity—of Activities; (2) Awareness of Overloading on AP/IB Courses; (3) Discouraging "Overcoaching"; (4) Options for Reducing Test Pressure; and (5) Expanding Students' Thinking About "Good" Colleges (Harvard Graduate School of Education, Making Caring Common Project, 2017).

4. Athletic Eligibility

"We have to do this so students are eligible for sports and other co-curricular activities."

I became more aware of the impact of athletic eligibility requirements on grading practices several years ago when I led a daylong series of small-group presentations about moving to more effective grading practices to all of the teachers in a high school in an American state. This session took place toward the end of the second week of school, and at the end of the day, all of the teachers came together in a plenary session where there appeared to be general agreement with the guidelines I had presented, including, most importantly, that grades should be determined from summative assessment evidence. After I had finished, various administrators made announcements about other mostly logistical concerns; the last person to speak was the athletic director, who reminded teachers that grades for athletic eligibility were due on the following Tuesday so that students could participate in fall sports. Teachers clearly would not have had enough evidence from summative assessments to determine meaningful grades so soon in the school year, but an external pressure required them.

The Ohio High School Athletic Association website says that "each student shall meet all requirements in Bylaw 4, Student Eligibility, to be eligible to participate in interscholastic athletic competition at an OHSAA member school." The introduction to that bylaw states that

> the eligibility rules in this Bylaw 4 are an integral part of the member schools of the OHSAA and the Commissioner's Office in order to create, administer and maintain the valuable and unique form of competition interscholastic athletics has to offer. This unique form of competition is a carefully constructed system that promotes competitive balance and serves the mission and purpose of education-based sports and activities. Interscholastic sports and activities are intended to foster a sense of community as well as to teach teamwork, citizenship and discipline. (Ohio High School Athletic Association, 2017, p. 42)

Following that statement are almost *20 pages* of complex requirements that control who plays high school and middle school sports in Ohio. Similar requirements are found in every state in the United States. According to Bukowski (2008), "All forty-eight state athletic associations recommended some form of academic eligibility requirements for student participation in interscholastic sports; however, most were very limited. The requirements ranged from just being enrolled in a minimum number of courses, to a combination of a minimum number of courses, no Fs, a minimum grade point average, and an attendance policy." He also noted that many high schools impose stricter requirements than those mandated by their state association.

Ohio's Bylaw 4.4.1 states, "In order to be eligible in grades 9–12, a student must be currently enrolled and must have been enrolled in school the immediately preceding grading period. . . . Furthermore, during the preceding grading period, *the student must have received passing grades in a minimum of five (5) one-credit courses or the equivalent, each of which counts toward graduation*" (Ohio High School Athletic Association, 2017, p. 47). This is probably at the more severe end of the requirements identified by Bukowski, but it is typical of state or school requirements.

Grades and/or pass/failing are clearly a significant part of decisions about eligibility almost everywhere, and I believe this is wrong. The primary purpose of grades is to communicate achievement, and they shouldn't be used as punishments or rewards, except for decisions where the main criterion is academic merit. I do believe, however, that it is reasonable to have eligibility requirements so that students are attending school to learn, not just to play sports. I think eligibility should be determined by behavior and attendance, *not* academic achievement. The requirements should include regular attendance and engagement in the learning process. If students are attending regularly and are participating appropriately in the learning process, they should remain eligible for sports, regardless of academic achievement, because if these conditions apply, there is a strong likelihood that their academic achievement will improve. But if they are ineligible and attend sporadically or drop out, then there is no possibility of improved academic achievement.

CHAPTER 10

Communicating Student Achievement

Effective communication about assessment results means that the information we share helps (all) users make sound decisions that improve learning.

—Stiggins (2017, p. 82)

The primary purpose of grades is to communicate meaningful information to students, parents, teachers, potential employers, colleges, and other individuals and institutions concerning the achievement status of students. Although grades will be meaningful and will support learning if they are developed following the guidelines described in this book, much more is needed to communicate effectively with all those who need quality information about student achievement. Whether they are letters or numbers, grades are merely symbols; to provide real information, they should be seen as only a part—probably a very small part—of our communication system. In this age of instant communication, with e-mails and texting and parent portals as part of computer grading programs, it is necessary to consider what are the most effective and the most efficient ways to communicate student achievement to those who have a right to know about student performance in school, especially parents.

> Grades are merely symbols; to provide real information, they should be seen as only a part—probably a very small part—of our communication system.

All of the methods listed in Figure 10.1 have a place in effective communication systems. The most effective communication, however, takes place when several methods are used to form a coherent and informative system that meets the needs of all stakeholders. The key to an effective communication system is being clear about the purpose of the system and each of its parts.

REPORT CARDS

Traditionally, report cards, especially for secondary schools, have been little more than a list of grades and brief comments about student progress and behavior. Because comments were severely limited in length, they were frequently of little value. Comments such as "a pleasure to teach" or "try for honors next term" do little to provide understanding of student achievement or possible directions for the future.

FIGURE 10.1 The Communication System

	Limited → → → **Comprehensive**					
Report cards Conferencing	Grades	Report cards (limited information, usually grades and brief comments)	Informal communications (infrequent, usually criticism/warning)	Parent/teacher interviews (no student present)	Report cards (expanded format)	Informal communication (frequent and ongoing, usually positive)	Student-involved conferencing	Student-led conferencing
Other communication strategies		Standardized assessment reports, weekly/monthly progress reports	Phone calls, notes, letters, e-mails, texts	School open houses	School webpages, parent portals	E-mails, texts, phone calls, notes, letters, projects, assignments, homework, and homework hotlines	Portfolios—hard copy and digital	Portfolios—hard copy and digital
							Exhibitions	Exhibitions

For report cards to provide effective communication, they need to provide information on student achievement of specific learning goals and have an expanded format with information about behaviors/ learning skills/work habits. In addition, other reporting opportunities are provided by expanded-format reports, including the following:

- Sharing student achievement on cross-curricular or exit learning goals

- Reflection by students on their own strengths, weaknesses, and goals

- Acknowledging actions that need to be taken by partners in learning—students, parents, and teachers

- Giving teachers the opportunity to write an anecdotal summary comment on each student's strengths, areas for improvement, and next steps

- Meeting legal requirements, such as providing information on attendance, tardies, promotion status, and signatures

> What is provided must not overwhelm parents.
>
> What is expected must not overwhelm teachers.

Think About This . . .

"Today's report cards are missed opportunities. As a parent I want to understand my child with this window into a classroom that I rarely enter. Instead I read that my child 'makes appropriate choices to meet his personal and academic needs to achieve his goals.'

"It would be one thing if teachers had nothing to say, but I know that they do. In informal chats at pick-up, I've learned a lot from them; that one son seems afraid to make mistakes and ask questions, while another remains impervious to classroom rules and has outed himself in the religious wars of kindergarten as an atheist. These insights don't fit into the corset of the report card. Pity the teacher who has to write them.

"Education, as the word in French suggests, is about the formation of a person. It is not clinical, objective or impersonal. Wrapping it in that kind of language makes today's report cards impossible to savour."

—Buck (2016)

- Is this fair criticism of report cards?

- Can this criticism be leveled at the report cards in your school/district?

- If we acted on Ms. Buck's critique, how would we change report cards?

Expanded-format report cards can provide a great deal of information, but what is provided should not overwhelm parents. Two sides of letter-size paper is a sufficient maximum size; parents do not need, want, or benefit from a small book! Equally important is that what is expected must not overwhelm teachers; the reporting workload must not require so much time that teachers are virtually unable to teach in the week(s) just before report card time. Also, the number of formal reports per year must be reasonable; two or three high-quality, expanded-format, standards-based report cards are sufficient as long as other means of communication, described later, are also used.

Several examples illustrate the features of expanded-format report cards. While none of these report cards is perfect, they all have some key strengths, as well as some weaknesses. It is hoped that as schools and districts move to expanded-format reporting, these samples will be helpful.

Elementary

Figure 10.2 is an example (not a model) of an elementary standards-based, expanded-format report card from the Greene County Schools in North Carolina for Grade 3. To support this report, parents are provided with a "Checkpoint of Progress on Standards" (Figure 10.2a) for each grade level for each nine weeks that provides an explanation of the standards that will be the focus for teaching and learning in that quarter in English language arts and mathematics. Figure 10.2c shows the "Learner Behaviors and Work Standards" and "Universal Student Practices" from page two of the report card that also has standards achievement information for science, social studies, art, physical education, and music.

Standards are listed for each subject, and a grade symbol is provided for each of those standards. There are no grades for subjects, and teachers do not use traditional letter grades; there is a four-point scale for "Academic Performance Indicators." On page one (Figure 10.2b), there are nineteen standards for language arts in five categories, and ten standards for math in the five domains from the Common Core. On page two (Figure 10.2c), there are eight "Learner Behaviors and Work Standards" and fifteen "Universal Student Practices."

This is a very good report card, but I think it would be better if "excels" was used in place of "exceeds" and if the descriptors for the levels didn't mix achievement and progress (see Chapter 2). Other desirable improvements would include a significant reduction in the number of "Learner Behaviors" and "Work Standards" and "Universal Student Practices" and a reduction in the number of standards for English language arts. An interesting feature of the report card is the use of nontraditional symbols for the four levels of academic performance; in principle, it is good to move away from number and letter symbols, but I can't help wondering if this symbol set would be confusing and would take a long time for students and parents to get used to.

Middle School

Middle school report cards are interesting because sometimes, they are just like elementary report cards; sometimes, they are more like traditional high school report cards than in some high schools; and sometimes, they combine features of both.

Standards-based, expanded-format reporting has become common at the middle school level, but the big issue for middle schools is whether to have subject grades or not. Appropriately, some choose not to, but many feel the pressures of parent and student expectations ("We're big people now, so we should get grades!") and add a summary grade for each subject.

FIGURE 10.2a Greene County (NC) Grade 3 Standards-Based Report Card

Third Grade
Checkpoint of Progress on Standards
FIRST NINE WEEKS

English/Language Arts	Mathematics

English/Language Arts

Key Ideas and Details

- Ask and answer questions based on the details from a text.

- Determine the main idea and supporting details from a text.

- Describe and explain characteristics of a character in a story.

Craft and Structure

- Write from their own point of view.

Text Types and Purpose

- Write an opinion piece that has an opening, with at least two reasons to support the opinion.

- Write multiple paragraphs with a topic sentence, supporting details, and a closing statement.

Production and Distribution of Writing

- Refer directly to details and examples from texts when writing.

- Strengthen writing through planning, revising, editing, and rewriting.

Vocabulary Acquisition and Use

- Use grade level appropriate academic vocabulary.

- Use words meaningfully and correctly throughout the piece.

- Present material orally where the topic is clear and details refer to the topic. Academic vocabulary will be used.

Mathematics

Use Place Value Understanding and Properties of Operations to Perform Multi-Digit Arithmetic

- Add up to 1000 using strategies based on place value.

- Add up to 1000 using strategies using properties of operations $(4 + 1 = 1 + 4)$.

- Add up to 1000 using strategies using the relationship between addition and subtraction $(4 - 2 = 2$ using $2 + 2 = 4)$.

- Subtract up to 1000 using strategies based on place value.

- Subtract up to 1000 using strategies using properties of operations $(4 + 1 = 1 + 4)$.

- Subtract up to 1000 using strategies using the relationship between addition and subtraction $(4 - 2 = 2$ using $2 + 2 = 4)$.

Represent and Solve Problems Involving Multiplication and Division

- Interpret products of whole numbers as the total number of objects in a group (For example: 5×7 is the total number of objects in 5 groups with 7 objects in each.)

FIGURE 10.2b Greene County (NC) Grade 3 Standards-Based Report Card

GREENE COUNTY SCHOOLS

Teaching 21st Century Students 21st Century Skills

West Greene Elementary School 2013-2014 Standards-Based Report Card

Student Name: _____

White: 1st Nine Weeks; Yellow: 2nd Nine Weeks; Pink: 3rd Nine Weeks; Gold: 4th Nine Weeks

Grade Level: Third Grade

Teacher's Name: _____

Family Involvement	1	2	3	4
Days Absent				
Number of Tardies				
Homework Assignments Missing				

1. Comments:
2. Comments:
3. Comments:
4. Comments:

Academic Performance Indicators for Content Areas	
Exceeds Standard	+
Meets Standard	=
Progressing Toward Standard	<
Not Yet Making Sufficient Progress	-
Not Assessed This Marking Period	n

Reading 3D Benchmarks by Grade	BOY	MOY	EOY
Kindergarten	RB	C	D (6)
1st Grade	D	G	J (18)
2nd Grade	J	L	M (28)
3rd Grade	M	O	P (38)
4th Grade	P	R	S (44)
5th Grade	S	T	U (50)

Reading Level	1	2	3	4
Current Instructional Reading Level				

1. Comments:
2. Comments:
3. Comments:
4. Comments:

3rd Grade Common Core English Language Arts	1	2	3	4
Reading Informational & Literary Text				
Key Ideas & Details				
Craft & Structure				
Integration of Knowledge & Ideas				
Range of Reading & Level of Text Complexity				
Reading Foundational Skills				
Print Concepts				
Phonological Awareness				
Phonics & Word Recognition				
Fluency				
Writing				
Text Types & Purposes				
Production & Distribution of Writing				
Research to Build and Present Knowledge				
Range of Writing				
Speaking & Listening				
Comprehension & Collaboration				
Presentation of Knowledge & Ideas				
Language				
Conventions of Standard English				
Knowledge of Language				
Vocabulary Acquisition and Use				

1. Comments:
2. Comments:
3. Comments:
4. Comments:

3rd Grade Common Core Mathematics	1	2	3	4
Operations & Algebraic Thinking				
Represent & Solve Problems Involving Multiplication & Division				
Understand Properties of Multiplication & the Relationship Between Multiplication & Division				
Multiply & Divide within 100				
Solve Problems Involving the Four Operations, & Identify & Explain Patterns in Arithmetic				
Number & Operations in Base Ten				
Use Place Value Understanding & Properties of Operations to Perform Multi-Digit Arithmetic				
Number & Operations – Fractions				
Develop Understanding of Fractions as Numbers				
Measurement & Data				
Solve Problems Involving Measurement & Estimation of Intervals of Time, Liquid, Volumes, & Masses of Objects				
Represent & Interpret Data				
Geometric Measurement: Understand Concepts of Area & Relate Area to Multiplication & to Addition				
Geometric Measurement: Recognize Perimeter as an Attribute of Plane Figures & Distinguish Between Linear & Area Measures				
Geometry				
Reason with Shapes & Their Attributes				

1. Comments:
2. Comments:
3. Comments:
4. Comments:

FIGURE 10.2c Greene County (NC) Grade 3 Standards-Based Report Card

West Greene Elementary School 2013-2014 Standards-Based Report Card

Student Name: _____

White: 1st Nine Weeks; Yellow: 2nd Nine Weeks; Pink: 3rd Nine Weeks; Gold: 4th Nine Weeks

Key: Consistently – 3; Sometimes – 2; Rarely - 1

Learner Behaviors & Work Standards	1	2	3	4
Demonstrates Self-Control; Follows Directions				
Accepts Responsibility for Actions				
Asks Questions & Seeks Help when Needed				
Completes Work Thoughtfully				
Takes Care of School & Personal Property				
Works Independently at Appropriate Times				
Completes Assignments in a Timely Manner				
Contributes Appropriately as a Group Member				

Universal Student Practices	1	2	3	4
Makes Sense of Problems & Perseveres in Solving Them				
Reasons Abstractly & Quantitatively				
Constructs Viable Arguments & Critiques in the Reasoning of Others				
Models with Mathematics				
Uses Appropriate Tools Strategically				
Attends to Precision				
Looks for & makes use of structure				
Looks for & Expresses Regularity of Repeated Reasoning				
Demonstrates Independence				
Builds Strong Content Knowledge				
Responds to Varying Demands of Audience, Task, Purpose, & Discipline				
Comprehends as well as Critiques				
Values Evidence				
Uses Technology & Digital Media Strategically & Capably				
Comes to Understand Other Perspectives & Cultures				

1. Comments:
2. Comments:
3. Comments:
4. Comments:

3rd Grade Science Essential Standards

	1	2	3	4
Physical Science				
Understand Motion & Factors that Affect Motion				
Understand the Structure & Properties of Matter Before & After they Undergo a Change				
Recognize How Energy Can be Transferred From One Object to Another				
Earth Science				
Recognize the Major Components & Patterns Observed in the Earth/Moon/Sun System				
Compare the Structures of the Earth's Surface Using Models or Three-Dimensional Diagrams				
Life Science				
Understand Human Body Systems & How They are Essential for Life: Protection, Movement & Support				

1. Comments:
2. Comments:
3. Comments:
4. Comments:

3rd Grade Social Studies Essential Standards

	1	2	3	4
History				
Understand how Events, Individuals & Ideas have Influenced the History of Local & Regional Communities				
Use Historical Thinking Skills to Understand the Context of Events, People & Places				
Geography & Environmental Literacy				
Understand the Earth's Patterns by Using the 5 Themes of Geography				
Economics & Financial Literacy				
Understand how the location of regions affects activity in a market economy				
Understand Entrepreneurship in a Market Economy				
Civics & Government				
Understand the Development, Structure & Function of Local Government				
Understand how Citizens Participate in their Communities				
Culture				
Understand how Diverse Cultures are Visible in Local and Regional Communities				

1. Comments:
2. Comments:
3. Comments:
4. Comments:

Art	1	2	3	4
Visual Literacy				
Contextual Literacy				
Critical Response				

1. Comments:
2. Comments:
3. Comments:
4. Comments:

Physical Education	1	2	3	4
Demonstrates Sportsmanship & Participates Fully & Cooperatively				
Demonstrates Self-Control of Body, Voice, & Personal Space				
Demonstrates Age-Appropriate Movement/Motor Concepts & Manipulative Skills				
Demonstrates Age-Appropriate Understanding of Physical Fitness & Health Concepts				

1. Comments:
2. Comments:
3. Comments:
4. Comments:

Music	1	2	3	4
Musical Literacy				
Musical Response				

1. Comments:
2. Comments:
3. Comments:
4. Comments:

A more innovative approach is being developed at the American School in Doha, and it is described in the educator contribution from Rob Gohr, the middle school principal.

Educator Contribution

Rob Gohr
Middle School Principal, American School of Doha

Developing Effective Communication of Student Achievement at a Middle School

When the American School of Doha middle school first began working on developing a standards-based report card, we began by clarifying our purpose in sharing out student progress. We wanted to communicate student achievement and progress toward meeting school-identified learning standards, provide evidence of student learning habits and their impact on academic achievement, and provide students with a context for self-reflection and goal setting.

Our first step was to change the way we graded. Assessments had to be linked to specific standards that were to be assessed and were graded using four levels of proficiency: advanced (ADV), proficient (PRO), approaching (APP), and limited (LTP). This provided specific information on how students were performing in each assessed standard; however, with so many curricular standards, we decided to group like standards together into strands.

When reporting progress to parents, we initially shared information on each standard and each strand, as well as an overall letter grade (based on strand progress). Our report was around five to six pages long. Feedback from parents was mixed. Some liked the detailed information, as it told them exactly how their child was doing. Others found it confusing, as there was so much information, they weren't sure if they should be concerned about progress or not, so they only focused on the overall grade and ignored the rest.

Based on teacher, student, and parent feedback collected, we decided to make a few adjustments (see Figure 10.3). We kept information on subjects in our report and did so using a kind of heat map (colored indicators) to draw attention to areas of strength identified as advanced and proficient (dark and medium blue) and areas of concern (light blue and gray). [The original report card features shades of green for advanced and proficient, yellow for approaching, and red for limited.] We also included learning habit information, separate from academic progress (ready to learn, works hard to learn, and works with others to learn, with the proficiency level descriptors being IN = Independent, WR = With Reminders, and DE = Dependent). We no longer reported out on individual standards, thereby shortening our report down to two pages. If parents wanted to see standard information, they could go to our online gradebook and view this information, but it was too much for our reports.

We also removed the overall letter grade; however, we decided to keep an indicator of overall progress. For a many parents, a letter grade only compares students within their class. Many still see a grade of C as "average" instead of approaching grade-level expectations. To get past this, overall progress was communicated in our reports as a statement, indicating whether overall, a student was meeting grade-level expectations or approaching grade-level expectations (see Figure 10.4). Overall progress is based on the levels of proficiency achieved on each assessed standard during a grading period, not the average of strand performance.

FIGURE 10.3 Academic Strands and Learning Habits

Course	Strands/Learning Habits	Q1	Q2	S3
Computer 7 Exploration	COMMUNICATION & COLLABORATION - CC	PRO		
	RESEARCH & INFORMATION FLUENCY - RIF	PRO		
	TECHNOLOGY OPERATIONS & CONCEPTS - TOC	PRO		
	Ready to Learn	*IN*		
	Works Hard to Learn	*IN*		
	Works With Others to Learn	*IN*		
Drama 7 Exploration	DEVISING FROM STIMULUS-DS		ADV	
	CHEATING USING DRAMATIC FORM-DF		PRO	
	ANALYZING WORK-AW		ADV	
	Ready to Learn		*IN*	
	Works Hard to Learn		*IN*	
	Works With Others to Learn		*IN*	
Math 7	*Ready to Learn*	*IN*	*IN*	*IN*
	Works Hard to Learn	*IN*	*IN*	*IN*
	Works With Others to Learn	*IN*	*IN*	*IN*
Social Studies	TIME, CONTINUITY, & CHANGE - TCC	PRO	PRO	PRO
	CONNECTIONS & CONFLICT - CC		ADV	ADV
	GOVERNMENT & ECONOMY - GE	APP	PRO	PRO
	TEXT LITERACY - TL	PRO		PRO
	Ready to Learn	*WR*	*IN*	*IN*
	Works Hard to Learn	*WR*	*IN*	*IN*
	Works With Others to Learn	*WR*	*IN*	*IN*
French B	WRITING - W	APP	APP	APP
	SPEAKING - S	APP	APP	APP
	LISTENING - L	PRO	PRO	PRO
	READING COMPREHENSION - RC	LTP	LTP	LTP
	Ready to Learn	*IN*	*IN*	*IN*
	Works Hard to Learn	*WR*	*WR*	*WR*
	Works With Others to Learn	*WR*	*IN*	*IN*
Language Arts	READING LITERATURE - RL	PRO	PRO	PRO
	WRITING - W	APP	APP	APP
	LISTENING & SPEAKING - LS		PRO	PRO
	LANGUAGE FOUNDATION SKILLS - LF	APP	APP	APP
	Ready to Learn	*WR*	*WR*	*WR*
	Works Hard to Learn	*DE*	*IN*	*WR*
	Works With Others to Learn	*IN*	*IN*	*IN*

(Continued)

FIGURE 10.3 (Continued)

Course	Strands/Learning Habits	Q1	Q2	S3
Physical Education	PHYSICAL SKILLS - PS	PRO	ADV	ADV
	MOVEMENT CONCEPTS & PRINCIPLES - MCP		ADV	ADV
	PHYSICAL WELL-BEING - PW	PRO	ADV	PRO
	SOCIAL RESPONSIBILITY & WELL-BEING - SRW	ADV	ADV	ADV
	MENTAL 8 EMOTIONAL WELL-BEING - MEW	APP		PRO
	Ready to Learn	*IN*	*IN*	*IN*
	Works Hard to Learn	*IN*	*IN*	*IN*
	Works With Others to Learn	*IN*	*IN*	*IN*

FIGURE 10.4 Overall Performance

Drama 7 Exploration/Jennifer/Q2 *had a great quarter in drama. As we worked through a deeper understanding of improvisation, character development, blocking, and vocal projection, showed great growth.*	Meeting grade-level expectations
French B/Irene/S1 *occasionally demonstrates an understanding of the basic skills covered in class. She is sometimes able to write in simple sentences using familiar vocabulary and language structures. She requires ongoing support to speak clearly with expressions. She needs to spend more time and to put more focus when doing her tasks applying new vocabulary and grammar structures effectively.*	Below grade-level expectations
Language Arts/Alejandro/S1 *is progressing well in language arts. He has especially applied himself and shown growth during the second quarter. He is consistently early to class, has all materials, and asks questions when he needs guidance. In order to demonstrate proficiency on grade-level standards, needs to continue drawing on his new habits of applying himself fully and trying his best. There will be a continued emphasis on inferential thinking, and needs to work on developing this type of thinking.*	Approaching grade-level expectations
Math 7/Richie/S1 *is a positive member of the class, but sometimes struggles with the content. To improve, can continue to work on his Standards for Math Practice which include modeling, being precise, and using reasoning skills to solve problems. The semester letter grade is based on the current scores. Standards are assessed multiple times throughout the school year so students may reach proficiency at a later date.*	Approaching grade-level expectations
Physical Education/Elliott/S1 *has displayed an understanding of social responsibility in Physical Education by having a positive attitude and demonstrating sportsmanship toward teammates and opponents, consistently engages in the activities and puts forth his best effort. During our Floor Hockey and Striking Games units worked with his teammates to develop an offensive and defensive strategy.*	Exceeding grade-level expectations
Science/Madison/S1 *demonstrated achievement of some of the learning outcomes during this semester. She showed an understanding of writing scientific questions, hypotheses, variables, analyzing data and conclusions. Had difficulty expressing an understanding of the structure and function of organelles and cellular transport systems: osmosis, photosynthesis and cellular respiration. It is recommended that ask clarifying questions and get assistance when faced with difficult scientific concepts.*	Approaching grade-level expectations

High School

High school report cards have traditionally been very limited in the information they provide, as the focus has been on grades, credit accumulation, and GPAs. This started to change about twenty years ago with the increasing realization that grades were often inaccurate because of the mixing of achievement and behavior. This led to the development of expanded-format report cards that provided information on the behaviors that were highly valued in the school, district, province, or state. One of the first jurisdictions to do this, to my knowledge, at the secondary level was the province of Ontario, where the Ministry of Education introduced provincial report cards with a separate section for learning skills in 1999. These report cards had to be used in every publicly supported school. Figure 10.5 is the current high school report card that was revised slightly from the report first used in the 1999–2000 school year. There are six "Learning Skills and Work Habits" reported on for each subject, and the characteristics of each are provided on the report card. (See Figure 10.6.) The same six learning skills are found on the Grade 1 to Grade 8 report cards, so students and parents are familiar with them before high school, although from Grade 1 to 8, they are only reported on once for each student, not by subject. A rubric for these learning skills can be found at http://www.stillskin.ca/Files/Learning%20Skills%20Assessment%20Rubric.pdf (accessed on April 27, 2017).

The Ontario Grade 9–12 report card is a good example of a report card implementing Guideline 3 at the high school level, but unfortunately, it isn't a standards-based report card. More and more high schools are implementing standards-based report cards, and some private schools in Ontario use the provincial report card as a base to which they add standards. Generally, these report cards provide overall subject grades and grades for a number of standards for each subject, as well as a section on behaviors/learning skills. From the point of view of content, an excellent example of this is the high school report card in Figure 10.7 for South Medford High School in Medford, Oregon. It is not strong from a design point of view; it would have been better if the information was spread over more pages, as it would not look as if the information presented was so overwhelming. The information on symbols and abbreviations below the horizontal line in Figure 10.7 is on the second page of the report card.

One of the most important aspects of each of the report card examples is the separation of achievement and behavior and the inclusion of skills other than achievement in an expanded-format report card. Elias, Ferrito, and Moceri (2016) say that we must ask if "the other side" of the report card "address(es) the behaviors most worth talking about, that is, those most essential and best aligned with our ultimate goal of educating the future citizens of our society" (p. 2). They say that the Collaborative for Academic, Social, and Emotional Learning (CASEL) has conducted systematic research on this, and they "have found that there are specific social-emotional skills composing five major areas that improve academic achievement, increase positive behaviors, . . . and decrease negative behaviors. . . . Referred to as the CASEL 5, the skill areas are self-awareness, self-management, social awareness, relationship skills, and responsible decision making" (p. 2). This should provide guidance for schools/districts that are planning to add this feature to their reporting or review and revise their current report card. An example of a school district moving in this direction is the Madison Metropolitan School District in Wisconsin, which has this section on their elementary report cards.

Ontario — Ministry of Education

Provincial Report Card, Grades 9–12

| Semester | Reporting Period | Date |

STUDENT:

OEN: _____ Grade: _____ Homeroom: _____ Principal: _____

Address:

School Council Chair: _____

SCHOOL:

Telephone: _____

BOARD:

Email/Website: _____

Address:

Fax: _____

Address:

Courses	Reporting Period	Percentage Mark	Course Median	Credit Earned	Learning Skills and Work Habits — Responsibility	Organization	Independent Work	Collaboration	Initiative	Self-Regulation	Comments — Strengths/Next Steps for Improvement	Attendance — Classes Missed	Total Classes	Times Late
Course Title: Course Code: Teacher: ☐ ESL/ELD ☐ IEP ☐ French ☐ SHSM	First													
	Final													
Course Title: Course Code: Teacher: ☐ ESL/ELD ☐ IEP ☐ French ☐ SHSM	First													
	Final													
Course Title: Course Code: Teacher: ☐ ESL/ELD ☐ IEP ☐ French ☐ SHSM	First													
	Final													
Course Title: Course Code: Teacher: ☐ ESL/ELD ☐ IEP ☐ French ☐ SHSM	First													
	Final													

To parents/guardians and students: This copy of the report should be kept for reference. The original or an exact copy has been placed in the student's Ontario Student Record (OSR) folder and will be retained for five (5) years after the student leaves school.

To view provincial curriculum documents, visit the Ministry of Education's website: www.edu.gov.on.ca.

83-0470E (2010/01) © Queen's Printer for Ontario, 2010

FIGURE 10.6 Ontario Learning Skills and Work Habits

LEARNING SKILLS AND WORK HABITS	SAMPLE BEHAVIOURS
Responsibility	The student: • fulfils responsibilities and commitments within the learning environment; • completes and submits class work, homework, and assignments according to agreed-upon timelines; • takes responsibility for and manages own behaviour.
Organization	The student: • devises and follows a plan and process for completing work and tasks; • establishes priorities and manages time to complete tasks and achieve goals; • identifies, gathers, evaluates, and uses information, technology, and resources to complete tasks.
Independent Work	The student: • independently monitors, assesses, and revises plans to complete tasks and meet goals; • uses class time appropriately to complete tasks; • follows instructions with minimal supervision.
Collaboration	The student: • accepts various roles and an equitable share of work in a group; • responds positively to the ideas, opinions, values, and traditions of others; • builds healthy peer-to-peer relationships through personal and media-assisted interactions; • works with others to resolve conflicts and build consensus to achieve group goals; • shares information, resources, and expertise and promotes critical thinking to solve problems and make decisions.
Initiative	The student: • looks for and acts on new ideas and opportunities for learning; • demonstrates the capacity for innovation and a willingness to take risks; • demonstrates curiosity and interest in learning; • approaches new tasks with a positive attitude; • recognizes and advocates appropriately for the rights of self and others.
Self-regulation	The student: • sets own individual goals and monitors progress towards achieving them; • seeks clarification or assistance when needed; • assesses and reflects critically on own strengths, needs, and interests; • identifies learning opportunities, choices, and strategies to meet personal needs and achieve goals; • perseveres and makes an effort when responding to challenges.

SOURCE: Ontario Ministry of Education (2010, p. 11).

FIGURE 10.7 South Medford HS Report Card

SOUTH MEDFORD HIGH SCHOOL
1551 CUNNINGHAM AVE
MEDFORD OR 97501

Grade Report
Medford School District 549C
Medford, Oregon

TO THE PARENT / GUARDIAN OF:	APRIL MAY 123 MAIN STREET MEDFORD OR 97501

The purpose of this report card is to communicate with parents and students about the achievement or progress toward established learning goals. Grades reflect how well students have met these goals in each class, indicating areas of strength and areas where additional time and effort are required.

Student Name	ID	Grade	Counselor	Term	Period End Date	School Year
April May	111111	10	Staci Fischer	4	June 7, 2013	2012-2013

Period / Term(s)		Course	Teacher	Term			
1	1234	English 4	Davis	1	2	3	4
		Overall Grades		B	B	B	B
Achievement Standards	Reading Informational Text			MAS	MAS	MAS	MAS
	Reading Literary Text			MTS	MTS	MTS	MTS
	Writing			MTS	MTS	MTS	ADV
	Language			MAS	MAS	MAS	MAS
	Speaking and Listening			MTS	MTS	MTS	MTS
CRL Standards	Independence & Initiative			M	M	M	M
	Work Completion & Work Habits			NI	M	NI	M
	Cooperation & Participation			M	M	M	M
	Absences			4/M	2/M	12/NI	1M

Period / Term(s)		Course	Teacher	Term			
2	1234	Anatomy / Phys	Warren	1	2	3	4
		Overall Grades		C	C	B	C
Achievement Standards	Organization of Living Systems			BEG	BEG	ADV	ADV
	Matter and Energy			ADV	BEG	ADV	BEG
	Interdependence			BEG	BEG	BEG	ADV
	Scientific Writing			ADV	MTS	MTS	MTS
	Reading Scientific Texts			MTS	MTS	MTS	MTS
	Scientific Writing			APP	APP	ADV	APP
CRL Standards	Independence & Initiative			M	M	M	M
	Work Completion & Work Habits			NI	M	NI	M
	Cooperation & Participation			M	M	M	M
	Absences			4/M	2/M	12/NI	1M

Period / Term(s)		Course	Teacher	Term			
3	1234	Women's Choir	Weller	1	2	3	4
		Overall Grades		A	B	A	B
Achievement Standards	Vocal Performance			MAS	MAS	MAS	MAS
	Music Reading			MTS	MTS	MTS	MTS
	Musical Concept Analysis			ADV	ADV	ADV	ADV
CRL Standards	Independence & Initiative			M	M	M	M
	Work Completion & Work Habits			NI	M	NI	M
	Cooperation & Participation			M	M	M	M
	Absences			4/M	2/M	12/NI	1M

Period / Term(s)		Course	Teacher	Term			
4	1234	Spanish 2	Wallace	1	2	3	4
		Overall Grades		A	B	A	B
Achievement Standards	Communication			MAS	MAS	MAS	MAS
	Knowledge of Culture & Viewpoints			MTS	MTS	MTS	MTS
	Language (Vocab, Conjugation, etc.)			MTS	MTS	MTS	ADV
CRL Standards	Independence & Initiative			M	M	M	M
	Work Completion & Work Habits			NI	M	NI	M
	Cooperation & Participation			M	M	M	M
	Absences			4/M	2/M	12/NI	1M

Period / Term(s)		Course	Teacher	Term			
5	1	Basic Compt 2	Mr. Richmond	1	2	3	4
		Overall Grades		A	A		
Achievement Standards	Typing			MAS	MAS		
	Application Management			MTS	MTS		
	Basic Skills			MTS	MTS		
CRL Standards	Independence & Initiative			M	M		
	Work Completion & Work Habits			NI	M		
	Cooperation & Participation			M	M		
	Absences			4/M	2/M		

Period / Term(s)		Course	Teacher	Term			
5	24	Algebra Intermed	Reed	1	2	3	4
		Overall Grades			A		A
Achievement Standards	Number and Quantity				MTS		MTS
	Interpreting and Building Functions				MAS		MAS
	The Real Number System				MTS		MTS
	Linear, Quadratic, & Exponential Models				MTS		MTS
	Statistics and Probability				ADV		ADV
CRL Standards	Independence & Initiative				M		M
	Work Completion & Work Habits				M		M
	Cooperation & Participation				M		M
	Absences				2/M		1M

Period / Term(s)		Course	Teacher	Term			
5	4	Auto Service 1	Veverka	1	2	3	4
		Overall Grades		B			
Achievement Standards	Mechanics			MAS			
	Functional Skills			MTS			
CRL Standards	Independence & Initiative			M			
	Work Completion & Work Habits			NI			
	Cooperation & Participation			M			
	Absences			12/NI			

Period / Term(s)		Course	Teacher	Term			
6	13	Algebra Intermed	Reed	1	2	3	4
		Overall Grades		C		C	
Achievement Standards	Number and Quantity				MTS		MTS
	Interpreting and Building Functions				MAS		MAS
	The Real Number System				MTS		MTS
	Linear, Quadratic, & Exponential Models				MTS		MTS
	Statistics and Probability				ADV		ADV
CRL Standards	Independence & Initiative				M		M
	Work Completion & Work Habits				M		M
	Cooperation & Participation				M		M
	Absences				2/M		1M

2015 Graduation Requirements

Scale: 0.0 0.5 1.0 1.5 2.0 2.5 3.0 3.5 4.0 4.5

- American Studies
- Arts/Cte/2Nd Lang
- Basic Computer Skill
- Career Education
- Cont Issues/Gov'T
- Economics
- Elective
- Health Ed
- Language Arts
- Mathematics
- Physical Education
- Science
- World Studies

Credits Required / Credits Earned

Academic GPA

This Period	Accumulative
x.xx	x.xx

Typical Progress Toward Graduation (credits Earned)

0 3 6 9 12 15 18 21 24

April's Progress Toward Graduation

0 3 6 9 12 15 18 21 24

Eligibility for Activities

Eligible for activities: Academic

Achievement Grades

MAS	Mastery
ADV	Advanced
MTS	Meets
APP	Approaching
Beg	Beginning
NA	Not Assessed
*	Modified (SPED / ELL)

Career Related Learning (CRL) Grades

M	Meets Expectations
NI	Needs Improvement

Overall Academic Grades

A	Mastery of Subject	I	Incomplete
B	Good Quality of Work	W	Withdrawn
C	Completed Minimum	X	No Grade
F	Fail	P	Pass

SEL Strengths

Social Emotional Learning Standards

I can think and talk about how I feel and will act.

I can use strategies to calm myself.

I can predict how others might feel in different situations.

I can tell others what activities I do well and what I need help with.

I can name and explain different values.

I can set goals for home and school success.

I can recognize what I have in common with my classmates.

I can observe and respect each person's unique qualities.

I can explain how to recognize feelings, by words, tone, and body language.

SEL Growth

Social Emotional Learning Standard

I'm working on how to predict how others might feel in different situations.

PARENT PORTALS/ONLINE GRADEBOOKS

One of the main features of most computer grading programs is that the gradebook can be made accessible online. Many students and parents like having easy access to grades because they can see how the student is doing in each class at any time and not have to wait until the teacher chooses to make grades available. One impact is that in some cases, it has encouraged teachers to be more prompt in marking student work. There are, however, many who are critical of these portals because some parents and students check grades several times a day and have an almost manic focus on grades; this can put a lot of stress on students, especially if they have one early bad test score. My main problem with them is that in Week 2, a grade is calculated even when there isn't enough evidence to make a summary judgment and that it leads to a focus on the subject grade rather than the more detailed information about achievement on standards.

Teachers and parents often have reservations about parent portals. One teacher expressed the following reservations about parent portals:

1. It leaves little room for a student to slip and solve their own problem before Mom knows about it.

2. It will light a fire under my tush to grade at a quicker pace. (He also listed this as a positive!)

3. It will require all teachers to be on the same grade book program.

4. It will require educating parents in how to read the program itself. (Walpert-Gawron, 2011)

Beth Ewen (2013) described how she "dropped out" of the Minneapolis parent portal because she came to understand that by contacting the teacher every time she saw a poor score or a missing assignment, she was depriving her child of important learning opportunities and as an advocate on her own behalf. She found herself asking, "But what has she learned?" and her answer was, "That Mom (or Dad) will place the difficult phone call, hound her and otherwise avert the natural outcome of her actions if she is left alone. Which is: She gets her act together and passes the class, or she doesn't, and then she learns how that feels and decides which path to take next."

Her conclusion was this: "After many iterations of this scenario, and many discussions with other parents doing the same," she was convinced that "we parents should quit using the parent portal. We should stop e-mailing when the Spanish V test is skipped or the technology policy is unfair" (Ewen, 2013). Jessica Lahey, writing in *The Atlantic*, expressed similar reservations and said that she promised her fourteen-year-old son that she and her husband "will not be using the system to check on his grades or attendance (or anything else). In return, he promised to use the system himself and keep us apprised of anything we need to know" (Lahey, 2013).

Some schools that could make the parent portal available have chosen not to while others have used them and then stopped. Lois McGill, director of academics at Balmoral Hall in Winnipeg, a highly regarded K–12 girls school, said,

> We have removed access to the online gradebook for both parents and students. Years ago, with an increase in the use of online grading programs, there was a shift to give parents access to student marks throughout the year, without the need to wait on the report card to see where the student was sitting. Although this provides the parents with current, ongoing information, it has often only heightened the "grading culture." Parents, without the conversations that sometimes are needed to accompany marks, focus solely on the mark. We invite parents and students to have ongoing conversations with the teachers where all the information needed is available. (personal communication, March 2017)

On the other hand, some schools have come to use parent portals so extensively that they have virtually replaced report cards. Brian Stack, principal of Sanborn Regional High School in Kingston, New Hampshire, says, "Very few parents ever want the report card; they simply look at our online grade viewer at real-time grades. We spent a lot of time on that template (for the report card), but in the end, it is only as accurate as when you print it, and parents prefer real-time grades online" (personal communication, April 2017).

A rather more radical view of how we should be reporting in this digital age is provided in this contribution on the next page from Arthur Chiaravalli.

INFORMAL COMMUNICATIONS

Teachers can use brief meetings in the school, phone calls, postcards, and quick notes as informal communications. Increasingly this type of communication is being done by e-mail and texts. Although informal, they are part of the communication system. If communication is seen as a system, even informal communications are planned, at least to some extent. Planning involves the availability of e-mail addresses and cell phone numbers and postcards or quick notes so that it is easy for teachers to send informal written communications home.

Educator Contribution

Arthur Chiaravalli
English Teacher, Haslett High School, Michigan

Communicating Student Achievement More Effectively in a High School

As I have few grades for students, reporting student performance and progress needs to take another form than traditional report cards.

First of all, anyone wanting to go this (nontraditional) route needs to clearly articulate the rationale for the approach and explain how it will work. In addition to providing a description in my syllabus, I send home a detailed letter (https://goo.gl/Kb6iYD) and invite students and parents to express any questions, comments, or concerns. Throughout the year, I continually e-mail newsletters reiterating these ideas, especially when we are nearing the end of the term.

With every e-mail I send out, I invite parents who have not yet joined us on Seesaw to do so. Once they've joined, parents can view and comment on their student's work, as well as read or listen to any feedback. I find that many parents who join are much more actively engaged with this platform than they are with a traditional online gradebook. Even if they don't leave comments themselves, they tell me about specific items in the portfolio they found interesting. One parent, noticing her son slouching in a video of a class discussion, told him later to sit up straight and participate. He listened!

Obviously, little of this can fit inside a simple online gradebook, that reductive descendant of a bygone age. Back then, the wire-bound class record book was the only available means to gather student achievement evidence in one accessible place. Thanks to user-friendly platforms like Seesaw, this is no longer the case. Isn't it time we make room for the richness, no longer restricting ourselves to that which can be conveyed through numbers?

Although schools have always seen it as their duty to inform parents when students misbehave or are frequently tardy or absent, it is important that informal communication also be used for positive feedback. This is another aspect of planning for schools: seeking to ensure that each parent receives at least one positive informal communication each grading period. For this to happen, teachers need to keep brief records of their use of informal communications. Informal communication and the associated record-keeping must not be a major burden for teachers; as with other methods of communication, planning is needed to ensure that teacher workload is reasonable. In addition, teachers need flexibility in choosing a method that is most comfortable for them—some prefer to make phone calls; others prefer to write.

PARENT/TEACHER/STUDENT CONFERENCING

"What did they say, what did they say?"

—My children's question(s) before I even got in the door
on returning from parent–teacher conferences

I watch them come in, hands clenched, eyes downcast, not quite sure what to think. I tell them to take a deep breath, tell your story, there is nothing to be worried about. Our students lead their conferences and while it is not perfect, it is incredible to watch their story unfold. To see them decide what deserves their attention, to see what they find valuable. To see those that come from home ask them questions and see them truly realize what we have known for quite a while; they have grown, they have changed, and yes, they are almost ready to leave us.

—Pernille Ripp, describing seventh-grade student-led conferences (Ripp, 2017)

Another part of a communication system involves planned meetings between parents, teachers, and, increasingly, students. Traditionally, these meetings have been parent-teacher interviews with no student participation. Much valuable information can be exchanged in such interviews, and although sometimes privacy is necessary, almost always, parents, teachers, or both discuss the interview with students afterwards. How much better for the student to be present and participate in the conference rather than receive secondhand—and inevitably somewhat distorted—accounts of what occurred. This leads to the concept of student-involved conferencing.

The continuum shown in Figure 10.8 demonstrates that student-involved conferencing may vary from the student merely being present as a listener but not really participating through increasing student participation to conferences that are truly led by students. Schools and teachers may start at the point on the continuum that is comfortable for them and their community. There are a huge variety of possible formats, and it is hoped that teachers will move quickly toward increasing levels of student involvement.

> Schools and teachers may start at the point on the continuum that is comfortable for them and their community.

FIGURE 10.8 Student Involvement Continuum

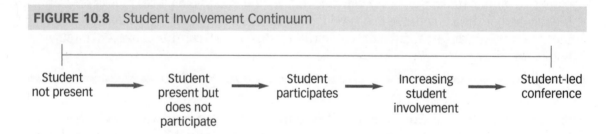

In one possible format, students share work samples that demonstrate their growth and their best work with their parent(s). Students identify for their parent(s) the strengths and weaknesses of the shared samples and what they could do to improve on a similar task in the future. Work samples may come from an organized portfolio assessment system, but it is not essential to have student portfolios to institute student-involved conferencing. Teachers can simply state the number of pieces of work that students are to share, some designated by the teacher and some chosen by the students. This approach applies particularly to interviews for middle and high school students (see Figure 10.9), where parents have many teachers to see, and teachers have very limited time with each student and his or her parent(s).

Students may lead conferences in the absence or presence of teachers. One of the most practical formats is to have a number of conferences occurring at the same time, with the number largely determined by the size of the available room. Students lead each conference by taking their parent(s) through each work sample and inviting their reactions to the work and the student's description and explanation. The teacher deals with any problems that

FIGURE 10.9 Parents' Night Interview—Science

Dear _____,

I look forward to meeting you on Thursday, _____ at _____ p.m. in Room _____. Your daughter/son is welcome to attend, too.

Before you come to see me, please find time to sit down with your daughter/son and ask her/him to show you the following from her/his SCIENCE NOTEBOOK:

1. Two pieces of work that she/he is particularly pleased with

2. One piece of work that she/he could have done better on

3. The self-tracking sheet outlining progress on the essential performance criteria

4. The self- and teacher evaluation of her/his participation in the learning process

Please discuss these pieces of work with her/him. I suggest you make several positive comments and outline one or two steps for improvement, if necessary. Please bring this sheet with you on parents' night.

Positive comments:

Steps for improvement:

Questions arising from your discussion:

Many thanks,

_____

SOURCE: Adapted by permission from Hilary Gerrard, former head of science, Thornlea, S.S. York Region District School Board, Ontario, Canada.

arise and spends a relatively short period with each student and parent(s). For example, conferences may be set for forty-five minutes, with four to eight different student–parent groups meeting simultaneously. The teacher rotates among the groups, giving about five minutes to each, a mix of two- and three-way conferences.

As with other parts of the communication system, student-involved conferencing requires a great deal of preparation and planning. Students have to be trained for whatever type of involvement they are to have, and parents need to be informed about how conferencing will be conducted and what is expected of them. Educator contributor Sarah Craig, the head of the junior school at Branksome Hall in Toronto, illustrates this and other aspects of student-led conferencing in her contribution that follows.

Educator Contribution

Sarah Craig
Head of Junior School, Branksome Hall
Toronto, Ontario

Student-Led Conferencing

Over the years, student involvement or student-centered approaches to assessment and evaluation have increased in popularity. As education has moved to more holistic and constructivist-based pedagogies, an increased focus on students having agency for their learning has resulted in new assessment approaches. Involving students in a component of the assessment process that has traditionally been between adults, teachers, and parents provides an opportunity for the adults to hear the students' authentic voice and their experience. Another powerful rationale for involving students is simply the idea that none of the adults typically understands the students' learning strengths and areas for growth better than the learners themselves. Having the students there, whether they are four or fourteen years old, provides the voices that are missing from traditional parent–teacher conference models.

Student involvement in conferencing can take many forms. Sometimes, it is a version of a traditional adult conference where the student is present, often referred to as a three-way conference. Another approach that yields great feedback from both students and their parents is a student-led conference. There are many models to consider, but one that I have found effective is an hour-long, portfolio-driven conference led by the student. In this model, teachers work with the students in their classes to plan in advance for the conference. Together, they decide on an agenda or program for the hour, with an eye to showcasing the students' most recent and consistent progress and accomplishments. Building the conference around a student's growth portfolio is a good way to provide a framework for the experience.

A student-led conference provides an opportunity for discussion about learning between a student and his or her parents. In these busy times, it is often rare for parents and children to have an uninterrupted hour to review learning progress and set goals together. It also can provide a "window" for parents into their child's daily classroom experience. Often, student-led conferences will involve a variety of assessment engagements that might include sharing, demonstrations, games, or engaging in learning experiences together.

At Branksome Hall, each student's conference will last approximately one hour,[1] and up to three other families will be engaged in conferences at the same time. Most of the time is spent in the student's grade-level classroom; however, they also take their parents to travel around the school to view artwork on display, to watch a demonstration of a physical education skill in the gym, or to hear a musical performance. Parents are encouraged to interact with their child by asking questions and making comments in support of the growth of learning skills, like responsibility and independence. As students share their pride in their accomplishments, they also are encouraged to be aware of areas for improvement. This type of approach is supportive of the development of a *growth mindset*, as defined by Carol Dweck. The enduring result is that over time, students learn to set reasonable goals for themselves in an age-appropriate manner, with increasing degrees of sophistication. They become their own best learning advocates.

---

[1] Sarah believes that one hour is the best amount of time and that thirty minutes is a desirable minimum, but I think it is important to recognize that the objectives of student-led conferencing can be met in a more limited ways, in as little as fifteen minutes.

If, for any reason, a parent is unable to attend, we welcome and encourage a caregiver, grandparent, or other adult family friend to participate. The process of sharing learning with an adult is highly motivating and empowering for students. Teachers act as facilitators during the conference by taking photos, interacting with families, offering encouragement, and answering questions if necessary. It is recommended that the school clarify expectations for parents. They need to stress that a student-led conference is not a time for a parent–teacher conference; rather, it is a student's time to share and celebrate his or her learning.[2]

After using this version of student-led conferences for more than twenty years in three different school settings, I can say with confidence that they are a unique and personal way for students to share their learning. As an assessment tool, they are helpful in the development of a growth mindset and a powerful way to support tangible targets for growth that are known and understood by both student and parent. As parents engage with their children, they often remark about the amount of specific and valuable information about their learning and development that the conference provides. The big smiles on the faces of the students and their parents say it all!

---

[2] The parent letter that clarifies expectations for parents can be found as Appendix G.

Student-involved conferencing has many benefits for students, parents, and teachers. Students hone their self-assessment abilities and develop their understanding and vocabulary about learning and assessment. They also learn, in a very powerful way, that they are responsible for their own learning.

Parents are able to see their children as learners and gain a much richer understanding of their children's growth and progress than is provided by report cards. Often, in fact, where student-involved conferencing is used, report cards play a very small part in the conference because the real information is in the shared work samples. Parents who do not speak the language used in the school benefit greatly from this approach because the student can conduct the conference in the parents' language.

> Student-involved conferencing has many benefits for students, parents, and teachers.

Think About This . . .

Student-led conferences:

- Encourage students to accept personal responsibility for their academic performance

- Help students recognize and take ownership for the things that interfered with their learning success

- Teach students the process of self-evaluation

- Develop students' oral communication skills and organizational skills

- Increase students' self-confidence

- Enhance communication between student and parents (Dyck, 2002, p. 39)

Teachers benefit from student-involved conferencing by improved communication with and among students, parents, and teachers, which develops a better understanding of their students' strengths and weaknesses and thus promotes dealing with them more effectively. Another major benefit for teachers (and schools) is that attendance by parents at student-involved conferences is almost always much better than at traditional parent interviews.

It is hard to think of any major problems with student-involved conferencing apart from logistical and time issues. It is obviously much easier to organize conferences for a self-contained Grade 2 class than for a Grade 8 class or a high school on a rotary timetable, but as indicated earlier, there are ways to adapt this approach for all grade levels. For example, universities have been using a version of student-involved conferencing (without parents) for centuries. They do this by having students attend lectures in large groups but then organizing students into small tutorial groups, where students meet with a leader (often a graduate student) to examine their understanding of the concepts and problems presented by the professor in the lecture.

One small problem with student-involved conferencing is that teachers lose some of the control they normally have with parent–teacher interviews. As with other aspects of communication, teachers should search to find a comfort zone in which they honor the principle (in this case, student involvement) to the extent that it is comfortable for them. Some teachers want to begin with the type of conference in which the students are just present, whereas others are happy to jump right into student-led conferencing. The important thing is that teachers involve students and, over time, move further to the right of the continuum (see Figure 10.8). At all times, parents should be offered the opportunity for a parent–teacher interview in place of or in addition to a student-involved conference.

PORTFOLIOS

Sharing of student work is an integral part of student-involved and student-led conferencing. Collections of student work can be organized into portfolios somewhat informally, or they can be highly organized, for example, by standards. Portfolios can be in hard copy, and we are now seeing increasing use of digital portfolios. Ian Landy, who has been a leader in the introduction of digital portfolios in British Columbia, provided a contribution in which he describes what he sees as the limitations of traditional report cards and the possibilities that are opened by the use of digital portfolios.

Educator Contribution

Ian Landy
Principal, North Shuswap Learning Community
British Columbia

The Benefits of Using E-Portfolios

One of the greatest challenges of using report cards is that they have traditionally been used to report out on how a student has succeeded based on achievement linked to a common task. This creates natural problems for students who have difficulty with written output and has often benefited students who could create nice-looking products. There are also great inconsistencies with terms of usage around weighting, averaging, missing work, and whether or not students should be able to redo work and how that should be factored in (which is why you are reading this book). The use of report cards has been debated since they were first implemented, which also is when the focus of learning became about what grade the student was going to see on the report.

Shifting to an e-portfolio, with a focus on descriptive feedback, allows the focus of learning to change. The focus is no longer about the mark that was received but on the feedback as to how the learning could be further improved. Consciously or unconsciously, those who are determining the curriculum delivery must ask themselves not what the learner should be graded on but on what the student (not the class) needs to learn. We need learners to seek the right answers to their questions, not worry about cramming for a memorization-focused test and focusing on the almighty grade, and ensure that they learned. This leads to a focus on learning standards being achieved rather than a set of tasks being completed.

Collating this information into a gradebook can be complex. It can help to have a running record of learning outcomes along the top with student names in rows (example from BC's curriculum) (see Figure 10.10).

FIGURE 10.10 Running Record of Learner Outcomes

ENGLISH LANGUAGE ARTS 7	BIG IDEA	CURRICULAR COMPETENCY	CONTENT
	Exploring and sharing multiple perspectives extends our thinking	Synthesize ideas from a variety of sources to build understanding	Metacognitive strategies
Student 1			
Student 2			

Where it becomes personalized is when we do not simply place a number or letter in the record (unless it connects to a rubric/learning standard where the definition of the number or letter is made explicit) but providing an exemplar, possibly including individual descriptive feedback, that can be referred back to. This is much easier when using an ongoing portfolio system so that examples of work linked to the standard can be improved upon throughout the learning term (see Figure 10.11).

This then leads to having a variety of learning artifacts that can be reviewed in order to see accomplishments and learnings that the student has made over time. Within the portfolio, there should be specific descriptive feedback that can be reviewed to see if the learner made progress based on the areas for growth identified by the teacher. The standards and learning outcomes do not have to change, but the way students show their ability to accomplish this can be very personalized.

The personalized feedback then becomes part of an ongoing feedback loop, where new information and learnings can be applied (or reapplied) to an artifact of learning. The focus then needs to turn toward how to provide the feedback in a meaningful manner. When starting out, it can be advantageous for both the teacher and the student to start simple by using "two stars and a wish," where you focus on two positives and one area to focus on improving. This can expand as both participants in the feedback loop become more comfortable with the process and establish what communication strategies work best for them.

(Continued)

(Continued)

FIGURE 10.11 Evidence of Learner Outcomes in a Portfolio System

ENGLISH LANGUAGE ARTS 7	BIG IDEA	CURRICULAR COMPETENCY	CONTENT
	Exploring and sharing multiple perspectives extends our thinking	Synthesize ideas from a variety of sources to build understanding	Metacognitive strategies
Student 1	Reading and watching a short story and video interpretation and imagining he or she was a minor character	E-portfolio example: speech to class comparing two versions	Student was working on seeing story from another character's perspective
Student 2	Reading two poems about the same topic	Exploring a video review of the poetry to get another point of view	E-portfolio share: student views compare/contrast to other reviewer

A summation of learning can also be provided to indicate if the level of work is within anticipated age/grade expectations; as an example, a project linked to a literature study could indicate what reading level the text is based on and what grade learning outcomes the strategies come from. When necessary, a grade can then be assigned based on a portfolio review of the learning represented based on specific subjects (Belanoff & Dickson, 1991). It does not need to factor in distractions, such as the amount of time it took, attendance, the amount of practice needed, or comparisons with how other students did on the same task. It allows differentiation to be shown authentically; whether students are gifted or have challenges, they are still being given descriptive feedback to improve their work based on what they have done and what they can do next.

If we are teaching differently, we must assess and communicate differently as well . . . and keep the focus on what has been learned and how that learning is best shared.

The varied methodologies of how to communicate student achievement are continuously debated. A recent shift in many reporting guidelines has been to de-emphasize the "reporting on achievement" and move toward "communicating student learning" (https:// curriculum.gov.bc.ca/sites/curriculum.gov.bc.ca/files/pdf/updates/educator_update_ student_progress_k-9.pdf). One of the most common interventions has been to focus on conferences with parents (either student-led or parent–teacher). Yet too often, the parents that the school wants to attend the conferences either can't or won't. Parents may also say they are more comfortable receiving traditional reports that are similar to what they received when they were in school. Sending a traditional report home may feel like a convenient way of connecting student achievement with families, but it is difficult for it to communicate how learning is happening within the classroom, and there is no guarantee that it will actually be read beyond looking at the summary letter grades and percentages.

The portfolio methodology continues to be an increasingly intriguing tool to replace the traditional report card that has many faults. A portfolio (electronic or hands-on) can enhance the necessary communication of how students are progressing in their learning.

This allows the focus to turn to the individual's accomplishments being compared to a learning outcome/objective rather than reporting on how she or he did on an activity. The learner and family can also observe the learning journey in a formative, ongoing way, rather than just reacting to a summation of scores.

As curriculum requirements continue to focus more on competencies, such as critical and creative thinking, problem solving, and communication, among others (depending on your jurisdiction), it becomes clear that it is not easy to "report" on these competencies with a number or grade. Instead, artifacts of learning can be included in an e-portfolio as a picture, video, audio, PDF, or even a note. There may be some shares of "moments of learning," but when an authentic assessment is being done, there should be the following:

a. A comment explaining what the learning objective was

b. Descriptive feedback about the student's accomplishment on a set of standards

c. A comment as to whether the work of the student is within an age/grade range or not

And when thinking about frequency, that can be aligned in a variety of ways. Some school districts in British Columbia have shared their "requirements with feedback" as a plan with an achievable number of posts of student work with meaningful descriptive feedback attached each year. The intention is to focus on the quality of the posts rather than the quantity. A "Portfolio Tracking Sheet" (see Figure 10.12) is one tool to help teachers preplan what and when posts about student learning in specific subject areas are to be communicated. The following are the *minimum* expectations for the number of posts provided in a portfolio over the course of the entire school year.

A focus on formative assessment through the e-portfolio necessitates the use of ongoing descriptive feedback loops, not a collection of numbers and percentages but meaningful feedback based on what the learner has accomplished at the time of assessment. This feedback can be done by writing or having conversations with the learners about what they have done and what they should be focusing on next. It works best when the feedback includes an area of strength, along with a focused area for further work. A score out of thirty does not communicate that a student is missing a key step in division, but comparing work with a set of standards can indicate where general and specific areas for growth exist.

At various times, it may be required (or requested) to provide a summation of learning, as shown in Figure 10.13. This can be provided by reviewing the portfolio and creating a written comment about their achievement at that point in time. There should be consistency in the language used (i.e., grade level or age level) to communicate how the student is generally doing in the subject area. If it is possible, common language (or numbers) between the performance standards and the subject summaries would be ideal!

Another option can be to have students provide their own self-assessment with the teacher's observations and comments connected to it. This can be a powerful part of the descriptive feedback loop, where teachers and students can confirm that they have the same view of what they have achieved and where their next focus should be. The focus is on the quality of student work over the quantity that has been accomplished. The accountability is that there are no surprises for anyone connected to the descriptive feedback because the portfolio has samples of the student work over time.

(Continued)

(Continued)

It cannot be said that portfolios are less work than report cards, but it is spread out throughout the term (throughout each week/day), instead of artificially created "due dates for learning." It is not about "bonus marks" or "doing more work for extra credit"; it is about the learning that has been done. It also enables better school–home communication. As one parent said after seeing her son play guitar, "He plays so much better at home," and the challenge was issued: record him at home, and we will add that to the archive to show what he is able to do because portfolios help support that learning happens at all hours and in multiple environments.

FIGURE 10.12 Portfolio Tracking Sheet

Portfolio Tracking Sheet	Student Name:
	Grade:
	Teacher:

Category	Post #	Details	Date completed
Language Arts Artifacts	1		
	2		
	3		
	4		
	5		
Mathematics Artifacts	1		
	2		
	3		
Physical and Health Education Artifacts	1		
	2		
Arts Artifacts	1		
	2		
Science Artifacts	1		
	2		
Social Studies Artifacts	1		
	2		
Other	1		
	2		
Summary of Learning	February Suggested		
	June Required		

SOURCE: Original design from School District 71 Comox Valley.

NOTES: This is a tool designed to HELP teachers keep track of the portfolio posts they do throughout the year that include descriptive feedback.

You are free to design your own tracking mechanism.

The posting of competencies is embedded in the categories listed above, and additional posts are not required.

FIGURE 10.13 Summary of Learning

SUBJECT	ACHIEVEMENT DATE: JUNE 2017
Language Arts	Exceeding Expectations
Math	Meeting Expectations
Science	Meeting Expectations
Social Studies	Meeting Expectations
Physical Education	Meeting Expectations
Fine Arts	Meeting Expectations
Health and Career Education	Meeting Expectations
Work Habits, Attitude, and Effort	Meeting Expectations

General Comments

STUDENT has had a great year. She has developed many great friendships in class and at the school. She struggles to stay focused and on task because of her social nature. I think she is capable of more creative thinking than she puts in.

STUDENT has made significant improvements with spelling, reading, and writing this year. She is above grade level in reading accuracy and comprehension. She should focus on developing reading fluency over the summer by choosing some good-fit books to try to build stamina with reading for extended periods of time. She can also keep a journal and write about what she has done daily by focusing on making simple and complex sentences that are grammatically correct.

STUDENT has had a good year in math. She always does well on all of her assessments and projects that indicate her strong number sense and her ability to apply math concepts to problem solving. She can continue to build fluency in addition, subtraction, multiplication, and division by practicing with drills and playing card games and dice games.

I wish STUDENT much success in Grade 5 next year. Keep staying on task. Have a great summer!

SUMMARY

Schools and teachers have a responsibility to communicate effectively with parents and others who are interested in the achievement and progress of students. Traditionally, report cards with letter or percentage grades and brief comments have been the main vehicles for communication. This has led to a cult-like status for grades, but grades are only part of the communication system. In addition to these symbols (or where acceptable, in place of these symbols), teachers can provide parents with real information by using expanded-format reporting, informal communications, and student-involved conferencing.

School districts, schools, and teachers must plan their communication system carefully and train students, parents, and teachers to participate effectively in the system. Prime considerations in developing such systems are effective and clear communication, clear purpose(s), and reasonable workloads for teachers. This is not a situation where more is always better. Careful choices need to be made that are within the comfort zone of both teachers and the community and that move everyone involved toward more effective communication. Great strides have been made in this area by elementary schools; it is now time that expanded-format reporting and student-involved conferencing become a regular part of middle and high school communication systems.

The checklist provided in Figure 10.14 is intended to help schools/districts check where they are and where they want to go as they revise their communication system. Remember this: The weaker the rest of the communication system, the more of a burden that grades and reports cards carry; the stronger the rest of the communication system, the less of a burden grades and report cards carry.

FIGURE 10.14 Communication System Checklist

Communication System			
• Informal →	__ Conversations		
	__ Notes/postcards		
	__ Phone calls		
	__ E-mail and texts		
• Interim reports			
• Report cards			
• Parent portals			
• Parent–teacher interviews			
• Student involvement →	__ Present		
	__ Participate		
	__ Lead		
• Portfolios—hard copy or digital			

General Considerations (for Stakeholder Discussions)			
• Fair	• Credible		
• Honest	• Feasible		
• Useful	• User friendly		

Report Card			
Purpose			
• Clearly established			
• Clearly stated			
Amount/Type of Information			
• Multiple grades	• Achievement	• Learning skills	• Other
• Subject grades	__ One per subject		
• Standards grades	__ Several per subject by strands or benchmarks		
• Comments			
• Attendance and tardies			
• Clarity of layout			
Learning/Skills/Behaviors			
• Appropriate	• Number		
• Scale	• Criteria/descriptors		

Comments	
• Focus	
• Teacher generated	
• Computer "bank"	
Use of Technology	

THE FINAL WORDS

Kent Brewer provides a thoughtful analysis of the use in technology in education, especially in communicating student learning. Reflecting on this contribution is an effective way to synthesize your thoughts on the ideas about communicating student learning in this chapter.

Educator Contribution

Kent Brewer
Educational Technology Leader, River East School Division
Winnipeg, Manitoba

Issues in the Use of Technology for Communicating Student Achievement

I would argue that with the influence and integration of technology in today's educational environments, we have fostered an excitement around learning that speaks to the "unfinished line." Goals are an important aspect of all facets of education, including perspectives from learners, educators, and institutions. If learning is truly meant to be lifelong, then the power behind such a statement can be derived from the flexibility toward continually reaching and resetting new goals. Society, in 2017, is fully immersed in a world of self-driving vehicles, drone-delivered goods, virtual reality, augmented reality, artificial intelligence, brainwave-controlled robots, and sky-cabs via unmanned flying vehicles. These types of once futuristic ideas are now becoming commonplace in a world that our children are being educated in. As teachers, we need to embrace the fact that this should be and is, in fact, one of the most exciting, engaging times to be learning alongside our students. That's right, *alongside* is a bold but necessary shift away from teacher delivered and centers on students. Some might say that this shift has been brought about, in part, by the influence of technology and the need to no longer concentrate on content but the process by which students acquire and use new knowledge. As newly designed curriculums reinforce this student-centered focus, educators are now tasked with developing new and innovative ways with regard to assessment as, for, and of learning. Sound assessment practice should be flexible enough to support the "unfinished line" of learning within the ever-changing and evolving landscape of education.

The Jury's Still Out!

The research would suggest that the integration of technology in education hasn't lived up to the amount of capital that provinces, states, and countries have invested. A clear argument against this would include the fact that we are using outdated measurement to assess the impact on what learning should look like when supported through such advanced tool integration. Like no other resource/tool has done in the past, technology is now connecting education. Although there have been huge EdTech investments since the early to mid-1990s, educational systems have always been playing catch-up with society's need to push the boundaries of technological innovation. In any case, educators are constantly closing the tech gap and developing new ways to support and enhance learning through technology. One such way is connecting through collaborative digital

(*Continued*)

(*Continued*)

environments. Microsoft, Google, and Apple all have developed such environments that lend themselves to a number of aspects of assessment. Technology has broken the barrier of time and physical space when it comes to learning and assessment as such. One example includes educators that are no longer isolated and have the power to work together and develop assessment practice that is consistent not only within schools but divisions, districts, and even states and provinces. Another example would include students having the ability to complete work in a digital space and hence having it assessed within the same area. Additionally, teachers would have the ability to digitally insert handwritten, textual, audio, and/or video feedback; provide grading; or exhume data from either a diagnosis, formative, or summative nature. These digital collaborative spaces also lend themselves to the inclusion of students when developing clear targets in level- or age-appropriate language that can be easily shared with administrators or parents/guardians. These types of activities are no longer restricted internally to one particular class, as technology has afforded us the avenue to create and share and a much grander scale inclusive of most other educational institutions that have Internet connectivity. Through any of these digitally supported learning processes, the assessment aspects and evidence of achievement can be communicated, curated, and made available without the traditional barrier of time and/or physical space. Digital platforms that support the curation of learning evidence allow students to benefit from reflection on the journey traveled while providing a visual assessment of the learning path that invested teachers/educators can utilize when planning next steps with regard to curricular outcomes. If anything, technology integration has the potential to provide a new level of transparency in assessment. It provides easy access to things such as benchmarks, targets, or even standardized rubrics (both internally or externally developed) while supporting through a documenting and/or sharing perspective(s).

Traditional Assessment Methods in a Digital World?

Personal communication, performance assessment, and paper-and-pencil testing can all exist in tech-rich classrooms and schools. In fact, retooling these assessments may increase engagement in learning. Observation, conversation, product, performance, and process can all be created, reflected upon, developed, communicated, curated, and shared through any number of technology options. As teachers utilize EdTech as part of a balanced assessment process, they are actively incorporating a part of students' daily lives within their learning. Customary paper-and-pencil testing is also an area in which technology has been highly invested from both web- and app-based perspectives. Formatively, assessments can be quickly developed and distributed through methods such as apps, QR codes, or, in some cases, augmented reality, allowing teachers a quick insight into next steps. Until recently, summative assessments were seen as "fluffy" at best in a digital space. However, some of the latest developments have allowed students to participate in such assessments, restricting access to resources that may sway actual results.

What's next? Well, we are already transporting ourselves to virtual worlds that may allow assessments to take place with any number of participants, including subject matter experts, parents, peers, administrators, teachers, and students, all in the same learning space, while never really leaving the comfort of the home base.

What do you think?

CHAPTER 11

Implementing Changes in Grading and Reporting

It ain't easy anymore
No, it ain't easy, that's for sure

—Blake Shelton song

None of this is easy, or guaranteed.
It is system change, it is messy,
it is flawed and vulnerable.
But it is worth the effort, if you can get it right.

—Gerry Varty, Facebook post, April 5, 2017

Traditional grading and reporting has been the way it was for most adults, especially for those who were successful in the traditional system (as most teachers were), so suggesting that there is a need to change a familiar system that has high stakes for many students and parents "ain't easy." In fact, it is usually extremely difficult, and it needs informed and capable leadership and a clear plan for how to get to the desired system—that is, standards-based grading (and reporting). There are examples of schools/districts that have been unsuccessful and either abandoned or drastically altered what they planned to do because of opposition from parents, teachers, and students, but fortunately, there are also many schools/districts that have been successful at least, at the elementary level, and sometimes at the middle school level. Although, as has been shown in examples in earlier chapters, there are schools/districts that are successful at the high school level, there are far too many that haven't even tried or that gave up too easily at the first sign of resistance.

To show the way, this chapter includes eight contributions from educators who have led or who are right in the middle of leading successful change in grading and reporting or who are experts on the change process, so you need to get reading.

As you read, try to identify commonalities in these change scenarios so that you can see what are the most important things to do—and not do. I have italicized what I see as the keys to effective implementation.

Educator Contribution

Lori Jeschke
Director of Education
Prairie Spirit School Division
Saskatchewan, Canada

Leading Change

Over the past nine years, I have had the privilege of being a part of the leadership team in Prairie Spirit School Division, focusing on assessment and learning. We were initially tasked with the building of *systemic beliefs and commitments* in the area of assessment and evaluation, with longer-term goals of providing a *supporting document* that would get at the research and the practice associated with those beliefs and commitments and, finally, the development and implementation of a *new report card* that would align how we gather evidence of learning and how we report it. This quote from Davies, Herbst, and Reynolds (2012) captures the essence of our journey: "Leading change requires *courage*. We must consciously and deliberately work through it with grace, honesty, and humor. We do that together with our colleagues, as a team. As leaders, we must acknowledge that we will make mistakes. We must actively seek solutions, while modeling how assessment for learning supports and guides our daily work."

A *team* of administrators, classroom teachers, a counselor, a special ed teacher, coordinators, and superintendents[1] was formed to lead the work within the division. One of our first steps in this journey was to gather voice from all of the stakeholders in our division: students, teachers, educational associates, parents, board members, and administrators. We created a document that captured what we believed, as well as four commitments we held. The commitments are to collaboration, communication, clarity, and consideration. This document became foundational to the work ahead of us. The committee worked with facilitators and leading assessment experts, such as Ken O'Connor, Damian Cooper, Anne Davies, and Sandra Herbst. We *looked at research and practice* and created a document called "Quality Assessment Practices," mainly based on the work of Ken O'Connor. This document was shared with our administrators, and schools were given a *"chewing" year* to get to know it better before we began implementing the practices into our classrooms.

One of the biggest shifts we faced was that of changing the focus in practice from earning to learning. This became a common theme for us in conversations with all of our stakeholders, including students, parents, and teachers. "Percentage grades give the community (students, parents, and community members) the wrong message of what school's all about, that it's the accumulation of points, when we should be doing everything to make clear that school is about learning" (Ken O'Connor, personal communication, 2014). *Learning for our students and for our adults became the focus of all we did.*

---

[1] In Canada, the chief educational administrator for a school district usually has the title of "director," with the second level identified as "superintendent(s)."

The implementation of a new report card was our next step. We looked at research and at samples from across Canada, consulted, and built drafts. The work was messy and often filled with emotion. We were reminded again and again that there is no perfect report card. In the process, we looked for a way in which we could sit side by side with our adults as they sat side by side with their students in the pursuit of learning. We wanted to embody the essence of the word *assess*—to sit side by side. Davies, Herbst, and Reynolds (2012) remind us that

> it seems no matter how much we know or think we know, every initiative that involves learning and change (and they all do) will at some point cause us to flounder or stop in our tracks . . . but . . . because children and their learning are at stake, we take the time and make the effort to reflect on the work and keep going!

As a division, we created documents that framed our practice. We were excited to work and learn alongside our Board of Trustees, our administrators, our teachers, our students, and our parents. We sought to communicate our work and to share our key messages. We worked hard to build a common understanding. We attended staff meetings, sat with student and parent focus groups, held parent forums with panels and Q&As, and gathered feedback through surveys and exit slips. We invited our administrators to *self-assess* their leadership stance as they led the work in their buildings. We knew that in order to learn and grow together, we needed to "find ways to collect ongoing information and use frequent feedback loops. Leadership literature has long promoted feedback loops as being incredibly important to system change and learning" (Herbst, 2015).

We realized we were asking our teachers to open up their practices and their gradebooks. We were mindful of the importance of trust and respect. As an assessment team, we sat beside our teachers in their schools to support and to model with and for them. We could not ask them to make changes in how they were assessing and gathering evidence if we were not willing to do the same. A favorite quote of mine is from McGuey (2007): "You cannot NOT model." If we were asking our students to create portfolios with evidence of their learning, and our administrators were asking our teachers to create portfolios of evidence of their learning, then I too needed to have a portfolio with evidence of my learning. As philosopher and physician Albert Schweitzer has been quoted saying, "Example is not the main thing in influencing others, it is the only thing." I needed to ask myself questions like, *As a leader of adult learning, what do I need to pay attention to in myself?*

We continue to *learn and grow* in our work as learning leaders. We focus on the qualities of assessment for learning: identifying the learning destination, describing what quality looks like, self-assessment, feedback and goal setting, collecting and selecting evidence, and determining next steps. We know that as leaders, we are always learning. Fullan would endorse learning as our moral responsibility. As leaders, change is always a part of our work. "Meaningful change—change we feel compelled to implement because of the empirically sound research and the potential benefits to our students—is our professional responsibility" (Schimmer, 2012).

Michael Lees
Director
International School of Havana

Changing Toward Standards-Based Reporting at the International School of Havana

In our efforts to move our school away from a traditional letter-based grading system, ISH has rolled out its first iteration of a standards-based reporting system that focuses on four learning competencies and four learning behaviors.

Such a move has not been without its *challenges*, as it has fundamentally questioned some fixed mindsets about grading among students, teachers, and parents. Further, as an IGCSE and IB Diploma Programme school, the decision was made for our reports in secondary to be a hybrid presentation of the standards-based competencies and behaviors, as well as the required letter and number grades of both programs. To some degree, this has mitigated the *inherent skepticism and pushback* in such a change initiative. Our goal is to shift the community's fixation on letter and number grades as the end in itself to more of a *focus on deep learning and continual improvement as the vision for the future.*

Upon reflection of the development and rollout of our new approach, a number of areas are worthy of consideration. First, in spite of our campaign to educate all stakeholders of the rationale and need for change, we still have far to go. For example, there still appears to be a *lack of common understanding* among teachers as to the timing of proficiency we expect as a school. Although we thought we were explicit in our aim to assess proficiency using expected levels at the end of each semester, what resulted was a range of interpretations, including a single end-of-year level of proficiency and, in one case, one for the end of middle school! Are we reporting on what students should know, understand, and be able to do by the end of the first semester, or are we reporting out on their progress toward the expectations of meeting the standards by the end of the year? This was one major gap that had not been resolved in spite of the *leadership team's perception* that everyone was "on board."

Another takeaway was the timing and participation of the change effort. Although the seeds of this change were planted in the spring of 2016, with our first report taking place approximately eight months later, based on the depth of understanding of where stakeholders currently are, the leadership team has concluded that *a more robust and longer-term development process*, which included considerably more voices in the development process, might have ensured less angst at this stage of our journey. Clearly, our timeline was far too ambitious, as we were essentially building the plane as we were flying it.

One of the persistent areas of feedback from both parents and students has been the degree to which our new reporting system will serve to de-motivate and disadvantage our high-performing students and will tend toward a degradation of rigor in our school. While these outcomes are certainly not the intention and do need to be carefully considered as we move forward, they are worthy of consideration, particularly when we hear some of these students continue to acknowledge that they are motivated fundamentally on high grades, as opposed to focusing first and foremost on learning. To them and many of their parents, they see high grades as the only path to quality higher education institutions.

Based on the premise that one's perception is one's reality, we have recognized that the *de-motivation factor* is a very real danger. It reminds us that maintaining highly rigorous programs that challenge students with higher-level thinking tasks and that employ authentic and relevant assessments is going to be critical to our success. Standards-based assessment and reporting does not mean dumbing down the curriculum, but we need to ensure that we remain vigilant in continually holding learners to high standards. To foster that *paradigm shift*, many students and parents need help to understand that traditional grading may be one of the factors that gets them into college while a well-designed standards-based assessment and reporting system coupled with a highly rigorous program prepares them to be successful in college and beyond. That's because it is more conducive to developing students as self-directed learners. And isn't that the real goal?

Although we have *much more to do* to support our students, parents, and teachers in shifting their perspectives of grading and reporting, we are confident that we have taken *solid steps* in the right direction in our vision to refocus our *attention on learning* as the prime motivator in our school. That being said, we'll be the first to admit that we still have a *long way to go* to change that culture.

Educator Contribution

Becca Lindahl, EdD
Professional Learning and Leadership Consultant
Heartland AEA 11, Johnston, Iowa

How Do We Even Start All of This?

Some schools and districts, in their beginning stages of standards-based grading, study and then figure out how to implement SBG practices with a model or a framework in mind. But many more do not. I have worked with schools and districts in my consultative/coaching support role, have worked with districts and schools in states outside my own, have listened to participants at conferences, and have read books on standards-based grading. Lots of educators understand the principles, but they often have a big question or two that they cannot get their heads around easily: How do we even start all this? How long does implementation last? Many educators read good books on this subject; find the standards-based grading guidelines and principles kind of fascinating, logical, and sensible; and strive to implement those right away. They don't necessarily plan to do anything beyond implementing the guiding principles because this is how their initiatives and professional development have gone in the past. I'd offer that for this particular educational change of standards-based grading, it is imperative to, yes, do the reading and study, but then, *plan* to create goals and build a framework or model in order to implement well.

First, let's think big picture through key components of large-scale implementation, then get some details into a framework, with a timeline embedded. You'll read through the key components a little further down. For just a moment, let's think solely of the key component of *vision*. Remember: hold off on a timeline, and hold off on simply implementing the SBG guidelines and principles. Think in terms of key components. Alright . . . *vision before timeline*.

(Continued)

(Continued)

It's critical to establish *vision and support* for the vision before establishing a timeline. Many districts and schools make a misstep when they try to outline the next three years and then fill in those three years with what they think fits in the timeline. Many schools are not used to having the implementation of a new initiative last beyond a couple years, maybe three at most. I'd offer that for a break from the past, as standards-based learning and grading is, it is important to articulate a vision of the work—what classrooms will look like and sound like when the work is in full implementation—and other components and then figure out how progression of work will happen over time. *Let the work drive the timeline*, not vice versa.

The framework outlined and described further on reflects how the "big-picture" key components play out in a school year's time, year after year. For example, when the *vision* of changing over to a standards-based learning system (including grading and reporting) is articulated for a district, it is articulated not only by top leadership but then by other key people as well, such as building leaders, teacher leaders, and perhaps even student and parent leaders. Maybe there's a representative *task force* gathered from the beginning of the vision. Over time, this task force, which helped articulate and relay the vision, still has a role to play. Perhaps some adjustments need to be made to the vision. Perhaps some work they did at the very beginning, concerning the vision, needs to be reviewed and updated over time.

As you read through the key components, you see the definitions, players, and actions. You then read through the framework—which is the outline of the implementation of standards-based learning and grading—and you will see the key components explained in detail through the years of implementation. Let's get started.

Key Components

Vision: clarity of vision means a model that is scalable and easily communicated; contains guiding practices; work of task force; needs to be done prior to implementation and stakeholder communication; contains clear outcomes for transition and case for change

Leadership: superintendent and director of teaching and learning; coalition of the willing; specifically identified teachers with social influence

Curriculum and Assessment: most significant piece of the puzzle; overhaul of course organization (topics, scales, and assessment creation and alignment); redefine role of instructional materials

Stakeholder Communication: critical but we must have clarity of vision before we communicate; clarity builds confidence; common literature in multiple languages; teacher and student testimonials

Professional Development: training structured around guiding practices; principals/school leaders first; methods include face to face, online, and job embedded

Monitoring and Program Evaluation: metrics need to be identified during the planning for implementation and shared with stakeholders

Reporting Student Learning: SIS (student information system) compatibility; custom report card; separating behavior from academics

FRAMEWORK: IMPLEMENTATION OUTLINE

KEY COMPONENTS	2012–2013 Preparing to Implement	2013–2014 Middle School Teacher Leaders	2014–2015 All Middle Schools + Ninth-Grade Courses	2015–2016 Tenth-Grade Courses + Fourth and Fifth Grades (can include elementary extended core/specials such as art, music, PE, and world languages)	2016–2017 Eleventh-Grade Courses + Grades K–1 and 2–3	2017–2018 Twelfth-Grade Courses All Elementary
VISION	• Task force made up of teachers, administrator, ELL, SPED, GT, curriculum, assessment • Adopted six guiding practices and outlined classroom application in a common teacher handbook • Addressed the "how" in the teacher handbook	• Task force updates handbook based on teacher feedback throughout implementation	• Task force updates handbook based on teacher feedback throughout implementation	• Task force updates handbook based on teacher feedback throughout implementation	• Task force updates handbook based on teacher feedback throughout implementation	• Task force updates handbook based on teacher feedback throughout implementation
LEADERSHIP	• Focus on mindset and guiding practices (developed by task force) • Prepare for stakeholder communication • Identification of the willing teachers (socially influential)	• Administrators attend training with teachers • Support and monitor implementation • Conduct parent meetings • Respond to community concerns and keep school board updated (see monitoring) • Allow first implementers to share their learning with school leadership team • Begin leading school-based PD (professional development) to prepare for next year • High school—focus on mindset	• Lead teachers (five) and administrators facilitate training with teachers in middle schools • Support and monitor implementation • Conduct parent meetings • Respond to community concerns • Teaching & Learning Department leads first cohort of ninth-grade teachers through SRG training • Continuous cycle of feedback and revision	• Ongoing support of implementation • Conduct parent meetings • Respond to community concerns • Continuous cycle of feedback and revision	• Ongoing support of implementation • Conduct parent meetings • Respond to community concerns • Continuous cycle of feedback and revision	• Ongoing support of implementation • Conduct parent meetings • Respond to community concerns • Continuous cycle of feedback and revision

(Continued)

FRAMEWORK: IMPLEMENTATION OUTLINE

KEY COMPONENTS	2012–2013 Preparing to Implement	2013–2014 Middle School Teacher Leaders	2014–2015 All Middle Schools + Ninth-Grade Courses	2015–2016 Tenth-Grade Courses + Fourth and Fifth Grades (can include elementary extended core/specials such as art, music, PE, and world languages)	2016–2017 Eleventh-Grade Courses + Grades K–1 and 2–3	2017–2018 Twelfth-Grade Courses All Elementary
CURRICULUM AND ASSESSMENT	• Identify teams of teacher leaders to work on curriculum revision (middle school courses) • Divide courses into reporting topics (on report card) • Develop common four-point proficiency scales for each topic • Develop common formative assessments for each scale	• Identify which courses will convert each year and develop timeline (K–12) • Identify teams of teacher leaders to work on curriculum revision for identified courses • Divide courses into reporting topics (on report card) • Develop common four-level scales for each topic • Develop common formative assessments for each scale	• Identify which courses will convert each year and develop timeline (K–12) • Identify teams of teacher leaders to work on curriculum revision for identified courses • Divide courses into reporting topics (on report card) • Develop common four-level scales for each topic • Develop common formative assessments for each scale • Revise scales for previous years' courses based on teacher feedback and implementation	• Identify which courses will convert each year and develop timeline (K–12) • Develop elementary instructional materials usage guidance (tight on standards, loose on materials) • Identify teams of teacher leaders to work on curriculum revision for identified courses • Divide courses into reporting topics (on report card) • Develop common four-level scales for each topic • Develop common formative assessments for each scale • Revise scales for previous years' courses based on teacher feedback and implementation	• Identify which courses will convert each year and develop timeline (K–12) • Identify teams of teacher leaders to work on curriculum revision for identified courses • Divide courses into reporting topics (on report card) • Develop common four-level scales for each topic • Develop common formative assessments for each scale • Revise scales for previous years' courses based on teacher feedback and implementation	• Identify which courses will convert each year and develop timeline (K–12) • Identify teams of teacher leaders to work on curriculum revision for identified courses • Divide courses into reporting topics (on report card) • Develop common four-level scales for each topic • Develop common formative assessments for each scale • Revise scales for previous years' courses based on teacher feedback and implementation

STAKEHOLDER COMMUNICATION					
• Communication is internal only while visioning is happening (task force, school leaders) • Clearly articulated implementation plan • Create case for change: grade correlation studies, number of grading scales in SIS, research on best practices, equity, failure rates • Develop website to house all information for teachers and stakeholders	• Work with school board to communicate case for change, clear vision, and implementation plan • Develop district-wide written communication for parents in multiple languages • Create common PowerPoints for parent meetings at schools • Develop student orientation videos to ensure common message • Parent portal guidance	• Each school leads parent meetings using district-created literature and resources • Parent surveys • One-on-one parent meetings as needed • Parent portal guidance • Provide updates to school board • Update website with teacher and student testimonials	• Each school leads parent meetings using district-created literature and resources • Parent surveys • One-on-one parent meetings as needed • Parent portal guidance • Elementary begins parent communication (spring) for fall launch • Provide updates to school board • Update website with teacher and student testimonials	• School-based communication • Provide updates to school board	• School-based communication • Provide updates to school board

PROFESSIONAL DEVELOPMENT					
• PD for task force = book studies + external experts	• Monthly PD and support for middle school teacher leaders • PD based on guiding practices and cognitive complexity + Infinite Campus	• Monthly PD and support for high school teachers • PD based on guiding practices and cognitive complexity + Infinite Campus • School-based PLCs (collaborative teams) • District PLCs	• Summer and monthly PD and support for high school and Grades 4/5 teachers • PD based on guiding practices and cognitive complexity + Infinite Campus • School-based PLCs • District PLCs • Office of Schools (OOS) directors support and coach principals	• Summer and monthly PD and support for high schools and Grades 2/3, K/1 teachers • PD based on guiding practices and cognitive complexity + Infinite Campus • School-based PLCs • District PLCs • Office of Schools directors support and coach principals	• Summer and monthly PD and support for high school teachers • PD based on guiding practices and cognitive complexity + Infinite Campus • School-based PLCs • District PLCs • Office of Schools directors support and coach principals

MONITORING AND PROGRAM EVALUATION					
• Establish baseline: grade correlation, failure rates, teacher beliefs inventory • Articulate action plan	• Report to stakeholders: • teacher perceptions, • student perceptions, • grade correlation, • failure rates • Monitor action plan and make adjustments	• Report to stakeholders: • teacher perceptions, • student perceptions, • grade correlation, • failure rates • Monitor action plan and make adjustments	• Report to stakeholders: • teacher perceptions, • student perceptions, • grade correlation, • failure rates • Monitor action plan and make adjustments	• Report to stakeholders: • teacher perceptions, • student perceptions, • grade correlation, • failure rates • Monitor action plan and make adjustments	• Report to stakeholders: • teacher perceptions, • student perceptions, • grade correlation, • failure rates • Monitor action plan and make adjustments

(Continued)

FRAMEWORK: IMPLEMENTATION OUTLINE

KEY COMPONENTS / REPORTING STUDENT LEARNING	2012–2013 Preparing to Implement	2013–2014 Middle School Teacher Leaders	2014–2015 All Middle Schools + Ninth-Grade Courses	2015–2016 Tenth-Grade Courses + Fourth and Fifth Grades (can include elementary extended core/specials such as art, music, PE, and world languages)	2016–2017 Eleventh-Grade Courses + Grades K–1 and 2–3	2017–2018 Twelfth-Grade Courses All Elementary
KEY COMPONENTS	• SIS (Infinite Campus) programming and SRG report card design (most significant amount of time) • Clean up course numbers so they are consistent from school to school • Curriculum/technology teams create custom gradebooks to be pushed out by course number	• Clean up course numbers so they are consistent from school to school • Curriculum/technology teams create custom gradebooks to be pushed out by course number • Begin teacher training on Infinite Campus • Troubleshooting based on frequent feedback • Onsite support and system for reporting issues to technology team	• Clean up course numbers so they are consistent from school to school • Curriculum/technology teams create custom gradebooks to be pushed out by course number	• Clean up course numbers so they are consistent from school to school • Curriculum/technology teams create custom grade books to be pushed out by course number	• Clean up course numbers so they are consistent from school to school • Curriculum/technology teams create custom gradebooks to be pushed out by course number	• Curriculum/technology teams create custom gradebooks to be pushed out by course number
REPORTING STUDENT LEARNING		• Two report cards: traditional and standards based • Parent Portal training and support	• Standards-based report card for middle school • 2 report cards for high school: traditional and standards-based (some SRG courses and some non-SRG)	• 2 report cards for high school: traditional and standards-based (some SRG courses and some non-SRG courses) • Teacher training on Infinite Campus • Parent Portal training and support	• Two report cards for high school: traditional and standards based (some SRG courses and some non-SRG courses) • Teacher training on Infinite Campus • Grades 4/5 report card converts to standards based	• One standards-based report card for high school • K–3 report cards convert to standards based • Teacher training on Infinite Campus • Parent Portal training and support

SOURCE: Adapted from Des Moines (Iowa) Public Schools Standards-Referenced Grading System, with permission, 2016.

Educator Contribution

Michelle Kuhns, *Director of Learning*
Dr. Michelle Remington, *Associate Superintendent*
American School of Dubai

Leadership Dispositions and Considerations in Moving to a Standards-Based System

1. Allow stakeholders to name their *hopes and fears*.

2. Make *learning the focus* of every conversation.

3. Remember that teachers care deeply about their students.

4. *Listen*, listen, listen!

5. Be transparent, and *engage* as many teachers as possible throughout the process.

6. Be comfortable with ambiguity and be a learning leader.

Implementing Grading and Reporting Change in a High School

When implementing a grading and reporting change, you need to understand the *why* first and foremost. At the American School of Dubai, our *why* was because we were hoping to improve the feedback that our students received. We wanted to offer clarity about strengths, opportunities to grow, and next steps in learning. We had a faculty that was uncomfortable with the degree to which students' dispositions or learning habits were affecting their academic marks, and there was a sincere desire to separate these behaviors from grades. We wanted to develop a focus on learning, rather than on points or grades. We also saw that our assessment practices needed to be improved and refined. Students weren't always being pushed to think critically and independently, and we trusted that a focus on planning and assessing proficiency toward the standards would improve our teaching and learning cycle.

With the energy of our teaching faculty focused on separating behaviors from academic grades, we started leading more comprehensive discussions framed with the latest research on standards-based grading. First, we established our *purpose* of reporting:

> The purpose of this report is to communicate to parents and students specific and useful information about students' level of proficiency in meeting learning goals, development of learning habits and identified areas of strength as well as areas for growth.

Once we were able to develop our statement, it was easy to identify what the purposes for reporting were NOT. They were not to punish, reward, or motivate students but to share an update on their most recent learning.

(Continued)

(Continued)

At any school, once the purpose of the reporting process is clear, the next steps become easier to navigate. We began with identifying which behaviors our teachers were currently incorporating into academic grades so that we could honor their importance and look for ways to report this information without confusing it with the subject grade.

Leading a high school faculty we knew that some discussions would be more contentious than others. It was important to go for the *early wins* and to identify the early adopters. It was important to delay the "hot topics," so we allowed those topics to simmer in a "parking lot" while we addressed others. The more *teachers' understanding* grew for how standards-based grading and reporting could work, the easier it was for them to find answers to the more contentious questions.

In addition to using Ken O'Connor's books, we *read articles* before each faculty meeting, including "The Case Against Zeros" by Douglas Reeves, and we watched videos on grading practices by Rick Wormeli. We used these as a basis for our *discussions*. Teachers were encouraged to share their *hopes and fears* and to debate the merits of the claims made in the research. Often teachers wanted to see the theory in practice; therefore, teachers were encouraged to be risk-takers and to do some action research in their classes. For example, the math department stopped grading homework and stopped reducing grades for late work. The English department realigned their gradebook to grade for skills (reading, writing, speaking/listening, and language) and moved away from the traditional grade book of tests, quizzes, homework, and participation. These teachers were then able to *share their success stories, as well as challenges*, which helped lead to the next phase of implementation.

There were many facets to the implementation that had to be managed by multiple people simultaneously. We worked hard to ensure transparency, including the full faculty for input whenever appropriate and using smaller groups to draft and troubleshoot. We had a *focus group* take faculty input and define the levels of academic proficiency. Department chairs took on the task of developing a rubric to evaluate the learning habits that were identified in the process of separating behaviors from grades. We utilized Guskey and Bailey's (2009) *Developing Standards-Based Report Cards* to provide guidance with word choice and examples. Our technology team members were developing the new report card template and were attending additional training on our online grading and reporting program in order to transition to a standards-based interface with our online system. This multidimensional approach served to build understanding and capacity across the school.

We have issued standards-based report cards for nearly four years at this point, and we *continue to work to improve* our assessment practices. Students are able to track and speak about their learning in a much different manner than they were able to four years ago. We have seen improvement in the teaching and assessment of critical-thinking skills, as this is what is necessary to achieve the highest proficiency level. Students are able to reassess when necessary and continue to make progress toward the standards. Though we still have some refining to do, the steps that we have taken to transition to standards-based grading and reporting have resulted in significant improvement in our teaching and learning cycle. Students understand their role in assessment better than before, teachers are better assessors, and grades have more meaning.

Educator Contribution

Derek Oldfield
Assistant Principal
Wirt County High School, West Virginia

Providing Learning Experiences for Teachers

When I kicked off this journey with my staff at Wirt County High School in West Virginia, I knew I had to start by exposing the fallacies of our current grading practices. My *goal* was to improve the way we measured and communicated learning. Though we started by reflecting on the roles of formative and summative assessment, ultimately, I knew that I was choreographing experiences for my staff to reflect on how they were currently grading. Grading is so entrenched in many schools that *how* or *why* is rarely ever questioned.

As I designed *learning experiences* for my staff, I did so utilizing a backwards design model. The end target was for my staff to design learning experiences for their students using the same template I used throughout this process. In order to reach their target, the staff would have to begin thinking about learning as a target or destination derived from a standard. Everyone in education takes kids from Point A to Point B, but the paths we take and the instruments used to measure and communicate that journey are often flawed. It was my intention to unify the instruments and the design. You can access my backwards design plan I used with my staff at http://tinyurl.com/jxbq641.

We put in some work around learning targets. I had to bathe my staff with opportunities to learn and *reflect* on their own practice in nonevaluative ways. Each learning experience included a formative piece that informed me about which steps to take next. For example, I utilized an archive from a recent #sblchat on Twitter as a means for my staff to hear from educators across the country going through the same journey. They posted a 3-2-1 reflection to Padlet after they took some time to read through the archive in small groups. My staff connected, through video chat, with students from Highland Local Schools in Ohio to hear their perspective on classes operating under standards-based principles. At this point, we've taken no formal action to initiate change in policies or language that appears in handbooks. We aren't there yet. What we've done well is we've chipped away at century-old ways of thinking about measuring and communicating learning. My teachers are beginning to see the importance of ultraclear and visible learning targets derived from content standards.

Educator Contribution

Garnet Hillman
Instructional Coach
Caruso Middle School, Deerfield, Illinois

Standards-Based Grading Implementation

In my personal experience as both a classroom teacher and an instructional coach, I have seen two very different sides of the implementation of standards-based grading. In the classroom, my shift from traditional grading to standards based was made in isolation with

(Continued)

(*Continued*)

only one other teacher at the high school level. As an instructional coach, the change was scaled district-wide, from the elementary schools to the middle level. This change can be successful either way, but the processes vary. My experiences in working with the shift in grading practices span from kindergarten through high school and from small to large scale. This has given me a broad view of how standards-based grading practices can be implemented.

I taught in a large high school with approximately 3,800 students in total. As a district, we were not ready to discuss grading practices with the entire staff, but myself and one other teacher were given the go ahead to shift to standards-based grading. The change in practice was sparked by a feeling of misalignment between our *learning-centered* classroom environments and our assessment and grading practices. It was a process of *researching*, learning, and, in the end, making some decisions about how this could work at the high school level and within a traditional reporting system. My colleague and I made the decisions, and as we implemented standards-based practices, changes and tweaks could be easily made. With only two of us, it was easy to meet frequently and *reflect* on the process. We were in control of the implementation, and reaching consensus between two is much easier than working within a larger group. We determined everything from our *purpose* for grading to standards, scales to assessment practices, and rubrics to reporting methods.

The most notable challenges of implementing on this small scale were (1) *communication* with students and parents and (2) *consistency* throughout the school day for the students. Students were in a standards-based grading environment for one or maybe two classes and then spent the rest of the day in a traditional system. Frequent communication with both students and parents about *why* we made the change, how the system worked, and information on student proficiency levels was absolutely necessary. Grading practices have been historically inconsistent in traditional systems, and because of this, students are accustomed to adapting to multiple systems. This particular adaptation was a little different, as it was not figuring out the game of points and percentages. In the end, the response from a majority of students was very positive. They felt supported in their learning and knew where they were in their learning and what their next steps should be.

I currently serve as an instructional coach at a middle school of about 560 students. Standards-based grading had been implemented in the K–8 district four years ago at the elementary level and this year at the two middle schools. When scaling standards-based grading to the school or district level, collective *discussions* are an essential practice to build consistency. When teachers are left to interpret standards-based grading on their own, inconsistencies will develop that could have been avoided at the outset. Making the change with over one hundred teachers, compared with two, creates a very different dynamic. With the larger-scale change, there were many more voices at the table. It makes for a wonderful and, at times, *challenging conversation* but also makes consensus more difficult to find. Some of the decisions were made by administration—for example, separation of behaviors and academics, four-level scale, and inclusion of a narrative on the report card. Other decisions were made by a standards-based grading *committee*. The committee was composed of teachers, instructional coaches, and administrators. Decisions made by the committee included the language of the purpose statement for grades, behaviors that would be included on the report card, and which academic standards would be used for summative assessment. Once those decisions were made, a foundation was made for the larger-scale implementation.

The challenges in this implementation are not limited to reaching consensus on implementation. Creating *buy-in* with a large group is much different than with two people who were seeking a solution. Therefore, a lot of *communication* about why the district was moving in this direction was necessary. The transition had a lot more setbacks and bumps in the road simply because of the varying levels of understanding with standards-based grading and buy-in that the change would be worth it. This will be a *continuous process*, with teachers at many places with their learning (just like the students we serve), and new staff arriving yearly that may need support with this type of grading practice.

Whether a few teachers are piloting standards-based grading or an entire building or school is gearing up for the change, *a plan for implementation* is critical for success. Overcoming the specific challenges each implementation creates is worth the outcome of healthy grading practices that support student learning.

Educator Contribution

Lois McGill
Director of Academics
Balmoral Hall School, Winnipeg, Manitoba

Changing Assessment and Communication of Student Achievement

We began to rethink assessment about five years ago. At that time, we knew the direction we wanted to go but were struggling with how to get there. Now, many years later, we have come a long way but have such a long way to go to truly make learning meaningful for all students. We have learned so much along the way.

Buy-in from all of the stakeholders involved is so important. Without that, you may have an administration that isn't able to support their faculty at a critical time, you will have pockets of teachers innovating and assessing in creative and forward-thinking ways while others are teaching in traditional ways behind closed doors, and you will have pushback from vocal parents who want to see a mark/grade—not feedback and parents demanding what they believe to be "fairness."

Manitoba has what I feel is a very forward-thinking assessment policy. It supports and encourages the use of professional judgment after examining a wide range of assessment tasks; it encourages teachers to consider most consistent achievement, with an eye to the most recent when determining a grade; and it puts the responsibility of completing all assessments in a timely manner on the student. However, in a quick poll of friends who are teachers in both public and private education, most feel that their administration does not know how to support the use of professional judgment because it may not be as easy/safe to defend when questioned. It is so imperative that administrators have a very clear understanding of assessment as, for, and of learning. If teachers don't feel they will be supported by the administration, it is very unlikely that they will take a risk and move away from the safe, mathematically calculated summative mark/grade. *Rethinking Classroom Assessment With Purpose in Mind,* by Dr. Lorna Earl and Dr. Steven Katz and the WNCP

(Continued)

(Continued)

team, was developed in 2006 and continues to be an outstanding and relevant guide. As we enter the last few months of 2017, I question how effective it has been in guiding schools to rethink assessment. Where is the disconnect between the relevance of this document, easily accessible to every school, and what is happening in the majority of middle and senior school classrooms?

There has never been more need for teacher *professional development*. Not only do teachers need to learn effective assessment strategies to support all learners, but they also need to rethink what and how they are teaching. Asking traditional teachers to assess in meaningful ways that may look different for every student—to become activators of student learning and give up some ownership of their classrooms—but not support them in developing strategies to teach differently will be counterproductive. Once behind closed doors, it is very likely that traditional teaching and assessment will be the norm. The organization of our faculty into *professional learning communities*, rather than by departments, has played a huge part in our shift from a grading culture to a *learning culture*. Our PLCs are made up of mixed-grade groupings and mixed disciplines, so now conversations are about how to assess and support learning—not how to assess math or assess English. The faculty challenges each other to think deeply and support those who are struggling to move away from traditional assessment. Time is often a common reason why teachers find it difficult to assess for learning and provide feedback along the way. "If I pause to give feedback, I'll never get through all the units by June!" Although there are curricular outcomes that are required, teachers need to rethink how learning outcomes can be met. Professor David Perkins, from the Harvard Graduate School of Education, asks teachers to consider that deeper and more purposeful learning can occur when it is a mile deep and an inch wide versus an inch deep and a mile wide. Studies have shown that students who achieve A's early in their learning often have gaps in their conceptual understanding. They know what they know, but they don't know what to do with what they know.

Students need to be equally involved in the conversation surrounding assessment, so they understand the why and not just the how. Students, for the most part, embrace the chance to take ownership for their learning, set learning goals, and reflect along the way. It is so important for teachers to guide students to learn how to scaffold, reflect, and revise as they work toward their learning goals and to recognize that feedback is just as important as a mark. Students who lack the confidence and sometimes the motivation to take ownership are the students who will say, "Just tell me what you want me to do and I'll do it! What will it take for me to get a good mark?" One of the biggest obstacles teachers face is students who view choice in deciding learning outcomes and deadlines as an opportunity to consistently turn assessments in late. Rules for consequences must be well thought out and clearly communicated to parents and students. Consequences cannot be an ever-moving target or the willingness for students who are embracing a learning culture will diminish. Students must be able to trust the process and not find out that the teacher has changed his or her mind about allowing a rewrite or an opportunity to revise and redo. A consistent message from all teachers, as students move from classroom to classroom, is a necessary component for a successful shift away from a grading culture. (I could write a whole paper on why they shouldn't be moving from classroom to classroom, from silo to silo, but that is a different discussion!)

Parents, like many teachers, need to "unlearn" how they were taught, and for this reason, it is so important to involve them in open and frequent *conversations* about assessment. Without a common language and understanding about assessment, some view choice and flexible deadlines as not "fair." Why do some students get more time than others to complete an assessment task or receive more help along the way? It is a lack of understanding that often results in demands for more rigor or consequences, such as a reduction of marks for students who can't pull their weight. Conversations with parents need to occur more than just during curriculum information sessions at the beginning of the year, and they will feel more comfortable and confident in changes being made when they hear the same information from the administration, from teachers, and, ultimately, from their children.

There are three things that we have done that have helped change the mindset of the students and the parents:

1. We have eliminated subject area awards at the end of the year that focus only on academic achievement. Our faculty requested this because it was counterproductive to all of the work they were doing throughout the year to help students focus on their *learning*. Rather, criteria have been created in each subject area that aligns to our Profile of a Graduate, and students are chosen based on their ability to meet the criteria (risk-takers, lifelong learners, resilient, etc.). Students in Grades 11 and 12, rather than being chosen, have to apply for an award and learn to recognize their strengths and advocate for themselves.

2. We have *ongoing discussions* and share all relevant research with our parents and students. Providing parents with information, studies, and research has helped to change the mindset of many who believe the traditional approach to learning and assessing is the right way. This takes a tremendous amount of time, and it isn't always a comfortable conversation, but it is helping us to move forward to becoming a school community with a shared understanding of assessment and learning.

3. We have removed access to the online gradebook for both parents and students (see page 270 for rationale).

Educator Contribution

Douglas Reeves
Founder
Creative Leadership Solutions
Boston, Massachusetts

Dealing With the Fear of Grading for Learning

In my advocacy of grading for learning, my greatest errors have been to pursue the *hearts and minds* of teachers and administrators without considering the *fears* of parents, community members, and governing board members. Here are some guidelines for successful implementation of grading reform.

1. Shift the Conversation From "Either/Or" to "Both/And"

Much of the rhetoric of grading reform, while thrilling to its advocates, is threatening to parents, who have been well served by traditional grading systems. Rather than engage in

(Continued)

an all-or-nothing fight in which, almost always, the traditionalists win, a better approach is to lower the collective blood pressure of the community by addressing *what will not change*. For secondary schools in particular, it is important to reassure parents and community members that students will continue to have transcripts and grade point averages. The key distinction that can bring both sides in the grading debate together is "what gets you into the room"—transcripts and grade point averages—and "what gets you into the class"—the passion, commitment, and exceptional learning that is best described in a nontraditional report card. It's not an "either/or" debate but must be reframed as "both/and." I have seen too many promising grading reform initiatives defeated—sometimes with the dismissal of the senior administrators involved—because parents and board members perceived grading reform as the enemy of opportunity for their children. Effective reform initiatives retain what parents value most, including not only transcripts but also academic honors, individualized education plans, and grade point averages.

2. Engage Students in the Grading Process

When *students are active participants* in the grading process, they understand the "rules of the game." When grading policies are mysterious and Byzantine in complexity, students abdicate their responsibility and assume that the role of the teacher is that of factory foreman, accepting or rejecting the products of the workers. But in the context of grading for learning, students themselves must understand the learning journey and their personal responsibilities for progressing from one level to the next. Moreover, students should bear responsibility for communicating their progress to parents. Contrast the conversation of, "The teacher didn't like me," with, "The reason I earned a 2 is that I didn't have transitions in my paragraphs and didn't use powerful vocabulary words, but I know that I can earn a higher score next time."

3. Address Teacher Needs

The workload for teachers is already extraordinary, and many of them perceive grading for learning as one more burden on top of an already overloaded schedule. This situation has been exacerbated by well-intentioned but futile grading systems that turn classroom teachers into data entry clerks, matching a grade to every conceivable academic standard. An effective approach to grading for learning recognizes the *time constraints of teachers* and limits the number of standards to be addressed in the grading system. In addition, because grading for learning is strongly associated with a lower failure rate, it is essential to show teachers that the results of a lower failure rate include better discipline and more electives.

4. Cheer the Champion

Perhaps the most common challenge I receive is, "Show me where grading for learning is working!" The answer is almost always, "In your own school." Teachers around the world have been using Ken O'Connor's work for years—eliminating the average, avoiding the zeros on hundred-point scales, and more—yet they have done so in a low-key and nearly anonymous way in order to avoid creating controversy. The best advocates for grading for learning are the teachers in your own school, who are already adopting effective grading practices and who have positive results. While there is an abundance of research on the positive impact of grading for learning, the most persuasive evidence is what teachers are already doing with their students in your schools.

NOTE: More about how to win the "Grading-Reform Debate" can be found in Reeves (2016a), especially pages xv–xix, 1–9, 47–51, and 153–155.

SYNTHESIS

From these seven contributions and my own twenty-plus years of experience helping schools and districts move to more effective grading and reporting practices, it seems to me that the following are the critical things that must be done for the implementation of change in grading and reporting to be successful.

1. Communicate, communicate, communicate with every method you have available.

2. Ensure that there is clarity and consensus about the purpose, which should be to create a culture of learning.

3. Determine the appropriate balance of pressure (policies/procedures and timelines) and support (studying, reading, talking, and professional development).

4. Plan with the end in mind, but be willing to adjust.

5. Utilize diverse committees/task forces/teams, but be transparent about which decisions will be made by administrators and which decisions will be reached by consensus.

6. Be clear about what will change and what will not change.

7. Be courageous and persistent. Non illegitimi carborundum.

CHAPTER 12

The Way Ahead

Grading for learning is . . . rather like bombing for peace.

—Kohn (2011)

I first heard Alfie Kohn say this in a keynote presentation at an ATI conference in Portland, Oregon, in (I think) July 2006. He made this observation just before I was to present several sessions that included "How to Grade for Learning" in the title. I was offended then, and I remain offended to this day because, with no intention here of examining the right or wrong of "bombing for peace," he obviously was being dismissive of the idea of "grading for learning" (and maybe me), and I believed then and I still believe that "grading for learning" does happen if the guidelines in this book are used with fidelity in schools/classrooms that have a culture of learning and support for student learning above all else. Proof of this can be provided by spending time in the classrooms of many practitioners, and if further proof is required, I suggest participation in the #sblchat (Wednesday 9 p.m. ET) on Twitter, where passionate, committed educators describe their practices and give testimonials to the positive results in their classrooms in 140 characters or less!

I acknowledge that portfolios, descriptive feedback—hard copy or digital—narratives—written or oral—ongoing informal communication, and student-involved conferencing each provide better information than grades. Grades are—and can never be anything more than—symbols that summarize achievement. These other methods of communication provide real information about student learning far more effectively than grades because each contains a wealth of information and provides an effective method to communicate the information. One *way ahead* is to promote these methods and make their use more widespread and more effective across at least K–12 education but hopefully the whole spectrum of K–20 education.

But whether we like it or not, grades are going to be with us, at least in high school and college, for the foreseeable future, so educators (and the media) have a responsibility to educate parents and the community about the place of grades in the communication system. This frequently has not been done well, as can be seen in an article published by the *Bangor Daily News* from the Maine Public with the headline "Maine Families Worry That New Grading System Will Harm College Chances." The headline is accurate, in as far as the article includes quotes from concerned parents and students (who clearly don't understand Maine's proficiency-based program), but it is extremely misleading because the article also quotes Chris Richards, the director of recruitment at the University of Maine in Orono, who says, "Colleges have always dealt with unusual grading systems from private or progressive schools. . . . And you've got to decipher all of that and work through that to make *the best choice for a candidate*" (My italics). The article continues, "To do that, he says, his university relies on a lot more than just grades. Extracurriculars, letters of recommendation, and standardized test scores are all incorporated, too. And Richards says counselors are also in constant contact with area high schools to stay up to date, so they can understand these new grading systems and accurately assess students" (Feinberg, 2017). Furthermore, the article ignores the fact that sixty-nine New England colleges and universities have signed a declaration that proficiency-based transcripts will not harm students in the admissions process.

In this chapter, in the first edition of *How to Grade for Learning*, written in 1998, and in each of the subsequent editions, I included the following quote, and I believe it has just as much, if not more, relevance now as it did when it was written in 1993:

> The time has come to de-emphasize traditional grades and to demystify the entire grading process. We need to focus instead on the process of learning and the progress of the individual student. (Burke, 1993, viii)

I used this quote because it brilliantly summarizes the intent and message of this book. Let us look at this by discussing each of the main ideas.

DE-EMPHASIZING TRADITIONAL GRADES

Grades have both too little and too much meaning. They have too little meaning because there are so many things mixed into them, in such idiosyncratic ways by different teachers, that their meaning is very unclear. They have too much meaning because of the cult-like status accorded them and because of their importance in high-stakes educational decisions. Grades can—and should—be de-emphasized by doing the following:

1. Eliminating subject grades at least from kindergarten to Grade 8—and preferably to Grade 10—so that students and parents come to understand and appreciate the better information provided by descriptive feedback—hard copy or digital—narratives—written or oral—ongoing informal communication, and student-involved conferencing.

2. Providing subject grades only for Grades 11 and 12 and only for a few days at the end of each grading period or when students need them for external purposes so that most conversations about student achievement are focused on words, not symbols. This should be accompanied by the summarizing function of online grading programs being turned off, except for those few days. (I realize that in most high schools, there will continue to be subject grades for each year of high school, and mainly because of tradition and community pressure, subject grades will continue to be used in many middle schools and some elementary schools, so this applies anywhere where there are subject grades.)

3. Reducing the number of grading periods each year to no more than three and preferably only two.

4. Eliminating the use of grades for external purposes, such as athletic eligibility, obtaining driver's licenses, and getting free pizza and gifts from parents, and especially from grandparents, for straight A's.

5. Providing high-quality, easily understandable, standards-based, expanded-format report cards twice a year in hard copy or online.

6. Eliminating class rank and revising how GPAs are determined.

DEMYSTIFYING THE ENTIRE GRADING PROCESS

"Grading still remains an aspect of school that is clothed in myth, mystery and magic" (O'Connor, 2009) to students and parents because the explanations we have provided have largely been about the relationship between percentages and letter grades, complicated mathematical formulas, and sometimes lengthy lists of how students will be penalized for what are deemed to be inappropriate behaviors.

The use of standards-based grading through applying the guidelines described and analyzed in this book produces grades that are understandable and that are accurate, consistent, meaningful, and more supportive of learning. Grades are demystified when

1. they are based on standards and provide a profile of student achievement with—or preferably without—subject grades;
2. they identify performance relative to proficiency with a limited number of levels;
3. they are based on individual achievement and are not contaminated by behaviors, penalties, extra credit, and group scores;
4. they are for performance, not practice—that is, determined primarily from assessments *of* learning (summative assessments), not assessments *for* learning (formative assessment);
5. they are determined by emphasizing more recent evidence, not by averaging everything students have done throughout the school year;
6. they are determined by logic rules and professional judgment rather than tortuous numerical formulas and calculations;
7. they use evidence from high-quality assessments; and
8. they have been thoroughly discussed with and understood by students.

Grading has also been a mystery for teachers because until recently, so little discussion about grading has taken place in education courses, staff development, and conference workshops or staff rooms. For the most part, grading has been the preserve of individual teachers operating in the isolation of their own classrooms, with minimal direction from school or district policies and minimal guidance from administrators. Teachers have basically done what was done to them as students or relied on individual help from a more experienced colleague. These grading guidelines demystify the process for teachers because they provide them with a clear, practical process to follow in their classrooms—and in their gradebooks. When these guidelines are adopted, it is expected that they will be given status as required procedures at both the school and district levels. This means that grading practices are no longer a mystery, and teachers can be held accountable for the procedures they follow. A grading policy based on the guidelines is provided in Appendix C.

Grading with these guidelines demystifies grades and de-emphasizes grades and differs from traditional grades in the ways shown in Figure 12.1.

FOCUS ON THE PROCESS OF LEARNING

Although grades always ultimately focus on the results of learning, use of the grading guidelines, expanded-format reporting, and the other methods of communication advocated in this book honor the process of learning far more than traditional grading. Guidelines 4 and 5, in particular, acknowledge learning as a process, as these guidelines

- require that formative assessment be seen as a process that provides information to adjust and improve learning (and teaching), not be used in the determination of grades;

- emphasize the more recent information rather than early information or first attempts; and

- strongly suggest that reassessment opportunities be available for students.

Seeing grades as only part of the communication system and emphasizing other methods of communication that provide more detailed information also move the focus more to the process of learning.

FIGURE 12.1 Traditional Grading Contrasted With Standards-Based Grading

GUIDELINE	TRADITIONAL SYSTEMS	STANDARDS-BASED SYSTEMS
1.	Based on assessment methods One grade per subject	Based on learning goals/standards One grade for each learning goal Subject grades only if required
2.	Often norm referenced or a mix of norm and criterion referenced Percentage system (101 levels) Criteria often unclear or assumed to be known	Criterion-referenced standards Proficiency based (limited number of levels, usually two to five) Publicly published criteria/targets
3.	Uncertain mix of achievement, attitude, effort, and behavior Penalties and extra credit used Includes group scores	Achievement only No penalties or bonuses Individual evidence only
4.	Everything scored included, regardless of purpose Homework major factor	Summative assessments only Homework rarely included
5.	Everything scored included, regardless of when Multiple assessments recorded as average, not best	More recent evidence emphasized Reassessment without penalty
6.	The mean is the measure Grades "calculated"	Metrics, including median and mode, used sparingly Grades "determined" using professional judgment
7.	Varied quality of assessments Some evidence only in teachers' heads	Quality assessments only Data carefully recorded
8.	Teacher decides and announces	All aspects discussed with and understood by students

FOCUS ON THE PROGRESS OF THE INDIVIDUAL STUDENT

There are many ways in which the guidelines focus on the individual student. First and foremost, Guideline 3 emphasizes individual achievement. Although it is critically important that teachers use cooperative learning structures in their classrooms, it is even more important that any marks that students receive from cooperative learning activities (either process or product) be based on each individual's contribution, not the achievement or lack of achievement of others. Group grades are inappropriate and should not be used, both because they are so unfair and because they contribute in a significant and unfortunate way to giving cooperative learning a bad reputation.

The guidelines also acknowledge students as individuals and enable individuals to progress because each student's learning preferences, strengths, and areas for improvement are taken into account. Guideline 5 acknowledges that students learn at different rates and need varying amounts of time to demonstrate adequately their knowledge and skills. Guideline 6 suggests using professional judgment rather than strict numerical calculation, which allows teachers to discount a few stumbles without the poorer performances detracting from their normal level of achievement. Guideline 2 leads to each individual student having the opportunity to succeed at the highest level. Criterion-referenced standards foster learning that is not competitive, and the standards also prevent success from being artificially rationed by a mathematical formula. Guideline 7 requires that teachers record assessment data accurately and consistently—producing quality information that communicates to students and parents the progress of each student. Guideline 8 gives every individual the best opportunities to progress because it requires that students be involved in and clearly understand how assessment and grading will be carried out.

Finally, this information is provided in ways that can contribute to the growth of individuals. Because grades are seen as only part of the communication system, other methods of communication that give rich information about the strengths and weaknesses of each student are used. This rich information enables students to be effective self-assessors and assists them, their parents, and their teachers with setting goals and identifying needed actions to reach those goals.

COMPETENCY-BASED TRANSCRIPTS

Apart from the guidelines, what can bring de-emphasizing and demystifying grades and focusing on the learning process and the progress of each individual student together? I believe that it is proficiency-based transcripts. They are very new, but as they are developed further, I think that they truly are *the way ahead*. And I would like to share two versions here.

The innovators and early implementers of standards-based grading in Champlain Valley Union High School in Hinesburg, Vermont, have proposed one draft. Their development process and a sample transcript follow.

Educator Contribution

Emily Rinkema, *Instructional Coach*
Stan Williams, *Social Studies Teacher*
Champlain Valley Union High School, Hinesburg, Vermont

Developing a Proficiency-Based Transcript

Champlain Valley Union High School is a large, public high school in Vermont, and as of the 2016–2017 school year we are completely standards based. We have been moving toward this for over five years and, throughout that time, have developed systems and structures that not only support teachers in changes in grading and reporting but also encourage the significant and necessary changes in instruction and assessment that come as a result of the shift to focusing on proficiency. Using state and national standards as a guide, we worked over these years to develop a dozen graduation standards that drive what we do in and out of the classroom. These are transferable skill standards, so they are not attached to specific discipline areas. Teachers and/or departments write more specific learning targets to drive instruction and assessment in the classroom and throughout nontraditional learning experiences. For example, an English teacher may create a learning target about the analysis of literature in an American lit class that would provide evidence for the following graduation standard: "Use evidence and reasoning to effectively support ideas or solutions." In this way, the specific learning targets provide evidence of the larger graduation standards over time and across disciplines.

At the beginning of the 2016–2017 school year, our principal asked us to research proficiency-based transcripts that could help us communicate what we were implementing. Our current ninth graders will graduate based on demonstrated proficiency in the graduation standards, not on credits, and yet we didn't have a model of a transcript that would help us envision where and how to make this significant change. As we began to look at transcripts, we struggled to find any that met our particular needs. Most examples we found looked remarkably similar to the one we have used for decades, and we wanted a way to communicate clearly about student learning, not just grades or course credits. We were looking to de-emphasize the traditional GPA but, at the same time, provide quantifiable evidence so as to not disadvantage our students as they competed for spaces in large, traditional, and selective colleges. We needed something easy to read but that put our transferable graduation standards at the center.

Unable to find what we wanted, we developed our own model (see Figure 12.2), which flipped the focus from course to standard but still maintained some traditional conventions that allow it to be easily read and understood by colleges and universities. The two major shifts in this proficiency-based transcript are the GPA and the Learning Experiences:

- **GPA:** There's still a grade point average, but the significant change is that this GPA is calculated based on the underlying graduation standards, not composite scores from courses. For example, the first graduation standard on the transcript includes evidence from a variety of courses over the student's four years. Note that in eleventh grade, the student took U.S. history and received a composite score of 3.8 for that standard. That composite came from the underlying learning targets tagged to that particular graduation standard. These learning targets were instructed, practiced, and assessed in U.S. history, ultimately determining the overall score. It's important that the 3.8 is not the overall score for the course itself. In fact, nowhere on the transcript is there a composite score for courses. We wanted to emphasize the importance of the graduation standards and increase the integrity of the numerical scores by only averaging within a particular skill.

- **Learning Experiences:** In addition to flipping the GPA, we wanted to highlight the change from course to learning experience. As we move to more personalized approaches to teaching and learning, students are beginning to demonstrate and learn in nontraditional ways. The Learning Experiences box at the top of the transcript lists how the student chose to travel through high school; some students will have mostly courses, but others will have a mix of learning experiences that provide evidence of proficiency.

We have so much more to learn and figure out over the next few years (and beyond). Do we include ninth through twelfth grade in the overall determination or just eleventh and twelfth? Do we take an average, or is the mean or mode more accurate? Are all Learning Experiences equal? Despite not having all of the details worked out yet, having a model of a transcript that emphasizes our graduation standards and our shift to personalization and communicates clearly about learning can help guide us as we continue to strive to improve learning and engagement for all students.

(Continued)

FIGURE 12.2 CVUHS High School Transcript

Champlain Valley Union High School
Official Transcript

369 CVU Road
Hinesburg, VT 05461

Phone: 802-482-7100 Fax: 802-482-7108 Website: www.cvuhs.org

Student Information	
Student Name: George Martin	DOB: 8/10/2002
Address: 5420 Shelburne Road	
Shelburne, VT 05482	
Student ID#:	
Grade Level: 12	
Date of Enrollment: 8/28/2016	
House: Nichols Advisor: Bunting, A	

Graduation Date:	Cumulative GPA:

Overview of Experiences by Grade Level

Grade 9	Type	Grade 10	Type	Grade 11	Type	Grade 12	Type
Humanities 9	Course	Humanities 10	Course	US History	Online	Physics I	Course
Yr 1 Science	Course	Year 2 Science	Course	American Lit	Course	French III	Course
French II	Course	Algebra II	Course	Nexus: Chem	Hybrid	Holocaust/Human Behavior	Course
Wellness	Course	Cooking/Eating Well	Course	Ceramics	Course	AP Government	AP
Geometry	Course	Nexus: Chinese	Hybrid	SCS 4th Gr. Teach	Internship	UVM - Statistics	College
Intro to Art	Course	Beginning Acting	Course	Pre-Calculus	AP	Riding Academy	Independent
Crew	Sport	Personal Finance		Personal Fitness	Course		

Informed & Integrative Thinking a: Use evidence & reasoning to effectively support ideas or solutions							**3.2**

Grade 9		Grade 10		Grade 11		Grade 12	
Humanities	3.0	Humanities 10	3.4	US History	3.8	Holocaust/Human	3.4
Year 1 Sci	3.4	Year 2 Science	2.8	American Lit	4.0	AP Government	3.5
French II	2.1	Algebra II	4.0	Ceramics	3.2	Physics I	3.2
		Cooking/Eating Well	2.6	Nexus: Chem	3.0	French III	2.7

Informed & Integrative Thinking b: Identify main & supporting ideas, patterns, trends, clues, & relationships in sources of information							**3.1**

Grade 9		Grade 10		Grade 11		Grade 12	
Humanities	3.2	Humanities 10	3.8	US History	3.3	Holocaust/Human	3.0
Year 1 Sci	3.0	Year 2 Science	3.0	American Lit	3.6	AP Government	2.0
Wellness	2.5	Algebra II	4.0	Nexus: Chem	3.0	Physics I	3.4
		Cooking/Eating Well	2.8	Personal Fitness	3.2		

Informed & Integrative Thinking c: Analyze, evaluate, and synthesize information to build on knowledge.							**3.2**

Grade 9		Grade 10		Grade 11		Grade 12	
Geometry	3.0	Humanities 10	3.0	SCS 4th gr teach	3.0	Holocaust/Human	3.5
Wellness	3.4	Year 2 Science	2.6	American Lit	3.5	UVM-Statistics	3.5
French II	2.6	Algebra II	3.5	Ceramics	3.6	Physics I	3.0
				Nexus: Chem	3.5	French III	2.8

Informed & Integrative Thinking d: Evaluate the accuracy, bias, and usefulness of information .							**3.8**

Grade 9		Grade 10		Grade 11		Grade 12	
Humanities	3.0	Nexus: Chinese	3.4	US History	3.8	Riding Academy	3.8
Year 1 Sci	3.4	Year 2 Science	2.8	American Lit	4.0	AP Government	3.5
Intro to Art	2.1	Geometry	4.0	Pre Calc	3.2	French III	3.0
				Personal Fitness	3.0		

Creative & Practical Problem Solving a: Generate a variety of possible solutions supported by evidence.							**3.6**

Grade 9		Grade 10		Grade 11		Grade 12	
Humanities	3.5	Humanities 10	3.8	SCS 4th gr tch	4.0	Holocaust/Human	3.9
Wellness	3.8	Beginning Acting	2.5	American Lit	3.8	French III	3.5
French II	3.6	Algebra II	4.0	Ceramics	3.6	Physics I	3.2
		Cooking/Eating Well	3.7	Nexus: Chem	3.5		

Learning Experiences

	Experiences Completed	Experiences Required
Humanities	7.5	7
STEM	7.5	6
Wellness	2	2
Arts	2.5	2
Global Literacy	3	2
Exploratory	2	2

Proficiency System

Cumulative scores for each standard are determined by the summary of evidence within the experiences tagged to that standard over time and across discipline. The scores next to each course/experience reflect the student's achievement of that transferable skill using specific content. The overall GPA is determined not by averaging course scores, but by averaging *standard* scores, thus putting the emphasis on the transferable skills. Students choose content-rich, rigorous learning experiences to help them grow and show excellence in skills that will transfer beyond school and throughout their lifetimes.

Academic Summary

Honors/Awards:

Signature:_____ Title:_____ Date:_____

The second version comes from a consortium called the Mastery Transcript Consortium™ (see Figure 12.3 on page 312). It is developing a very different but very interesting transcript. It is planning for a membership of at least one hundred independent schools with the aim of developing a transcript that is based on what they call microcredits in eight skills, such as complex communication—oral and written—global perspective, and habits of mind. The consortium has agreed on three core principles: no standardization of content, no grades, and a consistent transcript format. The plan is to host the transcript on a technology platform that produces a transcript that a college admissions counselor could

FIGURE 12.2 (Continued)

Creative and Practical Problem Solving b: Interpret information and derive meaning through the use of inference, empathy, metaphor and imagination							**3.2**
Grade 9		**Grade 10**		**Grade 11**		**Grade 12**	
Wellness	3.0	Beginning Acting	3.4	Pre Calc	3.8	UVM-Statistics	3.4
Year 1 Sci	3.4	Year 2 Science	2.8	American Lit	4.0	AP Government	3.5
French II	2.1	Algebra II	4.0	Nexus:Chem	3.2	Physics I	3.2
		Cooking/Eating Well	2.6			French III	2.7

Creative and Practical Problem Solving c: Frame questions, make predictions, experiment with possibility, and design strategies							**3.3**
Grade 9		**Grade 10**		**Grade 11**		**Grade 12**	
Intro to Art	3.2	Humanities 10	3.0	US History	2.6	Riding Academy	3.5
Year 1 Sci	3.6	Beginning Acting	3.4	SCS 4th gr tch	3.5	Physics I	3.0
Geometry	2.8	Algebra II	3.5	Ceramics	3.5	French III	3.3
				Nexus: Chem	3.6		

Creative and Practical Problem Solving d: Develop and use generalizations, models, and abstractions							**3.5**
Grade 9		**Grade 10**		**Grade 11**		**Grade 12**	
Humanities	3.0	Humanities 10	3.8	Nexus :Chem	4.0	Holocaust/Human	3.6
Year 1 Sci	3.2	Year 2 Science	3.8	American Lit	3.2	French III	3.7
French II	3.1	Algebra II	3.2				
		Personal Finance	3.6				

Clear and Effective Communication a: Understand and use discipline-specific vocabulary							**3.3**
Grade 9		**Grade 10**		**Grade 11**		**Grade 12**	
Wellness	3.3	Humanities 10	3.6	US History	3.6	UVM-Statistics	3.8
Year 1 Sci	3.2	Personal Finance	2.8	American Lit	4.0	AP Government	3.2
Intro to Art	2.8	Cooking/Eating Well	2.6	Personal Fitness	3.0		
				Nexus: Chem	3.5		

Clear and Effective Communication b: Demonstrate organized and purposeful communication							**2.7**
Grade 9		**Grade 10**		**Grade 11**		**Grade 12**	
Humanities	3.0	Humanities 10	2.4	Nexus:Chem	3.0	Holocaust/Human	3.0
Year 1 Sci	2.4	Year 2 Science	2.8	Ceramics	2.2	AP Government	2.5
French II	2.1	Personal Finance	3.0			Physics I	3.0

Clear and Effective Communication c: Adjust communication to suit the purpose, context, and audience							**3.0**
Grade 9		**Grade 10**		**Grade 11**		**Grade 12**	
Geometry	3.0	Algebra II	3.4	US History	3.8	Holocaust/Human	3.4
Wellness	2.8	Year 2 Science	2.8	American Lit	3.0	AP Government	3.0
French II	2.1			Personal Fit.	2.6	French III	3.2
Crew	3.0			Nexus:Chem	3.0		

Clear and Effective Communication d: Demonstrate standard conventions of expression including oral, written, performed, and emerging technologies							**2.8**
Grade 9		**Grade 10**		**Grade 11**		**Grade 12**	
Humanities	2.8	Humanities 10	3.0	Nexus :Chem	2.6	French III	3.1
Year 1 Sci	2.6	Year 2 Science	3.0	American Lit	2.8	AP Government	3.2
French II	2.1	Geometry	3.1	Ceramics	3.1		
		Cooking/Eating Well	2.6				

Personal Learning Plan

This is where we would put a general description of CVU's PLP process and overall goal.

PLP Exhibition Reflection:

PLP Roundtable Reflection:

PLP Defense Reflection:

read and understand in two minutes. "(The current idea, likely to change) is a sort of multi-colored spider web with featured credits listed at the side). Admissions officers can even click down into every skill the student has to see the standard, and then click down further to see individual items of student work (videos, art work, writing) supporting the standard" (Wehner, 2017). (See the transcript—without the color—in Figure 12.3, on the next page, and note that the transcript's design has not been finalized. That's part of what the MTC will do.) Ross Wehner, founder of the World Leadership School in Boulder, Colorado, in support of this transcript says, "Our students are stressed out; teachers

(Continued)

(Continued)

have inflated grades almost to the point where grades are meaningless; schools are held back from innovating; and even college admissions officers admit the whole system is broken." While I disagree with his second point, I do agree that a transcript that provides a picture of students' achievement in a number of skills would be very powerful and would help to create a culture of learning.

FIGURE 12.3 Current Version of the MTC Transcript (as of July 2017)

Smith, Joseph '17

Parents: Scott and Gina Smith
Student Residence Address & Phone:
1234 Cleveland Avenue
Cleveland, OH 44108
(555) 555-5555

Date of Birth: 10/11/1998
Entered:
Today's Date: 1/16/2017
Status: Current Student
Sex: Male

Hawken School
CEEB Code: 361262
12456 County Line Road, P.O. Box 8002
Gates Mills, Ohio 44040-8002
(440) 423-2916, fax (440) 423-2994

Featured Credits:

7b Foster integrity, honesty, fairness and respect

3b Lead through influence

3c Build trust, resolve conflicts, and provide support for others

3g Coordinate tasks, manage groups, delegate responsibilities

3h Implement decisions and meet goals

8e Persistence

Earned Credits:

1 Analytical and Creative Thinking
b. Detect bias, and distinguish between reliable and unsound information
e. Analyze and create ideas and knowledge

2 Complex Communication—Oral and Written
a. Understand and express ideas in two or more languages
c. Listen attentively
d. Speak effectively

3 Leadership and Teamwork:
a. Initiate new ideas
b. Lead through influence
c. Build trust, resolve conflicts, and provide support for others
d. Facilitate group discussions, forge consensus, and negotiate outcomes
f. Enlist help
g. Coordinate tasks, manage groups, and delegate responsibilities
h. Implement decisions and meet goals
i. Share the credit

4 Digital and Quantitative Literacy:
a. Understand, use, and apply digital technologies
c. Use multimedia resources to communicate ideas effectively in a variety of forms
d. Master and use higher-level mathematics
e. Understand traditional and emerging topics in math, science, and technology, environmental sciences, robotics, fractals, cellular automata, nanotechnology, and biotechnology

5 Global Perspective
b. Understand non-western history, politics, religion and culture
e. Develop social and intellectual skills to navigate effectively across cultures
h. Leverage social and cultural differences to create new ideas and achieve success

6 Adaptability, Initiative, and Risk-Taking
a. Develop flexibility, agility, and adaptability

b. Bring a sense of courage to unfamiliar situations
d. Work effectively in a climate of ambiguity and changing priorities
g. Develop entrepreneurial literacy

7 Integrity and Ethical Decision-Making
a. Sustain an empathetic and compassionate outlook
b. Foster integrity, honesty, fairness and respect
c. Exhibit moral courage in confronting unjust situations
d. Act responsibly, with the interests and well-being of the larger community in mind
e. Develop a fundamental understanding of emerging ethical issues and dilemmas regarding new media and technologies

8 Habits of Mind
b. Creativity
e. Persistence

Digital transcript: hawken.edu/joseph.smith
access code: 2F371AX4LT

SIGNATURE OF SCHOOL OFFICIAL

NOTE: Prototype as of July 2017. View ongoing work at http://www.mastery.org/a-new-model.

SUMMARY

Using the grading guidelines and the communication methods described in this book is a different approach than traditional grading and reporting. The guidelines and methods go a long way toward providing the student-involved assessment advocated by Stiggins (2001) and the honesty and fairness in grading and reporting that the late great Grant Wiggins (1996) advocated for many years. They also clearly acknowledge that grading and reporting must be directly related to learning goals and standards, which have become such a large part of education. This approach to grading and communication does what Burke advocates—"de-emphasize traditional grades," "demystify the entire grading process," and "focus on the process of learning and the progress of the individual student." All of these desirable characteristics occur because (1) the prime purpose of grades is recognized as communication, not competition, and (2) determining student grades is based on a pedagogy that views the teacher's role as supporting learning and encouraging student success. Keri Helgren, a high school English teacher in Calmar, Alberta, Canada, who has put these practices in place in her classroom, demonstrates the power of these approaches in her testimonial in Appendix A.

> The prime purpose of grades is recognized as communication, not competition.

Although the focus of this book is grading, it is important to acknowledge that many things are more important than grading in education. It is essential that everyone involved first develops a standards-based mindset and that schools and teachers provide high-quality standards-based curriculum, instruction, and assessment. Teachers should take many steps to implement the grading guidelines advocated in this book. They require that teachers have a laser-like focus on learning and have an orientation to do everything possible to support each student's learning. Their approach to assessment should include the following six action steps (only one of which is grading itself!):

1. Use a variety of assessment methods that meet the needs of all students.

2. Match assessment methods with learning goals. Generally, this will require more use of performance assessment and clearer identification of formative assessment.

3. With student involvement, develop clear criteria (rubrics) and provide models (exemplars or anchor papers) illustrating the levels of performance.

4. Provide reteaching and reassessment opportunities.

5. Encourage peer assessment and self-assessment reflection and goal setting by all students.

6. Base grades on the most consistent, more recent, summative, individual achievement data.

What is suggested in this book requires significant changes in many schools, especially high schools. DuFour, Eaker, and DuFour (2005) note that this will require "more than changes in structure—the policies, programs and procedures of a school. Substantive and lasting change will ultimately require a transformation of culture—the beliefs, assumptions, expectations and habits that constitute the norm for people throughout the organization" (p. 11). This means that teachers and administrators have to become reflective practitioners, especially as it relates to the practice of grading. The rubric for sound grading practices found in Appendix H is an excellent vehicle for such reflection.

WHAT'S MY THINKING NOW?

Having now reached this point in the book (and, it is hoped, having read all of it!), readers are in a position to consider two things: how the ideas presented will influence their own practices and what the links are between the grading guidelines. With this in mind, two final activities are suggested below.

Task

Examine your own grading practices, and consider changes that will benefit your students. Answer the questions, and discuss the results with your colleagues and/or administrators.

Activity 1: Reflecting on Your Grading Practices

1. Which of your grading practices were affirmed by the book?

2. What revisions to your grading practices do you need to make?

3. What points of uncertainty still exist?

4. What actions do you want to take now?

Activity 2: Grading Rubric (Appendix H, pages 329–332)

1. Identify where you are individually or collectively on each guideline on the rubric.

2. Focus on the guidelines/aspects where you are not fluent. What do you need to do to move from where you are to fluency?

Appendix A

A Testimonial on the Impact of Assessment and Grading for Learning

Author's note: Keri first wrote her testimonial in 2008 for the third edition of this book. I'm very grateful that nine years later, here she was willing to provide a current reflection on her assessment and grading journey.

AN ALBERTA TEACHER'S SELF-REFLECTION ON ENGLISH LANGUAGE ARTS ASSESSMENT

Keri Helgren
ELA Teacher
John Maland High School
Black Gold Regional Schools
Alberta, Canada

It has been about fifteen years since I first began my journey with assessment-for-learning strategies in my secondary English classroom. I've come up against a number of obstacles, such as rigid deadlines, government diploma examinations, university admissions offices, and skeptical colleagues and parents who still believe that zeros are valid, and late work should be punished. And let's not forget struggles to adopt report card templates to reflect our new commitment to assessment-for-learning practices—struggles that existed primarily because of a lack of resources, consensus, and will.

However, all of these roadblocks have not daunted me—instead, they have solidified the principles I believe are the most important for students to become empowered learners.

Despite all of my efforts, the greatest challenge I face to implementing all of the assessment-for-learning strategies I value can be found in the uncontrollable variable of time. How can I be able to hold students accountable for incomplete work when the semester is over? When the year is over? There is little I can do to move the mountain that is our school year calendar.

Knowing I would have to deal with incomplete assignments, I decided to reevaluate how much I was taking in as summative assessments. How many classroom assignments were "essential" in order to report students' achievement, based on curricular outcomes, as accurately as I could? Since asking that question, I have significantly reduced my summative assessments and turned my focus to formative assessments. I spend much more of my time scaffolding learning through practice and classroom activities. I also strive to help students recognize and develop their strengths and gain an awareness of their learning needs. I use Google Docs, Kaizena, and audio to provide guiding feedback on assignments. I refocus students as they work on annotating challenging texts, both independently or in group discussions. I challenge them to extend their thinking as they create proposals for creative projects or examine scholarship for new ideas on the novel we are studying. And when they've practiced—tried, failed, taken risks, and demonstrated growth and readiness—I then provide a summative assessment, all the while balancing their learning requirements with that ever-present obstacle of time.

Alongside the concern about what I was choosing to ask students to complete as "essential learning tasks," I also began eliminating or de-emphasizing assignments in my gradebook. In my ELA 10-1 class, as students are adjusting to the demands of critical/analytical writing, the early writing tasks do not demonstrate how much their skills develop toward the end of the term. So rather than maintain the weighting on those early assignments, I either exempt them or reduce their weighting. I am able to individualize learning and not penalize students for early weaknesses or mistakes.

Not only was I concerned about assessment weightings and types, but I was also troubled by the fixation both parents and students had about numbers. In the gradebook, parents and students have instant access to their raw scores and percentages on individual assignments across multiple courses. Emails would flow in after every mark entry, and the questions seemed never ending about the "mark" or the "grade." There had to be more I could share than just a stack of often meaningless numbers.

The score inspector has become my most powerful tool, as I am able to provide information about student learning daily if I choose. As each task, formative or summative, is entered into my gradebook, I am able to provide specific written comments for each individual student. These comments can be seen by both parents and students and have come to be very valuable in painting a picture of a student's learning over time. Parents are now able to see more clearly their child's approach to the practice they've been provided, gaining insight into the ways in which classroom activities directly relate to learner outcomes. Parents also gain a better understanding of the distinctions between formative and summative assessment and learn to value them as much as their children do. As the semester begins, I get a bit of, "Is this for marks?" but that question quickly disappears as students begin to understand the type of learning environment I am creating for them—something my colleague describes as their "roadmap to success." And yes, parents at first find it confusing, wondering why there is so much information in the gradebook without a "grade" attached. However, I now find that I have much more fruitful student–teacher–parent conferences as there is so much more to talk about now rather than just what 80 percent means (because what does that really mean, anyway?).

Has my marking load been affected? Absolutely. In reflection, I think I have less than a quarter of the total raw score marks I had my first year of teaching, twenty-five years ago. Why? Because the majority of my time is spent helping my students understand themselves as learners and develop their skills over the limited five months I have with them until they move on. Instead of sitting at my desk with a red pen grading stacks upon stacks of assigned tasks, I see my classroom as a dynamic practice space—a place where you warm up before you engage in your cerebral workout. A place where mistake making and risk taking go hand in hand. The first attempt at any task is done without the risk of a number being attached and is done in a supportive, collaborative, noncompetitive environment where students can fail and succeed—all in the same class—but, most importantly, learn. Feedback comes from all directions—peer, self, and, of course, from me—their guide. I use exemplars to make criteria in rubrics clear, so both feedback and assessment are two-way conversations, not top-down exercises. Assessment and learning are no longer words solely attached to marks and grades but have become as individualized as I can make them.

I no longer teach Shakespeare or poetry or the short story—they are just vehicles to teach the students to be resilient critical thinkers who are not afraid of failure or a challenge.

Despite all of these challenges, I know that the learning environment I have created now is far superior to the one I had when I first started my professional career twenty-five years ago. Conversations about fair approaches to teaching, learning, and assessment must continue—and metacognition must be at the center. Without stirring up change, even in the face of resistance, we will fall back on what has worked in the past, instead of striving to do better.

Appendix B

Guidelines for Grading in Standards-Based Systems

1. Relate grading procedures to learning goals (i.e., standards).

   a. Use learning goals (standards or some clustering of standards [e.g., domains, strands]) as basis for grade determination and grade reporting.

   b. Use assessment methods as the subset, *not* the set (i.e., standards, learning results, expectations, outcomes).

2. Use clearly described criterion-referenced performance standards.

   a. The meaning of grades (letters or numbers) should come from clear descriptions of a limited number of levels.

   b. If they hit the goal, they get the grade (i.e., no bell curve)!

3. Limit the valued attributes included in grades to individual achievement.

   a. Grades should be based on achievement (i.e., demonstration of the knowledge and skill components of the standards). Effort, participation, attitude, and other behaviors should be reported separately.

   b. Grades should be based on individual achievement.

4. Sample student performance—do not include all scores in grades.

   a. Do not include *formative* assessment in grades—provide feedback on formative performance using words, rubrics, or checklists, *not* scores.

   b. Include information primarily from a variety of *summative* assessments in grades.

5. Grade in pencil—keep records so they can be updated easily.

   a. Use the most consistent level of achievement, with special consideration for the more recent evidence.

   b. Provide several assessment opportunities (varying in method and number).

6. Determine, don't just calculate, grades.

   a. Crunch numbers carefully—if at all.

   b. Think "body of evidence" and professional judgment.

7. Use quality assessment(s), and properly record evidence of achievement.

   a. Meet standards for accurate assessment: clear targets, clear purpose, and sound design (which requires that assessments be well written, use appropriate target–method match, use appropriate sampling, and avoid bias and distortion).

   b. Record and maintain evidence of achievement (e.g., tracking sheets, spreadsheets, gradebooks—hard copy and/or electronic—portfolios—hard copy and electronic).

8. Discuss and involve students in assessment, including grading, throughout the teaching/learning process.

   a. Ensure (age appropriately) that students understand how their achievement will be assessed and how their grades will be determined.

   b. Involve students in the assessment process, in self-assessment, reflection and goal setting, and in communicating about their achievement and progress.

Appendix C

A Proposed Grading Policy

If the ideas and guidelines presented in this book were to be included in a school or district grading policy, the wording should be similar to the following. (The number of each section parallels the grading guidelines.)

1. Grading procedures shall be related directly to stated learning goals.

2. a. Performance standards will be identified and described using a limited number of levels of proficiency.

   b. Criterion-referenced standards shall be used to distribute grades and marks.

3. a. Individual achievement of stated learning goals shall be the only basis for grades.

   b. Effort, participation, attitude, and other behaviors shall not be included in grades but shall be reported separately, unless they are a stated part of a learning goal.

   c. Late submission of assessment evidence shall be handled as follows:

      1. Teachers may set due dates and deadlines for all marked assessment evidence that will be part of a student grade.

      2. There shall be no penalties for late submission of assessment evidence.

      3. Late submission of assessment evidence may lead to parent contact and will be noted for inclusion in comments and/or learning skills section of report card.

      4. Late submission of assessment evidence may lead to an invitation or the requirement to attend a support session during the school day, before school, at lunchtime, or after school hours.

      5. Students may request and receive extensions of timelines.

   d. Absences shall be handled as follows:

      1. Students shall not be penalized only for absence.

      2. Absent students shall be given makeup opportunities for all missed summative assessments (marked assessment evidence that will be part of student grades) without penalty.

   e. Extra credit and bonus points/questions will not be used.

   f. Academic dishonesty will be dealt with

      1. As set out in the Code of Conduct, not with mark reductions.

      2. Students will be required to resubmit any assessment identified as academically dishonest, certifying that it was completed honestly.

g. 1. No group scores will be included in grades unless collaboration is required by the standard being addressed.

   2. Parents and students shall be notified in advance of why and how group scores will be used.

4 a. Teachers shall provide descriptive feedback orally or in writing on formative assessment.

b. Formal assessments used in the formative assessment process shall not be included directly in grades.

c. Teachers shall provide students with a written overview of assessment in clear, easily understandable language, indicating how each summative assessment throughout the course will be evaluated before each such assessment is administered.

d. Marks/scores from summative assessments shall be used primarily to determine grades.

5. a. Where repetitive measures are made of the same or similar knowledge, skills, or behaviors, the more recent mark or marks shall replace the previous marks for grade determination.

b. Second chance (or more) assessment opportunities shall be made available to students; students shall receive the highest mark, not an average mark, for any such multiple opportunities.

6. a. Grading is an exercise in professional judgment in which the educator seeks to ensure that the grade each student receives is an accurate representation of his or her performance.

b. Consideration shall be given to the use of statistical measures other than the mean for grade determination—for example, the median, mode, weighted mean, highest, or more recent.

7. a. Teachers shall use quality assessment instruments. Each assessment must meet standards of quality. It must arise from a clearly articulated set of achievement expectations, serve an instructionally relevant purpose, rely on a proper method, sample student achievement in an appropriate manner, and control for all relevant sources of bias and distortion that can lead to inaccurate assessment. All assessments must be reviewed and adjusted as needed to meet these standards.

b. Teachers shall properly record evidence of student achievement on an ongoing basis.

8. a. Teachers shall discuss assessment with students, in an age-appropriate manner, at the beginning of instruction. Where feasible, students shall be involved in decisions about methods of assessment and scoring scales.

b. Teachers shall provide to students and parents a written overview of assessment, including grading, in clear, easily understandable language during the first week of classes in each course or grade.

c. Teachers will provide students with opportunities for self-assessment, reflection, and goal setting and will transition from parent–teacher conferences to student-led conferences.

Appendix D

Bay District Schools Assessment Principles and Practices

PRINCIPLE 1

The primary purpose of assessment is to measure student progress toward mastery of standards.

> Practice 1.1: Schools and teachers use a variety of standards-based assessments as a basis for instructional planning as well as the diagnosis, grading, and placement of students.

> Practice 1.2: Teachers provide opportunities for students to take ownership of learning by setting, meeting, and/or modifying individual goals.

> Practice 1.3: Teachers systematically collect and record standards-based assessment information regarding student achievement and progress and communicate information to the appropriate audience.

> Practice 1.4: Teachers interpret and analyze formative and summative assessment information (descriptive and evaluative) to plan and modify instruction and assessment to meet individual student needs.

> Practice 1.5: Teachers use summative assessments to indicate mastery of standards giving consideration to the most recent cumulative knowledge and skills.

PRINCIPLE 2

Grading is fair, consistent, and meaningful.

> Practice 2.1: Standards-based grading is a system of assessing and reporting that describes student progress in relation to standards

> Practice 2.2: Grading is consistent for ALL students across the district.

SOURCE: Retrieved from https://sites.google.com/a/bay.k12.fl.us/assessment

Appendix E

NGSS Performance Expectations for a High School Chemistry Course

HS-PS1 MATTER AND ITS INTERACTIONS

1. Use the periodic table as a model to predict the relative properties of elements based on the patterns of electrons in the outermost energy level of atoms.

2. Construct and revise an explanation for the outcome of a simple chemical reaction based on the outermost electron states of atoms, trends in the periodic table, and knowledge of the patterns of chemical properties.

3. Plan and conduct an investigation to gather evidence to compare the structure of substances at the bulk scale to infer the strength of electrical forces between particles.

4. Develop a model to illustrate that the release or absorption of energy from a chemical reaction system depends upon the changes in total bond energy.

5. Apply scientific principles and evidence to provide an explanation about the effects of changing the temperature or concentration of the reacting particles on the rate at which a reaction occurs.

6. Refine the design of a chemical system by specifying a change in conditions that would produce increased amounts of products at equilibrium.

7. Use mathematical representations to support the claim that atoms, and therefore mass, are conserved during a chemical reaction.

HS-LS1 FROM MOLECULES TO ORGANISMS: STRUCTURES AND PROCESSES

5. Use a model to illustrate how photosynthesis transforms light energy into stored chemical energy.

6. Construct and revise an explanation based on evidence for how carbon, hydrogen, and oxygen from sugar molecules may combine with other elements to form amino acids and/or other large carbon-based molecules.

7. Use a model to illustrate that cellular respiration is a chemical process whereby the bonds of food molecules and oxygen molecules are broken and the bonds in new compounds are formed resulting in a net transfer of energy.

HS-LS2-5 ECOSYSTEMS: INTERACTIONS, ENERGY, AND DYNAMICS

5. Develop a model to illustrate the role of photosynthesis and cellular respiration in the cycling of carbon among the biosphere, atmosphere, hydrosphere, and geosphere.

HS-ETS-1 ENGINEERING DESIGN

4. Use a computer simulation to model the impact of proposed solutions to a complex real-world problem with numerous criteria and constraints on interactions within and between systems relevant to the problem.

Appendix F

Ontario Achievement Chart for Canadian and World Studies

CATEGORIES	LEVEL 1	LEVEL 2	LEVEL 3	LEVEL 4
Knowledge and Understanding – Subject-specific content acquired in each grade (knowledge), and the comprehension of its meaning and significance (understanding)				
	The student:			
Knowledge of content (e.g., facts, terms, definitions)	demonstrates limited knowledge of content	demonstrates some knowledge of content	demonstrates considerable knowledge of content	demonstrates thorough knowledge of content
Understanding of content (e.g., concepts, ideas, theories, interrelationships, procedures, processes, methodologies, spatial technologies)	demonstrates limited understanding of content	demonstrates some understanding of content	demonstrates considerable understanding of content	demonstrates thorough understanding of content
Thinking – The use of critical and creative thinking skills and/or processes				
	The student:			
Use of planning skills (e.g., organizing an inquiry; formulating questions; gathering and organizing data, evidence, and information; setting goals; focusing research)	uses planning skills with limited effectiveness	uses planning skills with some effectiveness	uses planning skills with considerable effectiveness	uses planning skills with a high degree of effectiveness
Use of processing skills (e.g., interpreting, analysing, synthesizing, and evaluating data, evidence, and information; analysing maps; detecting point of view and bias; formulating conclusions)	uses processing skills with limited effectiveness	uses processing skills with some effectiveness	uses processing skills with considerable effectiveness	uses processing skills with a high degree of effectiveness
Use of critical/creative thinking processes (e.g., applying concepts of disciplinary thinking; using inquiry, problem-solving, and decision-making processes)	uses critical/ creative thinking processes with limited effectiveness	uses critical/ creative thinking processes with some effectiveness	uses critical/ creative thinking processes with considerable effectiveness	uses critical/ creative thinking processes with a high degree of effectiveness

(Continued)

(Continued)

CATEGORIES	LEVEL 1	LEVEL 2	LEVEL 3	LEVEL 4
Communication – The conveying of meaning through various forms				
	The student:			
Expression and organization of ideas and information (e.g., clear expression, logical organization) in oral, visual, and written forms	expresses and organizes ideas and information with limited effectiveness	expresses and organizes ideas and information with some effectiveness	expresses and organizes ideas and information with considerable effectiveness	expresses and organizes ideas and information with a high degree of effectiveness
Communication for different audiences (e.g., peers, adults) and purposes (e.g., to inform, to persuade) in oral, visual, and written forms	communicates for different audiences and purposes with limited effectiveness	communicates for different audiences and purposes with some effectiveness	communicates for different audiences and purposes with considerable effectiveness	communicates for different audiences and purposes with a high degree of effectiveness
Use of conventions (e.g., mapping and graphing conventions, communication conventions), vocabulary, and terminology of the discipline in oral, visual, and written forms	uses conventions, vocabulary, and terminology of the discipline with limited effectiveness	uses conventions, vocabulary, and terminology of the discipline with some effectiveness	uses conventions, vocabulary, and terminology of the discipline with considerable effectiveness	uses conventions, vocabulary, and terminology of the discipline with a high degree of effectiveness
Application – The use of knowledge and skills to make connections within and between various contexts				
	The student:			
Application of knowledge and skills (e.g., concepts, procedures, spatial skills, processes, technologies) in familiar contexts	applies knowledge and skills in familiar contexts with limited effectiveness	applies knowledge and skills in familiar contexts with some effectiveness	applies knowledge and skills in familiar contexts with considerable effectiveness	applies knowledge and skills in familiar contexts with a high degree of effectiveness
Transfer of knowledge and skills (e.g., concepts of thinking, procedures, spatial skills, methodologies, technologies) to new contexts	transfers knowledge and skills to new contexts with limited effectiveness	transfers knowledge and skills to new contexts with some effectiveness	transfers knowledge and skills to new contexts with considerable effectiveness	transfers knowledge and skills to new contexts with a high degree of effectiveness
Making connections within and between various contexts (e.g., between topics/issues being studied and everyday life; between disciplines; between past, present, and future contexts; in different spatial, cultural, or environmental contexts; in proposing and/or taking action to address related issues; in making predictions)	makes connections within and between various contexts with limited effectiveness	makes connections within and between various contexts with some effectiveness	makes connections within and between various contexts with considerable effectiveness	makes connections within and between various contexts with a high degree of effectiveness

SOURCE: Government of Ontario. 2015. *The Ontario Curriculum Grades 11 and 12: Canadian and World Studies*, pp. 42–43. Retrieved July 19, 2017, from http://www.edu.gov.on.ca/eng/curriculum/secondary/2015cws11and12.pdf

HOW TO GRADE FOR LEARNING

Appendix G

Letter to Parents About Student-Led Conferencing

BRANKSOME HALL JUNIOR SCHOOL, TORONTO, ONTARIO

November 16, 2016

Dear Junior School Parents:

Student-Led Conferences will be held on Friday, December 9, 2016, between 8:00 a.m. and 4:00 p.m. Please access our online registration system to book a conference time for each of your daughters. As this will not be a regular school day, students attend only for their scheduled conference. The After School Program will be open all day to provide programming at our usual PD day rate for families needing supervision.

Each student's conference will last approximately one hour, and up to three other families will be engaged in conferences at the same time. Most of your time will be spent in your daughter's classroom; however, she will ask you to travel around the school to view artwork on display, to watch her demonstrate a skill in the gym, or to hear her perform in the PAR. If, for any reason, you are unable to attend, we welcome and encourage a caregiver, grandparent, or other adult family friend to participate.

JK Student-Led Conferences will be scheduled on the hour between 8:00 a.m. and 12:00 p.m. SK to Grade 3 conferences will be scheduled on the hour between 8:00 a.m. and 12:00 p.m. and again between 1:00–3:00 p.m. An additional time slot from 3:00–4:00 p.m. will be available for Grades 4–6 students. Two household families wishing to have individual conferences with their daughter(s) are encouraged to book more than one conference time, as needed.

Student-Led Conferences are a unique and personal way for students to share their learning, and they are an important assessment tool within the Primary Years Program. The conference provides an opportunity for families to celebrate and appreciate students' hard work and accomplishments, and it presents a window into the daily classroom experience. In conjunction with a student's portfolio, a conference allows each student to demonstrate and reflect on her growth as a learner since the beginning of the school year.

Your daughter is preparing to demonstrate and share her learning with you through her personal growth portfolio. She may ask you to participate in a number of different activities or centres in the classroom, where she will share knowledge and demonstrate skills. Her teachers will act as facilitators during the conference.

Teachers will take photos, interact with families, offer encouragement, and answer questions if necessary. This is not a time for a Parent–Teacher interview; it is your daughter's time to share her learning.

Please plan to interact with your daughter by asking questions and making comments to encourage her and show her how much you appreciate her successes! One goal of the conference is to make students responsible for their own learning.

They should be proud of their accomplishments, aware of areas for improvement, and be able to set reasonable goals for themselves in an age-appropriate manner. As you listen to your daughter, consider the amount of information about her learning and development that the conference is providing. At the end of the conference, students and parents will be asked to share their reflections on the experience.

Once your daughter completes her conference, she should either head home with you or join the After School Program. There will be no Co-Curriculars, Athletics, or Study Hall on conference day.

In a few minutes, you will receive an individualized e-mail with the online booking system to reserve your conference time. It is the same system we used in October for booking Parent–Teacher Interviews.

If you have any further questions about Student-Led Conferences, please feel free to contact me, Evita Strobele, or your daughter's teacher.

Sincerely,

Sarah Craig, Head, Junior School

Evita Strobele, Assistant Head, PYP Coordinator

Appendix H

Rubric for Sound Grading Practice

GUIDELINE	BEGINNING	DEVELOPMENT	FLUENT
1. Organizing the Gradebook	The evidence of learning (e.g., a gradebook) is entirely organized by sources of information (tests, quizzes, homework, labs).	The evidence of learning (e.g., a gradebook) is organized by sources of information mixed with specific content standards.	The evidence of learning (e.g., a gradebook) is completely organized by student learning outcomes (content standards, benchmarks, grade-level indicators, and curriculum expectations).
2. Identifying "How Good" and "How Good Is Good Enough"	Points and percentages with limited descriptors. Complicated conversion scales. Little consistency between teachers.	Mix of points and percentages and levels of proficiency. Reduced use of conversion scales. Increasing consistency between teachers.	Clear descriptions of a limited number of levels of proficiency. No conversion between levels and points and percentages. Considerable consistency between teachers.
3. Including Factors in the Grade	Overall summary grades are based on a mix of achievement and nonachievement factors (e.g., timeliness of work, attitude, effort, and cheating). Nonachievement factors have a major impact on grades.	Overall summary grades are based on a mix of achievement and nonachievement factors, but achievement counts a lot more.	Overall summary grades are based on achievement only.
	Extra credit points are given for extra work completed, without connection to extra learning.	Some extra credit points are given for extra work completed; some extra credit work is used to provide extra evidence of student learning.	Extra credit work is evaluated for quality and is only used to provide extra evidence of learning. Credit is not awarded merely for completion of work.
	Cheating, late work, and missing work result in a zero (or lower score) in the gradebook. There is no opportunity to make up work, except in a few cases.	Cheating, late work, and missing work result in a zero (or lower score) in the gradebook. But there is an opportunity to make up work and replace the zero or raise the lower score.	Cheating, late work, and missing work is recorded as "incomplete" or "not enough information" rather than "0." There is an opportunity to replace an incomplete with a score without penalty.

(Continued)

GUIDELINE	BEGINNING	DEVELOPMENT	FLUENT
3. Including Factors in the Grade (continued)	Borderline cases are handled by considering nonachievement factors.	Borderline cases are handled by considering a combination of nonachievement factors and collecting evidence of student learning.	Borderline grade cases are handled by collecting additional evidence of student achievement, not by counting nonachievement factors.
4. Considering Assessment Purpose	Everything each student does is given a score, and every score goes into the final grade. There is no distinction between scores on practice work (formative assessment or many types of homework) and scores on work to demonstrate level of achievement (summative assessment).	Some distinctions are made between formative (practice such as homework) and summative assessment, but practice work still constitutes a significant part of the grade.	Student work is assessed frequently (formative assessment) and graded occasionally (summative assessment). Scores on formative assessments and other practice work (e.g., homework) are used descriptively to inform teachers and students of what has been learned and the next steps in learning. Grades are based only on summative assessments.
5. Considering Most Recent Information	All assessment data is cumulative and used in calculating a final summative grade. No consideration is given to identifying or using the most current information.	More current evidence is given consideration at times but does not entirely replace out-of-date evidence.	Most recent evidence completely replaces out-of-date evidence when it is reasonable to do so. For example, how well students write at the end of the grading period is more important than how well they wrote at the beginning, and later evidence of improved content understanding is more important than early evidence.
6. Summarizing Information and Determining Final Grade	The gradebook has a mixture of ABC, percentages, +/−, and/or rubric scores with no explanation of how they are to be combined into a final summary grade.	The gradebook may or may not have a mixture of symbols, but there is some attempt, even if incomplete, to explain how to combine them.	The gradebook may or may not have a mix of symbol types, but there is a sound explanation of how to combine them.
	Rubric scores are converted to percentages when averaged with other scores, or there is no provision for combining rubric and percentage scores.	Rubric scores are not directly converted to percentages; some type of logic rule is used; the final grade, many times, does not best depict level of student achievement.	Rubric scores are converted to a final grade using a logic rule that results in an accurate depiction of the level of student attainment of the learning targets.

GUIDELINE	BEGINNING	DEVELOPMENT	FLUENT
6. Summarizing Information and Determining Final Grade (continued)	Final summary grades are based on a curve—a student's place in the rank order of student achievement.	Final grades are criterion referenced, not norm referenced. They are based on preset standards, such as A = 90%–100% and B = 80%–89%. But there is no indication of the necessity to ensure shared meaning of symbols—that is, there is no definition of each standard.	Final grades are criterion referenced, not norm referenced. They are based on preset standards, with clear descriptions of what each symbol means. These descriptions go beyond A = 90%–100% and B = 80%–89%; they describe what A, B, and so on performance looks like.
	Final grades for special needs students are not based on learning targets as specified in the individual education program (IEP).	There is an attempt to base final grades for special needs students on learning targets in the IEP, but the attempt is not always successful, or it is not clear to all parties that modified learning targets are used to assign a grade.	Final grades for special needs students are criterion referenced and indicate level of attainment of the learning goals as specified in the IEP. The targets on which grades are based are clear to all parties.
	Final summary grades are based on calculation of mean (average) only.	The teacher understands various measures of central tendency but may not always choose the best one to accurately describe student achievement.	The teacher understands various measures of central tendency (average, median, and mode) and understands when each is the most appropriate one to use to accurately describe student learning.
7. Verifying Assessment Quality	There is little evidence of consideration of the accuracy/quality of the individual assessments on which grades are based.	The teacher tries to base grades on accurate assessment results only but may not consciously understand all of the features of a sound assessment.	Grades are based only on accurate assessment results. Questionable results are not included.
	Quality standards for classroom assessment are not considered, and the teacher has trouble articulating standards for quality.	Some standards of quality are adhered to in judging the accuracy of the assessment results on which grades are based. The teacher can articulate some of these standards or uses standards for quality assessment intuitively but has trouble articulating why an assessment is sound.	The teacher can articulate standards of quality and can show evidence of consideration of these standards in his or her classroom assessments: • Clear and appropriate learning targets • Clear and appropriate for users and uses • Sound assessment design (proper method, quality exercises, sound sampling, and minimum bias) • Effective communication of results

(Continued)

GUIDELINE	BEGINNING	DEVELOPMENT	FLUENT
7. Verifying Assessment Quality (continued)	Assessments are rarely modified for special needs students when such modifications would provide much more accurate information about student learning.	Assessments are modified for special needs students, but the procedures used may not result in accurate information and/or match provisions in the IEP.	Assessments are modified for special needs students in ways that match instructional modifications described in IEPs. Such modifications result in generating accurate information on student achievement.
8. Student Involvement	Grades are a surprise to students because (a) students don't understand the bases on which grades are determined; (b) students have not been involved in their own assessment (learning targets are not clear to them, and/or they do not self-assess and track progress toward the targets); or (c) teacher feedback is only evaluative (a judgment of level of quality) and includes no descriptive component.	Grades are somewhat of a surprise to students because student involvement practices and descriptive feedback are too limited to give them insights into the nature of the learning targets being pursued and their own performance.	Grades are not a surprise to students because (a) students understand the basis for the grades received; (b) students have been involved in their own assessment throughout the process (they understand the learning targets they are to hit, self-assess in relation to the targets, track their own progress toward the targets, and/or talk about their progress); and/or (c) teacher communication to students is frequent, descriptive, and focuses on what they have learned, as well as the next steps in learning. Descriptive feedback is related directly to specific and clear learning targets.

SOURCE: Adapted from Chappuis (2017, pp. 82–84).

Appendix I
Glossary

The glossary is an explanation of the way terms are used in this book.

achievement. The demonstration of student performance on learning goals measured against established criteria (performance standards).

assessment. Gathering and interpreting information about student achievement (group or individual) using a variety of tools and techniques. It is the act of describing student performance, primarily for the purpose of enhancing learning. As part of assessment, teachers provide students with feedback that guides their efforts toward improved achievement. (N.B. assessment has come to most commonly be used as both assessment and evaluation as defined here.)

content standards. What students are expected to know and be able to do.

criteria. Characteristics or dimensions of student performance.

criterion referenced. Assessment of students' success in meeting stated objectives, learning goals, expectations, or criteria based on absolute standards. (See also *norm referenced* and *self-referenced*.)

diagnostic. Assessment usually carried out prior to instruction that is designed to determine a student's attitude, skills, or knowledge to identify specific student needs. (See also *formative* and *summative*.)

evaluation. Making judgments about the quality of student achievement over a period of time, primarily for the purposes of certification and communicating student achievement.

formative. Assessment designed to provide direction for improvement and/or adjustment to a program for individual students or for a whole class (e.g., quizzes, initial drafts/attempts, homework [usually], and questions during instruction). (See also *diagnostic* and *summative*.)

grade. The number or letter reported at the end of a period of time as a summary statement of student performance. (See also *mark*.)

learning goal. An observable result demonstrated by a student's knowledge, skills, or behavior; a generic term. (See also *standard*.)

mark. The "score" (number or letter) given on any single test or performance. (See also *grade*.)

norm referenced. Assessment/evaluation in relation to other students within a class or across classes/schools or a segment of the population. (See also *criterion referenced* and *self-referenced*.)

performance standards. How well students are expected to demonstrate knowledge and skill.

reliability. The consistency with which an assessment strategy measures whatever it is meant to measure. (See also *validity*.)

rubric. A set of guidelines for assessment that states the characteristics and/or the dimensions being assessed with clear performance criteria and a rating scale.

self-referenced. Assessment designed to compare an individual's performance with his or her previous performance. (See also *criterion referenced* and *norm referenced*.)

standard. Statement that describes what (content standard) and/or how well (performance standard) students are expected to understand and perform.

summative. Assessment designed to provide information about a student's achievement at or toward the end of a period of instruction (e.g., tests, exams, final drafts/attempts, assignments, projects, performances). (See also *diagnostic* and *formative*.)

validity. The degree to which an assessment strategy measures what it is intended to measure. (See also *reliability*.)

References

Absolum, M. (2006). *Clarity in the classroom*. Auckland, New Zealand: Hodder Education.

Airasian, P. W. (1994). *Classroom assessment* (2nd ed.). New York: McGraw Hill.

Anderson, K. E., & Wendel, F. C. (1988). Pain relief: Make consistency the cornerstone of your policy on grading. *American School Board Journal, 175*(10), 36–37.

Armstrong, T. (2000). *Multiple intelligences in the classroom* (2nd ed.) Alexandria, VA: Association for Supervision and Curriculum Development.

Arter, J. A., & Chappuis, J. (2006). *Creating and recognizing quality rubrics*. Portland, OR: Educational Testing Service.

ASCD. (2007–2008). Theme issue "Informative assessment." *Educational Leadership, 66*(4).

ASCD. (2011). Theme issue "Effective grading practices." *Educational Leadership, 69*(3).

Assessment Reform Group. (2002). *Assessment for learning: 10 principles: Research-based principles to guide classroom practice*. London, UK: Author.

Assessment Reform Group. (2003). *The role of teachers in the assessment of learning*. London: CPA Office, Institute of Education, University of London. Retrieved from http://www.assessment-reform-group.org

Azzam, A. M. (2007). Special report: Why students drop out. *Educational Leadership, 64*(7), 91–93.

Azzam, A. M. (2014). Motivated to learn: A conversation with Daniel Pink. *Educational Leadership, 72*(1), 12–17.

Bailey, J., & McTighe, J. (1996). Reporting achievement at the secondary level: What and how. In T. R. Guskey (Ed.), *Communicating student learning: Association for Supervision and Curriculum Development yearbook 1996* (pp. 119–140). Alexandria, VA: Association for Supervision and Curriculum Development.

Beatty, I. D. (2013). Standards-based grading in introductory university physics. *Journal of the Scholarship of Teaching and Learning, 13*(2), 1–22. Retrieved from http://josotl.indiana.edu/article/view/3264/3382

Belanoff, P., & Dickson, M. (1991). *Portfolios: Process and product*. Portsmouth, NH: Boynton/Cook Publishers.

Bellanca, J. (1992). How to grade (if you must). In A. L. Costa, J. Bellanca, & R. Fogarty (Eds.), *If minds matter: A foreword to the future* (Vol. 2, pp. 297–311). Palatine, IL: Skylight.

Black, P., & Wiliam, D. (1998a). Inside the black box: Raising standards through classroom assessment. *Phi Delta Kappan, 80*(2), 139–148.

Black, P., & Wiliam, D. (1998b). *Inside the black box: Raising standards through classroom assessment*. London, UK: School of Education, King's College.

Black, P. J., & Wiliam, D. (2009). Developing the theory of formative assessment. *Educational Assessment, Evaluation and Accountability, 21*(1), 5–31.

Boaler, J. (2016). *Mathematical mindsets: Unleashing students' potential through creative math, inspiring messages, and innovative teaching.* San Francisco, CA: Jossey-Bass.

Bonstingl, J. J. (1992). *Schools of quality: An introduction to total quality management in education.* Alexandria, VA: Association for Supervision and Curriculum Development.

Brookhart, S. M. (1994). Teacher's grading: Theory and practice. *Applied Measurement in Education,* 7(4), 279–301.

Brookhart, S. M. (2004). *Grading.* Upper Saddle River, NJ: Pearson Merrill Prentice Hall.

Brookhart, S. M. (2007/2008). Feedback that fits. *Educational Leadership,* 65(4), 54–59.

Brookhart, S. M. (2011). Starting the conversation about grading. *Educational Leadership,* 69(3), 10–14.

Brookhart, S. M. (2013). *Grading and group work: How do I assess individual learning when students work together?* Alexandria, VA: ASCD

Brookhart, S. M., Guskey, T. R., Bowers, A. J., McMillan, J. H., Smith, J. K., Smith, L. F., . . . Welsh, M. E. (2016). A century of grading research: Meaning and value in the most common educational measure. *Review of Educational Research,* 86(4), 803–848. http://doi.org/10.3102/0034654316672069

Bruno, L. (2007, March 28). Princeton leads in grade deflation. *USA Today,* 9D.

Buck, N. (2016, June 27). Report cards are failing parents, kids. *Globe and Mail* (Toronto, ON), A11.

Buckmiller, T., Peters, R., & Kruse, J. (2017). Questioning points and percentages: Standards-based grading in higher education. *Journal of College Teaching.* Published online on March 31, 2017.

Bukowski, B. J. (2008). A comparison of academic athletic eligibility in interscholastic sports in American high schools. *Sport Journal, 19.* Retrieved from http://thesportjournal.org/article/a-comparison-of-academic-athletic-eligibility-in-interscholastic-sports-in-american-high-schools

Burke, K. (1993). *The mindful school: How to assess thoughtful outcomes: K–college.* Arlington Heights, IL: Skylight.

Burke, K., Fogarty, R., & Belgrad, S. (2001). *The portfolio connection: Student work linked to standards* (2nd ed.). Thousand Oaks, CA: Corwin.

Burkett, E. (2002). *Another planet: A year in the life of a suburban high school.* New York: Perennial.

Busick, K. U. (2000). Grading and standards-based assessment. In E. Trumbull & B. Farr (Eds.), *Grading and reporting student progress in an age of standards* (pp. 71–86). Norwood, MA: Christopher Gordon.

Cameron, C., & Gregory, K. (2014). *Rethinking letter grades: A five-step approach for aligning letter grades to learning standards* (2nd ed.). Winnipeg, MB, Canada: Portage and Main Press.

Canady, R. L. (1993, March). Current grading practices that decrease the odds of student success. Workshop given for the Association for Supervision and Curriculum Development annual meeting, Toronto, ON.

Canady, R. L., & Hotchkiss, P. R. (1989). It's a good score: Just a bad grade. *Phi Delta Kappan,* 73(4), 68–71.

Cash, R. M. (2016). *Self-regulation in the classroom: Helping students learn how to learn.* Golden Valley, MN: Free Spirit Publishing.

Chappuis, J. (2015). *Seven strategies of assessment for learning* (2nd ed.). Boston, MA: Pearson.

Chappuis, J., & Chappuis, S. (2002). *Understanding school assessment: A parent and community guide to helping students learn.* Portland, OR: Educational Testing Service.

Chappuis, J., Stiggins, R., Chappuis, S., & Arter, J. (2012). *Classroom assessment for student learning: Doing it right—doing it well* (2nd ed.). Boston, MA: Pearson

Chappuis, S., Commodore, C., & Stiggins, R. (2017). *Balanced assessment systems: Leadership, quality, and the role of classroom assessment*. Thousand Oaks, CA: Corwin.

Christodoulou, D. (2016). *Making progress: The future of assessment for learning*. Oxford, UK: Oxford University Press.

Cizek, G. J. (1996). Grades: The final frontier in assessment reform. *NASSP Bulletin, 80*(584), 103–110.

Clinedinst, M., Koranteng, A.-M., & Nicola, T. (2015). *2015 state of college admission*. Arlington, VA: National Association of College Admission Counseling.

Coates, J., & Draves, W. A. (2015). *Smart boys, bad grades*. River Falls, WI: LERN.

College Board. (2017). *Admission decisions: What matters*. Retrieved April 4, 2017, from https://professionals.collegeboard.org/guidance/applications/decisions

Cooper, D. (2007). *Talk about assessment: Strategies and tools to improve learning*. Toronto, Canada: Thomson Nelson.

Cooper, D. (2011). *Redefining fair: How to plan, assess, and grade for excellence in mixed-ability classrooms*. Bloomington, IN: Solution Tree.

Cooper, R., & Murphy, E. (2016). *Hacking project based learning: 10 easy steps to PBL and inquiry in the classroom*. Cleveland, OH: Times 10.

Costa, A. L., & Kallick, B. (1992). Reassessing assessment. In A. L. Costa, J. Bellanca, & R. Fogarty (Eds.), *If minds matter: A foreword to the future: Vol. 2* (pp. 275–280). Palatine, IL: IRI/Skylight.

Costa, A. L., & Kallick, B. (2000). *Assessing and reporting habits of mind*. Alexandria, VA: Association for Supervision and Curriculum Development.

Costello, C., & McKillop, B. (2000). Dealing with lates and absences. *Orbit, 30*(4), 43–46.

Crooks, T. (1998). The impact of classroom evaluation practices on students. *Review of Educational Research, 58*(4), 438–481.

Davies, A. (2000). *Making classroom assessment work*. Merville, Canada: Connections.

Davies, A., Herbst, S., & Reynolds, B. P. (2012). *Transforming schools and systems using assessment: A practical guide* (2nd ed.). Bloomington, IN: Solution Tree.

Depka, E. (2015). *Bringing homework into focus: Tools and tips to enhance practices, design, and feedback*. Bloomington, IN: Solution Tree.

DeZouche, D. (1945). The wound is mortal: Marks, honors unsound activities. *Clearing House, 19*, 339–344.

Dorfman, L. (2016). A look at the relationship between policy and practice in K–12 education reform: Insights for state and district leaders. New England Board of Higher Education. Retrieved April 18, 2017, from http://www.nebhe.org/info/pdf/policy/Policy_Spotlight_Relationship_between_Policy_and_Practice_K12_Ed_Reform_May_2016.pdf

Dueck, M. (2014). *Grading smarter, not harder: Assessment strategies that motivate kids and help them learn*. Alexandria, VA; ASCD

DuFour, R. (2007). Once upon a time: A tale of excellence in assessment. In D. Reeves (Ed.), *Ahead of the curve: The power of assessment to transform teaching and learning* (pp. 256–263). Bloomington, IN: Solution Tree.

DuFour R., Eaker, R., & DuFour, R. (2005). Recurring themes of professional learning communities and the assumptions they challenge. In R. DuFour, R. Eaker, & R. DuFour (Eds.), *On common ground: The power of professional learning communities* (pp. 7–29). Bloomington, IN: Solution Tree.

Dunbar, D. (1996). *Letter to Runkel* (26IEDLR387). Washington, DC: U.S. Department of Education, Office for Civil Rights.

Dweck, C. (2008). *Mindset*. New York, NY; Ballantine Books.

Dweck, C. (2015, September 22). Carol Dweck revisits the "growth mindset." *Education Week*. Retrieved from http://www.edweek.org/ew/articles/2015/09/23/carol-dweck-revisits-the-growth-mindset.html

Dyck, B. A. (2002). Student-led conferences up close and personal. *Middle Ground*, 6(2), 39–41.

Earl, L. (2003). *Assessment as learning: Using classroom assessment to maximize student learning*. Thousand Oaks, CA: Corwin.

Earl, L. M., & Katz, S. (2006). *Rethinking classroom assessment with purpose in mind: Assessment for learning, assessment as learning, assessment of learning*. Winnipeg, Canada: Manitoba Education, Citizenship and Youth.

Earl, L., & Katz, S. (2008). Getting to the core of learning: Using assessment for self-monitoring and self-regulation. In S. Swaffield (Ed.), *Unlocking assessment: Understanding for reflection and application* (pp. 90–104). London, UK: Routledge.

Ebert, C. (1992, December). So when can I take the retest? *Quality Outcomes-Driven Education*, 32–34.

Education World. (2017). *National standards*. Retrieved April 24, 2017, from http://www.education-world.com/standards

Elias, M. J, Ferrito, J. J., & Moceri, D. C. (2016). *The other side of the report card*. Thousand Oaks, CA: Corwin.

Ewen, B. (2013, May 31). Dropping out of the Minneapolis "parent portal": As graduation season arrives, a parent confesses. *Minneapolis Star Tribune*. Retrieved from http://www.startribune.com/dropping-out-of-the-minneapolis-parent-portal/209734321

Farr, B. (2000). Grading practices: An overview of the issues. In E. Trumbull & B. Farr (Eds.), *Grading and reporting student progress in an age of standards* (pp. 1–21). Norwood, MA: Christopher Gordon.

Feinberg, R. (2017, April 18). Maine families worry that new grading system will harm college chances. *Maine Public*. Retrieved from http://bangordailynews.com/2017/04/18/news/state/maine-families-concerned-about-proficiency-based-diplomas-harming-kids-college-chances

Frisbie, D. A., & Waltman, K. K. (1992, Fall). Developing a personal grading plan. *Educational Issues: Measurement and Practice*, 35–42.

Frith, J., & Briceno, E. (2017, April 7). Learning and Performance Zones in sports. *Mindset Works*. Retrieved April 25, 2017, from http://blog.mindsetworks.com/entry/learning-and-performance-zones-in-sports-2

Fullan, M. (2005). *Leadership and sustainability: System thinking in action*. Thousand Oaks, CA: Corwin.

G2 Crowd. (2017). Best student information system (SIS) software. Retrieved April 16, 2017, from https://www.g2crowd.com/categories/student-information-systems-sis?segment=all

Gardner, H. (1983). *Frames of mind: The theory of multiple intelligences*. New York, NY: HarperCollins.

Gardner, H. (2002, July 18). Test for aptitude, not for speed. *New York Times*. Retrieved from http://www.nytimes.com/2002/07/18/opinion/test-for-aptitude-not-for-speed.html

Gathercoal, F. (2004). *Judicious discipline* (6th ed.). San Francisco, CA: Caddo Gap Press.

Goodwin, D., & Hein, H. (2017). Learning styles: It's complicated. *Educational Leadership*, 74(7), 79–80

Gottlieb, M. (2006). *Assessing English language learners: Bridges from language proficiency to academic achievement*. Thousand Oaks, CA: Corwin.

Gronlund, N. E., & Linn, R. L. (1990). *Measurement and evaluation in teaching* (6th ed.). New York, NY: Macmillan.

Guskey, T. R. (1994). Making the grade: What benefits students? *Educational Leadership, 52*(2), 14–20.

Guskey, T. R. (1996). Reporting on student learning: Lessons from the past—prescriptions for the future. In T. R. Guskey (Ed.), *Communicating student learning: The Association for Supervision and Curriculum Development yearbook 1996* (pp. 13–24). Alexandria, VA: Association for Supervision and Curriculum Development.

Guskey, T. R. (2000). Grading policies that work against standards . . . and how to fix them. *NASSP Bulletin, 84*(620), 20–29.

Guskey, T. R. (2004). 0 Alternatives. *Principal Leadership, 5*(2), 49–53.

Guskey, T. R. (2013). The case against percentage grades. *Educational Leadership, 71*(1), 68–72.

Guskey, T. R. (2015). *On your mark: Challenging the conventions of grading and reporting.* Bloomington, IN: Solution Tree.

Guskey, T. R., & Bailey, J. M. (2001). *Developing grading and reporting systems for student learning.* Thousand Oaks, CA: Corwin.

Guskey, T. R., & Bailey, J. M. (2009). *Developing standards-based report cards.* Thousand Oaks, CA: Corwin.

Habeeb, S. (2016, October 6). Redos and retakes? Sure. But don't forget to loop [Web log post]. Assessment Network. Retrieved April 6, 2017, from http://salemafl.ning.com/m/blogpost? id=3850522%3ABlogPost%3A39915

Haladyna, T. M. (1999). *A complete guide to student grading.* Boston, MA: Allyn & Bacon.

Hart, G. (1996). Grades: Both a cause and result of fear. *Middle School Journal, 27*(4), 59–60.

Harvard Graduate School of Education, Making Caring Common Project. (2017). Inspiring concern for others and the common good through college admissions. Retrieved April 17, 2017, from http://mcc.gse.harvard.edu/collegeadmissions

Hattie, J. (2012). *Visible learning for teachers: Maximizing impact on learning.* London, UK: Routledge.

Hattie, J., & Timperley, H. (2007). The power of feedback. *Review of Educational Research, 77*(1), 81–112.

Herbst, S. (2015, January 19). Stop SHOULD-ING on others: Three actions successful leaders take [Web log post]. Retrieved April 28, 2017, from http://sandraherbst.blogspot.ca/2015/01/stop-should-ing-on-others-three-actions.html

Herbst, S., & Davies, A. (2014). *A fresh look at grading and reporting in high schools.* Courtenay, BC, Canada: Connect2learning.

Hierck, T., & Larson, G. (2016). *Target-based grading in collaborative teams: 13 steps to moving beyond standards.* Naples, FL: National Professional Resources.

Hill, D., & Nave, J. (2009). *The power of ICU: The end of student apathy: Reviving engagement and responsibility.* Nashville, TN: NTLB Publishing.

Hobbs, G. J. (1992). The legality of reducing student grades as a disciplinary measure. *Clearing House, 65*(4), 204–205.

Huhn, C. (2005). How many points is it worth? *Educational Leadership, 63*(3), 81–82.

Jensen, E. (1998). *Teaching with the brain in mind.* Alexandria, VA: Association for Supervision and Curriculum Development.

Juarez, T. (1990). Revitalizing teacher planning: Grade eggs, not learners. *Holistic Education Review, 3*(4), 36–39.

Jung, L. A. (2009). The challenges of grading and reporting in special education: An inclusive grading model. In T. R. Guskey (Ed.), *Practical solutions for serious problems in standards-based grading* (pp. 27–40). Thousand Oaks, CA: Corwin.

Jung, L. A. (2017a, May 17). Differentiated Assessment and Grading Model (DiAGraM). Retrieved from https://www.studentgrowth.org/2017/05/17/differentiatedgrading

Jung, L. A. (2017b). In providing supports for students, language matters. *Educational Leadership*, 74(7), 42–45.

Jung, L. A. (in press). *Supporting and measuring growth for students with learning differences* [working title]. Alexandria, VA: ASCD.

Jung, L. A., & Guskey, T. R. (2007). Standards-based grading and reporting: A model for special education. *Teaching Exceptional Children*, 40(2), 48–53.

Jung, L. A., & Guskey, T. R. (2012). *Grading exceptional and struggling learners*. Thousand Oaks, CA: Corwin.

Kagan, S. (1995). Group grades miss the mark. *Educational Leadership*, 52(8), 68–71.

Kain, D. L. (1996). Looking beneath the surface: Teacher collaboration through the lens of grading practices. *Teachers College Record*, 97(4), 569–587.

Karmasek, J. M. (2007, May 9). Teacher expresses relief she says that she and the student who sued her get along fine. *Charleston Daily Mail*, 1A. Retrieved December 8, 2008, from http://library.cnpapers.com

Katz, S. (2000). Competency, epistemology and pedagogy: Curriculum's holy trinity. *Curriculum Journal*, 11, 133–144.

Kelly, M. (2016, January 19). Traditional grading flaws and fixes. Principal MKellys EduMic. Retrieved April 14, 2017, from at https://principalmkelly.com

Kentucky Department of Education. (2011a). *English language arts deconstructed standards*. Retrieved from http://education.ky.gov/curriculum/conpro/engla/Pages/ELA-Deconstructed-Standards.aspx

Kentucky Department of Education. (2011b). *Mathematics deconstructed standards*. Retrieved from http://education.ky.gov/curriculum/conpro/Math/Pages/Mathematics-Deconstructed-Standards.aspx

Kohn, A. (1993). *Punished by rewards: The trouble with gold stars, incentive plans, A's, praise, and other bribes*. New York, NY: Houghton Mifflin.

Kohn, A. (2011). The case against grades. *Educational Leadership*, 69(3), 28–33.

Krakovsky, M. (2007, March/April). The effort effect. *Stanford Magazine*, 1–6. Retrieved from http://www.stanfordalumni.org/news/magazine/2007/marapr/features/dweck.html

Lahey, J. (2013, September 6). I will not check my son's grades online 5 times a day. *The Atlantic*. Retrieved from https://www.theatlantic.com/national/archive/2013/09/i-will-not-check-my-sons-grades-online-five-times-a-day/279385

Leahy, J., Lyon, C., Thompson, M., & Wiliam, D. (2005). Classroom assessment: Minute by minute, day by day. *Educational Leadership*, 63(3), 19–24.

Madison Metropolitan School District. (2017). *Supplemental guidelines for grading—middle/high school*. Retrieved April 16, 2017, from https://specialed.madison.k12.wi.us/files/specialed/Grading Supplem.doc

Maine Department of Education. (2017). *Guiding principles*. Retrieved April 17, 2017, from http://www.maine.gov/doe/proficiency/standards/guiding-principles.html

Manitoba Education, Citizenship and Youth. (2006). *Rethinking classroom assessment with purpose in mind: Assessment* for *learning; assessment* as *learning; assessment* of *learning*. Winnipeg, Canada: Author. Retrieved December 8, 2008, from http://www.edu.gov.mb.ca/k12/assess/wncp/index.html

Manon, J. R. (1995). The mathematics test: A new role for an old friend. *Mathematics Teacher*, *88*(2), 138–141.

Massachusetts Institute of Technology. (2016–2017). Academic procedures. *MIT Course Catalog Bulletin 2016–17*. Retrieved April 17, 2017, from http://catalog.mit.edu/mit/procedures/academic-performance-grades/#gradestext

Mathews, J. (2005, February 17). Math of the new grading scale adds up for some but not for others. *Washington Post*, GZ06.

Maxwell, J. C. (2000). *Failing forward: Turning mistakes into stepping-stones for success*. Nashville, TN: Thomas Nelson.

McColskey, W., & McMunn, N. (2000). Strategies for dealing with high-stakes tests. *Phi Delta Kappan*, *82*(2), 115–120.

McGuey, G., & Moore, L. (2007). *The inspirational teacher*. New York: Routledge/Eye on Education.

McKibben, S. (2016). The ins and outs of academic help seeking. *Education Update*, *58*(12), 1–5.

McTighe, J. (1996/1997). What happens between assessments. *Educational Leadership*, *54*(4), 6–12.

McTighe, J., & Ferrara, S. (1995). Assessing learning in the classroom. *Journal of Quality Learning*, *5*(2), 11–27.

McTighe, J., & O'Connor, K. (2005). Seven practices for effective learning. *Educational Leadership*, *63*(3), 10–17.

Melograno, V. J. (2007). Grading and report cards for standards-based physical education. *JOPERD: The Journal of Physical Education, Recreation & Dance*, *78*(6), 45–53.

Michigan 21st Century Education Commission. (2017). *The best education system for Michigan's success*. Retrieved April 18, 2017, from http://mieducationcommission.com/sites/mieducationcommission.com/files/document/pdf/Final%20Report%20-%20The%20Best%20Education%20System%20for%20Michigan%27s%20Success.pdf

Midwood, D., O'Connor, K., & Simpson, M. (1993). *Assess for success: Assessment, evaluation and reporting for successful learning*. Toronto, ON, Canada: Ontario Secondary School Teachers' Federation.

Miller, M. (2017, February 23). 10 strategies for lightning-quick feedback students can REALLY use [Web log post]. *Ditch That Textbook*. Retrieved from http://ditchthattextbook.com/2017/02/23/10-strategies-for-lightning-quick-feedback-students-can-really-use

Monroe, S. J. (2008). Dear colleague letter. Retrieved from https://www2.ed.gov/about/offices/list/ocr/letters/colleague-20081017.pdf

Moore, C., Garst, L., & Marzano, R. (2015). *Creating and using learning targets and performance scales: How teachers make better instructional decisions*. West Palm Beach, FL: Learning Sciences.

Nagel, D. (2015). *Effective grading practices for secondary teachers*. Thousand Oaks, CA: Corwin.

National Research Council. (2012). *A framework for K–12 science education*. Washington, DC: National Academies Press.

New England Secondary School Consortium. (2017). *College admissions*. Retrieved April 17, 2017, from http://newenglandssc.org/resources/college-admissions

NGSS Lead States. (2013). *Next Generation Science Standards: For states, by states*. Retrieved from http://www.nextgenscience.org/sites/default/files/Final%20Release%20NGSS%20Front%20Matter%20-%206.17.13%20Update_0.pdf

O'Connor, K. (1995). Guidelines for grading that support learning and student success. *NASSP Bulletin*, *79*(571), 91–101.

O'Connor, K. (2009). *How to grade for learning, K–12* (3rd ed.). Thousand Oaks, CA: Corwin.

O'Connor, K. (2011). *A repair kit for grading: 15 fixes for broken grades* (2nd ed.). Boston, MA: Pearson.

O'Connor, K. (2013). *The school leader's guide to grading.* Bloomington, IN: Solution Tree.

O'Connor, K. (2017, January). A case for standards-based grading and reporting. *School Administrator,* 24–28.

Ohio High School Athletic Association. (2017). Bylaws. Retrieved April 16, 2017, from http://ohsaa .org/Portals/0/Eligibility/OtherEligibiltyDocs/Bylaws.pdf

Ohio State Department of Education. (2017). *Ohio learning standards: Terminology definitions.* Retrieved from http://education.ohio.gov/Topics/Learning-in-Ohio/Ohios-Learning-Standards/Ohio-Learning-Standards-Resources/Ohio-Learning-Standards-Terminology

Ontario Ministry of Education. (2004). *The Ontario curriculum—Grades 1-12; Achievement charts (draft).* Retrieved from http://www.edu.gov.on.ca/eng/document/policy/achievement

Ontario Ministry of Education. (2010). *Growing success: Assessment, evaluation, and reporting in Ontario schools.* Toronto: Author. Retrieved April 27, 2017, from http://www.edu.gov.on.ca/eng/policyfunding/growSuccess.pdf

Owens, K. (2015, November 20). A beginners guide to standards-based grading [Web log post]. AMS blog on teaching and learning mathematics. Retrieved from http://blogs.ams.org/matheducation/2015/11/20/a-beginners-guide-to-standards-based-grading

Pink, D. (2009). *Drive: The surprising truth about what motivates us.* New York, NY: Riverhead Books.

Polloway, E. A., Epstein, M. H., Bursuck, W. D., Roderique, T. W., McConeghy, J. L., & Jayanthi, M. (1994). Classroom grading: A national survey of policies. *Remedial and Special Education, 15,* 162–170.

Popham, W. J. (2017). *The ABCs of educational testing: Demystifying the tools that shape our schools.* Thousand Oaks, CA: Corwin.

Pratt, D. (1980). *Curriculum design and development.* New York, NY: Harcourt Brace Jovanovich.

Princeton University. (2014). *Report from the Ad Hoc Committee to Review Policies Regarding Assessment and Grading.* Retrieved March 6, 2017, from https://www.princeton.edu/main/news/archive/S40/73/33I92/PU_Grading_Policy_Report_2014_Aug.pdf

Reeves, D. B. (2000). Standards are not enough: Essential transformations for school success. *NASSP Bulletin, 84*(10), 5–19.

Reeves, D. B. (2004, December). The case against the zero. *Phi Delta Kappan,* 324–325.

Reeves, D. B. (2006). *The learning leader: How to focus school improvement for better results.* Alexandria, VA: Association for Supervision and Curriculum Development.

Reeves, D. B. (2007). Challenges and choices: The role of educational leaders in effective assessment. In D. Reeves (Ed.), *Ahead of the curve: The power of assessment to transform teaching and learning* (pp. 227–247). Bloomington, IN: Solution Tree.

Reeves, D. B. (2016a). *Elements of grading: A guide to effective practice* (2nd ed.). Bloomington, IN: Solution Tree.

Reeves, D. B. (2016b). *FAST grading.* Bloomington, IN: Solution Tree.

Reeves, D. B., Jung, L. A., & O'Connor, K. (2017). What's worth fighting for in grading. *Educational Leadership, 74*(8), 42–45.

Ripp, P. (2017, April 18). What I have to tell them [Web log post]. *Blogging Through the Fourth Dimension.* Retrieved from at https://pernillesripp.com

Rothstein-Fisch, C., & Trumbull, E. (2008). *Managing diverse classrooms: How to build on students' cultural strengths.* Alexandria, VA: Association for Supervision and Curriculum Development.

Ryan, M. (2017, March 17). Iowa bill would ban extra credit for school supplies. *Des Moines Register*. Retrieved from http://www.desmoinesregister.com/story/news/education/2017/03/17/iowa-bill-would-ban-extra-credit-school-supplies/99312126

Sackstein, S. (2015). *Teaching students to self-assess*. Alexandria, VA: ASCD.

Sackstein, S., & Hamilton, C. (2016). *Hacking homework: 10 strategies that inspire learning outside the classroom*. Cleveland, OH: Times 10 Publications.

Schimmer, T. (2012). *Ten things that matter from assessment to grading*. Toronto, ON: Pearson Canada.

Schimmer, T. (2016). *Grading from the inside out: Bringing accuracy to student assessment through a standards-based mindset*. Bloomington, IN; Solution Tree.

Silva, M., Munk, D. D., & Bursuck, W. D. (2005). Grading adaptations for students with disabilities. *Intervention in School and Clinic, 41*, 87–98.

Spady, W. G. (1987). On grades, grading and school reform. *Outcomes, 6*(1), 7–12.

Starsinic, J. (2003, November 21). Letter to the editor. *Patriot News* (Harrisburg, PA).

Steele-Carlin, S. (2000, June 7). Grading software: Sorting through the choices [Web log post]. Education World. Retrieved April 16, 2017, from http://www.educationworld.com/a_tech/tech/tech031.shtml

Stephens, K., & Davis, S. (2001). Traditional group work versus cooperative learning. *Crucible* (Science Teachers Association of Ontario), *33*(1), 24–26.

Stiggins, R. J. (1997). *Student-centered classroom assessment* (2nd ed.). Upper Saddle River, NJ: Merrill/Prentice Hall.

Stiggins, R. J. (2001). *Student-involved classroom assessment* (3rd ed.). Upper Saddle River, NJ: Merrill Prentice Hall.

Stiggins, R. J. (2017). *The perfect assessment system*. Alexandria, VA: ASCD.

Stiggins, R. J., Arter, J. A., Chappuis, J., & Chappuis, S. (2004). *Classroom assessment for student learning: Doing it right—using it well*. Portland, OR: Assessment Training Institute.

Stiggins, R. J., & Chappuis, J. (2012). *An introduction to student-involved assessment for learning* (6th ed.). New York, NY: Pearson.

Stiggins, R. J., Frisbie, D. A., & Griswold, P. A. (1989). Inside high school grading practices: Building a research agenda. *Educational Measurement: Issues and Practices, 8*(2), 5–14.

Stigler, J. W., & Stevenson, H. W. (1991). How Asian teachers polish each lesson to perfection. *American Educator, 15*(1), 12–20, 43–47.

Strauss, V. (2017, April 24). Betsy DeVos said, "There isn't really any Common Core any more." Um, yes, there is. *Washington Post*. Retrieved from https://www.washingtonpost.com/news/answer-sheet/wp/2017/04/24/betsy-devos-said-there-isnt-really-any-common-core-any-more-um-yes-there-is/? utm_term=.eb55573565fb

Stuart, L. F. (2003). *Assessment in practice: A view from the school*. Newton, MA: Teachers 21.

Sturgis, C. (2014). *Progress and proficiency: Redesigning grading for competency education*. Vienna, VA: International Association for K–12 Online Learning (iNACOL).

Sutton, R. (1991). *Assessment: A framework for teachers*. Abingdon, UK: Routledge.

Tarte, J. (2015, February 2). Students' bill of assessment rights. Retrieved March 30, 2017, from https://twitter.com/justintarte/status/719254669092999168

Thayer, J. D. (1991, April). *Use of observed, true, and scale variability in combining student scores in grading*. Paper presented at the Annual Meeting of the National Council on Measurement on Education, Chicago, IL.

Tombari, M., & Borich, G. (1999). *Authentic assessment in the classroom: Applications and practice.* Upper Saddle River, NJ: Merrill Prentice Hall.

Tomlinson, C. A., & McTighe, J. (2006). *Integrating differentiated instruction and understanding by design.* Alexandria, VA: Association for Supervision and Curriculum Development.

Tough, P. (2012). *How children succeed: Confidence, curiosity and the hidden power of character.* New York, NY: Houghton Mifflin.

Townsley, M. (2014, November 11). What is the difference between standards-based grading (or reporting) and competency-based education? [Web log post]. *MeTA Musings.* Retrieved April 17, 2017, from http://mctownsley.blogspot.ca/2012/02/what-is-difference-between-standards.html

University of Alberta. (2006). 61.6 Marking and Grading Guidelines. Retrieved March 6, 2017, from http://www.chem.ualberta.ca/~vederas/Chem_164/Information/MarkingGrading.pdf

Vagle, N. D. (2015). *Design in 5: Essential phases to create engaging assessment practice.* Bloomington, IN: Solution Tree.

Vatterott, C. (2015). *Rethinking grading: Meaningful assessment for standards-based learning.* Alexandria, VA: ASCD.

Walpert-Gawron, H. (2011, October 29). The parent portal: The pros and cons of transparent gradebooks [Web log post]. Retrieved from http://tweenteacher.com/2011/10/29/the-parent-portal-the-pros-and-cons-of-transparent-gradebooks

Wehner, R. (2017, March 1). Mastery Transcript Consortium: Big idea to upend college admissions process. *World Leadership School.* Retrieved from https://medium.com/@worldleadershipschool/mastery-transcript-consortium-big-idea-at-naisac-8989eb3594a4

Westerberg, T. R. (2016). *Charting a course to standards-based grading.* Bloomington, IN: Solution Tree.

White, K. (2017). *Softening the edges: Assessment practices that honor K–12 teachers and students.* Bloomington, IN: Solution Tree.

Wiggins, G. (1996). Honesty and fairness: Toward better grading and reporting. In T. R. Guskey (Ed.), *Communicating student learning: The Association for Supervision and Curriculum Development yearbook 1996* (pp 141–176). Arlington, VA: Association for Supervision and Curriculum Development.

Wiggins, G. (2000, January 19). Response to question on chatserver.ascd.org

Wiggins, G. (2004, November). On grading: Toward more "rational numbers." Presentation at the annual conference of the Independent Schools Association of the Central States, Chicago. Retrieved December 5, 2008, from http://www.grantwiggins.org/documents/grading04.pdf

Wiggins, G. (2008, January 22). Feedback: How learning occurs. *Big Ideas.* Retrieved December 5, 2008, from http://www.authenticeducation.org/bigideas/article.lasso?artid=61

Wikipedia. (2017). Grading systems by country. Retrieved March 6, 2017, from https://en.wikipedia.org/wiki/Grading_systems_by_country

Wiliam, D. (2011a). *Embedded formative assessment.* Bloomington, IN: Solution Tree.

Wiliam, D. (2011b). What is assessment for learning? *Studies in Educational Evaluation, 37,* 3–14.

Willis, J. (2007). Which brain research can educators trust? *Phi Delta Kappan, 88*(9), 697–699.

Willis, S. (1993). Are letter grades obsolete? *Association for Supervision and Curriculum Development Update, 35,* 1, 4, 8.

Wormeli, R. (2006). *Fair isn't equal: Assessing and grading in the differentiated classroom.* Portland, ME: Stenhouse and the National Middle School Association.

Wright, R. G. (1994). Success for all: The median is the key. *Phi Delta Kappan, 75*(9), 723–725.

Additional Resources

(These are references not quoted in the book that have significance in the study of the history and development of grading or that have a particularly interesting view of grading or that have some unique characteristics that make them worth reading.)

Arter, J. A., & McTighe, J. (2001). *Scoring rubrics in the classroom*. Thousand Oaks, CA: Corwin.

Ashenfelter, J. W. (1990). Our schools grappled with grade-point politics and lost. *Executive Educator, 12*(1), 21–23.

Assessment Reform Group. (1999). *Assessment for learning: Beyond the black box*. Cambridge, England: Cambridge University School of Education.

Bailey, J. M., & Guskey, T. R. (2001). *Implementing student-led conferences*. Thousand Oaks, CA: Corwin

Bateman, C. F. (1988). Goldy's coffee. *Phi Delta Kappan, 70*(3), 252–254.

Benson, J. (2015). *10 steps to managing change in schools*. Alexandria, VA: ASCD.

Bissinger, H. G. (1990). *Friday night lights*. New York: Harper Perennial.

Black, P., Harrison, C., Lee, C., Marshall B., & Wiliam, D. (2003). *Assessment for learning: Putting it into practice*. Maidenhead, England: Open University Press.

Brandt, R. (1995). Punished by rewards: A conversation with Alfie Kohn. *Educational Leadership, 53*(1), 252–254.

Brown, J. (2004). Grade-A perfect. *Principal Leadership, 5*(2), 28–32.

Burns, M. (2000). *About teaching mathematics: A K–8 resource*. Sausalito, CA: Math Solutions.

Bursuck, W., Polloway, E. A., Plante, L., Epstein, M. H., Jayanthi, M., & McConeghy, J. (1996). Report card grading and adaptations: A national survey of classroom practices. *Exceptional Children, 62*(4), 301–318.

Butler, S. M., & McMunn, N. D. (2006). *A teacher's guide to classroom assessment: Understanding and using assessment to improve student learning*. San Francisco, CA: Jossey-Bass.

Carr, J. F., & Harris, D. E. (2001). *Succeeding with standards: Linking curriculum, assessment and action planning*. Alexandria, VA: Association for Supervision and Curriculum Development.

Chappuis, J., & Chappuis, S. (2007/2008). The best value in formative assessment. *Educational Leadership, 65*(4), 14–19.

Cizek, G. J. (1996). Setting passing scores. *Educational Measurement: Issues and Practices, 15*(2), 20–31.

Cizek, G. J. (2003). *Detecting and preventing cheating: Promoting integrity in assessment*. Thousand Oaks, CA: Corwin.

Clymer, J., & Wiliam, D. (2006/2007). Improving the way we grade science. *Educational Leadership, 64*(4), 36–42.

Curren, R. R. (1995). Coercion and the ethics of grading and testing. *Educational Theory, 45*(4), 425–441.

Darling-Hammond, L., Ancess, R., & Falk, B. (1995). *Authentic assessment in action.* New York, NY: Teachers College Press.

Davies, A. (2001). Involving students in communicating about their learning. *NASSP Bulletin, 85*(621), 47–52.

Davies, A. (2007). *Making classroom assessment work* (2nd ed.). Courtenay, Canada: Connections.

Davies, A., Cameron, C., Politano, C., & Gregory, K. (1992). *Together is better: Collaborative assessment, evaluation and reporting.* Winnipeg, Canada: Peguis.

Doran, R., Chan, F., & Tamir, P. (1998). *Science educators' guide to assessment.* Arlington, VA: National Science Teachers Association.

Earl, L., & Cousins, J. B. (1995). *Classroom assessment: Changing the face, facing the change.* Toronto, Canada: Ontario Public School Teachers Federation.

Friedman, S. J. (1998). Grading teachers' grading policies. *NASSP Bulletin, 82*(597), 77–83.

Friedman, S. J., & Manley, M. (1992). Improving high school grading practices: "Experts" vs. "practitioners." *NASSP Bulletin, 76*(544), 100–104.

Glasser, W. (1990). *The quality school.* New York, NY: Harper Perennial.

Goodrich, H. (1996/1997). Understanding rubrics. *Educational Leadership, 54*(4), 14–17.

Gregory, K., Cameron, C., & Davies, A. (2000). *Knowing what counts: Self-assessment and goal-setting.* Merville, Canada: Connections.

Guskey, T. R. (2002). Computerized gradebooks and the myth of objectivity. *Phi Delta Kappan, 83*(10), 775–780.

Guskey, T. R. (2004). The communication challenge of standards-based reporting. *Phi Delta Kappan, 86*(4), 326–329.

Guskey, T. R. (2006). Making high school grades meaningful. *Phi Delta Kappan, 87*(9), 670–675.

Guskey, T. R. (Ed). (2009). *Practical solutions for serious problems in standards-based grading.* Thousand Oaks, CA: Corwin.

Haley, B. (1988). Does an A really equal learning? *NASSP Bulletin, 72*(507), 35–41.

Hargis, C. H. (1990). *Grades and grading practices: Obstacles to improving education and to helping at-risk students.* Springfield, IL: Charles C. Thomas.

Herman, J. L., Aschbacher, P. R., & Winters, L. (1992). *A practical guide to alternative assessment.* Alexandria, VA: Association for Supervision and Curriculum Development.

Hobbs, G. J. (1989, February). The issuance of student grades and the courts. Paper presented to the Annual Meeting of the Eastern Educational Research Association, Savannah, GA.

Johnson, D. W., & Johnson, R. T. (2004). *Assessing students in groups: Promoting responsibility and individual accountability.* Thousand Oaks, CA: Corwin.

Jones, L. H., Jr. (1995). Recipe for assessment: How Arty cooked his goose while grading art. *Art Education, 48*(2), 12–17.

Jongsma, K. S. (1991). Rethinking grading practices. *Reading Teacher, 45*(4), 318–320.

Juarez, T. (1996). Why any grades at all, father? *Phi Delta Kappan, 77,* 374–377.

Jung, L. A. (2009). The challenges of grading and reporting in special education. In T. R. Guskey (Ed.), *Practical solutions for serious problems in standards-based grading* (pp. 27–40). Thousand Oaks, CA: Corwin.

Kagan, S. (1994). *Cooperative learning.* San Clemente, CA: Kagan Cooperative Learning.

Kagan, S. (1996). Avoiding the group-grades trap. *Learning, 24*(4), 56–58.

Kirschenbaum, H., Napier, R., & Simon, S. B. (1971). *Wad-ja-get? The grading game in American education*. New York, NY: Hart.

Kohn, A. (1994). Grading: The issue is not how but why. *Educational Leadership, 52*(2), 38–41.

Laska, J. A., & Juarez, T. (Eds.). (1992). *Grading and marking in American schools*. Springfield, IL: Charles C. Thomas.

Leahy, S., Lyon, C., Thompson, M., & Wiliam, D. (2005). Classroom assessment: Minute by minute, day by day. *Educational Leadership, 63*(3), 18–24.

Littky, D. (2004). *The big picture: Education is everyone's business* (with S. Grabelle). Alexandria, VA: Association for Supervision and Curriculum Development.

Madgic, R. F. (1988). The point system of grading: A critical appraisal. *NASSP Bulletin, 72*(507), 29–34.

Malehorn, H. (1994). Ten measures better than grading. *Clearing House, 67*(6), 323–324.

Mazzarella, D. (1997, March 25). When everyone gets an A, grades are meaningless. *USA Today*.

McMillan, J. H. (2000). *Essential assessment concepts for teachers and administrators*. Thousand Oaks, CA: Corwin.

McMillan, J. H. (2001). Secondary teachers' classroom assessment and grading practices. *Educational Measurement: Issues and Practice, 20*(1), 20–32.

Midwood, D., O'Connor, K., & Simpson, M. (1993). *Assess for success: Assessment, evaluation and reporting for successful learning*. Toronto, Canada: Ontario Secondary Teachers Federation.

Millar Grant, J., Heffler, B., & Mereweather, K. (1995). *Student-led conferences: Using portfolios to share learning with parents*. Markham, Canada: Pembroke.

National Association of Secondary School Principals. (1996). *Breaking ranks: Changing an American institution*. Reston, VA: National Association of Secondary School Principals.

National Council of Teachers of English. (2000). Teacher talk: How do you handle late work? *Classroom Notes Plus, 17*(3), 18–21.

Nava, F. J. G., & Loyd, B. A. (1992, April). *An investigation of achievement and nonachievement criteria in elementary and secondary school grading*. Paper presented at the Annual Meeting of the American Educational Research Association, San Francisco, CA.

Nemecek, P. M. (1994). Constructing weighted grading systems. *Clearing House, 67*(6), 325–326.

O'Connor, K. (1996, April). Grading: Myth, mystery or magic. *Research Speaks to Teachers* [newsletter].

Ohlhausen, M. M., Powell, R. R., & Reitz, B. S. (1994). Parents' views of traditional and alternative report cards. *School Community Journal, 4*(1), 81–97.

Ontario Institute for Studies in Education of the University of Toronto. (2000). Classroom assessment [Entire issue]. *Orbit, 31*(4).

Ornstein, A. C. (1989). The nature of grading. *Clearing House, 62*(8), 365–369.

Patterson, W. (2003). Breaking out of our boxes. *Phi Delta Kappan, 84*(8), 568–574.

Popham, W. J. (1995). *Classroom assessment: What teachers need to know*. Needham Heights, MA: Allyn & Bacon.

Popham, W. J. (2000). Assessing mastery of wish-list content standards. *NASSP Bulletin, 84*(620), 30–36.

Reeves, D. B. (2007). From the bell curve to the mountain: A new vision for achievement, assessment and equity. In D. B. Reeves (Ed.), *Ahead of the curve: The power of assessment to transform teaching and learning* (pp. 1–10). Bloomington, IN: Solution Tree.

Seeley, M. (1994). The mismatch between assessment and grading. *Educational Leadership*, *52*(2), 4–6.

Sizer, T. (1996). *Horace's hope: What works for the American high school*. New York, NY: Houghton Mifflin.

Spady, W. G. (1991). Shifting the grading paradigm that pervades education. *Outcomes*, *9*(4), 39–45.

Sperling, D. (1993). What's worth an "A"? Setting standards together. *Educational Leadership*, *50*(5), 73–75.

Stiggins, R. J. (1990). *Developing sound grading practices (classroom assessment training)*. Portland, OR: Northwest Regional Educational Laboratory.

Stiggins, R. J. (2006). Assessment for learning: A key to motivation and achievement. *Edge*, *2*(2), 3–19.

Terwilliger, J. S. (1989). Classroom standard setting and grading practices. *Educational Measurement: Issues and Practices*, *8*(2), 15–19.

Thomas, W. C. (1996). Grading: Why are school policies necessary? What are the issues? *NASSP Bulletin*, *70*(487), 23–26.

Tomlinson, C. A. (2001). Standards and the art of teaching: Crafting high quality classrooms. *NASSP Bulletin*, *85*(622), 38–47.

Trotter, A. (1990). What to do if you're worried about how students are graded. *Executive Educator*, *12*(1), 24–25.

Walvoord, B. E., & Anderson, V. J. (1998). *Effective grading: A tool for learning and assessment*. San Francisco, CA: Jossey-Bass.

Wiggins, G. (1991). Standards, not standardization: Evoking quality student work. *Educational Leadership*, *48*(5), 18–25.

Wiggins, G. (1994). Toward better report cards. *Educational Leadership*, *52*(2), 28–37.

Wiggins, G., & McTighe, J. (2005). *Understanding by design* (exp. 2nd ed.). Alexandria, VA: Association for Supervision and Curriculum Development.

Wilson, R. J. (1994, June). Back to basics: A revisionist model of classroom-based assessment. Invited presidential address to the Annual Meeting of the Canadian Educational Researchers Association, Calgary, Canada.

Wilson, R. J. (1996). *Assessing students in classrooms and schools*. Scarborough, Canada: Allyn & Bacon.

Winger, T. (2005). Grading to communicate. *Educational Leadership*, *63*(3), 61–65.

Wright, R. G. (1989). Don't be a mean teacher. *Science Teacher*, *56*(1), 38–41.

Zmuda, A., & Tomaino, M. (2001). *The competent classroom: Aligning high school curriculum, standards, and assessment—a creative teaching guide*. New York & Washington, DC: Teachers College Press & National Education Association Professional Library.

Index

Notes

Notes

Notes

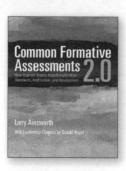
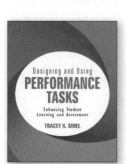

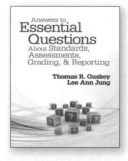

Driving Instruction That Impacts Learning

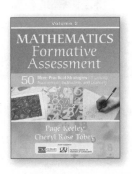

A SAGE Publishing Company

CORWIN HAS ONE MISSION: to enhance education through intentional professional learning.

We build long-term relationships with our authors, educators, clients, and associations who partner with us to develop and continuously improve the best evidence-based practices that establish and support lifelong learning.